BULGARIA

INVESTMENT AND BUSINESS GUIDE

VOLUME 1

STRATEGIC AND PRACTICAL INFORMATION

International Business Publications, USA
Washington DC, USA - Bulgaria

BULGARIA

INVESTMENT AND BUSINESS GUIDE

VOLUME 1 STRATEGIC AND PRACTICAL INFORMATION

UPDATED ANNUALLY

We express our sincere appreciation to all government agencies and international organizations, which provided information and other materials for this guide

Cover Design: **International Business Publications, USA**

2014 Edition Updated Reprint International Business Publications, USA
ISBN 1-57751-850-0

For customer service and information, please contact:
in the USA: **International Business Publications, USA**
P.O.Box 15343, Washington, DC 20043
Phone: (202) 546-2103, Fax: (202) 546-3275.
E-mail: rusric@erols.com

Printed in the USA

BULGARIA
INVESTMENT AND BUSINESS GUIDE
VOLUME 1
STRATEGIC AND PRACTICAL INFORMATION

TABLE OF CONTENTS

STRATEGIC AND DEVELOPMENT PROFILE

Capital and largest city	Sofia 42°41′N 23°19′E42.683°N 23.317°E
Official languages	Bulgarian
Official script	Cyrillic
Ethnic groups (2011[1])	84.6% Bulgarians 8.9% Turks 4.8% Roma 1.7% others
Demonym	Bulgarian
Government	Unitary parliamentary republic
- President	Rosen Plevneliev
- Acting Prime Minister	Georgi Bliznashki
Legislature	National Assembly
Formation	
- Medieval states:	
- First Bulgarian Empire	681-1018
- Second Bulgarian Empire	1185-1396
- Modern state:	
- Principality of Bulgaria	13 July 1878
- Independence from the Ottoman Empire	5 October 1908[note 1]
Area	
- Total	110,994 km² (105th) 42,823 sq mi
- Water (%)	0.3
Population	
- 2011 census	7,364,570[2] (98th)
- Density	66.2/km² (139th) 171/sq mi
GDP (PPP)	2013 estimate
- Total	$106.8 billion[3] (66th)
- Per capita	$16,041[3] (67th)
GDP (nominal)	2013 estimate
- Total	$54.446 billion[3] (75th)
- Per capita	$7,582[3] (76th)
Gini	35.1[4] medium
HDI	0.777[5] high · 58th
Currency	Lev (BGN)
Time zone	EET (UTC+2)

- Summer (DST)	EEST (UTC+3)
Drives on the	right
Calling code	+359
ISO 3166 code	BG
Internet TLD	.bg

Bulgaria officially the **Republic of Bulgaria** is a country in southeastern Europe. It is bordered by Romania to the north, Serbia and Macedonia to the west, Greece and Turkey to the south, and the Black Sea to the east. With a territory of 110,994 square kilometres (42,855 sq mi), Bulgaria is Europe's 14th-largest country.

Organised prehistoric cultures began developing on Bulgarian lands during the Neolithic period. Its ancient history saw the presence of the Thracians and later the Greeks and Romans. The emergence of a unified Bulgarian state dates back to the establishment of the First Bulgarian Empire in 681 CE, which dominated most of the Balkans and functioned as a cultural hub for Slavs during the Middle Ages. With the downfall of the Second Bulgarian Empire in 1396, its territories came under Ottoman rule for nearly five centuries. The Russo-Turkish War (1877–78) led to the formation of the Third Bulgarian State. The following years saw several conflicts with its neighbours, which prompted Bulgaria to align with Germany in both world wars. In 1946 it became a single-party socialist state as part of the Soviet-led Eastern Bloc. In December 1989 the ruling Communist Party allowed multi-party elections, which subsequently led to Bulgaria's transition into a democracy and a market-based economy.

Bulgaria's population of 7.4 million people is predominantly urbanised and mainly concentrated in the administrative centres of its 28 provinces. Most commercial and cultural activities are centred on the capital and largest city, Sofia. The strongest sectors of the economy are heavy industry, power engineering, and agriculture, all of which rely on local natural resources.

The country's current political structure dates to the adoption of a democratic constitution in 1991. Bulgaria is a unitary parliamentary republic with a high degree of political, administrative, and economic centralisation. It is a member of the European Union, NATO, and the Council of Europe; a founding state of the Organization for Security and Co-operation in Europe (OSCE); and has taken a seat at the UN Security Council three times.

GENERAL INFORMATION

Bulgaria (Bulgarian: България, officially the **Republic of Bulgaria** (Bulgarian: Република България, is a country in Southeastern Europe, and a member state of the European Union. It borders the Black Sea to the east, Greece and Turkey to the south, Serbia and the Republic of Macedonia to the west, and Romania to the north, mostly along the Danube. Bulgaria also shares a maritime border with Turkey, Romania, Ukraine, Russia, and Georgia. The capital of Bulgaria is Sofia.

Bulgaria is a country with an ancient history dating back to prehistoric times, the Thracian, Greek and Roman worlds of antiquity and the powerful Bulgarian Empire of the Middle Ages founded in 681. Geographically and climatically, Bulgaria is noted for its diversity, with the landscape ranging from the Alpine snow-capped peaks in Rila, Pirin and the Balkan Mountains to the mild and sunny weather of the Black Sea coast, from the typically continental Danubian Plain (ancient Moesia) in the north to the strong Mediterranean influence in the valleys of Macedonia and the lowlands in the southernmost parts of Thrace.

Bulgaria joined NATO on March 29, 2004 and the European Union on January 1, 2007. The country has been a member of the United Nations since 1955, and is a founding member of OSCE. As a Consultative Party to the Antarctic Treaty, Bulgaria takes part in the governing of the territories situated south of 60° south latitude.

GEOGRAPHY

Location: Southeastern Europe, bordering the Black Sea, between Romania and Turkey

Geographic coordinates: 43 00 N, 25 00 E

Map references: Europe

Area:
total area: 110,910 sq km
land area: 110,550 sq km
comparative area: slightly larger than Tennessee

Land boundaries:
total: 1,808 km
border countries: Greece 494 km, The Former Yugoslav Republic of Macedonia 148 km, Romania 608 km, Serbia and Montenegro 318 km (all with Serbia), Turkey 240 km
Coastline: 354 km

Maritime claims:
contiguous zone: 24 nm
exclusive economic zone: 200 nm
territorial sea: 12 nm

International disputes: none

Climate: temperate; cold, damp winters; hot, dry summers

Terrain: mostly mountains with lowlands in north and southeast
lowest point: Black Sea 0 m
highest point: Musala 2,925 m

Natural resources: bauxite, copper, lead, zinc, coal, timber, arable land

Land use:
arable land: 34%
permanent crops: 3%
meadows and pastures: 18%
forest and woodland: 35%
other: 10%

Irrigated land: 10 sq km

Environment:
current issues: air pollution from industrial emissions; rivers polluted from raw sewage, heavy metals, detergents; deforestation; forest damage from air pollution and resulting acid rain; soil contamination from heavy metals from metallurgical plants and industrial wastes
natural hazards: earthquakes, landslides

international agreements: party to - Air Pollution, Air Pollution-Nitrogen Oxides, Air Pollution-Sulphur 85, Antarctic Treaty, Climate Change, Endangered Species, Environmental Modification, Nuclear Test Ban, Ozone Layer Protection, Ship Pollution, Wetlands; signed, but not ratified - Air Pollution-Sulphur 94, Air Pollution-Volatile Organic Compounds, Antarctic-Environmental Protocol, Biodiversity, Law of the Sea
Geographic note: strategic location near Turkish Straits; controls key land routes from Europe to Middle East and Asia

PEOPLE

Population: 8,612,757

Base 802231 (R01234) 6-94

Age structure:
0-14 years: 17% (male 769,025; female 732,119)
15-64 years: 68% (male 2,891,197; female 2,923,440)
65 years and over: 15% (male 561,944; female 735,032)

Population growth rate: 0.46%
Birth rate: 8.33 births/1,000 population
Death rate: 13.55 deaths/1,000 population
Net migration rate: 9.81 migrant(s)/1,000 population
Sex ratio:
at birth: 1.05 male(s)/female
under 15 years: 1.05 male(s)/female

15-64 years: 0.99 male(s)/female
65 years and over: 0.76 male(s)/female
all ages: 0.96 male(s)/female
Infant mortality rate: 15.7 deaths/1,000 live births
Life expectancy at birth:
total population: 71 years
male: 67.07 years
female: 75.12 years
Total fertility rate: 1.17 children born/woman
Nationality:
noun: Bulgarian(s)
adjective: Bulgarian

Ethnic divisions: Bulgarian 85.3%, Turk 8.5%, Gypsy 2.6%, Macedonian 2.5%, Armenian 0.3%, Russian 0.2%, other 0.6%
Religions: Bulgarian Orthodox 85%, Muslim 13%, Jewish 0.8%, Roman Catholic 0.5%, Uniate Catholic 0.2%, Protestant, Gregorian-Armenian, and other 0.5%
Languages: Bulgarian, secondary languages closely correspond to ethnic breakdown
Literacy: age 15 and over can read and write (1992 est.)
total population: 98%
male: 99%
female: 97%

GOVERNMENT

Country name:
conventional long form: Republic of Bulgaria
conventional short form: Bulgaria
local long form: Republika Balgariya
local short form: Balgariya

Government type:
parliamentary democracy

Capital:
name: Sofia
geographic coordinates: 42 41 N, 23 19 E
time difference: UTC+2 (7 hours ahead of Washington, DC, during Standard Time)
daylight saving time: +1hr, begins last Sunday in March; ends last Sunday in October

Administrative divisions:
28 provinces (oblasti, singular - oblast); Blagoevgrad, Burgas, Dobrich, Gabrovo, Khaskovo, Kurdzhali, Kyustendil, Lovech, Montana, Pazardzhik, Pernik, Pleven, Plovdiv, Razgrad, Ruse, Shumen, Silistra, Sliven, Smolyan, Sofiya (Sofia), Sofiya-Grad (Sofia City), Stara Zagora, Turgovishte, Varna, Veliko Turnovo, Vidin, Vratsa, Yambol

Independence:

3 March 1878 (as an autonomous principality within the Ottoman Empire); 22 September 1908 (complete independence from the Ottoman Empire)

National holiday:
Liberation Day, 3 March (1878)

Constitution:
several previous; latest drafted between late 1990 and early 1991, adopted 12 July 1991; amended several times, last in 2007

Legal system:
civil law

International law organization participation:
accepts compulsory ICJ jurisdiction with reservations; accepts ICCt jurisdiction

Suffrage:
18 years of age; universal

Executive branch:
chief of state: President Rosen PLEVNELIEV (since 22 January 2012); Vice President Margarita POPOVA (since 22 January 2012)
head of government: Prime Minister Plamen ORESHARSKI (since 29 May 2013), Deputy Prime Ministers Zinaida ZLATANOVA (since 29 May 2013), Tsvetlin YOVCHEV (since June 2013), and Daniela BOBEVA (since June 2013)
cabinet: Council of Ministers nominated by the prime minister and elected by the National Assembly
elections: president and vice president elected on the same ticket by popular vote for a five-year term (eligible for a second term); election last held on 23 and 30 October 2011 (next to be held in 2016); chairman of the Council of Ministers (prime minister) elected by the National Assembly; deputy prime ministers nominated by the prime minister and elected by the National Assembly
election results: Rosen PLEVNELIEV elected president in a runoff election; percent of vote - Rosen PLEVNELIEV 52.6%, Ivailo KALFIN 47.4%; Plamen ORESHARSKI elected prime minister; result of legislative vote - 120 to 97

Legislative branch:
unicameral National Assembly or Narodno Sabranie (240 seats; members elected by popular vote to serve four-year terms)
elections: last held on 12 May 2013 (next to be held spring 2017)
election results: percent of vote by party - GERB 30.5%, BSP 26.6%, MRF 11.3%, Ataka 7.3%; seats by party - GERB 97, BSP 84, MRF 36, Ataka 23

Judicial branch:
highest court(s): Supreme Court of Cassation (consists of a chairman and approximately 72 judges organized into penal, civil, and commercial colleges); Supreme Administrative Court (organized in 2 colleges with various panels of 5 judges each); Constitutional Court (consists of 12 justices); note - Constitutional Court resides outside the Judiciary
judge selection and term of office: Supreme Court of Cassation and Supreme Administrative judges elected by the Supreme Judicial Council or SJC (consists of 25 members with extensive legal experience) and appointed by the president; judge tenure NA; Constitutional Court justices elected by the National Assembly and appointed by the president and the SJC; justices appointed

for 9-year terms with renewal of four justices every 3 years
subordinate courts: appeals courts; regional and district courts; administrative courts; courts martial

Political parties and leaders:
Attack (Ataka) [Volen Nikolov SIDEROV]
Bulgarian Socialist Party or BSP [Sergei STANISHEV]
Bulgaria of the Citizens [Meglena KUNEVA]
Citizens for the European Development of Bulgaria or GERB [Boyko BORISOV]
Coalition for Bulgaria or CfB [Sergei STANISHEV] (coalition of parties dominated by BSP)
Democrats for a Strong Bulgaria or DSB [Radan KANEV]
Internal Macedonian Revolutionary Organization or IMRO [Krasimir KARAKACHANOV]
Movement for Rights and Freedoms or MRF [Lyutvi MESTAN]
National Front for the Salvation of Bulgaria or NFSB [Valeri SIMEONOV]
National Movement for Stability and Progress or NDSV [Hristina HRISTOVA] (formerly National Movement Simeon II or NMS2)
Order, Law, and Justice or RZS [Yane YANEV]
Union of Democratic Forces or UDF [Bozhidar LUKARSKI]

Political pressure groups and leaders:
Confederation of Independent Trade Unions of Bulgaria or CITUB
Podkrepa Labor Confederation
other: numerous regional, ethnic, and national interest groups with various agendas

International organization participation:
Australia Group, BIS, BSEC, CD, CE, CEI, CERN, EAPC, EBRD, EIB, EU, FAO, G- 9, IAEA, IBRD, ICAO, ICC (national committees), ICRM, IDA, IFC, IFRCS, IHO (pending member), ILO, IMF, IMO, IMSO, Interpol, IOC, IOM, IPU, ISO, ITSO, ITU, ITUC (NGOs), MIGA, NATO, NSG, OAS (observer), OIF, OPCW, OSCE, PCA, SELEC, UN, UNCTAD, UNESCO, UNHCR, UNIDO, UNMIL, UNWTO, UPU, WCO, WFTU (NGOs), WHO, WIPO, WMO, WTO, ZC

Diplomatic representation in the US:
chief of mission: Ambassador Elena POPTODOROVA (since 4 August 2010)
chancery: 1621 22nd Street NW, Washington, DC 20008
telephone: [1] (202) 387-0174
FAX: [1] (202) 234-7973
consulate(s) general: Chicago, Los Angeles, New York

Diplomatic representation from the US:
chief of mission: Ambassador Marcie B. RIES (since 5 September 2012)
embassy: 16 Kozyak Street, Sofia 1408
mailing address: American Embassy Sofia, US Department of State, 5740 Sofia Place, Washington, DC 20521-5740
telephone: [359] (2) 937-5100
FAX: [359] (2) 937-5320

Flag description:
three equal horizontal bands of white (top), green, and red; the pan-Slavic white-blue-red colors were modified by substituting a green band (representing freedom) for the blue
note:the national emblem, formerly on the hoist side of the white stripe, has been removed

National symbol(s):
lion

National anthem:
name: "Mila Rodino" (Dear Homeland)

ECONOMY

Bulgaria, a former Communist country that entered the EU on 1 January 2007, averaged more than 6% annual growth from 2004 to 2008, driven by significant amounts of bank lending, consumption, and foreign direct investment. Successive governments have demonstrated a commitment to economic reforms and responsible fiscal planning, but the global downturn sharply reduced domestic demand, exports, capital inflows, and industrial production. GDP contracted by 5.5% in 2009, and has been slow to recover in the years since. Despite having a favorable investment regime, including low, flat corporate income taxes, significant challenges remain. Corruption in public administration, a weak judiciary, and the presence of organized crime continue to hamper the country's investment climate and economic prospects.

GDP (purchasing power parity):
$104.6 billion (2013 est.)
country comparison to the world: 74
$104.1 billion (2012 est.)
$103.3 billion (2011 est.)
note:data are in 2013 US dollars

GDP (official exchange rate):
$53.7 billion (2013 est.)

GDP - real growth rate:
0.5% (2013 est.)
country comparison to the world: 186
0.8% (2012 est.)
1.8% (2011 est.)

GDP - per capita (PPP):
$14,400 (2013 est.)
country comparison to the world: 93
$14,300 (2012 est.)
$14,100 (2011 est.)
note:data are in 2013 US dollars

Gross national saving:
23.5% of GDP (2013 est.)
country comparison to the world: 60
22.5% of GDP (2012 est.)
22% of GDP (2011 est.)

GDP - composition, by end use:
household consumption: 70.4%
government consumption: 7.9%
investment in fixed capital: 21.3%

investment in inventories: 2.5%
exports of goods and services: 69.7%
imports of goods and services: -71.8%
(2013 est.)

GDP - composition, by sector of origin:
agriculture: 6.7%
industry: 30.3%
services: 63% (2013 est.)

Agriculture - products:
vegetables, fruits, tobacco, wine, wheat, barley, sunflowers, sugar beets; livestock

Industries:
electricity, gas, water; food, beverages, tobacco; machinery and equipment, base metals, chemical products, coke, refined petroleum, nuclear fuel

Industrial production growth rate:
1% (2013 est.)
country comparison to the world: 147

Labor force:
2.551 million (2013 est.)
country comparison to the world: 112

Labor force - by occupation:
agriculture: 7.1%
industry: 35.2%
services: 57.7%

Unemployment rate:
11.6% (2013 est.)
country comparison to the world: 120
11.1% (2012 est.)

Population below poverty line:
21.8%

Household income or consumption by percentage share:
lowest 10%: 2%
highest 10%: 35.2%

Distribution of family income - Gini index:
45.3
country comparison to the world: 39
26 (2001)

Budget:
revenues: $18.81 billion
expenditures: $20.12 billion (2013 est.)

Taxes and other revenues:
35% of GDP (2013 est.)
country comparison to the world: 67

Budget surplus (+) or deficit (-):
-2.4% of GDP (2013 est.)
country comparison to the world: 98

Public debt:
18.4% of GDP (2013 est.)
country comparison to the world: 138
16.3% of GDP (2012 est.)
defined by the EU's Maastricht Treaty as consolidated general government gross debt at nominal value, outstanding at the end of the year in the following categories of government liabilities: currency and deposits, securities other than shares excluding financial derivatives, and loans; general government sector comprises the subsectors: central government, state government, local government, and social security funds

Fiscal year:
calendar year

Inflation rate (consumer prices):
1.5% (2013 est.)
country comparison to the world: 41
3% (2012 est.)

Central bank discount rate:
$NA (31 December 2012 est.)
country comparison to the world: 141
0.22% (31 December 2011 est.)
note: Bulgarian National Bank (BNB) has had no independent monetary policy since the introduction of the Currency Board regime in 1997; this is BNB's base interest rate

Commercial bank prime lending rate:
9.1% (31 December 2013 est.)
country comparison to the world: 88
9.72% (31 December 2012 est.)

Stock of narrow money:
$17.55 billion (31 December 2013 est.)
country comparison to the world: 65
$15.51 billion (31 December 2012 est.)

Stock of broad money:
$45.84 billion (31 December 2013 est.)
country comparison to the world: 72
$41.53 billion (31 December 2012 est.)

Stock of domestic credit:
$37.6 billion (31 December 2013 est.)

country comparison to the world: 66
$37.12 billion (31 December 2012 est.)

Market value of publicly traded shares:
$6.666 billion (31 December 2012 est.)
country comparison to the world: 69
$8.253 billion (31 December 2011)
$7.276 billion (31 December 2010 est.)

Current account balance:
-$182.3 million (2013 est.)
country comparison to the world: 83
-$669.5 million (2012 est.)

Exports:
$27.9 billion (2013 est.)
country comparison to the world: 67
$26.7 billion (2012 est.)

Exports - commodities:
clothing, footwear, iron and steel, machinery and equipment, fuels

Exports - partners:
Germany 10.4%, Turkey 9.1%, Italy 8.7%, Romania 8.2%, Greece 7.3%, France 4%

Imports:
$32.88 billion (2013 est.)
country comparison to the world: 65
$31.15 billion (2012 est.)

Imports - commodities:
machinery and equipment; metals and ores; chemicals and plastics; fuels, minerals, and raw materials

Imports - partners:
Russia 20.9%, Germany 11.3%, Italy 6.7%, Romania 6.6%, Greece 6.1%, Turkey 4.6%, Spain 4.5%

Reserves of foreign exchange and gold:
$20.69 billion (31 December 2013 est.)
country comparison to the world: 59
$20.5 billion (31 December 2012 est.)

Debt - external:
$37.85 billion (31 December 2013 est.)
country comparison to the world: 67
$36.52 billion (31 December 2012 est.)

Stock of direct foreign investment - at home:
$54.21 billion (31 December 2013 est.)

country comparison to the world: 53
$52.21 billion (31 December 2012 est.)

Stock of direct foreign investment - abroad:
$1.939 billion (31 December 2013 est.)
country comparison to the world: 72
$1.82 billion (31 December 2012 est.)

Exchange rates:
leva (BGN) per US dollar -
1.478 (2013 est.)
1.5221 (2012 est.)
1.4774 (2010 est.)
1.404
1.3171

ENERGY

Electricity - production:
43.39 billion kWh
country comparison to the world: 57

Electricity - consumption:
30.46 billion kWh
country comparison to the world: 62

Electricity - exports:
12.11 billion kWh
country comparison to the world: 17

Electricity - imports:
1.45 billion kWh
country comparison to the world: 58

Electricity - installed generating capacity:
10.01 million kW
country comparison to the world: 57

Electricity - from fossil fuels:
45.7% of total installed capacity
country comparison to the world: 163

Electricity - from nuclear fuels:
19% of total installed capacity
country comparison to the world: 11

Electricity - from hydroelectric plants:
21.8% of total installed capacity
country comparison to the world: 86

Electricity - from other renewable sources:
4.8% of total installed capacity
country comparison to the world: 48

Crude oil - production:
3,384 bbl/day
country comparison to the world: 101

Crude oil - exports:
0 bbl/day (2012 est.)
country comparison to the world: 92

Crude oil - imports:
124,700 bbl/day
country comparison to the world: 43

Crude oil - proved reserves:
15 million bbl
country comparison to the world: 85

Refined petroleum products - production:
128,500 bbl/day
country comparison to the world: 68

Refined petroleum products - consumption:
112,700 bbl/day
country comparison to the world: 73

Refined petroleum products - exports:
73,740 bbl/day
country comparison to the world: 52

Refined petroleum products - imports:
50,130 bbl/day
country comparison to the world: 69

Natural gas - production:
410 million cu m
country comparison to the world: 73

Natural gas - consumption:
2.54 billion cu m
country comparison to the world: 77

Natural gas - exports:
0 cu m
country comparison to the world: 72

Natural gas - imports:
2.64 billion cu m
country comparison to the world: 44

Natural gas - proved reserves:
5.663 billion cu m
country comparison to the world: 93

Carbon dioxide emissions from consumption of energy:
52.44 million Mt

COMMUNICATION

Telephones - main lines in use:
2.253 million
country comparison to the world: 55

Telephones - mobile cellular:
10.78 million
country comparison to the world: 74

Telephone system:
general assessment: inherited an extensive but antiquated telecommunications network from the Soviet era; quality has improved with a modern digital trunk line now connecting switching centers in most of the regions; remaining areas are connected by digital microwave radio relay
domestic: the Bulgaria Telecommunications Company's fixed-line monopoly terminated in 2005 in an effort to upgrade fixed-line services; mobile-cellular teledensity, fostered by multiple service providers, has reached 150 telephones per 100 persons
international: country code - 359; submarine cable provides connectivity to Ukraine and Russia; a combination submarine cable and land fiber-optic system provides connectivity to Italy, Albania, and Macedonia; satellite earth stations - 3 (1 Intersputnik in the Atlantic Ocean region, 2 Intelsat in the Atlantic and Indian Ocean regions)

Broadcast media:
4 national terrestrial TV stations with 1 state-owned and 3 privately owned; a vast array of TV stations are available from cable and satellite TV providers; state-owned national radio broadcasts over 3 networks; large number of private radio stations broadcasting, especially in urban areas

Internet country code:
.bg

Internet hosts:

976,277
country comparison to the world: 47

Internet users:
3.395 million
country comparison to the world: 63

TRANSPORTATION

Airports:
68
country comparison to the world: 74

Airports - with paved runways:
total: 57
over 3,047 m: 2
2,438 to 3,047 m: 17
1,524 to 2,437 m: 12
under 914 m: 26

Airports - with unpaved runways:
total: 11
914 to 1,523 m: 2
under 914 m:
9

Heliports:
1

Pipelines:
gas 2,887 km; oil 346 km; refined products 378 km

Railways:
total: 4,152 km
country comparison to the world: 41
standard gauge: 4,072 km 1.435-m gauge (2,863 km electrified)
narrow gauge: 80 km 0.760-m gauge

Roadways:
total: 19,512 km
country comparison to the world: 111
paved: 19,235 km (includes 458 km of expressways)
unpaved: 277 km
note:does not include Category IV local roads

Waterways:
470 km
country comparison to the world: 84

Merchant marine:
total: 22

Inflation rate: 1.6% ; 7.2% ; 11.6% , 6.1% (2006); 7.4% (2005); 4.0% (2004); 5.6% (2003).
Unemployment rate: 9.1% ; 6.3% ; 6.9% ; 9.1% (2006); 10.7% (2005); 12.2% (2004); 14.3% (2003).
Natural resources: Bauxite, copper, lead, zinc, coal, and timber.
Official exchange rate: Lev per $1 U.S. = 1.36 ; 1.39 ; 1.33 ; 1.49 (2006); 1.66 (2005); 1.44 (2004).

GEOGRAPHY AND PEOPLE

Bulgaria shares a border with Turkey and Greece to the south, Macedonia and Serbia to the west, Romania to the north, and the Black Sea to the east. The capital, Sofia, lies in the western region of the country. Ethnic groups include Bulgarian, Turkish, Roma, and others. The official language is Bulgarian.

HISTORICAL HIGHLIGHTS

Ancient Thrace was partially located on the territory of modern Bulgaria, and Thracian culture provides a wealth of archeological sites within Bulgaria. In the second century A.D., the Bulgars came to Europe from their old homeland, the Kingdom of Balhara situated in the Mount Imeon area (present Hindu Kush in northern Afghanistan).

The first Bulgarian state was established in 635 A.D., located along the north coast of the Black Sea. In 681 A.D. the first Bulgarian state on the territory of modern Bulgaria was founded. This state consisted of a mixture of Slav and Bulgar peoples. In 864, Bulgaria adopted Orthodox Christianity. The First Bulgarian Kingdom, considered to be Bulgaria's "Golden Age," emerged under Tsar Simeon I in 893-927. During this time, Bulgarian art and literature flourished. Followers of Saints Cyril and Methodius are believed to have developed the Cyrillic alphabet in Bulgaria in the early 10th century.

In 1018, the Byzantine Empire conquered Bulgaria. In 1185 the Bulgarians broke free of Byzantine rule and established the Second Bulgarian Kingdom. A number of Bulgaria's famous monasteries were founded during this period. Following the 1242 Mongol invasion, this kingdom began losing territory to its neighbors. Ottoman expansion into the Balkan Peninsula eventually reached Bulgaria, and in 1396 Bulgaria became part of the Ottoman Empire. During the five centuries of Ottoman rule, most of Bulgaria's indigenous cultural centers were destroyed. Several Bulgarian uprisings were brutally suppressed and a great many people fled abroad. The April uprising of 1876, the Russo-Turkish War (1877-78), and the Treaty of San Stefano (March 3, 1878, the date of Bulgaria's national holiday), began Bulgaria's liberation from the Ottoman Empire, but complete independence was not recognized until 1908.

During the first half of the 20th century, Bulgaria was marred by social and political unrest. Bulgaria participated in the First and Second Balkan Wars (1912 and 1913) and sided with the Central Powers, and later the Axis Powers, during the two World Wars. Although allied with Germany during World War II, Bulgaria never declared war on the Soviet Union and never sent troops abroad to fight under Nazi command. Near the end of World War II, Bulgaria changed sides to fight the German army all the way to Austria; 30,000 Bulgarian troops were killed.

Bulgaria had a mixed record during World War II, when it was allied with Nazi Germany under a March 1941 agreement. The Law for the Protection of the Nation, enacted in January 1941, divested Jews of property, livelihood, civil rights, and personal security. Despite a February 1943 agreement requiring Bulgaria to transfer Bulgaria's Jews to Nazi extermination camps in Poland, Bulgaria did not actually deport any Bulgarian Jews or Roma to Nazi concentration camps. Under that agreement, however, Bulgarian forces transferred approximately 11,000 Jews from Bulgarian-occupied territory (Thrace and Macedonia) to Nazi concentration camps. In June 1943 the government "re-settled" Sofia's 25,000 Jews to rural areas. Tsar Boris--supported by the parliament (especially its prominent Deputy Speaker, Dimitar Peshev), the Orthodox Church, and the general public--aided the Jewish community and helped its 50,000 members survive the war, despite harsh conditions. The Bulgarian Jews remained safe, and when they were permitted to emigrate to Israel after the war, most of them did.

King Simeon II assumed control of the throne in 1943 at the age of six following the death of his father Boris III. With the entry of Soviet troops into Bulgaria in September 1944 and the defeat of the Axis Powers in World War II, communism emerged as the dominant political force within Bulgaria. Simeon, who later returned and served as Prime Minister, was forced into exile in 1946 and resided primarily in Madrid, Spain. By 1946, Bulgaria had become a satellite of the Soviet Union, remaining so throughout the Cold War period. Todor Zhivkov, the head of the Bulgarian Communist Party, ruled the country for much of this period. During his 27 years as leader of Bulgaria, democratic opposition was crushed; agriculture was collectivized and industry was nationalized; and the Bulgarian Orthodox Church fell under the control of the state.

In 1989, Zhivkov was removed from power, and democratic change began. The first multi-party elections since World War II were held in 1990. The ruling communist party changed its name to the Bulgarian Socialist Party and won the June 1990 elections. Following a period of social unrest and passage of a new constitution, the first fully democratic parliamentary elections were held in 1991 in which the Union of Democratic Forces won. The first direct presidential elections were held the next year.

As Bulgaria emerged from the throes of communism, it experienced a period of social and economic turmoil that culminated in a severe economic and financial crisis in late 1996-early 1997. With the help of the international community, former Prime Minister Ivan Kostov initiated a series of reforms in 1997 that helped stabilize the country's economy and put Bulgaria on the Euro-Atlantic path. Elections in 2001 ushered in a new government and president. In July 2001, Bulgaria's ex-king Simeon Saxe-Coburg-Gotha became the first former monarch in post-communist Eastern Europe to become Prime Minister. His government continued to pursue Euro-Atlantic integration, democratic reform, and development of a market economy. Bulgaria became a member of the North Atlantic Treaty Organization on March 29, 2004, and a member of the European Union (EU) on January 1, 2007.

Following June 2005 general elections, Sergei Stanishev of the Bulgarian Socialist Party became the new Prime Minister of a coalition government on August 16, 2005. In October 2006, Georgi Parvanov, the former leader of the Bulgarian Socialist Party, became the first Bulgarian president to win re-election. Despite his limited constitutional powers, President Parvanov has played an important role in helping to ensure a consistent, pro-Western foreign policy. The Stanishev government continued Bulgaria's integration with the Euro-Atlantic world and its close partnership with the United States. Bulgaria has attracted large amounts of American and European investment, and is an active partner in coalition operations in Afghanistan as well as in UN-led peacekeeping operations in the Balkans.

In the July 2009 general elections, Bulgarian voters punished the Socialist-led government for corruption scandals and frozen EU funds. GERB took 116 of 240 seats in parliament, and its leader (and former Sofia mayor) Boyko Borissov became the Prime Minister. Borissov formed a minority government supported by the Blue Coalition, Ataka, and RZS. The government's priorities include: promoting economic stability, unblocking the frozen EU funds, and fighting corruption. According to the latest opinion polls, Borissov's government is the most popular government since the beginning of the transition in 1989.

GOVERNMENT AND POLITICAL CONDITIONS

Bulgaria is a parliamentary republic. The unicameral National Assembly, or Narodno Subranie, consists of 240 deputies who are elected for 4-year terms through a mixed electoral system: 209 members of parliament (MPs) elected according to the classic proportional representation system (voters vote for fixed, rank-ordered party lists for each of the 31 electoral districts, with a different list for each district), and 31 majority MPs elected individually under the majority representation system in each and every district (the winning candidate receives a plurality of the votes in the region). Parliament selects and dismisses government ministers, including the prime minister, exercises control over the government, and sanctions deployment of troops abroad. It is responsible for enactment of laws, approval of the budget, scheduling of presidential elections, declaration of war, and ratification of international treaties and agreements.

A one-month official campaign period precedes general elections. The voting age is 18. Preliminary results are available within hours of poll closings. Parties and coalitions must win a minimum 4% of the national vote to enter parliament. Seats are then allocated to the parties in proportion to the distribution of votes in their respective electoral districts. Votes belonging to parties not passing the 4% threshold are distributed to other parties using the method of the smallest remainder. The lists of newly elected members of parliament are announced 7 days after the elections. The president must convene the new parliament within one month after the elections, and calls upon parties, coalitions, or political groups to nominate a prime minister and form a government. If the three largest parties, coalitions, or political groups fail to nominate a prime minister, the president can dissolve parliament and schedule new elections. In recent years, it has taken approximately a month for the new government to form.

A general election was held in Bulgaria July 5, 2009; turnout was 60.20%. Results were as follows: GERB 39.7%, BSP 17.7%, MRF 14.4%, ATAKA 9.4%, Blue Coalition 6.8%, RZS 4.1%, other 7.9%; seats by party were GERB 116, BSP 40, MRF 38, ATAKA 21, Blue Coalition 15, RZS 10.

Results of the June 7, 2009 European Parliament elections were GERB 24.36%, 5 seats; BSP 18.5%, 4 seats; DPS 14.14%, 3 seats; ATAKA 11.96%, 2 seats; NDSV 7.96%, 2 seats; Blue Coalition (SDS-DSB and other right-wing parties) 7.95%, 1 seat (turnout: 37.49%).

The president of Bulgaria is directly elected for a 5-year term with the right to one re-election. The president serves as the head of state and commander in chief of the armed forces. The president is the head of the Consultative Council for National Security and while unable to initiate legislation, the president can return a bill for further debate. Parliament can overturn the president's veto with a simple majority vote. Bulgarian Socialist Party candidate Georgi Parvanov won the November 2001 presidential election and was re-elected in October 2006 as an independent candidate in a run-off against Volen Siderov, the leader of extreme nationalist Ataka Party. The next presidential election will be held in 2011.

The prime minister is head of the Council of Ministers, which is the primary component of the executive branch. In addition to the prime minister and deputy prime ministers, the Council is composed of ministers who head the various agencies within the government and usually come from the majority/ruling party or from a member party of the ruling coalition in parliament. The Council is responsible for carrying out state policy, managing the state budget and maintaining law and order. The Council must resign if the National Assembly passes a vote of no confidence in the Council or prime minister.

The Bulgarian judicial system became an independent branch of the government following passage of the 1991 constitution. Reform within this branch has been slow, with political influence, widespread corruption, and long delays continuously plaguing the system. In 1994, the National Assembly passed the Judicial System Act to further delineate the role of the judiciary. In 2003, Bulgaria adopted amendments to the constitution, which aimed to improve the effectiveness of the judicial system by limiting magistrates' irremovability and immunity against criminal prosecution. Additional amendments to the constitution in 2006 and 2007 further increased oversight of the judicial system by the legislative branch. They introduced the Supreme Judicial Council as a permanently operating supervisory body, as well as an Inspectorate responsible for overseeing the performance of the judicial system as a whole and its individual members. The prosecution service was given absolute authority over all investigations, and the police received a mandate to investigate 95% of all crimes, which reduced the role of the investigative service.

The trial, appellate, and cassation (highest appellate) courts comprise the three tiers of the judicial system. Military courts (at trial and appeal level) handle cases involving military and Ministry of Interior personnel. Administrative courts, effective since March 2007, specialize in reviewing appeals of government acts.

The Supreme Administrative Court and the Supreme Court of Cassation are the highest courts of appeal and determine the application of all laws.

The Supreme Judicial Council (SJC) is composed of 25 members serving 5-year terms. Those who serve on the council are experienced legal professionals and are either appointed by the National Assembly, selected by the judicial system, or serve on the SJC as a result of their position in government. The SJC manages the judiciary and is responsible for appointing judges. In 2007 parliament revised the Judicial System Act to make it compliant with the latest constitutional amendments, which provided for the establishment of the Inspectorate with the Supreme Judicial Council: a standing body with 11 members who investigate complaints of magistrates' misconduct, with no right to rule on the substance of judicial acts.

The Constitutional Court, which is separate from the rest of the judiciary, interprets the constitution and constitutionality of laws and treaties. Its 12 justices serve 9-year terms and are selected by the president, the National Assembly, and the Supreme Courts.

Principal Government Officials

Office	Incumbent	Since	Party
Prime Minister	Georgi Bliznashki	August 6, 2014	Independent
Deputy Prime Minister and Minister of Regional Development and Infrastructure Design	Ekaterina Zakharieva	August 6, 2014	Independent
Deputy Prime Minister and Minister of Labor and Social Policy	Yordan Hristoskov	August 6, 2014	Independent

Deputy Prime Minister and Minister of Justice	Hristo Ivanov	August 6, 2014	Independent
Deputy Prime Minister and Management of EU Funds	Iliyana Tsanova	August 6, 2014	Independent
Minister of Interior	Yordan Bakalov	August 6, 2014	Independent
Minister of Foreign Affairs	Daniel Mitov	August 6, 2014	Independent
Minister of Finance	Rumen Porozhanov	August 6, 2014	Independent
Minister of Economy, Energy and Tourism	Asen Vasilev	August 6, 2014	Independent
Minister of Economy and Energy	Rumen Porozhanov	August 6, 2014	Independent
Minister of Education and Science	Rumyana Kolarova	August 6, 2014	Independent
Minister of Defence	Velizar Shalamanov	August 6, 2014	Independent
Minister of Agriculture and Food	Vasil Grudev	August 6, 2014	Independent
Minister of Transport, Information Technology and Communications	Nikolina Angelkova	August 6, 2014	Independent
Minister of Environment and Water	Svetlana Zhekova	August 6, 2014	Independent
Minister of Health	Miroslav Nenkov	August 6, 2014	Independent
Minister of Culture	Martin Ivanov	August 6, 2014	Independent
Minister of Youth and Sports	Evgenia Radanova	August 6, 2014	Independent

Bulgaria maintains an **embassy** in the United States at 1621 22nd Street, NW, Washington DC 20008 (tel. 202-387-0174; fax: 202-234-7973).

ECONOMY

Rank	74th (nominal) / 72nd (PPP)
Currency	1 Bulgarian lev (BGN) = 100 stotinki
Fiscal year	Calendar year
Trade organisations	EU, WTO, OSCE and BSEC
Statistics	
GDP	▲$103.15 billion (PPP) ▲$50.78 billion (nominal)
GDP growth	▼1.0% (Real)
GDP per capita	▲$6,903 (nominal) ▲$14,020 (PPP)
GDP by sector	Agriculture (5.6%), industry (31.2%), services (63.2%)
Inflation (CPI)	▼3%
Population below poverty line	21%
Gini coefficient	45.3

Labour force	▲2.551 million
Labour force by occupation	Agriculture 7.1%, industry 35.2%, services 57.7%
Unemployment	▲12,5%
Average gross salary	754 BGN 509 $
Average net salary	591 BGN 400 $
Main industries	Electricity, gas and water; food, beverages and tobacco; machinery and equipment, base metals, chemical products, refined petroleum, nuclear fuel
Ease-of-doing-business rank	58th[6]
External	
Exports	▲$27.9 billion
Export goods	clothing, footwear, iron and steel, machinery and equipment, fuels
Main export partners	Germany 10.4% Turkey 9.1% Italy 8.7% Romania 8.2% Greece 7.3% France 4.0%
Imports	▲$32.88 billion
Import goods	machinery and equipment, metals and ores, chemicals and plastics, fuels, minerals, and raw materials
Main import partners	Russia 20.9% Germany 11.3% Italy 6.7% Romania 6.6% Greece 6.1% Turkey 4.6% Spain 4.5%
Gross external debt	▼$43.24 billion
Public finances	
Public debt	▼15.0% of GDP
Revenues	BGN 30.55 billion (2013) ($20.13B)
Expenses	BGN 31.65 billion (2013) ($21.63B)
Economic aid	$475 million
Credit rating	BBB (Domestic) BBB (Foreign) A (T&C Assessment) (Standard & Poor's)
Foreign reserves	▲$20.5 billion

The **economy of Bulgaria** functions on the principles of the free market, having a large private sector and a smaller public one. Bulgaria is an industrialised upper-middle-income country according to the World Bank.[13] Recently, it has experienced rapid economic growth in recent yearswith an average monthly wage of 812 leva (554 USD).[14] GDP per capita is estimated at $14,400 (PPP, 2013).

Since 2001, Bulgaria has managed to attract considerable amounts of Foreign Direct Investment (FDI). During the Financial crisis of 2007–2010, Bulgaria marked a decline in its economy of 5.5% in 2009, but quickly restored positive growth levels to 0.2% in 2010, in contrast to other Balkan countries.[16]

The currency of the country is the lev (plural leva), pegged to the euro at a rate of 1.95583 leva for 1 euro.[17] The lev is the strongest and most stable currency in Eastern Europe.[18][19] The strongest sectors are energy, mining, metallurgy, machine building, agriculture and tourism. Primary industrial exports are clothing, iron and steel, machinery and refined fuels.[20] Low productivity and competitiveness on the European and world markets alike due to inadequate R&D funding and a lack of a clearly defined development policy remain a significant obstacle for foreign investment and economic growth

Bulgaria's economy contracted dramatically after 1989 with the collapse of the COMECON system and the loss of the Soviet market, to which the Bulgarian economy had been closely tied. The standard of living fell by about 40%. In addition, UN sanctions against Yugoslavia and Iraq took a heavy toll on the Bulgarian economy. The first signs of recovery emerged when GDP grew in 1994 for the first time since 1988, by 1.4% and then by 2.5% in 1995. Inflation, which surged in 1994 to 122%, fell to 32.9% in 1995. During 1996, however, the economy collapsed due to shortsighted economic reforms and an unstable and de-capitalized banking system.

Under the leadership of former Prime Minister Ivan Kostov (UDF), who came to power in 1997, an ambitious set of reforms was launched, including introduction of a currency board regime, bringing growth and stability to the Bulgarian economy. The currency board contained inflationary pressures and the three-digit inflation in 1997 was cut to only 1% in 1998. Following declines in GDP in both 1996 and 1997, the Bulgarian Government delivered strong, steady GDP growth in real terms in recent years. Prime Minister Simeon Saxe-Coburg's economic team of young, Western-educated financiers continued to implement measures that helped sustain stable economic growth and curb unemployment. Measures introduced by the government were targeted at reducing corporate and individual taxes, curtailing corruption, and attracting foreign investment. The government also restructured the country's foreign debt, revived the local stock market, and moved ahead with long-delayed privatization of some major state monopolies. As a result of this progress, in October 2002 the European Commission declared Bulgaria had a "Functioning Market Economy."

Successive governments continued these reforms, and in 2007 the country joined the European Union. According to the World Bank, in 2006 Bulgaria attracted the highest levels of foreign direct investment, as a share of GDP, among Eastern European countries. In early 2007, to attract additional foreign investment, the Bulgarian Government lowered corporate tax rates to 10%, reportedly the lowest rate in Europe. A flat-tax rate of 10% for personal income, in place as of January 1, 2008, has helped to bring down domestic labor costs and reduce the share of the "gray" economy. In response to local governments' demand for financial independence in 2006, parliament passed fiscal decentralization of municipalities, granting them authority over collection and administration of some taxes, thus further enhancing local economic stability. The 2007-2009 global financial and economic crisis erased many of the gains attributed to conservative fiscal policies and tax reforms. After 10 years of steady growth, Bulgaria's economy fell into recession in the fourth quarter of 2008, causing an increase in both unemployment and household debt. The new government responded with an 82-point "anti-crisis" plan to maintain fiscal stability and promote economic recovery. The government also committed itself to strengthening control over EU funds and fighting organized crime and corruption.

DEFENSE

Bulgaria became a member of NATO on March 29, 2004. Bulgaria's military is currently undergoing an ambitious restructuring program which aims to bring the army up to NATO standards, modernize equipment, and bring about full integration of the civilian and armed components. In 2008, Bulgaria made the transition to an all-volunteer force. Since 1994, the U.S. Government has provided approximately $134 million in foreign military financing assistance to support training and procurement of military equipment.

As of June 2010, Bulgaria had approximately 670 troops serving abroad in support of NATO, EU, and UN missions. It currently has company-sized units working with coalition forces in Afghanistan and has maintained small contingents of troops deployed with international forces in Bosnia and Herzegovina and Kosovo. It deployed a frigate to Lebanon with UNIFIL in late 2006 and has several military observers serving in support of United Nations missions in Ethiopia, Liberia, and Kosovo.

There are three Bulgarian bases identified as “joint-use facilities” (meaning the U.S. has the right to station troops and conduct training in them) in the U.S.-Bulgarian Defense Cooperation Agreement (DCA) signed April 28, 2006 by Secretary of State Condoleezza Rice: Novo Selo Training Area (including the Aytos Storage Facility), Bezmer Air Base, and Graf Ignatievo Air Base.

FOREIGN RELATIONS

Bulgaria became a member of the North Atlantic Treaty Organization on March 29, 2004, and a member of the European Union on January 1, 2007. Bulgaria is a member of the United Nations, and in 2002-2003 served a 2-year term as a nonpermanent member on the UN Security Council. Bulgaria served as Chair-In-

Office of the Organization for Security and Cooperation in Europe (OSCE) in 2004.

Bulgaria joined the World Trade Organization in 1996. In July 1998, Bulgaria became a full member of the Central European Free Trade Agreement (CEFTA), which called for the reduction of tariffs by 2002 on most industrial and agricultural goods traded between CEFTA countries. Bulgaria has initialed free trade agreements with Turkey, Macedonia, Croatia, Lithuania, Estonia, Israel, Albania, and Latvia.

On September 22, 2009, UNESCO's Executive Board nominated Bulgarian diplomat Irina Bokova to become its next Director General; she took office in November 2009.

Bulgaria's relationship with its neighbors has generally been good. Bulgaria has proven to be a constructive force in the region and has played an important role in promoting regional security. Pursuing its initiative as a partner in the South-East European regional cooperation, Bulgaria held the chairmanship-in-office of the South-East European Cooperation Process (SEECP) for the period May 2007-May 2008.

U.S.-BULGARIAN RELATIONS

The year 2003 marked the 100th anniversary of diplomatic relations between the United States and Bulgaria. U.S.-Bulgarian relations were severed in 1950 but were restored a decade later. Bilateral relations between the two nations improved dramatically after the fall of communism. The United States moved quickly to encourage development of multi-party democracy and a market economy. The U.S. signed a Bilateral Investment Treaty in 1994 and gave Bulgaria most-favored-nation trade status in October 1996.

In 1989, the U.S. Congress passed the Support for East European Democracies Act (SEED), authorizing financial support to facilitate development of democratic institutions, political pluralism, and free market economies in the Balkan region. Since 1990, Bulgaria has received over $600 million in SEED assistance. In 2007, after its EU accession, Bulgaria graduated from the SEED program.

In May 2005 the United States and the Republic of Bulgaria signed a Defense Cooperation Agreement, which gives the United States military access to and shared use of several Bulgarian military facilities. The United States military intends to use this access to facilitate joint training with the Bulgarian and Romanian militaries. In January 2009 a treaty on avoidance of double taxation came into effect.

American citizens traveling on a U.S. passport for business or tourism purposes can enter and stay in Bulgaria for up to 90 days in a 6-month period without requiring issuance of a visa.

Bulgaria hosts the only fully American university in the region, the American University of Bulgaria in Blagoevgrad, established in 1991, drawing students from throughout southeast Europe and beyond. As of 2007, the American University of Bulgaria had over 1,000 students.

In June 2007, President George W. Bush visited Sofia following the first visit of a U.S. President, Bill Clinton, in 1999.

Principal U.S. Official
Ambassador--James B. Warlick, Jr.
Deputy Chief of Mission--Susan Sutton
Political-Economic Counselor--Kelly Adams-Smith
Legal Attache--Timothy Langan, Jr.
Public Affairs Counselor--Kenneth Moskowitz
Management Counselor--Steve Adams-Smith
Regional Security Officer--Thomas Huey
Defense Attache--Col. David Wilcot
Office of Defense Cooperation--Ltc Eric Hartman
Commercial Counselor--Scott Pozil
Agriculture Counselor--Hoa Huynh
Consul General--Eric Alexander

The **U.S. Embassy** is located at 16 Kozyak Street, Sofia; tel: [359] (2) 937-5100; facsimile: [359] (2) 9375-320.

TRAVEL AND BUSINESS INFORMATION

The U.S. Department of State's Consular Information Program advises Americans traveling and residing abroad through Country Specific Information, Travel Alerts, and Travel Warnings. **Country Specific Information** exists for all countries and includes information on entry and exit requirements, currency regulations, health conditions, safety and security, crime, political disturbances, and the addresses of the U.S. embassies and consulates abroad. **Travel Alerts** are issued to disseminate information quickly about terrorist threats and other relatively short-term conditions overseas that pose significant risks to the security of American travelers. **Travel Warnings** are issued when the State Department recommends that Americans avoid travel to a certain country because the situation is dangerous or unstable.

For the latest security information, Americans living and traveling abroad should regularly monitor the Department's Bureau of Consular Affairs Internet web site at http://www.travel.state.gov, where the current Worldwide Caution, Travel Alerts, and Travel Warnings can be found. Consular Affairs Publications, which contain information on obtaining passports and planning a safe trip abroad, are also available at http://www.travel.state.gov. For additional information on international travel, see http://www.usa.gov/Citizen/Topics/Travel/International.shtml.

The Department of State encourages all U.S. citizens traveling or residing abroad to register via the State Department's travel registration website or at the nearest U.S. embassy or consulate abroad. Registration will make your presence and whereabouts known in case it is necessary to contact you in an emergency and will enable you to receive up-to-date information on security conditions.

Emergency information concerning Americans traveling abroad may be obtained by calling 1-888-407-4747 toll free in the U.S. and Canada or the regular toll line 1-202-501-4444 for callers outside the U.S. and Canada.

The National Passport Information Center (NPIC) is the U.S. Department of State's single, centralized public contact center for U.S. passport information. Telephone: 1-877-4-USA-PPT (1-877-487-2778); TDD/TTY: 1-888-874-7793. Passport information is available 24 hours, 7 days a week. You may speak with a representative Monday-Friday, 8 a.m. to 10 p.m., Eastern Time, excluding federal holidays.

Travelers can check the latest health information with the U.S. Centers for Disease Control and Prevention in Atlanta, Georgia. A hotline at 800-CDC-INFO (800-232-4636) and a web site at http://wwwn.cdc.gov/travel/default.aspx give the most recent health advisories, immunization recommendations or requirements, and advice on food and drinking water safety for regions and countries.

PRACTICAL INFORMATION FOR DOING BUSINESS[2]

DOING BUSINESS IN BULGARIA

MARKET OVERVIEW

Three years after joining the European Union (EU), Bulgaria is on the radar screen of U.S. firms for investments and business opportunities. The country enjoys political stability, and forecasts are for slight or flat economic growth in 2010. The Bulgarian Government introduced the lowest tax rates in the region – ten per cent rate both on personal income and on corporate income, which contributed to strong foreign investment inflows. The global financial crisis has slowed investment growth somewhat, particularly in the real estate and manufacturing sectors. So far, Bulgaria has weathered the global financial downturn through strict fiscal discipline. The currency peg to the Euro and fixed exchange rate are seen as an obstacle to export of Bulgarian products, especially in the context of currency devaluation in neighboring countries. Home demand will remain low due to limited allocation of consumer loans and a 11% jobless rate. Other risks include high foreign debt and another gas crisis due to dependency on Russia for supply.

U.S. companies are successfully conducting business across the major industry sectors. The top two foreign investors in Bulgaria are U.S. companies. EU membership will continue to result in funding for infrastructure projects, provided that the Bulgarian government procedures are efficient and transparent. Due to geographical location, Bulgaria is an excellent launching pad for sales into the European Union, Russia, Turkey and the Middle East.

Bulgaria joined NATO in 2004 and is participating in joint operations. The general attitude in Bulgaria is pro-American and the Bulgarian market is receptive to American goods and services.

MARKET CHALLENGES

Bulgaria offers excellent opportunities for U.S. firms, but there are challenges. While the business climate is generally positive, there are factors that inhibit trade and investment. The major challenges include: inefficient bureaucracy; a slow moving court system, organized crime influence in some sectors of the economy; corruption; intellectual property rights violations; and a complicated and often non transparent tendering process.

Although Bulgaria has experienced growth for 9 of the last 10 years, the country remains one of the EU's poorest countries with limited consumer disposable income.

Upon its EU accession, Bulgaria adopted regulations and standards that conform to EU norms. While this is good news for many U.S. firms, American companies sometimes find these EU regulations and standards difficult to understand. The U.S. mission to the EU provides assistance to U.S. companies. Please refer to their website for more information: http://www.buyusa.gov/europeanunion/

MARKET OPPORTUNITIES

Bulgaria boasts a talented labor force, one of the lowest wage rates in EU, and a convenient geographical location. EU membership offers additional opportunities as Structural and Cohesion funds are funding major infrastructure projects. Please refer to: http://www.buyusa.gov/europeanunion/eu_funds.html

[2] US Governmetn materials. Doing Business in Bulgaria Commercial Guide

Good prospects for exports to Bulgaria are listed below (in alphabetical order). A more

detailed analysis of these sectors can be found in Chapter Four of this Guide:

Financing from the U.S. Export-Import Bank (Exim Bank) http://www.exim.gov and the Overseas Private Investment Corporation (OPIC) http://www.opic.gov is available. The U.S. Trade and Development Agency (USTDA) http://www.ustda.gov offers financing for technical assistance, feasibility studies, orientation visits, and training grants.

MARKET ENTRY STRATEGY

Finding a good, reputable local representative is key in order to successfully enter the market, and conducting due diligence before selecting a representative is essential. Enlisting qualified local legal services for contract negotiations is also highly recommended. The U.S. Commercial Service located in the U.S. Embassy in Sofia can assist with market research, contact facilitation, contact evaluation, and service providers – refer to: http://www.buyusa.gov/bulgaria

SELLING PRODUCTS AND SERVICES

USING AN AGENT OR DISTRIBUTOR

Bulgarian law stipulates that representation in court and before administrative agencies must be performed by duly licensed members of the Bulgarian Bar Association, who are independent practitioners in law firms or who are certain employees of corporations.

Bulgaria does not allow foreign (i.e., non-EU) lawyers to practice in Bulgarian courts, except as defense counsel of a national of his/her own country in civil and criminal action, while accompanied by a Bulgarian lawyer, where this has been envisaged in an agreement between the Bulgarian and the respective foreign state, or on the basis of reciprocity, and in both cases after submitting a preliminary request to this effect to the Chairperson of the Supreme Bar Council. In the case of a corporation, representation may be either by an authorized senior executive of the firm such as executive director, or by an employee who has passed the practical examination of the Ministry of Justice and who has a power of attorney from the corporation to represent it as "in-house counsel".

A Bulgarian patent representative who specializes in intellectual property rights and who is admitted to practice before the Bulgarian Patent Office is also essential for preparing documents to protect intellectual property rights. Some lawyers are patent representatives.

Other services such as filing corporate documents with the courts or the Commercial Registry, legal opinions, and legal consultations, are in practice performed by self-styled "legal consultants" whose qualifications and experience may vary. Some legal consultants may be former in-house counsel. Attorneys who are members of the

Bulgarian Bar Association also provide such services. Additionally, some of the larger international accounting and consultancy firms have established legal offices, which perform some of the services offered by a law firm.

The AmCham membership list at http://www.amcham.bg and the Commercial Service Business Service Provider http://www.buyusa.gov/bulgaria/en/serviceproviderlist.html are good places to start when looking for legal and other business services in Bulgaria.

The EU regulations and legislation for this topic can be found in the European Country

ESTABLISHING AN OFFICE

The Law on Encouragement of Investments sets forth preferential treatment measures for foreign or local investments. The measures are differentiated according to the class of the investments, and include two levels of benefits, depending on the amount of the investment. For more information, see http://www.investbg.government.bg/index.php

A representative office for information gathering and non-proprietary activities, such as performing promotions, exhibitions, demonstrations, training or advertising of products or services, is established by registration with the Bulgarian Chamber of Commerce and Industry http://www.bcci.bg/index.htm

A representative office is not a legal entity in Bulgaria. The Law on Encouragement of Investments places certain restrictions on the office's activities, and in particular, a representative office may not carry out commercial activities. The Law on Commerce defines the various forms of economic associations and regulates their foundation, organization, and termination. While it is possible to register a branch of a foreign entity in Bulgaria, the most common type of organization for foreign investors is a limited liability company (OOD), or a one-person owned limited liability company (EOOD) respectively.

FRANCHISING

More than half of the franchise chains present in Bulgaria have entered the market during the last five or six years, and significant surge has been seen during 2007 and 2008. This trend will accelerate even more as disposable income and understanding of the franchise business model grows. Due to the growth in this sector, we have added Franchising to our top sectors in Chapter 4 of this guide. Among the most visible brands in Bulgaria are: KFC, Dunkin Donuts, Subway, Pizza Hut, Berlitz, ERA, Centrury 21, Remax, GNC, Wilson Learning and others. The recent entry of Curves, Subway, and Starbucks demonstrate that the American frinchase concept is becoming popular as the local market matures..

The Bulgarian legal system accommodates franchise agreements. Laws on labor relations are clearly spelled out, leases can be freely negotiated, and laws protect trademarks, patents and copyrights.

DIRECT MARKETING

Direct marketing is not popular in Bulgaria. There are few Bulgarian mail-order catalogs. Vacuum cleaners, small kitchen appliances, home healthcare products and consumables, hospitality, catering and cosmetics are being sold fairly successfully door-to-door. Companies employ different marketing techniques. A Slovenian company, which offers direct marketing of U.S. products, and an Austrian company are currently using television home shopping "infomercials" to sell kitchen tools and fittness appliances not available in local shops. Home demonstrations are not popular and have generated little success. Avon and the Swedish company Oriflame report success in the direct sale of cosmetics.

Direct marketing through catalogs, telemarketing and the Internet from the U.S. to

Bulgaria is still quite difficult. Bulgarians are switching to debit and credit cards but still prefer to use cash. Catalog and internet shopping are still in their infancy due to low purchasing power, the high cost of shipping, and lack of security for parcels.

The EU regulations and legislation for this topic can be found in the European Country

JOINT VENTURES/LICENSING

In addition to establishing their own companies, U.S. companies can also invest in existing companies.

Joint ventures with state-owned companies (i.e., wholly owned by the Bulgarian State) must be approved by the Council of Ministers or by the relevant minister. The negotiation phase usually addresses the evaluation of existing assets and contribution of the foreign partner. The foreign contribution can be in cash and/or in-kind (e.g., knowledge sharing). The contribution of the local partner is usually in long-term assets (i.e., existing equipment, and facilities).

Joint ventures with private companies do not follow the same procedures. No government involvement or approval is necessary. After completion of negotiations, the new legal entity must be registered in the Commercial Registry. Joint ventures are subject to the provisions of the Law on Protection of Competition regulating concentration of economic activity.

SELLING TO THE GOVERNMENT

Public procurement procedures used by state agencies and state controlled companies for purchases are prescribed by the Law on Public Procurement. The law harmonizes Bulgarian legislation with the two major public procurement directives of the EU. According to the said law, a government procurement agency was established, responsible for public procurement and reporting to the Minister of Economy, Energy and Tourism. The most often used form of procurement is a public tender.

All Bulgarian and foreign companies are eligible to participate in public procurement tenders in Bulgaria. The Commission on Protection of Competition (CPC) is the authority enforcing the Law on Public Procurement and the Law on Protection of Competition . Appeals are no longer under the direct competence of the civil courts.

Regarding public tenders funded by EU funds, see http://www.buyusa.gov/europeanunion/eu_funds.html

DISTRIBUTION AND SALES CHANNELS

Recent developments in retail sales channels are worth noting.

By the end of 2009, the following retail chains had established a network of stores throughout Bulgaria: Fantastiko (33), Billa (40), Metro (11), Picadilly (22), Praktiker (8), Hit (2), Mr. Bricolage (10), Baumax (2), German discounters Penny (20), Kaufland (19), T Market (28), PLUS (2).

Como (1) and Aiko (4) are furniture and houseware retail chains. Technopolis (23), Technomarket (43), Densi (6) and Domo are retail chains for consumer electronics.

The German food retail chains Lidl and Carrefour, the world's second-largest retailer after Wal-Mart, are expected to start operations sometime in 2010.

According to GfK Shopping Monitor, Bulgarian consumers still prefer to shop at the local store near their homes. There are three major factors, which influence the choice of the place for shopping: the proximity to home and the working place, the level of prices, and the range of goods. The Bulgarian consumer is still not very mobile – less than 30 per cent of consumers go shopping by automobile, which limits the choice of stores. The percentage of consumers who read promotional brochures is barely 26 per cent.

Shopping malls in Sofia (4), Plovdiv (2), Veliko Turnovo (1), Stara Zagora (1) and Varna(1) are becoming very popular among the urban population. Several others shopping malls are in process of being built.

SELLING FACTORS/TECHNIQUES

Bulgarian consumers and companies have low purchasing power, which means that price is a major consideration in developing a market strategy. American companies are widely recognized for their quality and reasonable price, and value sells well in Bulgaria.

Available market size statistics are usually unreliable and do not assist in accurately predicting market responses.

ELECTRONIC COMMERCE

Shopping over the Internet is not very popular in Bulgaria and most people still prefer to shop at local stores. Despite these difficulties, some companies are already offering goods for sale over the Internet.

TRADE PROMOTION AND ADVERTISING

The 1998 Law on the Protection of Competition, and the 2006 Law on Protection of the

Consumers and on Trading Rules regulate advertising. These laws prohibit advertisements that disseminate misleading information to consumers or malign the reputation of competitors. Separate legislation regulates advertising for specific products such as tobacco products, pharmaceuticals, and alcoholic beverages.

All the normal channels for advertising are available and are widely used in Bulgaria, including newspapers, internet banners, magazines, television, radio, and outdoor billboards/signs.

Trade fair activities in Bulgaria grew rapidly to a full year's schedule of industry and product specific events in major cities around the country. Bulgaria has a number of industry-specific trade shows. Many U.S. products are displayed through local agents, distributors and dealers.

PRICING

Due to low per capita income and purchasing power, consumers are highly price sensitive. Consumers are willing to spend more in return for higher quality.

Most people restrict purchasing to basic necessities. Imported products are typically higher priced than locally produced goods. Small niche markets exist where consumers demand high-end luxury goods.

SALES SERVICE/CUSTOMER SUPPORT

Bulgarian consumers expect good after-sales service and customer support when purchasing products. New private companies understand the importance of customer support and follow through on promises.

Companies expect support from the U.S. exporter when purchasing imported products.

Emphasis on customer support is an initial step in developing customer loyalty.

Most American companies operating in Bulgaria provide training to their distributors/agents. In many cases, agents and distributors are trained in the U.S. in order to communicate the firm's distinctive corporate policies, behavior, and standards.

PROTECTING YOUR INTELLECTUAL PROPERTY

Several general principles are important for effective management of intellectual property rights in Bulgaria. First, it is important to have an overall strategy to protect IPR. Second, IPR is protected differently in Bulgaria than in the U.S. Third, rights must be registered and enforced in Bulgaria, under local laws. Companies may wish to seek advice from local attorneys or IP consultants. A Bulgarian patent representative who specializes in intellectual property rights and who is admitted to practice before the Bulgarian Patent Office is also essential for preparing documents to protect intellectual property rights. Some lawyers are patent representatives as well.

It is vital that companies understand that intellectual property is primarily a private right and that the U.S. government generally cannot enforce rights for private individuals in Bulgaria. It is the responsibility of the rights' holders to register, protect, and enforce their rights where relevant, retaining their own counsel and advisors. While the U.S. Government is willing to assist, there is little it can do if the rights holders have not taken these fundamental steps necessary to securing and enforcing their IPR in a timely fashion. It is also recommended that companies understand the importance of working together with trade associations and international organizations to support efforts to protect IPR and stop counterfeiting.

IPR Resources

A wealth of information on protecting IPR is freely available to U.S. rights holders. Some excellent resources for companies regarding intellectual property include the following:

Bulgarian law protects intellectual property rights, but enforcement is often problematic.

Bulgaria is a member of the World Intellectual Property Organization (WIPO) and a signatory to the following agreements:

-- Paris Convention for the Protection of Intellectual Property;

-- Rome Convention for the Protection of Performers, Producers of Phonograms and Broadcast Organizations;

-- Geneva Phonograms Convention;

-- Madrid Agreement for the Repression of False or Deceptive Indications of Source of Goods;

-- Madrid Agreement on the International Classification and Registration of Trademarks;

-- Patent Cooperation Treaty;

-- Universal Copyright Convention;

-- Bern Convention for the Protection of Literary and Artistic Works;

-- Lisbon Agreement for the Protection of Appellations of Origin and their International Registration;

-- Budapest Treaty on the International Recognition of the Deposit of Microorganisms for the Purpose of Patent Protection;

-- Nairobi Treaty on the Protection of the Olympic Symbol;

-- Vienna Agreement Establishing an International Classification of the Figurative Elements of Marks;

-- Nice Agreement Concerning the International Classification of Goods and Services for the Purposes of the Registration of Marks;

-- Strasbourg Agreement Concerning the International Patent Classification;

-- Locarno Agreement Establishing an International Classification for Industrial Designs;

-- WIPO Copyright Treaty; and

-- WIPO Performances and Phonograms Treaty.

DUE DILIGENCE

The U.S. Commercial Service offers the International Company Profile service for evaluating potential business partners. See www.buyusa.gov/bulgaria for more information.

There is only one internationally recognized credit-reporting agency in Bulgaria, Credit

Reform Bulgaria http://www.creditreform.bg/en/index.jsp , headquartered in Germany, although there are new companies that have advertised their ability to check corporate references and provide corporate financial data.

The official database online source called DAXY (www.daxy.com) provides information on official court, tax, address registration of Bulgarian companies, major shareholders, balance sheets, direct and indirect connections between and among managers and other Bulgarian companies and other public information.

An agency called the Financial Intelligence Agency http://www.fia.minfin.bg/?cat=2&lang=1 (member of the international EGMONT Group) was established in the Ministry of Finance in 2001 by virtue of the Law on Amendments and Complements to the Law on Measures against Money Laundering (LMML). Under December 2007 legislation, FIA was transferred to the new State Agency for National Security (DANS) and became the Financial Intelligence Directorate (FID). The FID receives, preserves, examines, analyses and discloses to law enforcement bodies information, connected with suspicion of money laundering or financing of terrorist activities. The Directorate also carries out international exchange of financial intelligence information and performs control over the persons under article 3, paragraphs 1 and 2 of the LMML with regard to the compliance with the anti-money laundering measures and measures against financing terrorist activities.

LOCAL PROFESSIONAL SERVICES

The American Chamber of Commerce in Bulgaria (AmCham) maintains a membership list that can be sorted by product and service. The AmCham web site http://www.amcham.bg is a good place to start when looking for legal and other business services in Bulgaria. From the AmCham home page, click on "About us" then "Members list" for a directory of local professional services.

WEB RESOURCES

http://sofia.usembassy.gov/ (U.S. Embassy, Sofia)

http://www.buyUSA.gov/bulgaria (U.S. Commercial Service, Sofia)

http://www.buyusa.gov/europeanunion (U.S. Mission to the EU, Brussels)

http://www.government.bg (Bulgarian Government English language site)

http://www.amcham.bg (American Chamber of Commerce in Bulgaria)

http://www.bcci.bg (Bulgarian Chamber of Commerce and Industry)

http://b2b.bia-bg.com/index.asp (Bulgarian Industrial Association)

http://www.sofiaecho.com (English language news service for Bulgaria)

http://www.daxy.com (business, financial and tax registration of Bulgarian companies)

http://www.creditreform.bg/en/index.jsp (credit-reporting agency)

LEADING SECTORS FOR U.S. EXPORT AND INVESTMENT

AUTOMOTIVE

OVERVIEW

The automotive market in Bulgaria, which was characterized with steady growth of new car imports and sales as well as steady imports of used cars through the end of August 2009, has suffered a nearly 50% decline since that time.

The number of new cars sold during the first 9 months of 2008 in Bulgaria was 39,926 compared to 45,145 for all of 2007 and 42,625 in 2006; the number of trucks and buses sold in 2008 was 2,923 compared to 2,851 for all of 2007 and 2,675 in 2006. For the three year period 2006 through 2008, the automotive import car market in Bulgaria registered growth of 16% for cars and 61.8% for trucks and busses.

Despite the stronger sales of new automobiles, the used car market in Bulgaria still dominates with approximately 150.000 cars entering the market each year. Almost 18% of the cars registered in Bulgaria are older than ten years. Since 2000, Bulgarian families prefer to buy cars not older than ten years. Now almost 70% of Bulgarian families own a car and almost 80% of the firms with business activities have motor pools, which depending on their activities, consists of cars, vans, minibuses, jeeps and light trucks. Companies prefer to use leasing schemes on the basis of return-replace.

The automotive aftermarket and collision repair car business is one of the fastest growing in Bulgaria. The growth in numbers of European cars will lead to a need for more sophisticated service and car body repair equipment, both mechanical and electronic, paint products, and application methods at an affordable price. The official distributors of all new car models maintain warranty service and repair stations within their company structures. For newer used cars, sophisticated electronic car equipment requires special analyzers, testers and experts to deal with it.

Best sales prospects include consumables, tuning equipment and accessories, service equipment for electronic diagnosis, monitoring, testing and analyzing and auto cosmetics for the second hand car market, year 2000 or later.

Very few Bulgarian companies import classic cars and/or tuning equipment. These companies suffer many tariff and non-tariff trade barriers.

In January 2010, the new Bulgarian government finally responded to the car importers' requirements for concurrence with the EU rules for eliminating level excise duties on cars with engine capacity of over 166 horse power.

For more information and market entry strategies contact:

Uliana Kanelli, Commercial Specialist
U.S. Commercial Service, Sofia, Bulgaria
Tel: 359-2-939-5706
Email: uliana.kanelli@mail.doc.gov
http://www.buyusa.gov/bulgaria

RESOURCES

Union of Car Importers in Bulgaria (UCIB) – www.svab.bg

Bulgarian Customs – www.customs.bg

Expoteam (organizer of the largest automotive market and aftermarket show in Sofia) – www.expoteam.org

Bulgarreklama (organizer of the International Plovdiv Fair) – www.bulgarreklama.bg and www.fair.bg

AEROSPACE AND DEFENSE

OVERVIEW

The total market for aviation, runway systems and air traffic control equipment and services for a short to medium five-year term is estimated at approximately $200 million. This market is supplied almost entirely by imports.

Growth in this market is influenced by the ICAO, IATA, IASA, EASA, Eurocontrol, Open Sky and Common European Sky agreements and requirements for sustainable development, quality improvements, safety and security upgrades and compliance to international standards.

The end user market includes 6 international airports, Aviation Administration (CAA), Air Traffic Services Authority (ATSA), the major air carriers and services companies licensed to provide ground-handling activities. The largest international airport is based in Sofia, and it operation is under the Ministry of Transportation.

The concessionaire for two airports – Varna and Bourgas, declared intentions to invest approximately Euro 500 million, 10% of which during the first three years of its management.

The procedure for privatization of the other two international airports (Rousse and Gorna Orjahovitza) by means of concession is expected to be determined in 2010 and officially announced on the web site of the Bulgarian Ministry of Transport (www.mt.government.bg)

The fifth airport - Plovdiv airport is designated to be jointly utilized by Ministry of Transport and Ministry of Defense/ Airforces. The infrastructure upgrades at this airport were completed in 2009.

The Air Traffic Services Authority (ATSA) completed the selection process for design of a new air traffic control tower and is preparing to announce its engineering and construction phase.

By the end of 2007, there were 10 licensed air operators in Bulgaria and 60 flying machines, all of them with a valid "CofA" (Certificate of Airworthiness) code. The total number of large aircrafts (over 5700 kg) is 38 with a valid "CofA" code. The total number of small aircrafts (below 5700 kg) is 13 with a valid "CofA" code. Separately there are 55 light jets up to 5.7 tones, 30% of which are second hand.

The fleet as specified consists of the following type and category by alphabetical ranking: Airbus 319, 320, ATR, Bae-146, Boeing 737, BE20, CE-550, CL60, CL64, L-410 and MD 80.

The helicopter fleet consists of large helicopters (over 3175 kg) type Mi-8, total number is 6, all of them with a valid "CofA" code and small helicopters (below 3175 kg) type BO105 and SA 365N1, total number is 3, all of them with a valid "CofA" code. Two private operators purchased Gulfstream and Bell helicopters, which depending on the onboard equipment, can be used for different purposes like agriculture, firefighting, courier, etc.

Demand is estimated to be highest for airport and air traffic control equipment and related services, for services related to concessioning of airport activities, to cargo handling outsourcing and management, runway systems improvement, and safety and security equipment.

For more information and market entry strategies contact:

Uliana Kanelli, Commercial Specialist
U.S. Commercial Service, Sofia, Bulgaria
Tel: 359-2-939-5706
Email: uliana.kanelli@mail.doc.gov
http://www.buyusa.gov/bulgaria

RESOURCES

Ministry of Transport and Communications --www.mtc.government.bg

Civil Aviation Administration – www.caa.bg

Airport Sofia – www.sofia-airport.bg

Bulgarian Aviation directory – www.aviation.bg

ENVIRONMENTAL TECHNOLOGIES

OVERVIEW

Bulgaria's accession to the EU was a major impetus for large-scale environmental remediation and implementation of new environmental standards in Bulgaria. Bulgaria will have to invest more than EUR11.6 billion by 2013 in order to meet EU environmental requirements, some of the funding coming from EU funds for environmental infrastructure projects. Bulgaria will need to import almost all of the technology for these requirements, and U.S. companies that possess world-class technology, equipment, services and systems at competitive prices will be best poised to benefit from these opportunities. There are no restrictions for U.S. firms to take advantage of EU funding for environmental projects.

Water and wastewater:

Most industries in Bulgaria need to construct or upgrade their wastewater treatment facilities in the next 3-4 years in order to meet the new EU requirement. Urban wastewater treatment plants are planned for more than 400 cities and towns with populations over 2,000, through 2015.

Solid waste:

Currently Bulgaria utilizes landfills for the disposal of municipal waste. The EU requires Bulgaria to decrease the number of landfills. There is a critical need to find more environmentally friendly ways to handle hazardous, solid, and industrial waste, such as waste-to-energy projects, recycling, and waste minimization. There are a few projects underway for the construction of solid waste treatment plants.

Air:

The air-pollution control sector will provide opportunities for construction of air-pollution control installations at large industrial facilities.

For more information and market entry strategies contact:

Stanislava Dimitrova, Commercial Specialist
U.S. Commercial Service, Sofia, Bulgaria
Tel: 359-2-939-5740
Email: Stanislava.Dimitrova@mail.doc.gov
http://www.buyusa.gov/bulgaria

FRANCHISING

OVERVIEW

More than half of the franchise chains present in Bulgaria have entered the market during the last five years, and a significant surge has been seen during 2007 and 2008. This trend will accelerate even more as disposable income and understanding of the franchise business model grows.

Franchising is most apparent in the fast-food sector with many local and internationally recognized fast-food franchises operating in Bulgaria. The Bulgarian retail market is now ready for the many products and services that are typically marketed and sold internationally through franchise stores. Bulgarian consumers are looking for retailers that can provide a consistent selection of quality products, reasonable prices and good service. Bulgarian entrepreneurs are also eager to obtain marketing and management expertise. The Bulgarian legal framework is very accommodating to foreign franchises. Currently, there are no franchise laws or specific regulations pertaining to this business model. In general, no specific registration or government approval is required in order to establish a franchise enterprise.

Among the most visible brands in Bulgaria are: KFC, Dunkin Donuts, Subway, Pizza

Hut, Berlitz, ERA, Century 21, Remax, GNC, and Wilson Learning. The recent entry of Curves, Subway and Starbucks, demonstrate that the American franchise concept is becoming popular as the local market matures. McDonald's is the most visible franchise around the country with nearly 30 restaurants that employ over 1,000 Bulgarians and serve over 6 million customers a year.

Sectors with the most significant potential for U.S. franchisers include automotive

products and services, restaurants, coffee shops, lodging (hotels), laundry/dry-cleaning, hotel management, real estate brokerage, nutrition and supplement industry products, and employment/educational/training services. Good franchise opportunities also include convenience stores, ice cream/yogurt stores, hardware stores, marketing/public relations, specialty retail stores, commercial and residential cleaning, recreation facilities/equipment and services, baked foods, candy and snacks.

For more information on market entry strategies contact:

Emily Taneva, Commercial Specialist
U.S. Commercial Service, Sofia, Bulgaria
Tel: 359-2-939-5770
Email: emily.taneva@mail.doc.gov
http://www.buyusa.gov/bulgaria

Resources

http://franchising.start.bg/ Franchising in Bulgaria

www.bulfa.org Bulgarian Franchise Association

HEALTHCARE/MEDICAL

Overview

The short and long term development of the healthcare sector in Bulgaria will be strongly determined by the new phase of the health sector reform.

The new government, which came to power in July 2009, is planning to introduce,reforms, which will include a revision and remodeling of hospitals' reimbursement method and format. These reforms will be based on the revision of the Disease Related Groups (DRG) principle, assigning new roles of the university hospitals as major players. Moreover, all hospitals will be incentivized to start implementing the latest high tech non-invasive surgery and monitoring equipment, laser equipment and other new methodology equipment, to increase and improve the knowledge of the entire healthcare society – doctors, general practitioners, medical equipment importers and distributors, NHIF and social institutions.

Beginning this year, the Ministry of Healthcare decided to close down 21 hospitals and optimize the scope of work of another 158 hospitals.

In times of overall worldwide economic crisis, Bulgarian Ministry of Healthcare is following its long-term labor and reimbursement strategy adjustment policy along with upgrading the other components of its overall operational system.

The Health Sector Reform Project has several components: the first is the reform and sustainability of the primary and ambulatory care sector. It provides practice equipment for primary health care, funds physician office information systems, provides training in general practitioner (GP) practice management, funds an information campaign, finances a health reform investment program to provide low-interest loans to physicians, and funds a labor adjustment strategy.

The second component targets reform of the hospital system, including funding hospital information systems, financing a health reform investment program, reducing the number of hospitals, optimizing their functionality and funding a labor adjustment strategy. Other tasks include implementation of a hospital accreditation system, introduction of healthcare electronic data and record management systems, coping with EU assigned duties such as improvement and expansion of HIV and tuberculosis prevention meausres, extending In-Vitro programs, improvement of emergency and ambulance systems, and a CRM system to handle emergency calls.

The third component aims at assisting the National Health Insurance Fund (NHIF) to establish the technological infrastructure to operate the insurance system, including the hardware and software systems needed as well as the training and technical assistance required. The final component aims at strengthening the management and institutional capacity of the health ministry, the NHIF, and the health system generally.

The health sector reform strategy will result in a demand for invasive and noninvasive surgery equipment, ultrasound equipment, in-vitro diagnostic equipment, urology equipment, laboratory and testing equipment, diagnostic imaging equipment, equipment for haemodilysis, tissue and blood bank related equipment, veterinary turnkey project equipment, hospital care equipment, information systems, modern patient monitoring systems, and hospital management systems.

For more information and market entry strategies contact:

Uliana Kanelli, Commercial Specialist
U.S. Commercial Service, Sofia, Bulgaria
Tel: 359-2-939-5706
Email: uliana.kanelli@mail.doc.gov
http://www.buyusa.gov/bulgaria

Resources

Ministry of Healthcare – www.mh.government.bg

Bulgarian Drug Agency – www.bda.bg

National Health Insurance Fund (NHIF) – www.nhif.bg

Bulgarreklama (agency organizing the international exhibition Bulmedica, Buldental,

Buloptics, Bullabor) – www.bulgarreklama.com

INFRASTRUCTURE PROJECTS AND REAL ESTATE DEVELOPMENT

Overview

The Bulgarian Government's goals to clean up the country's environment; modernize its infrastructure and further develop its real estate base represent an extraordinary business opportunity for U.S. companies.

After EU accession in January 2007, Bulgaria directed efforts, resources and initiatives to modernizing its outdated infrastructure and boost economic growth. The pessimism related to recent developments in the U.S. and Western Europe real estate sector shifted toward this small Balkan country, but the impact has been relatively small. Solid GDP growth and a real estate market propelled by a flood of foreign investors also fueled construction. EBRD, Raiffeisen and a few other international banks are actively supporting the large scale development and redevelopment projects in Bulgaria providing funds to businesses and municipalities. The construction sector is facing the challenges of rising material costs and a drop in demand. Local financial attention and foreign investments are being placed on the dilapidated road and rail networks, new metro stations construction, shopping centers, tourism industry, department store chains, telecommunications and infrastructure. The Bulgarian market for building materials is growing at more than 20% per year.

U.S. companies that specialize in road network upgrading, park development, golf course development, management and development of logistic, residential, shopping and industrial complexes, and airport development will find many opportunities. Real estate investors and firms providing public-private partnership solutions in the area of commercial and residential site development, water and wastewater treatment, earthmoving, road building, installation of underground utilities, construction material suppliers may have excellent opportunities to participate in the upgrade of major transport and tourism-related infrastructure facilities.

For more information on market entry strategies contact:

Emily Taneva, Commercial Specialist
U.S. Commercial Service, Sofia, Bulgaria
Tel: 359-2-939-5770
Email: emily.taneva@mail.doc.gov
http://www.buyusa.gov/bulgaria

RESOURCES

Ministry of Transport and Communications --www.mtc.government.bg

Ministry of Regional Development, Directorate for National Construction Supervision

www.mrrb.government.bg

Chamber of the Architects in Bulgaria - www.geocities.com/arch_art/kabinx.html

Bulgarian Construction Chamber - www.kcb.bg

INFORMATION AND COMMUNICATION TECHNOLOGIES

As Bulgarian companies must increase their competitiveness in the EU, and the Bulgarian Government must comply with EU directives and legislation on various aspects of the digital economy, new and expanded opportunities exist in the ICT sector.

International software companies find Bulgaria attractive because of the 0% export tax, low costs and local workforce skills. Both fixed and mobile segments of the Bulgarian ICT market still have high growth potential with large investments expected in both segments.

A number of foreign companies are opening call/service centers in Bulgaria. There are opportunities for participation in tenders for sale of computers, peripherals, and servers for government procurement. Moreover, the Bulgarian Government and private telecom companies have various information and communication initiatives that will provide major opportunities.

U.S. providers of advanced telephone service solutions and value-added telecommunications services are in demand. Other best prospects include Internet services, wireless and broadband Internet access technologies, cable television, and voice-over-Internet, routers, switches, access servers, equipment for mobile telephony, including WiMAX technologies, cable operators' equipment and fixed wireless equipment.

For more information and market entry strategies contact:

Stanislava Dimitrova, Commercial Specialist
U.S. Commercial Service, Sofia, Bulgaria
Tel: 359-2-939-5740
Email: Stanislava.Dimitrova@mail.doc.gov
http://www.buyusa.gov/bulgaria

RESOURCES

www.nsi.bg - National Statistical Institute of Bulgaria

www.daits.government.bg - State Agency on IT and Communications

www.crc.bg - Communications Regulation Commission

www.investbg.government.bg - Invest Bulgaria Agency

www.basscom.org - BASSCOM

www.bait.bg - Bulgarian Association of Information Technology

POWER GENERATION AND ENERGY EFFICIENCY

Bulgaria's EU membership means increased energy demand, decreased supply (the closure of Kozloduy's reactors 3 and 4), requirements for rehabilitation of the obsolete generation units, development of new thermal, nuclear power and co-generating capacities, development of alternative/renewable energy supply and increased energy efficiency.

Major rehabilitation and construction of new generating capacities are creating enormous opportunities for U.S. companies in Bulgaria. Firms providing solutions that will increase Bulgaria's energy independence and energy efficiency will also find good opportunities for equipment and services. Bulgaria is looking for energy providers other than Russia to secure its oil and natural gas supplies, amid continuous pressure from Gasprom and Lukoil. Having the worse energy intensity in Europe, Bulgaria offers significant opportunities for providing technology, services and solutions that will steadily decrease energy intensity in leading industrial sectors.

The best prospects for the U.S. companies are exports of electrical power systems and activities related to the construction of new power capacities; energy network design and construction; co-generation and district heating equipment and technologies; upgrading and maintenance of street lighting; electricity/heat consumption meter reading equipment; upgrading of boilers and electro precipitators (solid emission) and supply of Flu Gas desulphurization installations for the thermal energy sector. The coal mining sector and its rehabilitation also provide opportunities for American companies specialized in mining equipment and technologies and those than can improve the lignite mines' energy efficiency. In the gas sector opportunities include: technology and services for expanding of gas storage capacities; equipment for control of shipment and transit of gas via Ukraine; services related to construction of gas interconnections with Romania and Greece.

For more information on market entry strategies contact:

Emily Taneva, Commercial Specialist
U.S. Commercial Service, Sofia, Bulgaria
Tel: 359-2-939-5770
Email: emily.taneva@mail.doc.gov

For information on alternative/renewable energy and energy efficiency contact:
Andon Kalibatsev
U.S. Commercial Service, Sofia, Bulgaria
Tel: 359-2-939-5781
Email: andon.kalibatsev@mail.doc.gov

RESOURCES

Bulgargaz www.bulgargaz.bg

National Electric Company www.nek.bg

Kozloduy NPP www.kznpp.org

Ministry of Economy and Energy www.mi.government.bg/

State Energy and Water Regulatory Commission www.dker.bg

Energy Efficiency Agency www.SEEA.government.bg

SAFETY AND SECURITY

Safety and security are important issues for the Bulgarian government and businesses. The global threat for terrorist attacks, the EU accession of the country and the high number of thefts are affording good market opportunities for U.S. companies in this sector.

Bulgaria is an external EU border, and the country is expected to join the Schengen area in 2011 or 2012. Consequently, the government must develop projects to upgrade control on the EU's external borders and to integrate its system with the Schengen Information System (SIS). The EU pre-accession program PHARE allocated funds for the modernization of the Border Police equipment, but further upgrades are required.

The Bulgarian Ministry of Transportation and the U.S. Trade and Development Agency completed two technical assistance projects to upgrade and improve safety and security at Bulgarian international airports. In 2008, the Ministry of Interior launched a tender for design, building of a system and consultancy services for the issuance of new ID documents according to the EU requirements. The first biometrical ID documents will be issued in April, 2010.

The cities of Sofia and Varna completed projects for video surveillance in the central areas and other sensitive zones, including traffic safety and public safety. Video surveillance was launched in Varna, using 229 cameras, monitoring pedestrian areas, major crossings, and traffic safety. The budget of this project was $3 million, and the Municipality established a joint venture with the Austrian company Efkon to purchase and install the cameras. This is the first big scale monitoring system introduced in Bulgaria. Two other cities, Blagoevgrad and Lovech, have partially developed a video surveillance system.

The central area of Sofia is already under video monitoring, and the project will be extended to public schools and kindergartens. The public institutions under video surveillance are expected to reach approximately 140 at the final stages of the project. The number of installed cameras in the schools varies from 6 to 12. The network will be extended to other main boulevards, streets and entrance points in the city. The project is approximately $12 million.

Other cities are considering the opportunity to build CCTV systems. Remote control systems and information systems, including monitoring of the traffic lights, street lights, flood control were installed in some cities and similar projects will be considered in the future.

Besides video surveillance, demand is high for access control and perimeter security systems. Many private companies in the big cities offer real time monitoring of premises and physical control, and the number of clients using this technology is growing.

The Bulgarian Ministry of Interior together with Ministry of Finance, the Customs Agency and Border Police are looking for ways to improve border monitoring, security and customs database systems. Best prospects include X-ray, MR type of equipment, infrared mobile and stationary equipment, IP videosurveillance, on site field testing, access control equipment, CCTV, laboratory equipment, ID security application equipment, new IT and high tech equipment, programs and related services.

The private security sector is represented mostly by Bulgarian companies providing centralized security services by means of technical equipment via monitoring-centers and vehicle patrols, physical security, convoy of valuables and dangerous loads; delivery, installation and support of security systems. The number of companies, operating in the safety and security sector is around 1000, including guard/personal security services and detective agencies, 90% of them are small- and medium-sized companies. Most of the companies are service providers and do not directly acquire security equipment.

NAFTSO is a non-profit association and incorporates Bulgarian trading companies that provide security services. NAFTSO incorporates members - companies that provide security services. The members of the Association employ more than 17,900 workers (30.5% of the employees at the private security sector) and their turnover for the year 2007 exceeded $113.5 million (34.4% of the market). The number of guarded and secured sites exceeds 112,900. More than 60% of the commercial banks registered in the Republic of Bulgaria avail themselves of the cash collection services offered. The Association is a member of the Confederation of European Security Services (CoESS).

Local production may be found in the following areas: parts and accessories for telephones and installations, metal detectors, safe deposit boxes, intercoms, sirens, control panels, control alarm systems, electronic locking systems for elevators; electronic locking systems for external doors inputs, TV systems for day/night surveillance, systems for perimeter and outside perimeter guarding, cameras and lenses, communication cables, fire detectors, equipment and parts for access control, signaling devices and production of protective clothing with special purpose – fireproof, antistatic, water and oilproof, windproof and aggressiveproof. There is low local production in electronic security equipment, due to lack of investment in research and development of new technology.

The growth in the safety and security equipment and services sector in Bulgaria is related to the new investments made by financial institutions, airports, large industrial groups, multinational corporations, real estate companies, shopping centers, and retail chains. All commercial segments on Bulgaria's real estate market enjoyed significant growth in the past several years, so the need of safety and security equipment has increased substantially.

For more information and market entry strategies contact:

Andon Kalibatsev, Commercial Specialist
U.S. Commercial Service, Sofia, Bulgaria
Tel: 359-2-939-5781
Email: andon.kalibatsev@mail.doc.gov
http://www.buyusa.gov/bulgaria

Resources

Ministry of Finance, State Agency Customs – www.customs.bg

Ministry of Interior – www.mvr.bg

Ministry of Transport – www.mtc.government.bg

TRAVEL AND TOURISM

The tourism industry in Bulgaria plays a critical role in the country's economy. Accession to the EU has made a positive impact on the market, due to the improved facilities and hotels, great affordability and accessibility and increased exposure. Bulgaria is gaining popularity among business and leisure travelers around the world who spend over $3 billion annually here. The seaside summer resorts on the Black Sea coast and the winter mountain resorts are the main attractions. Alternative streams such as art, wine, spa-based travel, and a wide range of archaeological, historic, scenic and recreational attractions represent good potential. Building golf courses, marinas, and luxury spa facilities aims to shift a greater percentage of tourists away from low revenue package tours and into more luxurious and upscale resorts. The Bulgarian Government would like to increase off-season tourism, attracting higher spending travelers by further developing its convention and festival markets. New developments are making Bulgaria more attractive. The tourism industry accounts for 13% of GDP.

Among the primary reasons Bulgarians travel to the U.S. are leisure, incentive tours, holidays, and business including participation at conferences and exhibitions, and visits to relatives. More than 250,000 Bulgarian-Americans live in the U.S. and approximately 3,700 Bulgarian students study at American universities and colleges. Over 40,000 Bulgarian students experienced the „Work and Travel" Program that started back in the late 1990's. The primary information source for Bulgarian travelers remains their travel agent. The Internet is also considered a reliable source, especially by travelers aged 20-35. U.S. destinations have become very popular because of the weak dollar and the increased disposable income of Bulgarians.

Market segments with high potential for American firms are the development of wellness and spa complexes, golf courses, hotel management, development and expansion of marinas, high-end convention hotel development, amusement games and attractions. The sector offers opportunities for utilization of seasonally employed workers, it needs support and assistance for promotion of Bulgarian touristic sites and towns.

The U.S. Commercial Service can facilitate information exchange between U.S.-based tour operators and tourism establishments in Bulgaria. There are many mutually beneficial opportunities for business partnerships and/or collaborations. Also, regional business cooperation should be encouraged through business development (i.e. tours which combine several countries in the region).

For more information on market entry strategies contact:

Emily Taneva, Commercial Specialist
U.S. Commercial Service, Sofia, Bulgaria
Tel: 359-2-939-5770
Email: emily.taneva@mail.doc.gov
http://www.buyusa.gov/bulgaria

Resources

National Hospitality Management Club www.tourmarketing.org

International Tourism Conferences and tourist info www.bulgariantourism.com

National Tourist Info Center & Tourism Authority www.bulgariatravel.org

Bulgarian Tourist Chamber www.btch.org

Ministry of Economy and Energy – tourism sector www.mi.government.bg

State Agency for Tourism – www.bulgariatravel.org

AGRICULTURAL SECTORS

EU membership has had a significant impact on trade in food and agricultural products in Bulgaria. Certain opportunities for U.S. exporters have all but disappeared (beef, poultry) while others have expanded (below). There are also several new market opportunities for new food products. In general, Bulgarian agricultural and food imports from the U.S. will increasingly resemble the profile of U.S. exports to other EU member states that is heavily weighted toward consumer-oriented and high-value products. The demand for these products will grow due to the expanding share of disposable income that is taken by retail and food service sectors. At the end of 2008 and in early 2009, there was a visible shift in trade and consumption trends within certain product groups toward more expensive, higher-quality products, including distilled spirits, snack foods, tree nuts, seafood, and soft drinks. However, the current economic and financial crisis slowed down this trend in mid/late 2009 and most likely in 2010. In the medium and long term, lower-than-average consumer incomes will continue to be the major limiting factor in expanding U.S. sales.

In 2010, most importers will be able to operate more efficiently in the new business environment, in which convergence with EU norms is taking place gradually. Many Bulgarian importers are switching from importing directly from the U.S. to importing from wholesalers/importers within the EU which have longstanding links with U.S. exporters. For many Bulgarian importers this tends to be a relatively efficient way to buy U.S. products.

Due to growing investment and rising demand in the agricultural sector, U.S. export prospects are expected to continue to improve for agricultural inputs, including animal feed and feed additives, bovine and other animal genetic material, live animals, seeds, planting materials, and raw materials such as cotton, wool, powdered milk, and egg powder.

The major competitor for U.S. food exporters will be producers from other EU member states which have facilities in Bulgaria, as the result of a direct investment, or ship product to Bulgaria from other EU member states.

Good prospects exist for the following agricultural/food products:

1. Red meat (pork and beef)

Bulgaria is a net importer of red meats. Demand is growing both in volume and in value. While until 2007, this category represented the best opportunity for the U.S. exporters, the EU non-tariff veterinary restrictions made this trade difficult in 2007 when U.S. red meat exports to Bulgaria dropped by 50 percent. However, in 2008, as a result of collaborative promotion efforts between FAS/Sofia, U.S. Meat Export Federation and local meat industry, exports of U.S. red meat exceeded total U.S. red meat exports to Bulgaria over the last 5 years to reach $42 million. In 2009, due to the financial issues, these imports dropped to $11.6 million but were still the leading product category in U.S. agricultural exports to Bulgaria. Good market opportunities exist for U.S. exporters of price-competitive pork, mainly for processing; and hormone-free high quality beef for food service outlets. U.S. pork is also imported to the region (Romania) and from there is traded in the region.

2. Seafood

Bulgaria is a net importer of fish and seafood over the last ten years. The local market for imports in 2008 was estimated at 28,000 MT, valued at $50 million, compared to $31 million in 2007. More than 80 percent of total imports are frozen fish. In 2009 (January-October), seafood imports were 23,000 MT at $41 million. U.S. exports of seafood to Bulgaria were stable during the last three years. However, while domestic demand for all seafood products is not expected to have dropped, U.S. seafood exports to Bulgaria fell to around $3.0 million in 2007 due to the introduction of new EU regulatory requirements for imports and higher import duties on certain products from May to November. Despite this change, U.S. seafood exports in 2008 were stable at $2.5 million and increased in 2009 to $3.3 million since more high-value seafood products were imported (salmon, heck and lobsters). Prospects for 2010 are very good due to steady market development and Post having found some solutions to regulatory issues that were holding up some shipments. Demand for seafood is supported by the rapid expansion of retail and food service outlets which sell consumer-ready and ready-to-eat products. Higher value products have also seen sales increases.

3. Tree nuts

The Bulgarian market for tree nuts has had record growth over the past years: from $1.3 million in 2006, U.S. exports grew to $2.8 million in 2007 and $3.3 million in 2008. In 2009 (January-October), tree nuts exports dropped a little to $2.9 miillion. Demand is expanding due to the growing number of food service outlets, to tourism, and to an increase in the number of middle- and high-income consumers. Prospects for U.S. exporters in 2010 are good due to recognized U.S. quality, a favorable tariff and regulatory regime, a lack of local production of quality tree nuts, and growing demand.

EU tariff rates are far lower than were Bulgaria's pre-EU rates. For example, the import duty on almonds fell from 20-35 percent (2006) to 5.6 percent or zero ; for peanuts, the import tariff declined from 40 percent to zero; for walnuts, from 35 percent to 4.0-5.1 percent. In 2007, total tree nuts imports were 13,000 MT at a value of $15 million; 2008 -at 15,000 MT and $21 million and about the same size in 2009. The market is expected to be stable or with little growth in 2010.

4. Snacks/Cereals

U.S. companies face substantial competition from EU producers in the snack foods market. Snack foods generally are sourced from EU companies in the EU, or are produced locally as the result of foreign direct investment (including U.S.). Bulgaria does not have a tradition of either producing or consuming high-quality or price-competitive snack foods. Consumption has been growing thanks to changing consumer tastes due to travel, marketing by snack foods companies, rising incomes, and expanded tourism. Since production of snack foods has not kept up with demand, much of the local consumption is met by imports. In 2007, U.S. snack foods exports reached $1.1 million and increased further to $1.4 million in 2008. In 2009, due to the economic crisis, exports dropped to $0.7 million, however, it rebounded quickly in early 2010 and the prospects are optimistic for a full restoration of imports this year.

Recently, local production of confectionery products has grown thanks to investment by EU-based companies (the American-owned Kraft Foods and Nestle). Their products successfully compete with imports. Currently, there are only a few local Bulgarian producers of snack foods but their number has been rising. Local consumers perceive U.S. products as high quality and as having competitive prices. The most popular are U.S. microwave popcorn, breakfast cereals, and some types of confectionery products.

5. Distilled spirits

With Bulgaria's accession to the EU, certain export opportunities have expanded in this sector. Total imports of distilled spirits (whiskey) to Bulgaria in 2008 reached $56 million. In 2009 (January-October), imports dropped to $28 million. U.S. distilled spirits exports in 2007 were $3.0 million and a record $5.2 million in 2008 but dropped in 2009 (January-October) to $4.2 million percent due to general economic challenges . Tax regulations which were revised in 2007/08 made locally-produced spirits more expensive and less competitive compared to high-quality U.S. spirits. Import duties have declined to zero in many cases. EU competition is strong, since EU producers are benefitting from the same lower tariffs and stiffer regulatory requirements that are assisting U.S. exports.

6. Dairy genetics

Over the last two years, Bulgarian dairy farm industry has significantly increased its demand for high quality genetics materials, both for live animals, imported mainly from the EU, and for semen and embryos imported from the U.S. Farmers highly appreciate U.S. genetics and as of today, its market size is estimated at over 70 percent (in 2008) of total genetics market. In value, it is close to $1.0 million with a forecast to increase quickly to $3.0 million over the next two-three years. Trade regime (no import duties) and veterinary requirements are favorable, along with fast growing local demand.

7. Soft drinks/waters/juices

The soft drinks market is one of the most dynamic in Bulgaria. In 2008, total imports of soft drinks (HS#2201,2202) were $54.4 million followed by imports of juices (HS#2009) at $29 million, or total $83.4 million. In 2009 (January-October), imports dropped to total $55.4 million, $38.4 million and $17 million for the above two categories, respectively. Major competitors include companies in Austria, Germany, Romania, Poland, Hungary and Greece, which have more than 70 percent market share. These countries are competetive mainly due to their proximity (lower freight costs, traditional ties). Local consumption of waters, juices and energy drinks is increasing, especially in the last three years with the continued rapid development of hotel/restaurant sector. According to the local Association of Soft Drinks Producers, local consumption is expected to continue to increase over the next several years. U.S. producers can successfully compete with juice concentrates for local manufacturers (almost all concentrates are currently imported) as well as with some juices for direct consumption that are of higher quality and can be differentiated from local products. For example, cranberry juice and other frozen juices would be very popular with Bulgarian consumers if they were price competitive. EU tariffs are relatively high, however, compared with Bulgaria's pre-accession duties of 15-20 percent. EU duties are currently 15.2 percent + 20.6 Euro/100 kilos and 33.6 percent + 20.6 Euro/100 kilos.

If you would like more information, please contact the Office of Agricultural Affairs at the U.S. Embassy: agsofia@usda.gov

TRADE REGULATIONS AND STANDARDS

IMPORT TARIFFS

Bulgaria joined the EU on January 1, 2007, and became part of the EU customs union. Most Bulgarian customs provisions were replaced with the respective EU regulations including the Community Customs Code, the Integrated Community Tariff (TARIC) and implementing provisions. Please visit for more information: http://ec.europa.eu/taxation_customs/index_en.htm

TARIC rates can be found at: http://ec.europa.eu/taxation_customs/dds/tarhome_en.htm

TRADE BARRIERS

Bulgaria remains a relatively open market, but certain administrative requirements and processes are potential non-tariff trade barriers. The lack of adequate protection of intellectual property, and the need for greater transparency and predictability in the regulatory environment are common market access issues with U.S. firms. This Chapter and the section on standards describe import requirements that may be considered as trade barriers.

For information on existing trade barriers, please see the National Trade Estimate Report on Foreign Trade Barriers, published by USTR and available through the following website: http://www.ustr.gov/sites/default/files/uploads/reports/2009/NTE/asset_upload_file348_15473.pdf

Information on agricultural trade barriers can be found at the following website: http://www.fas.usda.gov/posthome/useu/

To report existing or new trade barriers and get assistance in removing them, contact either the Trade Compliance Center at http://www.trade.gov/tcc or the U.S. Mission to the European Union at http://www.buyusa.gov/europeanunion .

IMPORT REQUIREMENTS AND DOCUMENTATION

Customs valuation is based on the transaction value – the price actually paid or payable for the goods, defined in Bulgarian Leva. The dutiable value consists of the purchase price, transportation costs, insurance charges, commissions, royalties, license fees and all the transportation costs (e.g., loading and unloading). After the calculation of the customs duty, all U.S. imports are subject to a 20% Value Added Tax (VAT), levied at the time of customs clearance. Some commodities are also subject to excise duties.

Goods are declared by a customs declaration either by a commercial or other document. The customs authorities may carry out post-clearance examination of relevant documents or data. Besides the customs declaration, other required documents include an invoice or pro forma invoice, a certificate of origin or a certificate of the movement of the goods in order to take advantage from preferential customs treatment, transport documents, an insurance policy, a specification, and a packing list. A veterinary or phyto-sanitary certificate is necessary for goods of animal or plant of origin. Customs authorities may require other documents, such as a commercial treaty or a laboratory analysis.

A document issued by the competent State authority is required in case the goods are subject to a specific import procedure or a special import regulation is applied (permits, registration).

1.According to Decree 289/2009, a permit is required prior to the entry of the following products: nuclear materials, explosives, arms, dual use commodities, plant protection products, and pharmaceuticals for human medicine. This is a non-automatic licensing process. Authorization, in the form of an import license, is normally issued within five days of the Ministry's receipt of the application.

Bulgarian Customs exercises control over the export, import, re-export and transit of arms and dual-use goods and technologies. Bulgarian regulations follow the EU list of dual-use goods, which includes goods and technologies in the nuclear weapon, chemical and biological warfare and missile areas. A permit for each transaction (import, export and re-export) and transit with dual-use goods and arms issued by the Commission for Control and Permission for Foreign Transactions in Arms and Dual-use Goods and Technologies of the Ministry of Economy and Energy is required regardless of destination. More information on dual use and arms export control is available from the Military Economic Cooperation & Internationally Controlled Trade Directorate to the Ministry of Economy, Energy and Tourism, tel. 359-2-940-7030 http://www.mee.government.bg/eng/ or www.exportcontrol.bg

In case you need to know whether your item falls under control, you have to search for items that are comparable (similar) to yours from the Lists of the controlled items, namely:

for import: Decree (CoM) No. 289 / 2009
for export and re-export: Annex I to Council Regulation (EC) No. 428/2009
for transfer: Annex IV of Council Regulation (EC) No. 428/2009

2.Batteries

EU battery rules changed in September 2006 following the publication of the Directive on batteries and accumulators and waste batteries and accumulators (Directive 2006/66). This Directive replaces the original Battery Directive of 1991 (Directive 91/157). The updated Directive applies to all batteries and accumulators put on the EU market including automotive, industrial and portable batteries. It aims to protect the environment by restricting the sale of batteries and accumulators that contain mercury or cadmium (with an exemption for emergency and alarm systems, medical equipment and cordless power tools) and by promoting a high level of collection and recycling. It places the responsibility on producers to finance the costs associated with the collection, treatment, and recycling of used batteries and accumulators. The Directive also includes provisions on the labeling of batteries and their removability from equipment. For more information, see our market research report: http://www.buyusainfo.net/docs/x_8086174.pdf or

visit the CS EU website Batteries Direct page at:
http://www.buyusa.gov/europeanunion/batteries.html

REACH

REACH is a major reform of EU chemicals policy that was adopted in December 2006 and became national law in the 27 EU Member States in June 2007 (Regulation 1907/2006). Virtually every industrial sector, from automobiles to textiles, is affected by the new policy. REACH stands for the "Registration, Evaluation and Authorization and Restriction of Chemicals." Since June 1 2008, REACH requires chemicals produced or imported into the EU in volumes above 1 ton per year per to be registered with a central European Chemicals Agency (ECHA), including information on their properties, uses and safe ways of handling them. Chemicals pre-registered before December 1 2008, benefit from extended registration deadlines, from three to eleven years depending on the volume of the substance and its hazard properties. U.S. companies without a presence in Europe cannot register directly and must have their chemicals registered through their importer or EU-based 'Only Representative of non-EU manufacturer'. A list of Only Representatives can be found on the website of the U.S. Mission to the EU:
http://www.buyusa.gov/europeanunion/reach.html.

U.S. exporters to the EU should carefully consider the REACH 'Candidate List' of substances of very high concern. Substances on that list are subject to communication requirements and may at a later stage require Authorization for the EU market. For more information, see the ECHA website:

http://echa.europa.eu/chem_data/authorisation_process/candidate_list_table_en.asp

WEEE & RoHS

EU rules on waste electrical and electronic equipment (WEEE), while not requiring specific customs or import paperwork, may entail a financial obligation for U.S. exporters. They require U.S. exporters to register the products with the national WEEE authority which is the Ministry of Environment and Water, or arrange for this to be done by a local partner. Similarly, related rules for EEE restricting the use of the hazardous substances (RoHS) lead, cadmium, mercury, hexavalent chromium, PBBs, and PBDEs, do not entail customs or importation paperwork. However, U.S. exporters may be asked by the Bulgarian RoHS enforcement authority or by a customer to provide evidence of due diligence in compliance with the substance bans on a case-by-case basis. The WEEE and RoHS Directives are currently being revised to enlarge the scope and add substances to be banned in electrical and electronic equipment; the new rules could take effect as early as 2011. U.S. exporters seeking more information on WEEE and RoHS regulations should visit: http://www.buyusa.gov/europeanunion/weee.html

Products for human consumption should be analyzed in approved local laboratories in cooperation with local authorities. The State Agency for Standards and Metrology strictly enforces Bulgarian quality standards, which do not always coincide with generally accepted international standards. Foreign certificates may or may not be considered adequate. After approval is issued, the commodities may be sold on the local market

Agricultural Documentation

Phytosanitary Certificates: Phytosanitary certificates are required for most fresh fruits, vegetables, and other plant materials.

Sanitary Certificates: For commodities composed of animal products or by-products, EU countries require that shipments be accompanied by a certificate issued by the competent authority of the exporting country. This applies regardless of whether the product is for human consumption, for pharmaceutical use, or strictly for non-human use (e.g., veterinary biologicals, animal feeds, fertilizers, research). The vast majority of these certificates are uniform throughout the EU, but the harmonization process is not complete. During this transition period, certain member state import requirements continue to apply. In addition to the legally required EU health certificates, a number of other certificates are used in international trade. These certificates, which may also be harmonized in EU legislation, certify origin for customs purposes and certain quality attributes. Up-to-date information on harmonized import requirements can be found at the following website: http://www.fas.usda.gov/posthome/useu/certificates-overview.html

Sanitary Certificates (Fisheries): In April 2006, the European Union declared the U.S. seafood inspection system as equivalent to the European one. Consequently, a specific public health certificate must accompany U.S. seafood shipments. Commission Decision 2006/199/EC places specific conditions on imports of fishery products from the U.S. Sanitary certificates for live shellfish are covered by Commission Regulation (EC) 1664/2006 and must be used for gastropods, bivalve mollusks, tunicates and echinoderms. The two competent Authorities for issuing sanitary certificates are the FDA and the U.S. Department of Commerce, National Marine Fisheries Service (NMFS/NOAA/USDC).

Since May 1, 2007, with the implementation of the second Hygiene Package, aquaculture products coming from the United States must be accompanied by a public health certificate according to Commission Decision 2006/199/EC and the animal health attestation included in the new fishery products certificate covered by Regulation (EC) 1664/2006. This animal health attestation is not required in the case of live bivalve mollusks intended for immediate human consumption (retail).

U.S. EXPORT CONTROLS

For exports of sensitive technologies to Bulgaria, U.S. exporters should consult the U.S. Department of Commerce Bureau of Industry and Security web site http://www.bis.doc.gov for specific U.S. export licensing requirements.

TEMPORARY ENTRY

Products may be imported into Bulgaria on a temporary basis as long as they are not prohibited by law. The entry of samples and products for trade exhibitions is allowed. The commodities intended for re-export without being subject to any changes in their characteristics may be totally or partially exempt from customs duties. In practice, Customs requires a deposit equivalent to the assessed duties or a bank guarantee during the temporary import period. Bulgaria is a party to the Customs Convention on Carnet (ATA) for Temporary Import of Goods.

More information on ATA: *The purpose of the Convention on temporary admission is to simplify procedures on temporary imports of certain kinds of goods (professional equipment, goods for exhibitions, etc.). The ATA Carnet is a customs document to perform temporary importation and temporary exportation and it also serves as a transit document for transit of goods to the country of temporary importation.*

Apart from the temporary import, the law sets out procedures concerning transit, customs warehousing, inward processing, processing under customs control, and outward processing. The law provides for public and private bonded warehouses.

LABELING AND MARKING REQUIREMENTS

Manufacturers should be aware that all labels require metric units although dual labeling is also acceptable. Labels must contain the following information in Bulgarian:

The product must be clearly marked with the date of production, expiration date and the warranty period.

According to the new requirements for compliance with EU legislation, labels must include information on the recyclable content of packaging material.

PROHIBITED AND RESTRICTED IMPORTS

Bulgaria prohibits imports of ozone-depleting products and other internationally banned products.

The EU's Common External Customs Tariff - TARIC is designed to show various rules applying to specific products being imported into the customs territory of the EU or, in some cases, when exported from it. To determine if a product is prohibited or subject to restriction, check the TARIC for that product for the following codes:

CITES Convention on International Trade of Endangered Species

PROHI Import Suspension

RSTR Import Restriction

For information on how to access the TARIC, see the Import Requirements and Documentation Section above.

CUSTOMS REGULATIONS AND CONTACT INFORMATION

U.S. companies may direct inquiries to the Bulgarian Customs Agency.
Director: Mr. Vanio Tanov
1, Aksakov Street, 1000 Sofia
Phone: 359-2-9859-4210
Fax: 359-2-9859-4061
http://www.customs.bg/
e-mail: pr@customs.bg

STANDARDS

Products tested and certified in the United States to American standards are likely to have to be retested and re-certified to EU requirements as a result of the EU's different approach to the protection of the health and safety of consumers and the environment.

Bulgaria has its standardization, conformity assessment, accreditation and product certification bodies. In certain areas, such as processed foods, beverages and pharmaceutical products, individual ministries or agencies issue sector-specific standards and certificates. Bulgaria is making an effort to harmonize its national standards with international standards. Bulgaria is a participant in the International Organization for Standardization (ISO), the International Electrotechnical Commission (IEC) and International Technical Union (ITU).

The Bulgarian Institute for Standardization will answer questions regarding standards http://www.bds-bg.org/ or the State Agency for Metrology and Technical Surveillance http://www.damtn.government.bg/index_en.html

The major requirements for product safety are regulated in ordinances issued by the appropriate ministries and comply with the respective EU directives.

(see http://www.bds-bg.org/pages/?button_id=38)

STANDARDS ORGANIZATIONS

1. Ministry of Economy, Energy and Tourism through its department Eurointegration

http://www.mi.government.bg/integration/eu/harmonize.html is responsible for harmonizing the Bulgarian legislation with the EU legislation including everything related to ensuring the whole metrology, standardization, certification and testing, verification and accreditation process is in compliance with the EU requirements. The law on metrology can be reviewed on this web site as well.

2. Bulgarian Drug Agency http://www.bda.bg is responsible for registration, product testing & certification, and establishing standards for pharmaceutical products and implants. The Ministry of Healthcare http://www.mh.government.bg is responsible for certification, registration, import licensing and establishing standards for some medical equipment, medical and natural products. In some cases, the Ministry of Healthcare performs these activities jointly with the Drug Agency.

3. Ministry of Agriculture and Food Supply http://www.mzgar.government.bg is the authority responsible for agriculture and food products testing and certification, registration of technical documentation (former national standards BDS) for product certification, assessment of conformity, and establishing the national policy as to the Mutual Recognition Arrangement (MRA's) with international standardization institutions. It is responsible for the in-country and border control health and sanitary policy. The Ministry is performing its functions related to standards, certification, verification and conformity assessment through its National Services that are listed on its web site; the most important one being the State Agency National Veterinary Service http://www.nvms.government.bg/index.php through its Directorate State Veterinary Public Health Control.

The Executive Agency Bulgarian Accreditation Service http://www.nab-bas.bg has accredited the Central Laboratory for Veterinary, Sanitary Expertise and Ecology to perform laboratory testing, inspection, certification, auditing and verification of phyto and veterinary products.

4. The Bulgarian Institute for Standardization (www.bds-bg.org) performs all activities related to standardization, verification, editing and registration of standards for industrial commodities, machinery and transport equipment, construction and materials, chemistry, textiles, foodstuffs, electrical engineering commodities. The Bulgarian Institute for Standardization has signed Mutual Recognition Agreements (MRA's) with the following organizations:

DIN - Deutsches Institut für Normung

BSI - British Standards Institution

UNI - Ente Nazionale Italiano di Unificazione

ASTM International - American Society for Testing and Materials

The Bulgarian Institute for Standardization is a full member of the International Standard

Organization (ISO), which is the core international standardization body, and of

International Electrotechnical Commission (IEC). The Institute is also an affiliate member of the European Committee for Electrotechnical Standardization (CENELEC) and of the European Committee for Standardization (CEN).

Bulgaria as a Member country of the World Trade Organization (WTO) is required under the Agreement on Technical Barriers to Trade (TBT Agreement) to report to the WTO all proposed technical regulations that could affect trade with other Member countries.

NIST NOTIFY U.S. SERVICE

Member countries of the World Trade Organization (WTO) are required under the Agreement on Technical Barriers to Trade (TBT Agreement) to report to the WTO all proposed technical regulations that could affect trade with other Member countries. Notify U.S. is a free, web-based e-mail subscription service that offers an opportunity to review and comment on proposed foreign technical regulations that can affect your access to international markets. Register online at Internet URL: http://www.nist.gov/notifyus/

CONFORMITY ASSESSMENT

The conformity assessment body is the State Agency for Metrology and Technical Surveillance (SAMTS) http://www.damtn.government.bg/l The Agency is performing fundamental metrology, metrological control, monitoring and supervision; conformity assessment; technical inspection of high-risk equipment; market surveillance and quality control of liquid fuels.

PRODUCT CERTIFICATION

Product certification is performed by the Executive Agency for Certification and Testing

http://exact.e-gov.bg The Agency performs testing and certification of electrical

appliances, toys, electrical-magnetic compliance, tobacco and tobacco products, chemicals, cosmetics, foodstuffs, sugar and sugar products, dried fruits and vegetables, meat, and processed-meat products through a number of laboratories around Bulgaria.

There is a procedure for mutual recognition of international certificates issued by international certification bodies such as TUV and SGS.

ACCREDITATION

There is only one national accreditation body in Bulgaria – the Executive Agency Bulgarian Accreditation Service http://www.nab-bas.bg/index_en.php The Agency reports directly to the Minister of Economy, Energy and Tourism and is the only national institute for accreditation of laboratories, certification bodies and control bodies. The Agency web site lists all accredited organizations and laboratories nationwide. The accreditation bodies are structured in four main groups: laboratories, inspection bodies, certification bodies, and verifiers according to the Regulation of the National scheme for management of environment and auditing.

PUBLICATION OF TECHNICAL REGULATIONS

Each law, regulation, ordinance, Council of Ministers decree, decision, nationwide technical regulation, agreement etc. enters into force after official publication in the national gazette (State Gazette). Final regulations, ordinances and laws are published in State Gazette and in the official journals of every issuing authority. The State Gazette is issued only in Bulgarian. There are several information system database providers, which translate legislation published in State Gazette. See http://www.apis.bg/en/ , http:// www.ciela.bg or www.daxy.com

LABELING AND MARKING

General labeling and marking requirements are described previously in this Chapter under "Labeling and Marking."

CONTACTS

For more information on each group and its Bulgarian Standard Code (BDS) with EU cross-reference codes (ISO/IEC), please contact Andon Kalibatsev at the U.S. Commercial Service - email: andon.kalibatsev@mail.doc.gov

TRADE AGREEMENTS

Bulgaria joined the EU in January 2007; became a member of the World Trade Organization in December 1996 and joined the Central European Free Trade Agreement (CEFTA) in January 1999. Bulgaria has free trade agreements with the following countries: China (1995), Croatia (1998), Turkey (1999); Macedonia (signed in 1999); Israel (2002); Albania (2003), Serbia and Montenegro (2004), Bosnia and Herzegovina (2004).

WEB RESOURCES

http://www.mee.government.bg/eng/index.html (Ministry of Economy and Energy)

http://www.customs.bg (State Customs Agency)

http://www.bda.bg (Bulgarian Drug Agency)

http://www.mzgar.government.bg/mz_eng/default.asp (Ministry of Agriculture and Food Supply)

http://www.bds-bg.org (Bulgarian Institute for Standardization)

http://www.damtn.government.bg/index_en.html (State Agency for Metrology and Technical Surveillance - SAMTS)

http://exact.e-gov.bg (Executive Agency for Certification and Testing)

http://www.nab-bas.bg/index_en.php (Executive Agency Bulgarian Accreditation Service)

http://www.apis.bg/en/ (Law publications, law and business-information database management)

http://www.ciela.bg (Law publications, law and business-information database management)

The most common type of organization for foreign investors is a limited liability company. The required minimum for registering a limited liability company is one Euro. Other typical corporate entities include joint stock companies, joint ventures, business associations, general and limited partnerships, and sole proprietorships.

Foreign investors must comply with the 1991 Commercial Code, which regulates commercial and company law, and with the 1951 Law on Obligations and Contracts, which regulates civil transactions.

The 2003 Law on Special Purpose Investment Companies (SPIC) allows for public investment companies in real estate and receivables, essentially real estate investment trusts (REITs). Since a SPIC is considered a pass-through structure for corporate income tax purposes, at least 90 percent of its net income must be distributed to shareholders as taxable dividends. A SPIC must apply for an operational license from the Financial Supervision Commission within six months of registration.

The 2014 Offshore Company Act list 28 activities banned for business by companies registered in offshore jurisdictions. The law, however, allows those companies to do business if the physical owners of the parent company are Bulgarian citizens and known to the public, if the parent company's stock is publicly traded, or if the parent company is registered in a jurisdiction with which Bulgaria enjoys a treaty for the avoidance of double taxation (such as the United States).

Industrial Strategy

Bulgaria typically supports small and medium business creation and development through strategies focused on EU co-funded innovation and competitiveness policies. The current government has revived efforts to sell some previously-closed communist-era factories in the mining and chemical industries, viewing this as a way to reindustrialize the Bulgarian economy while attracting private money and new management in these enterprises.

Limits on Foreign Control

Foreign investors often encounter the following problems: a sluggish government bureaucracy, poor infrastructure, corruption, frequent changes in the legal framework, lack of transparency, and pre-determined public tenders. In addition, a weak judicial system limits investor confidence in the courts' ability to serve as an enforcement mechanism.

U.S. music, software, pharmaceutical, and other industries report continuing intellectual property rights (IPR) concerns in Bulgaria, particularly with respect to internet piracy, ineffective prosecution of IPR cases, and delays and conflicts of interest in enforcing trademark and patent protection. Current Bulgarian legislation effectively bans all biotech crop trials and production. Food legislation imposes voluntary standards which restrict the use of soy protein in processed meat products.

A previous seven-year ban on the purchase of Bulgarian agricultural land by foreigners expired in 2014. However, in April 2014 Parliament passed legislative changes that impose a new five-year residency requirement for non-EU foreign citizens before they may purchase Bulgarian agricultural land. Parliament is also considering a bill introduced in March 2014 that would require that the Competition Protection Commission approve any draft contract between a company with reported sales income above BGN 50 million and its suppliers. If passed, this law could limit the freedom of international retail chains to conclude certain contracts with their local suppliers. Foreign investors in Bulgaria have raised concerns that these pieces of proposed legislation, combined with the Offshore Companies Act and the new 20 percent fee on revenues from renewable energy production (a sector in which most investments have been by foreign companies) aim at limiting competition from foreign investors with certain Bulgarian business interests.

Privatization Program

Bulgaria completed its major privatizations in the 1990s and early 2000s. All state-owned property is eligible for privatization, with the exception of a specific list of companies including water management companies, state hospitals, and state sports facilities. Municipally-owned property is considered for privatization upon decision by the municipal council, or authorized body and upon publication of the municipal privatization list in the State Gazette. Privatization methods include: public auctions, public tenders, and public offerings. Foreign companies, including state-owned ones, may purchase Bulgarian state-owned firms and the privatization process is generally fair and transparent. The 2010 Privatization and Post-Privatization Act created a single Privatization and Post-Privatization Agency which makes privatization decisions regarding: hospitals; equity and shares in companies 50 percent or more owned by the state; state-owned property valued at between BGN 10,000 (USD 7,000) and BGN 500,000 (USD 352,000), following approval from the Minister of Regional Development and Public Works and the Minister of Finance; and state-owned property valued at over BGN 500,000 (USD 352,000), following approval from the Council of Ministers.

The Privatization and Post-Privatization Agency also oversees the implementation of privatization contracts and ensures that non-price privatization commitments (employee retention, technology transfer, environmental liability, and investment) in the privatization selection criteria are honored. In 2012, the government completed the sale of its minority interest in the three regional foreign owned electricity distributors. In April 2014, the State Energy and Water Regulatory Commission began a procedure to revoke these companies' licenses due to their alleged indebtedness to the NEC (which in turn was due to the NEC's indebtedness to the companies); a third hearing in this case is scheduled for May 12. The privatization of the arms factory VMZ-Sopot was halted in 2013 due to the change in government in May. The current government has listed for 2014 privatization: 50.05 percent of the capital of the Bulgarian Stock Exchange, 43.7 percent the Central Depository, 49.63 percent of the International Fair in Plovdiv, and 30 percent of the Bulgarian Maritime Fleet. Additionally, the government has plans to put for sale 100 percent of the capital of Diplomatic Properties Agency (ADIS) and the Free Trade Zone in Plovdiv. The expected 2014 privatization revenues have been estimated at USD 216 million.

Competition Law

The 2008 Law on the Protection of Competition (the "Competition Law") is intended to implement EU rules which promote competition and consumer protection. The Competition Law forbids monopolies, restrictive trade practices, abuse of market power, and unfair competition. Companies are prohibited from: direct or indirect abusive pricing practices, distribution of market shares and supply sources, limiting manufacturing development to the detriment of consumers, discriminatory treatment of competing customers, tying contracts to additional and unrelated obligations, and use of economic coercion to cause mergers. The law prohibits certain forms of unfair competition: damaging competitors' goodwill; misrepresentation with respect to goods or services; misrepresentation with respect to the origin, manufacturer, or other features of goods or services; use or disclosure of someone else's trade secrets in violation of good faith commercial practices; and "unfair solicitation of customers" (i.e., promotion through gifts and lotteries). Monopolies can only be legally established for certain categories of activities: railway and postal services, atomic energy, production of radioactive materials, and weapons production. The Competition Commission defines market concentration of 15 percent or more as potentially damaging to competition. It also defines market concentration of 25 percent or more as potentially damaging to competition if the companies involved are operating in different markets (and are not competitors).

In practice, the Competition Protection Act has been inconsistently applied. In one case, the Competition Committee charged with implementing the law ruled that it did not need to review the sale of Bulgaria's tobacco monopoly, Bulgartabac, to an unknown purchaser and also that the identity of the purchaser did not need to be revealed before the transaction. As of March 2014, Parliament was considering an amendment to the Competition Protection Act that would require stores with "substantial market power," which is defined in a way that applies mainly to retail chains, to seek approval from the Competition Commission for their contracts with suppliers.

Investment Trends

TABLE 1: The following chart summarizes several well-regarded indices and rankings.

Measure	Year	Rank or value	Website Address
TI Corruption Perceptions index	2013	(77 of 177)	http://cpi.transparency.org/cpi2013/results/
Heritage Foundation's Economic Freedom index	2014	(61 of 177)	http://www.heritage.org/index/ranking
World Bank's Doing Business Report "Ease of Doing Business"	2014	(58 of 189)	http//doingbusiness.org/rankings
Global Innovation Index	2013	(41 of 142)	http://www.globalinnovationindex.org/content.aspx?page=gii-full-report-2013#pdfopener
World Bank GNI per capita	2012	USD 6,840	http://data.worldbank.org/indicator/NY.GNP.PCAP.CD

CONVERSION AND TRANSFER POLICIES

Foreign Exchange

Foreign exchange is freely accessible. The 2011 amendments of the 1999 Foreign Currency Act stipulate that anyone may import or export up to EUR 10,000 (USD 13,700) or its foreign exchange equivalent without filling out a customs declaration. The import or export of over EUR 10,000 or its equivalent in BGN or another currency across the border to or from a third country must be declared to the customs authorities. The import or export of over EUR 10,000 or its equivalent in BGN or another currency across the border to or from an EU member state must be declared if requested by the customs authorities. Exporting over BGN 30,000 (USD 21,100) in cash requires a declaration about the source of the funds, supported by documents certifying that the exporter does not owe taxes. No tax certificate is required for foreigners exporting the cash equivalent of BGN 30,000 or greater provided the amount is equal to or less than the amount declared when imported. Bulgarian law requires all international payments over BGN 30,000 to be executed via bank transfer with supporting documentation detailing the purpose of the transaction. The central bank and commercial banks record every international transaction that is equal to or more than 100,000 BGN (USD 70,400).

EXPROPRIATION AND COMPENSATION

Private real property rights are legally protected by the Bulgarian Constitution. Only in a case where a public need cannot be met by other means, the Council of Ministers or a regional governor may expropriate land provided that the owner is compensated at fair market value. No taxes are levied on the expropriation transaction. Expropriation actions of the Council of Ministers can be appealed directly to the Supreme Administrative Court on the legality of the action itself, the property appraisal, or the amount of compensation. A regional governor's expropriation can be appealed in the appropriate local administrative court. In its Bilateral Investment Treaty (BIT) with the United States, Bulgaria committed itself to international arbitration in the event of expropriation and other investment disputes.

DISPUTE SETTLEMENT

Legal System, Specialized Courts, Judicial Independence, Judgments of Foreign Courts

The 1991 Constitution serves as the foundation of the legal system and creates an independent judicial branch comprised of judges, prosecutors, and investigators. Continued reform efforts have led to some improvements, particularly in the smaller courts. The busiest courts in Sofia, however, lack adequate resources and as a result suffer from serious backlogs and inefficient procedures that hamper the swift and fair administration of justice. Corruption remains a serious problem. The judiciary consistently scores among the least trusted institutions in the country with widespread allegations of nepotism, opaque selection procedures, and political and business influences.

There are three levels of courts. The 113 regional courts exercise jurisdiction over civil and criminal cases. Above them, 29 district courts (including the Sofia City Court and the Specialized Court for Organized Crime) serve as courts of appellate review for regional court decisions and have trial-level (first-instance) jurisdiction in serious criminal cases and in civil cases where claims exceed BGN 25,000 (USD 17,600), excluding alimony, labor disputes, and financial audit discrepancies, or in property cases where the property's value exceeds BGN 50,000 (USD 35,200). Six appellate courts review the first-instance decisions of the district courts. The Supreme Court of Cassation is the court of last resort for criminal and civil appeals. There is a separate system of 28 specialized administrative courts which rules on the legality of local and national government decisions with the Supreme Administrative Court serving as appeals instance. The Constitutional Court, which is separate from the rest of the judiciary, issues final rulings on the compliance of laws with the Constitution.

Bulgaria has effective means of enforcing property and contractual rights under local legislation. The government's record of handling investment disputes is generally slow and bureaucratic, but usually the issues are resolved. There are no outstanding investment disputes before Bulgarian courts involving U.S. companies. However, legislation is a constantly moving target that is sometimes used to eliminate competition, including from foreign investors.

Bankruptcy

The 1994 Commercial Code Chapter on Bankruptcy provides for reorganization or rehabilitation of a legal entity, maximizes asset recovery, and provides for fair and equal distribution among all creditors. The law applies to all commercial entities, except public monopolies or state-owned companies established by a special law. Bank failures are regulated under the 2002 Bank Insolvency Act and 2006 Credit Institutions Act; while, the 2005 Insurance Code regulates insurance company failures.

Non-performance of a monetary obligation must be adjudicated before the bankruptcy court can determine whether the debtor is insolvent. There is a presumption of insolvency when the debtor is unable to perform an executable obligation under a commercial transaction or public debt or related commercial activities, has suspended all payments, or is able to pay only the claims of certain creditors. The debtor is deemed over-indebted if its assets are insufficient to cover its short-term monetary obligations.

Bankruptcy proceedings may be initiated on two grounds: the debtor's insolvency, or the debtor's excessive indebtedness. Under Part IV of the Commercial Code, debtors or creditors, including state authorities such as the National Revenue Agency, can initiate bankruptcy proceedings. The debtor must declare bankruptcy within 30 days of becoming insolvent or over-indebted. The 2010 amendments to the Commercial Code increased protection for creditors in bankruptcy proceedings by prohibiting a debtor from falsifying the date of insolvency to avoid claims after a certain date. Despite this, cases involving bankruptcy frauds, including through transfer of capital to U.S.-registered shell companies, have increased recently. The application for bankruptcy submitted by the debtor is published in the Commercial Register, thus providing all creditors and contractual partners with information about the bankruptcy proceedings. Should any creditor or contractual partner file a request for bankruptcy in court, such a claim is heard in the presence of both the creditor and the debtor.

Once insolvency is determined, the court appoints an interim trustee to represent and manage the company, take inventory of property and assets, identify and convene the creditors, and develop a recovery plan. At the first meeting of the creditors, a trustee is nominated; usually this is just a reaffirmation of the court appointed interim trustee.

Bankruptcy proceedings supersede other court proceedings initiated against the debtor except for labor cases, enforcement proceedings, and cases related to receivables securitized by third parties' property. Such cases may be initiated even after bankruptcy proceedings begin. Third parties with securities seeking protection against a debtor's unfair activities may appeal the court decision to initiate a bankruptcy proceeding when securities have been entered in public registers before the date of the claim which started the bankruptcy procedure.

Creditors must declare to the trustee all debts owed to them within one month of the start of bankruptcy proceedings. The trustee then has seven days to compile a list of debts. A rehabilitation plan must be proposed within one month after publication of the list of debts in the Commercial Register. The 2010 amendments to the Commercial Code limit the application of the rehabilitation plan to debts approved up to the moment of submission of the rehabilitation plan.

After creditors' approval, the court endorses the rehabilitation plan, terminates the bankruptcy proceeding and appoints a supervisory body for overseeing the implementation of the rehabilitation plan. The court must endorse the plan within seven days and put it forward to the creditors for approval. The creditors shall convene to discuss the plan within a period of 45 days. The court may renew the bankruptcy proceedings if the debtor does not fulfill its obligations under the rehabilitation plan. June 2003 legislation required examinations for individuals applying to become trustees and obliged the Ministers of Justice and Economy to organize annual training courses for trustees. In June 2005, the ministries of Justice, Economy, and Finance published a regulation on the procedure for appointment, qualification, and control over the trustees.

The methods of liquidating assets were also revised by the June 2003 legislation to establish a legal framework for selling assets that accounts for the character of bankruptcy proceedings, thus avoiding the need to apply the Civil Procedure Code. The regime includes rules requiring publicity for asset sales.

Investment Disputes

To execute a judgment, a final ruling must be obtained. The court of first instance must then be petitioned for a writ of execution (based on the judgment). On the basis of the writ of execution, a specialized category of professionals, execution agents, seize the assets or ensure the performance of the ordered action. Both private and state execution agents operate in Bulgaria. A new Civil Procedure Code, effective since March 2008, streamlined civil procedures, including the execution of judgments. Foreign judgments can be executed in Bulgaria. Execution depends on reciprocity, as well as bilateral or multilateral agreements, as determined by an official list maintained by the Ministry of Justice. The United States does not currently have reciprocity with Bulgaria; Bulgarian courts are not obliged to honor decisions of U.S. courts. All foreign judgments are handled by the Sofia City Court, which must determine that the judgment does not violate public decrees, standards, or morals before it can be executed.

Voluntary mediation was first introduced in Bulgaria in 2004 with the adoption of the Mediation Act. The Bulgarian Chamber of Commerce and Industry and the American Chamber of Commerce (AmCham) opened commercial mediation centers with USAID-trained mediators. Several courts, including the biggest trial level court in Sofia, have established mediation centers where cases can be settled with the help of trained mediators. Judges are increasingly referring cases for mediation; however, it is still not widely used due to limited public awareness and general reluctance to seek alternative dispute resolution.

International Arbitration

Pursuant to its Bilateral Investment Treaty (BIT) with the United States, Bulgaria has committed to a range of dispute settlement procedures starting with notification and consultations. Bulgaria accepts binding international arbitration in disputes with foreign investors.

The most experienced arbitration institution in Bulgaria is the Arbitration Court (AC) of the Bulgarian Chamber of Commerce and Industry (BCCI). Established more than 110 years ago, the AC hears civil disputes between legal persons, one of whom must be seated outside Bulgaria. It began to act as a voluntary arbitration court between natural and/or legal persons domiciled in Bulgaria in 1989.

Arbitration is regulated by the 1988 Law on International Commercial Arbitration, which is based on the United Nations Commission on International Trade Law (UNCITRAL) Model Law. According to the Code of Civil Procedure, not all disputes may be resolved through arbitration. Disputes regarding rights over real estate situated in the country, alimony, or individual labor disputes may only be heard by the courts. In addition, under the Code of Private International Law of 2005, Bulgarian courts have exclusive competence over industrial property disputes regarding patents issued in Bulgaria.

Regarding arbitration clauses that select a foreign court of arbitration, the Code of Civil Procedure mandates that these clauses are only valid if at least one of the parties maintains its residence abroad. As a result, foreign-owned, Bulgarian-registered companies having a dispute with a Bulgarian entity can only have arbitration in Bulgaria. However, under the Law on International Commercial Arbitration, the arbitrator could be a foreign person. Under the same act, the parties can agree on the language to be used in the arbitration proceedings. Arbitral awards, both foreign and domestic, are enforced through the judicial system. The party must petition the Sofia City Court for a writ of execution. Having obtained a writ, however, the creditor then must execute the award using the general framework for execution of judgments in the country. Foreclosure proceedings may also be initiated.

Bulgaria is a member of the 1958 New York Convention on the Recognition and Enforcement of Foreign Arbitral Awards and the 1961 European Convention on International Commercial Arbitration. Bulgaria is also a signatory of the 1996 Convention on the Settlement of Investment Disputes between States and Nationals of Other States.

ICSID Convention and New York Convention

Bulgaria is a member of the 1958 New York Convention on the Recognition and Enforcement of Foreign Arbitral Awards and the 1961 European Convention on International Commercial Arbitration. Bulgaria is also a signatory of the 1996 Convention on the Settlement of Investment Disputes between States and Nationals of Other States.

PERFORMANCE REQUIREMENTS AND INVESTMENT INCENTIVES

Investment Incentives

The Invest Bulgaria Agency (IBA), the government's investment coordinating body, provides information, administrative services, and incentive assessments to prospective foreign investors. The 2004 Investment Promotion Act (IPA) is the primary legislation providing investment incentives to investors in Bulgaria. Foreign investments over BGN 20 million (USD 14.1 million) are deemed to be priority "Class A" investment projects. At the request of investors receiving Class A investment certificates, IBA can recommend that the competent authorities grant them free real estate (either state or municipal property). Class A investments are also eligible to apply for state financing for critical infrastructure deemed necessary for the investment plan's implementation. Additionally, IBA represents "Class B" investment projects (over BGN 10 million, or USD 6.8 million) before government authorities, and assists with processing all administrative documents. The government policy for investment promotion is not applicable to investments in coal mining, steel production, shipbuilding, synthetic production, agriculture, and fisheries. In addition, the IPA gives Class A or Class B status to certain investments in high-technology manufacturing and services and in regions with an unemployment rate equal to or higher than the country average. A two-year valued-added tax (VAT) exemption on equipment imports applies to investment projects over EUR 5 million (USD 6.7 million), provided the project will be implemented over a two-year period and creates at least 50 new jobs.

Additionally, investment projects that are particularly important for the economy and meet the legal requirement for a minimum investment commitment in the amount of BGN 100 million (USD 70.5 million) and for creating 200 new jobs are classified as priority projects. Such projects can be implemented in all sectors of the economy. In addition to the incentives granted to Class A investors, the priority investors can acquire limited rights on central or municipal government property at below market prices, receive government grants for projects on R&D and education, and institutional support for establishing PPPs.

Contact: InvestBulgaria Agency

31 Aksakov Street
Sofia 1000, Bulgaria
Tel.: (+359 2) 985-5500
Fax: (+359 2) 980-1320
E-mail: iba@investbg.government.bg
www.investbg.government.bg

Performance Requirements

Bulgaria does not impose export performance or local content requirements as a condition for establishing, maintaining, or expanding an investment. Employment visas and work permits are required for most expatriate personnel from non-EU countries. Permanent residence permits are often difficult to obtain. Private companies cannot exceed a 1:10 ratio of non-EU residents to Bulgarian employees. The law regulating gambling imposes other requirements for non-EU investors for organizing games of chance, including foreigners having to obtain an operating license.

Data Storage

Responding to long-standing industry concerns, the Bulgarian government included a provision to provide data exclusivity (i.e., protection of confidential data submitted to the government to obtain approval for market pharmaceutical products) in its Drug Law. Bulgaria grants supplemental protection certificates for pharmaceutical products and plant protection products under EU regulations. This protection is similar to that provided in the United States.

RIGHT TO PRIVATE OWNERSHIP AND ESTABLISHMENT

Article 19 of the Constitution states that the Bulgarian economy "shall be based on free economic initiative." Private entities, both foreign and domestic, can establish and own business enterprises engaging in any profit-making activities not expressly prohibited by law. Bulgaria's Commercial Code guarantees and regulates, for both foreign and domestic entities, the free establishment, acquisition, and disposition of private business enterprises. Competitive equality is the standard applied to private enterprises in competition with public enterprises.

PROTECTION OF PROPERTY RIGHTS

Bulgarian law protects the acquisition and disposition of property rights. The Bulgarian legal system protects and facilitates acquisition and disposition of all property rights, such as land, buildings, and mortgages.

Although Bulgarian intellectual property rights (IPR) legislation is generally adequate – and in some cases stronger than in other EU countries – industry representatives believe effective IPR protection requires stronger enforcement, including stricter penalties for offenders. The Law on Copyright and Related Rights, the Law on Patents and Registration of Utility Models, the Law on Marks and Geographical Indications, the Law on Industrial Design, and the Penal Code were all harmonized with international standards in 2006. Bulgaria is a member of the World Intellectual Property Organization (WIPO) and a signatory to key international agreements, including WIPO Internet treaties and the TRIPS Agreement.

The United State Trade Representative (USTR) placed Bulgaria back on the Special 301 Watch List in April 2013, noting the little progress made in fighting online piracy. In view of the few available legitimate platforms for purchasing licensed digital content, the illegal download of music and films stands out as the greatest enforcement issue for the relevant Bulgarian authorities and IP rights holders. The software piracy rate for end-users and businesses was 64 percent in 2012, according to the Business Software Alliance. The Bulgarian legal system has not kept pace with new internet-based technologies. Bulgaria's Penal Code and Copyright Law lack deterrent effect on Internet pirates and there has been little political will to adopt the necessary changes, or to cooperate with private stakeholders. As a result, Bulgarian courts have never successfully prosecuted Internet pirates, except in one case when the court imposed small (USD 600) administrative fines on four site operators, but the offenders eventually were acquitted by a higher instance court which ruled that the statute of limitations had expired before sentencing. Bulgaria has neither legal requirements nor voluntary agreements holding advertisers, Internet service providers, and payment service providers accountable for supporting or doing business with pirate sites.

Real Property

There are no legal restrictions against real property acquisition by locally-registered, majority foreign-owned companies, which is the method most foreigners use to purchase property in Bulgaria. A requirement for five-year residency in the country for foreign purchase of Bulgarian agricultural land was approved by Bulgarian Parliament in May 2014.

Intellectual Property Rights

The 1993 Law on Copyright and Related Rights protects literary, artistic, and scientific works. Article 3 provides a full listing of protected works including computer programs (which are protected as literary works). The use of protected works is prohibited without the author's permission, except in certain instances. Since 2000 the law has undergone major revisions to comply with EU and international legislation, including major changes in March 2011, which introduced government arbitration for contract negotiations between rights users and rights collection societies.

For films and other audio-visual works, copyrights are protected during the lives of the director, screenplay-writer, cameraman, or author of dialogue or music (if the music was created for the film) plus 70 years. Pursuant to 2014 Copyright Act amendments, the term of protection for producers and performing artists was extended to 70 years, starting from the day of the first recording or making the work first known to the public. However, Bulgarian law limits the duration of contracts on the use of copyrighted works to no more than ten years. Rights owners may file civil claims to terminate infringing activity and seek confiscation of equipment and pirated materials. The Copyright Office in the Ministry of Culture is responsible for copyright and related rights matters in Bulgaria. It is not adequately staffed. Bulgarian legislation provides for criminal, civil, and administrative remedies against copyright and related rights violations, but because of the small number of court judgments, administrative remedies enforced, and sentences, law enforcement is still inadequate.

Bulgarian patent law has been harmonized with EU law for patents and patent protection. However, in patent procedures, there are reports of conflicts of interest and delays in decision-making and informing patent holders. These issues, coupled with a lack of accountability of the Bulgarian Patent Office, have weakened patent protection in the country.

Bulgaria joined the Convention on Granting of European Patents (European Patent Convention) in 2002. Bulgaria is a contracting state of the European Patent Office (EPO), whereby a patent recognized by the European Patent Convention must immediately take effect in Bulgaria after validation, which includes a process of translation of the entire patent documentation into Bulgarian and payment of a fee (starting from BGN 130 or USD 92) within three months of the day the EPO issues the patent. Bulgaria has also signed the London agreement for facilitating the validation process, which allows rights holders to submit only a translation of the patent claim and not of the whole patent. But, Bulgarian law has still not been amended to correspond to this agreement. Bulgaria is also part of the Patent Cooperation Treaty (PCT). Bulgaria grants the right to exclusive use of inventions for 20 years from the date of patent application, subject to payment of annual fees, which range from BGN 50 (USD 35.20) to BGN 1,500 (USD 1,056), depending on the time remaining before the patent expires. Innovations can also be protected as utility models ("small inventions"). The term of validity of a utility model registration is four years from the date of filing with the Patent Office. It may be extended by two consecutive three-year periods, but the total term of validity may not exceed 10 years.

Inventions eligible for patent protection must be new, involve an inventive step, and be capable of industrial application. Article 6 of the Law on Patent and Utility Model Registration lists items not regarded as inventions and Article 7 lists the exceptions to patentability. With regard to utility models, no registration is granted for methods and objects in the field of biotechnology. There is no accessible database for the registered and valid patents and utility models in Bulgaria.

Located in the Ministry of Economy, Energy, and Tourism, the Patent Office is the competent authority with respect to industrial property rights (including patent matters). The Patent Act describes patent application procedures and the examination process. Patent applications are submitted directly to the Patent Office and recorded in the state register. Compulsory licensing (allowing competitors in the market despite a valid patent) may be ordered under certain conditions: if the patent has not been used within four years of filing the patent application or within three years from the date of issue, if the patent holder is unable to offer justification for not adequately supplying the national market, or in the case of a declaration of national emergency. Disputes arising from the creation, protection, or use of inventions and utility models can be heard and settled under administrative, civil, or arbitration procedures. Disputes are reviewed by specialized panels convened by the President of the Patent Office and may be appealed to the Sofia Administrative Court within three months of the panel's decision. The Customs Office conducts border seizures when there is reason to believe that the goods are infringing either a patent, a supplementary protection certificate (SPC), or a registered utility model. The regime is in compliance with Regulation 608/2013/EC.

Pursuant to the 1996 Protection of New Plant Varieties and Animal Breeds Act, the Patent Office can issue a certificate which protects new plant varieties and animal breeds for between 25 and 30 years. In 1998, Parliament ratified the 1991 International Convention for the Protection of New Varieties of Plants. In addition, all new types of plants registered by the EU's Community Plant Variety Office are considered effective in Bulgaria.

In 1999, Parliament passed a series of laws on trademarks and geographical indications, industrial designs, and integrated circuits in accordance with TRIPs (WTO's Trade Related Aspects of Intellectual Property) requirements and the EU Association Agreement. The Trademarks and Geographical Indications Act (TGIA), as amended in 2005 and 2006 to comply with EU standards, regulates the establishment, use, suspension, renewal, and protection of trademarks, collective and certificate marks, and geographic indications.

The right for marks (trademarks, service marks, and collective and certificate marks) is acquired through registration and is valid from the date of filing the application. The right of registration belongs to the first applicant. Co-ownership of marks is allowed.

With amendments to the TGIA that entered into force in March 2011, all applications which comply with the basic requirements of the law are published. Interested parties then have three months from the date the application is published in the national gazette to file an objection.

Bulgaria is a member of the Lisbon Agreement for the Protection of Appellations of Origin and their International Registration.

Right of priority with respect to trademarks that do not differ substantially is given to the application that was filed in compliance with Article 32 of the TGIA. Right of priority is also established on the basis of a request made in one of the member countries of the Paris Convention for the Protection of Industrial Property or of the WTO. To exercise the right of priority, the applicant must file a request within six months of the date the other party files.

A trademark is normally granted within eighteen months of filing a complete application. Refusals can be appealed to the Disputes Department of the Patent Office. Decisions of this department can be appealed to the Sofia Administrative Court within three months of the decision. The right of exclusive use of a trademark is granted for ten years from the date of submitting the application. Extension requests must be filed during the final year of validity and can be renewed up to six months after its expiration. Protection is terminated if a trademark is not used for a five-year period.

Trademark infringement is a significant problem in Bulgaria for U.S. cigarette and apparel producers, and smaller scale infringement affects other U.S. brands. Bulgarian legislation provides for criminal, civil, and administrative remedies against trademark violation. Civil legal infringement actions may be conducted, including seizure and destruction of the infringing products and compensation for damages. The claimant may request compensation ranging from BGN 500 to BGN 100,000 (USD 352 and USD 70,500). In addition, the claimant may request possession of the infringing articles and compensation for expenses incurred in destroying the articles. All civil actions are heard by Sofia City Court.

Bulgaria has no simplified border control procedure for the destruction of seized fake goods without civil or criminal trial.

The TGIA imposes a fine of BGN 500 (USD 352) to BGN 1,500 (USD 1,056) on any physical person who is selling goods or services that bear a sign that is identical or similar to a registered mark without the proprietor's consent. Legal entities are fined between BGN 1,000 (USD 700) and BGN 3,000 (USD 2,112). The fine for repeated offenses is between BGN 1,500 (USD 1,056) and BGN 3,000 (USD 2,112) for physical persons and between BGN 3,000 (USD 2,112) and BGN 5,000 (USD 3,520) for legal entities. The Criminal Code prohibits use of a third person's trademark without the proprietor's consent, punishable by imprisonment of up to five years and a fine of up to BGN 5,000 (USD 3,520). If the act is repeated or significant damages result, the punishment can be extended up to eight years of imprisonment and a fine between BGN 5,000 to BGN 8,000 (USD 5,634). In practice criminal court rulings are rare and sentencing is lenient.

In Bulgaria, trademarks, service-marks, and rights to geographic indications are only protected pursuant to registration with the Bulgarian Patent Office or an international registration (under the Madrid Agreement and the Madrid protocol) designating Bulgaria; they do not arise simply with "use in commerce" of the mark or indication. Bad faith registrations of well-known international marks are increasingly common in Bulgaria. In the past year, there have been at least two cases in which the Bulgarian Patent Office has upheld the rights of the bad-faith registrants with enforcement procedures against original U.S. mark holders.

Legal entities cannot be held liable under the Criminal Code. Criminal penalties for copyright infringement and willful trademark infringement are limited compared to enforcement mechanisms available under U.S. law.

Under Bulgarian law, industrial designs which are new and original can be granted certificates from the Patent Office and entered in the state register. The term of protection is 10 years, renewable up to 25 years. Bulgaria is a contracting state of The Hague Agreement Concerning the International Deposit of Industrial Designs. With respect to third parties, an international registration shall have effect in Bulgaria as of the date of expiration of the six-month period under Article 8 (1) of the Hague Agreement. Enforcement of industrial design is similar to trademarks enforcement.

For additional information about treaty obligations and points of contact at local IP offices, please see WIPO's country profiles at http://www.wipo.int/directory/en/.

Embassy point of contact: Robin Brooks BrooksRS@state.gov or Danko Tonev tonevdt@state.gov

TRANSPARENCY OF THE REGULATORY SYSTEM

In general, the regulatory environment in Bulgaria is characterized by complex regulations, lack of transparency, and arbitrary or weak enforcement. These factors create incentives for public corruption and, as a result, foreign investors may experience a cumbersome investment climate.

Bulgarian law defines 38 operations that must be licensed and includes registration and permit regimes. The law requires all regulations to be justified by defined need (in terms of national security, environmental protection, or personal and material rights of citizens), and prohibits restrictions incidental to the stated purposes of the regulation. The law also requires that the regulating authority perform a cost-benefit analysis of any proposed regulation. In addition, the law eliminates bureaucratic discretion in granting requests for routine economic activities, and provides for "silent consent" when the government does not respond to a request in the allotted time. While the law creates a ground-breaking normative framework, implementation and consistent enforcement are still lacking. Local companies in which foreign partners have controlling interests may be requested to provide additional information or meet mandatory requirements in order to engage in certain licensed activities including production and export of arms and ammunition; banking and insurance; and exploration, development, and exploitation of natural resources.

EFFICIENT CAPITAL MARKETS AND PORTFOLIO INVESTMENT

Money and Banking System, Hostile Takeovers

Since 1997, the Bulgarian Stock Exchange (BSE) has operated under a license from the Securities and Stock Exchange Commission (SSEC). The 1999 Law on Public Offering of Securities regulates the issuance of securities, securities transactions, stock exchanges, and investment intermediaries. The 2002 comprehensive amendments to this law established significant rights for minority shareholders of publicly-owned companies in Bulgaria. In addition, they created an important foundation for the adoption of international best practices for corporate governance principles in public companies. Since 2007, Bulgaria has aligned its regulation of securities markets to EU standards under the Markets in Financial Instruments Directive (MiFID) that seeks to integrate trading, clearing, settlement and depository functions of the EU securities markets.

The BSE is the only trading venue in Bulgaria. Its infrastructure has substantially improved in recent years, including the establishment of an official index (SOFIX), an Internet-based trading system, and a growing number of brokers. Investors access the BSE to trade corporate stock, government bonds, corporate bonds, Bulgarian Depositary Receipts, municipal bonds, and mortgage-backed bonds. The stock exchange operates three other indexes in addition to the official SOFIX: BG40, BG TR30, and BGREIT. The small domestic market is served by a large number of domestically oriented investment firms.

Total market capitalization only increased slightly to 12.67 percent of GDP in 2013, from 12.54 percent of GDP in 2012. The liquidity of the market remains relatively low. Annual trading turnover increased notably, from 9 percent of total market capitalization in 2012 to 15 percent in 2013. The majority of BSE's equity is still owned by the Ministry of Finance (50.05 percent) and by investment intermediaries and commercial banks (33 percent). The remaining BSE capital is allocated among other local and foreign legal entities, natural persons, and institutional investors. The government confirmed plans to sell its majority stake in BSE in 2014.

The Bulgarian banking system has undergone considerable transformation since its virtual collapse in 1996 and now demonstrates both high predictability and client and investor confidence. There are 30 commercial banks (24 subsidiaries and 6 branches), with total assets of BGN 85.7 billion (USD 60.4 billion) in 2013. Approximately 55 percent of bank assets are concentrated in the top five banks: UniCredit-Bulbank, DSK Bank, First Investment Bank, United Bulgarian Bank, and Corporate Commercial Bank.

In 2003, Bulgaria completed the privatization of its state-owned banks, attracting some strong foreign banks as strategic investors. Foreign investors drawn to the Bulgarian banking industry include UniCredito Italiano SpA (UCI), BNP PARIBAS, KBC, National Bank of Greece, Societe Generale, Raiffeisen International, OTP Group, and Citibank. Approximately 72 percent of the banking system is owned by foreign banking groups.

Bulgaria's banking system is well capitalized. The average capital adequacy ratio (capital base to risk-weighted credit exposures) for the banking system has steadily declined from 43 percent in 1998 to 16.8 percent in 2013, but still remains above the Bulgarian National Bank's requirement of 12 percent. Domestic banks have responded to the global financial crisis by reducing risk exposure through increased interest rates on both deposits and loans. Non-performing loans (those over 90 days overdue and written off) were 11 percent of banks' total loan portfolios in

2013. The Bulgarian government finances some of its expenditures by issuing bonds in capital markets. Commercial banks and private pension funds are the primary purchasers of these instruments. EU-based banks are eligible to be primary dealers of Bulgarian government bonds.

In order to acquire Bulgarian government bonds, a foreign bank must register with the Ministry of Finance and open a "custody account" in Bulgarian Leva.

The Investment Promotion Act defines securities, including treasury bills, with maturities over six months as investments. Repatriation of profits is possible after presenting documentation that taxes have been paid.

COMPETITION FROM STATE-OWNED ENTERPRISES

OECD Guidelines on Corporate Governance of SOEs

Upon EU accession, Bulgaria was recognized as a fully operating market economy, in which the majority of the companies are private. The state's monopoly in railway infrastructure is among the few exceptions. The state-owned Bulgarian Postal Service still holds a partial market monopoly, but the local market for postal services has been increasingly de-monopolized to include a number of privately managed courier companies. Though Bulgaria has separate state-owned companies for infrastructure ownership and distribution in both the electricity and gas markets, all of these companies are owned by the same state-owned holding company.

CORPORATE SOCIAL RESPONSIBILITY

OECD Guidelines for Multinational Enterprises

There is a growing awareness of corporate social responsibility among both producers and consumers, but it is not always clear that expectations are as high for domestic firms as for foreign investors.

POLITICAL VIOLENCE

There have been no incidents in recent years involving politically-motivated damage to projects or installations. Rather, violence in Bulgaria is primarily criminal in nature.

CORRUPTION

UN Anticorruption Convention, OECD Convention on Combatting Bribery

Widespread corruption continues to be one of the most difficult problems in Bulgaria's investment climate. Well-established human trafficking, narcotics, and contraband smuggling channels that contribute to corruption in Bulgaria still exist. Law enforcement capacity remains limited and the authorities opt for easy-to-prove, low-level corruption cases. As a result, progress on cases of high public interest, involving alleged siphoning of millions from the state coffers or EU funds, such as cases involving public procurements for big infrastructure projects, have not generally been pursued.

The Prosecution service, the State Agency for National Security, and the Ministry of Interior are the primary institutions responsible for combating corruption. A government analytical center for curbing corruption (BORCOR) was set up in 2011 but it has shown no concrete results, in spite of the resources which have been devoted to the project. Bulgaria has laws, regulations, and penalties to combat corruption. However internal oversight within institutions is often weak which contributes to the overall image of uncoordinated response to what is seen as a systemic problem throughout the public administration. Bribery is a criminal act under Bulgarian law for both the giver and the receiver. Individuals who mediate and facilitate a bribe are also held accountable. Penalties range from one to fifteen years imprisonment along with possible confiscation of property depending on the circumstances and seriousness of the case. In the most egregious cases, the Penal Code calls for prison terms of 10 to 30 years. Bribing a foreign official is also a criminal act. The government does not require companies to establish internal codes of conduct nor compliance programs to detect and prevent bribery. In the area of public procurement, a complex and ever-changing legislative framework has made it even more difficult to create a culture of objectivity and rigor.

Bulgaria has an NGO sector that monitors corruption and organized crime, including a local chapter of Transparency International (TI). Bulgaria ranks 77th of 177 countries in TI's Corruption Perception Index for 2013, down one place from 2012.

In 1998, Bulgaria was one of the first non-OECD nations to ratify the OECD Anti-Bribery Convention and is a participating member of the OECD Working Group on Bribery. Bulgaria has also ratified the Council of Europe's Convention on Laundering, Search, Seizure, and Confiscation of Proceeds of Crime (1994) and Civil Convention on Corruption (1999). Bulgaria has signed and ratified the UN Convention against Corruption (2003); the Additional Protocol to the Council of Europe's Criminal Law Convention on Corruption; and the UN Convention against Transnational Organized Crime.

BILATERAL INVESTMENT AGREEMENTS

Bulgaria has a Bilateral Investment Treaty (BIT) with the United States, which guarantees national treatment for U.S. investments and creates a dispute settlement process. The BIT also includes a side letter on protections for intellectual property rights. The Governments of Bulgaria and the United States exchanged notes in 2003 to make Bulgaria's obligations under the BIT compatible with its EU obligations, and finalized the process in January 2007.

As of 2012, Bulgaria has bilateral investment treaties signed with the United States and the following countries: Albania, Algeria, Argentina, Armenia, Austria, Azerbaijan, Bahrain, Belarus, Belgium, China, Croatia, Cuba, Cyprus, Czech Republic, Denmark, Egypt, Finland, France, Georgia, Germany, Ghana, Greece, Hungary, India, Indonesia, Iran, Israel, Italy, Jordan, Kazakhstan, Kuwait, Latvia, Lebanon, Libya, Lithuania, Luxembourg, Macedonia, Malta, Moldova, Mongolia, Montenegro, Morocco, Nigeria, North Korea, Oman, Pakistan, Poland, Portugal, Qatar, Romania, Russia, San Marino, Serbia, Singapore, Slovakia, Slovenia, South Korea, Spain, Sudan, Sweden, Switzerland, Syria, Thailand, The Netherlands, Tunisia, Turkey, Ukraine, United Kingdom and Northern Ireland, Uzbekistan, Vietnam, and Yemen.

Bilateral Taxation Treaties

As of 2012, Bulgaria has signed bilateral double taxation treaties with the United States and the following countries: Albania, Algeria, Armenia, Austria, Azerbaijan, Bahrain Belarus, Belgium, Canada, China, Croatia, Cyprus, Czech Republic, Denmark, Egypt, Estonia, Finland, France, Georgia, Germany, Greece, Hungary, India, Indonesia, Iran, Ireland, Israel, Italy, Japan, Kazakhstan, Kuwait, Latvia, Lebanon, Lithuania, Luxembourg, Macedonia, Malta, Moldova, Mongolia, Montenegro, Morocco, North Korea, Norway, Poland, Portugal, Qatar, Romania, Russia, Serbia, Singapore, Slovakia, Slovenia, South Africa, South Korea, Spain, Sweden, Switzerland, Syria, Thailand, The Netherlands Turkey, Ukraine, United Arab Emirates, United Kingdom and Northern Ireland, Uzbekistan, Vietnam, and Zimbabwe.

OPIC AND OTHER INVESTMENT INSURANCE PROGRAMS

In 1991, the Overseas Private Investment Corporation (OPIC) and the Bulgarian government signed an Investment Incentive Agreement, which governs OPIC's operations in Bulgaria. OPIC provides medium- to long-term funding through direct loans and loan guarantees to eligible investment projects in developing countries and emerging markets. OPIC also supports a number of privately owned and managed equity funds, including a regional fund for Southeast Europe created in 2005 for investments in companies in Bulgaria and other Balkan countries. OPIC's Small- and Medium-Size Financing is available for businesses with annual revenues under USD 250 million. OPIC's structured financing focuses on U.S. businesses with annual revenue over USD 250 million and supports large capital-intensive projects such as infrastructure, telecommunications, power, water, housing, airports, technology, and financial services.

OPIC offers U.S. investors insurance against currency inconvertibility, expropriation, and political violence. Political risk insurance is also available from the Multilateral Investment Guarantee Agency (MIGA), which is a World Bank affiliate, as well as from a number of private U.S. companies.

Bulgaria is a signatory to the Convention Establishing the Multilateral Investment Guarantee Agency.

LABOR

As of 2013, Bulgaria's workforce officially consisted of 3,371,200 men (53.3 percent) and women (46.7 percent), many of whom are skilled in sciences, information technology, customer service, and foreign languages. Officially registered unemployed were 11.8 percent of the labor force in December 2013, and the number increased to 12.2 percent in each of the first three months of 2014. About 25 percent of all youth are presently reported as unemployed, which poses a serious labor market issue that has prompted government to enact a set of measures addressing specifically youth unemployment.

The official adult literacy rate in Bulgaria is 98.3 percent. A high percentage of the workforce has completed some form of secondary, technical, or vocational education. Many Bulgarians have strong backgrounds in engineering, medicine, economics, and the sciences, but there is a shortage of professionals with Western management skills as well as of highly-skilled manual laborers. The aptitude of workers, the relatively high number of those who speak English, and the relatively low cost of labor are considerable incentives for foreign companies, especially those that are labor-intensive, to invest in Bulgaria. In recent years, many foreign investors have increasingly complained of the deteriorating quality of Bulgarian university education and the fact that it is training graduates for specialties that are not in line with the real labor market needs. In an attempt to reverse that trend, Bulgarian government is considering legislative changes that would introduce a vocational training track for some Bulgarian high school students. If this legislation is adopted, certain students would receive professional qualification while at school, but forego some of the humanities and social science prerequisites for a regular university education after graduation.

Another concern frequently raised by investors regards difficulties finding the appropriate skilled local laborers, because many well-trained Bulgarians, enabled by the generally unrestricted access to EU labor market, still choose to leave the country in pursuit of better paid jobs. However, the global financial and economic crisis has caused some the low skilled emigres such as Bulgarian construction workers working in other EU countries to temporarily return to Bulgaria. Meanwhile, the development of Bulgaria's digital technologies sector has provided opportunities for many local IT specialists to start working for large IT corporations from home.

The Bulgarian Constitution recognizes workers' rights to join trade unions and organize. The National Council for Tripartite Cooperation (NCTC) provides a forum for dialog among government, employer organizations, and trade unions on issues such as cost-of-living adjustments. An established practice of negotiating the so-called "social security thresholds" between trade unions and the employers organizations each year helps determine the formula for calculating the relative amount of employer and employee social security contributions.

Bulgaria has two large trade union confederations represented at the national level, the Confederation of Independent Trade Unions of Bulgaria (CITUB) and the Confederation of Labor "Podkrepa" ("Support"). As of 2012, estimated trade union membership was 300,000 for CITUB and over 150,500 for Podkrepa.

There are very few restrictions on trade union activity, but employees in smaller private firms are often not represented by trade unions. In addition, there are four nationally recognized employer organizations currently in Bulgaria that target different industry and company membership.

Under the Bulgarian Labor Code, employer-employee relations are regulated by employment contracts. The framework of the employment contracts can be shaped through collective bargaining. Collective labor contracts can be concluded at the sectoral level, enterprise level, and municipal level. The Labor Code addresses worker occupational safety and health issues, mandates a minimum wage (determined by the Council of Ministers), and prevents exploitation of workers, including child labor. It clearly delineates employer rights. Disputes between labor and management can be referred to the courts, but resolution is often subject to delays. Neither foreign companies nor majority foreign-owned Bulgarian companies are exempt from the requirements of the Labor Code.

Over the last ten years, the Labor Code has been amended to address labor market rigidities and bring labor legislation into compliance with EU requirements. In 2008, the Parliament passed changes in the labor legislation to increase fines to BGN 15,000 (USD 10,560) for Labor Code violations. The minimum annual paid leave is 20 days. The minimum wage is BGN 340 (USD 239.4) per month. In 2012, rules regulating the status of temporary workers and temporary employment agencies were introduced.

The National Institute for Conciliation and Arbitration (NICA) developed a framework for collective labor dispute mediation and arbitration. NICA includes representatives from labor, employers, and government. NICA-sponsored collective labor dispute resolutions are still few in number. Several of the appointed mediators received basic mediation skills training from the U.S. Federal Mediation and Conciliation Service. There are 31 appointed mediators and 30 arbiters, proposed by social partners and approved by NICA's Supervisory Board.

FOREIGN TRADE ZONES/FREE PORTS

There are six duty-free zones in Bulgaria: Ruse and Vidin ports on the Danube; Plovdiv; Svilengrad (near the Turkish border); Dragoman (near the Serbian border); and Burgas port on the Black Sea. They are all managed by joint stock or state-owned companies. The government provided land and infrastructure for each zone.

Foreign individuals and corporations, and Bulgarian companies with one percent or more foreign ownership may operate in a duty-free zone. Thus, foreign-owned firms have equal or better investment opportunities in the zones compared to Bulgarian firms. All forms of legal economic activity are permissible in duty-free zones. Foreign, non-EU goods delivered to the duty free zones for production, storage, processing, or re-export are VAT and duty exempt. Bulgarian goods may also be stored in duty free zones with permission from the customs authorities. With Bulgaria in the EU, the duty-free zones no longer apply tax and duty exemptions to exports from Bulgaria to other EU countries.

EU integration has encouraged regional authorities to attract outside investors to spur local economic development. In partnership with the private sector, they provide resources (i.e., land, infrastructure, etc.) for the development of industrial zones and technological parks, which are different from duty-free zones in that they do not provide for any form of preferential tax treatment. There are several industrial zones under construction in: Bozhurishte (outside Sofia), Burgas, Varna, Karlovo (near Plovdiv), and Telish (near Pleven). The high technology Sofia Tech Park has recently joined efforts with the Bulgarian Academy of Sciences in what is expected to become the largest center for high level R&D and incubator for high technology international and local business in Bulgaria. The government has established a National Industrial Zones Company to support the establishment of industrial zones and technological parks and enable a stable FDI inflow.

18. Foreign Direct Investment and Foreign Portfolio Investment Statistics

TABLE 2: Key Macroeconomic data, U.S. FDI in host country/economy

	Host Country Statistical source*		USG or international statistical source		USG or international Source of data (Source of Data: BEA; IMF; Eurostat; UNCTAD, Other)
Economic Data	Year	Amount	Year	Amount	
Host Country Gross Domestic Product (GDP) (Millions U.S. Dollars)	2012	52, 760	2012	50,970	http://www.worldbank.org/en/country
Foreign Direct Investment	Host Country Statistical source*		USG or international statistical source		USG or international Source of data: BEA; IMF; Eurostat; UNCTAD, Other
U.S. FDI in partner country (Millions U.S. Dollars, stock positions)	2012	1,841	2012	1,459	IMF
Host country's FDI in the United States (Millions U.S. Dollars, stock positions)	2012	73.4 million	2012	70 million	Eurostat
Total inbound stock of FDI as % host GDP (calculate)	2012	101.1	2012	87.2	IMF

TABLE 3: Sources and Destination of FDI

Data on inward direct investment reported by Bulgaria are shown side-by-side against data on outward direct investment reported by the counterpart economy. This allows reported data to be easily compared and to identify reporting inconsistencies. Bulgaria, 2012

From Top Eight Sources/To Top Eight Destinations *(US Dollars, Millions)*

Inward Direct Investment	Outward Direct Investment

Total Inward	44,443	100%	Total Outward	26,618	100%
The Netherlands	8,875	20%	Netherlands	6,094	23%
Austria	6,663	15%	Austria	5,600	21%
Greece	3,464	8%	Greece	2,578	10%
Cyprus	2,738	6%	Cyprus	c	
United Kingdom	2,576	6%	United Kingdom	183	0.7%
Germany	2,376	5%	Germany	2,964	11%
Russia	1,876	4%	Russia	2,835	11%
United States	1,459	3%	United States	c	

Source: http://cdis.imf.org

Local contact for FDI statistics: "Balance of Payments and External Debt" Department, Bulgarian National Bank (www.bnb.bg)

The Bulgarian National Bank ranks top eight investor countries in the same order as the table above, with the Netherlands listed as number one and the United States listed at number eight.

TABLE 4: Sources of Portfolio Investment

Bulgaria, 2012

Portfolio Investment Assets

Top Eight Partners (Millions, US Dollars)

Total			Equity Securities			Total Debt Securities		
All Countries	44,443	100%	All Countries	30,131	100%	All Countries	14,312	100%
Netherlands	8,875	20%	Netherlands	1,985	7%	Netherlands	6,889	48%
Austria	6,663	15%	Austria	5,646	19%	Austria	1,017	7%
Greece	3,464	8%	Greece	3,186	11%	Greece	278	2%
Cyprus	2,738	6%	Cyprus	1,753	6%	Cyprus	985	7%
United Kingdom	2,576	6%	United Kingdom	2,372	8%	United Kingdom	205	1%
Germany	2,376	5%	Germany	1,936	6%	Germany	440	3%
Russia	1,876	3%	Russia	1,469	5%	Russia	406	3%

United States	1,459	3%	United States	1,045	3%	United States	415	3%

Source: http://cpis.imf.org

IMPORTANT CONTACTS

Robin Brooks
Economic Officer
Embassy of the United States
16 Kozyak Street
Sofia 1407, Bulgaria
Tel: +359 937 5220
BrooksRS@state.gov

AK Vladimirov Law Office
Admiralty/maritime law, international law, franchising and distribution, insurance law, customs law, criminal law, corporate & commercial law, real estate law & construction, litigation & arbitration, family and inheritance law and U.S. immigration law.
Sofia Office: Tzar Boris III Blvd., 225A, 5th Floor, Office 13-14 1618 Sofia
Tel: +359 2 850 1601, +359 888 426040, +359 2 878 426092
Fax: +359 2 850 1601
E-mail: office@vladimirovlaw.com
Web Site: www.vladimirovlaw.com
Varna Office: 110 Vladislav Varnenchik Blvd, Office 6 9000 Varna
Tel: + 359 885 01 47 88
US Office (Washington DC Metro Area)
Tel:+1 910 551 0913
E-mail: ensley@vladimirovlaw.com
Offices in Sofia, Varna and Washington DC

Arsov Natchev Ganeva, Attorneys-at-Law
Corporate law, privatization, concessions, lending and finance, litigation, real estate, insolvency, EC law, aviation law, intellectual property, company and commercial law, business services, setting up new companies and partnerships, mergers & acquisitions, purchase and sale of businesses, liquidation, distribution and license agreements, employment, stockholder and partnership agreements, franchising, commercial contracts, banking, finance, securities and commodities, project financing, payment and bank guarantees, escrow accounts, debt collection and operations with securities, administrative and competition law, domestic and international arbitration, tax law, labor and social security, international engineering and construction projects, human rights protection law, foundations, associations, non-profit organizations law and draft legislation.
36 Shipka Street 1504 Sofia
Tel: +359 2 946 3349, 943 4066
Fax: +359 2 946 3348
E-mail: marsov@omega.bg; office@anglaw.com
Website: www.anglaw.com

Dimitar Blyangov, Esq.
U.S. immigration, U.S. taxation, U.S. customs; business and not -for-profit organizations; accounting, contracts, IP, sports and entertainment.
Sofia Office: Georgi Obretenov Street No. 9, 1000 Sofia
U.S. Office (New York): 419 Lafayette Street, 3rd Floor, New York, NY 10003 - USA
Tel.: +1 917 406 1533
Fax. : +1 212 228 6149
E-mail: dblyangov@dnbly.com
Website: www.dnbly.com

Svetlana Bogdanova, Attorney-at-Law
Commercial law, civil law, real estate law and property law, bank law, company law, administrative law, international law and litigation.
20 Knyaz Boris I Street, Floor 1, Apt 2 1463 Sofia

Tel: +359 2 965 0988
Fax: +359 2 965 0981
Mobile: +359 89 998 5578
E-mail: svetlana_bogdanova@abv.bg
Website: http://bglaw-consulting.com

Borislav Boyanov & Co. *Sofia Office* (Borislav T. Boyanov, Managing Partner)
Banking law, bankruptcy, company law, competition law, criminal and administrative law, energy and natural resources, finance, foreign investments, insurance law, intellectual property, litigation and arbitration, privatization, property, public procurement, securities, telecommunications and media.
82 Patriarch Evtimii Blvd., 1463 Sofia
Tel.: +359 2 805 5055
Fax: +359 2 805 5000
E-mail: mail@boyanov.com, b.boyanov@boyanov.com,
Website: www.boyanov.com

Braykov's Legal Office (Valentin Braykov, Senior Partner)
Contract law, commercial law, company law, intellectual property rights (no patents), commercial litigation, competition and employment.
15 Nikolai Gogol Street, 1504 Sofia
Tel: +359 2 943 0245, 943 0246
Fax: +359 2 944 9894
E-mail: office@braykov.com
Website: www.braykov.com

Bulgarian Consulting Group Ltd. (in cooperation with Anadolieva & Ilieva Law Office)
Insurance banking/financial, commercial/business law, foreign investments, marketing agreements, patents/trademarks/copyrights, civil law collections, commercial law, contracts, corporations, foreign claims, estates, taxes, government relations, labor relations and immigration
Regus Sofia City West, 53-55 Totleben Blvd, 1606 Sofia
Tel.: +359 89 2440199 +359 87 6228332, 88 451 3821, 88 704 7671
Fax: +359 2 805 7001
E-mail: office@bulgarianconsulting.eu
Website: www.bulgarianconsulting.eu

Bulgaria Legal Law Office
Family Law, Child Custody, Marriage/Divorce, Insurance, Banking/Financial, commercial/business law, foreign investments, marketing agreements, patents/trademarks/copyrights, civil law, damages, collections, commercial Law, contracts, transportation law, corporations, aeronautical/maritime, estates, taxes, government relations, immigration. Galina Georgieva is a practicing English solicitor, registered with the SRA of England and Wales.
8 Stefan Stambolov Street, Floor 1, Office 1, 9000 Varna
Tel: +359 0 52 604422
Mob: +359 0886 462040
Fax: +359 052 617226
E-mail: call@bulgaria-legal.com
UK Tel: 44 (0)191 640 8899, UK Fax: 44(0) 709 288 5817
Website: http://www.bulgaria-legal.com/
Offices in Varna and UK

COELER Legal Consulting (Dr. Cornelia Draganova LL.M)
Foreign investment, corporate & commercial law, real estate & construction, intellectual property, trademarks, taxation, insolvency and liquidation of companies, debt collection, litigation & arbitration, ADR, business services, domiciliation of companies, accountancy, notary and translation services.
1 Oborishte Str., 1504 Sofia
Tel: +359 2 489 08 67
Fax: +359 2 846 80 46
E-mail: info@coelerlegal.com
Website: www.coelerlegal.com

Damyanov Law Firm

Family law, parental child abduction, commercial/business law, foreign investments, patents/trademarks/copyrights, civil law, collections, contracts, foreign claims, estates, taxes, government relations and labor relations
63 Raiko Daskalov Street , Floor 1, 4000 Plovdiv
Tel.: +359 32 622 161
Fax. +359 32 622 163
E-mail: office@damyanovlaw.eu
Website: http://www.damyanovlaw.eu/

Dimitrov Ivanov & Partners, Attorneys-at-law
Insurance, banking/financial, commercial/business law, foreign investments, marketing Agreements, patents/trademarks/copyrights, civil law, contracts, transportation law, corporations, estates, labor relations.
31 Pirinski Prohod St., Apt. 12, 1618 Sofia
Tel.: +359 89 7922 715; +359 88 932 5272
E-mail: contactus@dipartners.bg
Website: http://www.dipartners.bg/

Dimitrov, Petrov & Co.
Corporate & commercial law, mergers & acquisitions, banking & securities law, ICT & IPR law, telecommunications & competition law, energy law & utilities, real estate law & construction, taxation, employment & social security, litigation & arbitration.
Sofia Office: 28 Todor Alexandrov Blvd, Floor 7, 1303 Sofia
Tel: +359 2 421 4201
Fax: +359 2 421 4202
Varna Office: 7 Krastyu Mirski Street, Floor 3, Office 9, 9000 Varna
Tel/ Fax: +359 52 912 986, +359 52 912 987, +359 52 694 505
E-mail: info@dpc.bg;
Website: www.dpc.bg
Offices in Sofia and Varna

Djingov, Gouginski, Kyutchukov & Velichkov *(Assen Djingov, Georgi Gouginski, Stephan Kyutchukov & Marius Velichkov)*
General corporate and foreign trade, joint ventures, mergers & acquisitions, privatization, banking, finance and securities, project finance & infrastructure, telecommunications, energy, oil and gas, employment and social security, intellectual property, trademarks, not-for-profit organizations, legal advice to the government.
10 Tsar Osvoboditel Blvd, 1000 Sofia
Tel: +359 2 932 1100
Fax: +359 2 980 3586
E-mail: dgkv@dgkv.com
Website: www.dgkv.com

Dobrev & Partners *(George P. Dobrev, Managing Partner)*
Commercial and property investment, residential conveyancing, property finance and mortgages, property litigation, commercial and corporate law, commercial agreements, partnerships and joint ventures, mergers and acquisitions, corporate and personal taxation, intellectual property, trademarks and brand protection, patents, design and copyright, franchising, licensing and distribution, competition and EU law, unfair competition, dispute resolution in all IP rights, environmental law, family law, personal injury, product liability, professional negligence, accidents at work, commercial crime, advise on commercial and regulated industries, public procurement, public/private partnerships, litigation, arbitration & mediation.
32, Antim I Street, 4000 Plovdiv
Tel.: +359 32 622 611
Cell: +359 898 611 416, +359 887 479 226
E-mail: ge.dobrev@gmail.com; gd@dobrevandpartners.com
Website: http://dobrevandpartners.com/

European Litigation Support EEIG *(Country Representative: Mrs. Sevda ROS)*
Family law, adoptions, child custody, parental child abduction, child protection, marriage/divorce, insurance, banking/financial, commercial/business law, foreign investments, marketing agreements, patents/trademarks/copyrights, civil law, criminal law, damages, narcotics, collections, commercial law, contracts, transportation law, corporations, aeronautical/maritime, foreign claims, estates, taxes, government relations, labor relations, immigration, auto/accidents.

D. Kovachev 21 A/10, 9300 Dobrich
Tel: +359 897 406 778
Fax: +359 897 406 778
E-mail: contact@litigation-support.eu

Georgiev, Todorov & Co.
Administrative appeals, arbitration, banking law, bankruptcy, concessions, construction, contracts, competition, corporate law, employment, energy, equities, foreign investments, insurance, IT law, licenses, litigation, media, M&As, privatization, project finance, public procurements, taxes, telecommunications, secured lending, securities, utilities, waste and waste management.
27 Parchevich Street, 1000 Sofia
Tel.: +359 2 9376527
Fax: +359 2 9376525
E-mail: office@georg-tod.com
Website: www.georg-tod.com

Yanko Georgiev, Attorney-at-Law
Medical law, administrative law, tort law, contract law, company law, family law, insurance law, property law and litigation
5 Tzar Asen 5 St., floor 2nd, office 11, 1000 Sofia
Tel.: +359 2 9819264
Fax: +359 2 9864338
E-mail: ygeorgiev@mbox.contact.bg

Harizanov Law Office
Legal services and online consultations for commercial and company law, real estate property investments, litigation, trademarks and brand protection, patents, design and copyright legal management and labor matters. Representation before all state institutions and court instances in relation to commercial, tax, labor, contractual and property litigation. Legal assistance in the conclusion of commercial deals with real estate properties, securities, leasing deals, contracts for transportation, sales, commissions and distribution agreements, agency agreements, franchising, etc.
Business Center Bulgaria, Vitosha Boulevard, 146 B, Floor 6, 1465 Sofia
Tel: +359 88 7397 106
Fax: +359 2 805 3033
E-mail: legal.consult.yv@gmail.com
Website: http://www.harizanov.net

Iliev & Partners Law Firm
Family law, adoptions, child custody, parental child abduction, child protection, marriage/divorce, insurance, banking/financial, commercial/business law, foreign investments, marketing agreements, patents/trademarks/copyrights, civil law, damages, collections, commercial law, contracts, transportation law, corporations, aeronautical/maritime, foreign claims, estates, taxes, government relations, labor relations, immigration, auto/accidents.
3 William Gladstone Street, Ground Floor, Office 2, 1000 Sofia
Tel: +359 2 851 7227
Fax: +359 2 851 7887
Mobile: +359 898 600 116
E-mail: office@ilievlawoffice.com
Website: http://www.ilievlawoffice.com/

Kambourov & Partners, Attorneys-at-Law
Infrastructure projects, public procurements, concessions, energy and natural resources, telecoms and media, intellectual property, multimedia and film production, banking and finance, capital markets, securities, receiverships and bad debt collection, corporate restructuring and insolvency, real estate and construction, green field Investments, corporate and commercial, M&A, joint ventures, competition, litigation and dispute resolution, mediation & arbitration; taxation, NGO's and private foundations
55 Neofit Rilski Street, 1000 Sofia
Tel.: +359 2 986 9999, 986 8888, 986 8885, 932 0032
Fax: +359 2 986 9995
E-mail: office@kambourov.biz
Website: www.kambourov.biz

Kreston BulMar *(Georgi Naydenov)*
Commercial and business law, foreign investments, civil law, contracts, corporations, foreign claims, estates, taxes, government relations, labor relations
172 Nishka Street, 1309 Sofia
Tel/ Fax: +359 2 8 12 06
Mobile: + 359 878 350 000
E-mail: bulmar@bulmar.com
Website: http://www.bulmar.com
Offices in Pernik, Silistra, Veliko Turrnovo, Sliven, Kyustendil, Plovdiv and Kurdzhali

Law Firm Georgieva & Georgiev
Family law, commercial/business law, foreign investments, marketing agreements, patents/trademarks/copyrights, civil law, contracts, corporations, foreign claims, estates, labor relations.
1A Kaimakchalan Street, 3 Floor, 14 Apt., 1505 Sofia
Tel.: + 359 2 9440311
E-mail: office@legaideas.eu
Website: http://www.legaideas.eu/

LEGACON – Bulgarian Law Company *(Angel Dinkov, Lawyer, Member of Burgas Bar Association Bulgaria)*
Tax, commercial and real law. judicial defense and arbitration in business and civil deals; judicial defense in real estate arguments; representation in privatization deals; representation in concession and procurement procedures; representation and consultation on the legal aspects of securities operations, franchising contracts and insurance contracts; performing deals with land in favor of foreign citizens and companies; establishing professional contacts with local and central authorities; procedures on the change of purpose of farming lands; companies registration, companies register amendments; taxation and optimization of tax expenditures for trade companies and citizens; PRE-IVESTMENT EXAMINATION: Analysis of legal status; analysis of financial status; valuation of the real market value of investment object; analysis of norms and regulations with regards to the activities, which the prospective investor would like to perform in the area of the Republic of Bulgaria.
15 B Han Krum Street, 8000 Burgas
Secretary: +359 56 814095
Tel: +359 56 857890
Mobile: +359 888 403262
Fax: +359 56 857881
E-mail: info@LegaConsult.com
Website: www.legaconsult.com

Lega InterConsult - Penkov, Markov & Partners, Law Offices *(Vladimir Penkov, Managing Partner)*
Commercial law, commercial contracts for sale and purchase, cooperation and joint activities, commercial representation, franchising, distribution, participation in negotiations, customs clearance procedures, protection of the competition, company law, incorporation, association agreements, joint venture agreements, notarial procedures, bankruptcy proceedings, creditors representation, privatization and foreign investments, due diligence reports, mergers and acquisitions, planning and consultancy on corporate and tax structures, participation in negotiations, due diligence reports, agreements on equity sales, tax law, employment contracts and contracts for services, management contracts, social security consultancy, real estate transactions, family and inheritance law, licensing and know-how agreements, litigation and arbitration.
Iztok Distr., Bldg. 22, Entr. A, 1113 Sofia
Tel.: +359 2 971 3935, 971 0323, 971 0254, 971 0261, 971 0283, 971 0279
Fax: +359 2 971 1191, 971 0162
E-mail: lawyers@penkov-markov.eu
Website: www.licpenkov-markov.com
Offices in Bourgas, Russe, Lovech, Dobrich, Pleven, Stara Zagora, Targovishte and Varna.

Legal Consultancy *(Hristo Dyankov, Attorney at Law)*
Construction & real estate, corporate & commercial Law, litigation & arbitration, competition law, energy & environmental law, labor and social security law.
47 Madrid Blvd., 2nd Floor, Office 2, 1505 Sofia
Tel.: +359 2 943 0801, 943 0802, 943 803

Fax: +359 2 943 0800
E-mail: office@legalconsultancy.net, dyankov@legalconsultancy.net
Website: www.legalconsultancy.net

Lex Americana Law Office *(Christian Schrobsdorff, Attorney-at-Law)*
United States law and New York State law, with a focus on international finance and corporate matters.
Sofia Office: Blvd. Vitosha 36, Et 4, #8A, 1000 Sofia
Tel: +359 897 919 965
Fax: +359 2 987 6887
US Address (New York): 21-12 Broadway, Queens, NY 11106
US Tel +1 646 582 0182
Fax: +1 786 292 3201
E-mail: cs@lexamericana.com
Website: www.lexamericana.com
Offices in Sofia and Queens, NY

Tatyana Mihaylova, Bar of Bourgas
Marriage, Divorce, Commercial, Business Law, Foreign Investments, Civil and Criminal Law, Damages, Narcotics, Collections, Commercial Law, Contracts, Estates, Adoptions, Child Custody, Parental Child Abduction, Child Protection, Insurance, Banking, Financial, Marketing Agreements, Patents, Trademarks, Copyrights, Transportation Law, Corporations, Aeronautical, Maritime, Foreign Claims, Taxes, Government Relations, Labor Relations, Immigration, Auto Accidents.
Address: Complex "Bratia Miladinovi" block 89A, entrance 1, floor 1, Burgas
Office Tel: +359 899 976 688
Home Tel: +359 56 54 16 40
Fax: +359 56 54 16 40
E-mail: terrymih@yahoo.ca

MH Legal Law Office *(Milen Hristov, LLM)*
EU transportation law, company and corporate law, real estate law, debt collection.
12 Konstantin Velichkov Street, Floor 1, Office 8, 9000 Varna
Tel/Fax: +359 52 605 997
E-mail: milen@mhlegal.eu
Website: http://mhlegal.eu

Stanislav Natzev, *Attorney at Law*
Family law, child custody, parental child abduction, child protection, marriage/divorce, insurance, banking/financial, commercial/business law, foreign investments, marketing agreements, civil law, damages, collections, commercial law, contracts, corporations, foreign claims, estates, labor relations, immigration
Graf Ignatiev Street No.38A, Floor 1, Apt.3, 1000 Sofia
Tel: +359 888 10 62 58
Fax: +359 2 986 73 37
E-mail: snatzev@gmail.com
Webpage: http://snatzev.googlepages.com/

New Balkans Law Office
Family law, adoptions, child custody, parental child abduction, child protection, marriage/divorce, insurance, banking/financial, commercial/business law, foreign investments, marketing agreements, patents/trademarks/copyrights, civil law, damages, collections, commercial law, contracts, transportation law, corporations, aeronautical/maritime, foreign claims, estates, taxes, government relations, labor relations, immigration and auto/accident.
14 Shesti Septemvri Street, 1000 Sofia
Tel: +359 2 403 1900
Fax: +359 2 489 4333
E-mail: sofia@newbalkanslawoffice.com
Website: http://www.newbalkanslawoffice.com/
Offices in Rousse and London, UK

Niesar Diamond & Todorova Law Offices *(Ms. Pavlina Todorova)*
Commercial law, civil law, competition law, foreign investment and privatization, tax, real estate and investments.

1 Yuri Venelin Street, 3rd Floor, 1000 Sofia
Tel.: +359 2 980 4136, 987 7097, 987 8747
Tel./Fax: +359 2 980 4136
Mobile: +359 888 527 337
E-mail: bbcelc@bbce-legalconsultancy.com, todorova@bbce-legalconsultancy.com, Konstantinova@bbce-legalconsultancy.com
Office in Sofia and San Francisco, CA

Nikolov Law Firm
Adoptions and immigration
66 Vitosha Blvd., 1463 Sofia
Tel.: +359 2 879 859990
E-mail: contact@esenlaw.com
Website: http://www.esenlaw.com/, www.esenlaw.com/bg
Offices in Sofia and Chicago, IL

Noblex Ltd.
Banking, business advice, corporate and commerical law, employment, litigation, maritime law, property, private clients, taxation, practice groups
Burgas (Head Office) (Stamen Cholakov, LLM, Stanislav Kassarov, LLM, Anna Ivanova, LLM, Sofia Radoslavova, LLM, Boyana Chilikova, LLM, Katyusha Ivanova, LLM, Daniel Cholakov, LLM)
1 Rilska Street, 8000 Burgas
Tel: +359 56 843 745, 843 746
Fax: +359 56 840 124
E-mail: bourgas@noblexgroup.com
Website: www.noblexgroup.com
Sofia: Valentina Bineva, LLM; Daniela Zareva, LLM; Dencho Slavov , LLM;
4 Dobrudja Street, 1000 Sofia
Tel: +359 2 9811809; 9877484
Fax: +359 2 9811806
E-mail:sofia@noblexgroup.com
Sredets: Daniel Cholakov, LLM
3 Spartak Street, 8300 Sredets
Tel.: +359 55 51 2142
Fax: +359 55 51 2141
Email: sredets@noblexgroup.com
Varna: Snejana Pasheva, LLM
1 Kotel Street, Floor 3, Apt. 3 9000 Varna
Tel: +359 52 617454
E-mail: varna@noblexgroup.com
Offices in Burgas, Sofia, Sredets, Varna, Oxford, UK and Athens, GR

Penev, LLP *(formerly known as Seplex Consulting Co.)*
Banking & finance, commercial arbitration, commercial law, company law, competition law, concession, intellectual property law, labor and social security, litigation, media, publishing, advertising, natural resources and energy, notary services, property and construction law, privatization, public procurement, representation of foreign companies, real estate, telecommunications and IT.
19-A, Patriarch Evtimii Blvd., 2nd Floor, 1142 Sofia
Tel.: +359 2 930 0970, 988 8036, 980 0838
Fax: +359 2 930 0978
E-mail:info@penev.eu
Website: www.seplex.com
Offices in Plovdiv, Varna, Geneva, CH and London, UK

Penkov, Markov & Partners, Law Offices *(Vladimir Penkov, Managing Partner)*
Commercial law, commercial contracts for sale and purchase, banking & finance, public procurement, cooperation and joint activities, commercial representation, energy law and renewables, IP & Trademarks, IT & media, franchising, distribution, participation in negotiations, customs clearance procedures, protection of competition, company law, incorporation, association agreements, joint venture agreements, notarial procedures, bankruptcy proceedings, creditors representation, privatization and foreign investments, due diligence reports, mergers and acquisitions, planning and consultancy on corporate and tax structures,

agreements on equity sales, tax law, employment contracts and contracts for services, management contracts, social security consultancy, real estate transactions, family and inheritance law, licensing and know-how agreements, administrative law, litigation and arbitration, pharmaceutical law.
Iztok District, Tintyava Street, 13B, Floor 6 1113 Sofia
Tel.: +359 2 971 3935
Fax: +359 2 971 1191
E-mail: lawyers@penkov-markov.eu
Website: www.penkov-markov.eu
Offices in Bourgas, Rousse, Lovech, Pleven, Stara Zagora, and Varna

Petkov, Pavel Plamenov
Insurance, banking/financial, commercial/business law, commercial law, contracts, corporations, estates, taxes, labor relations
9 Targovska Street, Floor 2, Office 1, 3700 Vidin
Tel.: +359 94 990 459
Cell: +359 876 990 459
E-mail: petkov@lawyer.com
Web site: http://www.yourlawyer.eu/

Latchezar Lubomirov Popov
Adoption, human rights, tax law, registration of Not-for-Profits, administrative law, import/export, commercial law, intellectual property, contracts, immigration and visas, criminal law, real estate, customs, restitution, family law, registration and businesses.
44 Parchevich Street, Floor 5, Apt. 15, Sofia
Tel. +359 2 980 8911
Fax: +359 2 981 4993
Mobile: +359 2 88 794 4473
E-mail: rlinet@ruleoflawinstitute.bg; lpopov@advocateseurope.org
Website: www.ruleoflawinstitute.bg
Offices in Plovdiv, Varna and Vidin

Rolinski & Suarez, LLC *(Skochev & Associates: Vladimir Skochev, Attorney at Law)*
Corporate law-US and foreign, international business negotiations, civil litigation and appeals, commercial transactions, joint ventures law-US and foreign. Represent U.S. and foreign corporations in international contract negotiations, litigation, and corporate formation. Joint venture consultation and negotiations, foreign investor negotiations.
3 N. Vapcarov Street, Entrance G, Floor 8, Office 21, 9000 Varna
Tel: 359 52 712 666
Fax: 359 52 712 533
E-mail: v.skochev@skochevandpartners.eu
U.S. Office: The Kentlands, 305 Main Street, Gaithersburg, MD 20878
Tel. +1 301 987 0202
Fax. +1 301 987 0295
E-mail: SRolinski@Rolinski.com
Website: www.Rolinski.com
Offices in Washington, DC and Longwood, FL

Rusev & Co. *(Valentin Rusev, Attorney at Law)*
Customs law, tax law, import, export, civil law, criminal law, administrative law, insurance law, commercial law, family law, finance law, arbitration law, labor law, Banking law, contract law, transportation law, copyrights law, notary law, environmental law
1 Vitosha Blvd, Floor 3, Office 369, 1000 Sofia
Tel. +359 2 987 1713
Fax/Tel.: +359 2 953 0160
Mobile: +359 2 898 686 224, 898 448 452
Skype: valentine.rusev1
E-mail: office@lawyer-bg.com, rusev@lawyer-bg.com
Website: www.lawyer-bg.com

Ruseva-Savova Law Office
Corporate law - Bulgarian and US, Public Procurement and EU Funding, M&A, private equity,

commercial/business law, contracts, international business negotiations, foreign investments, technology, data protection and security, IP&IT, renewable energy and natural resources, banking/financial law, capital markets, insurance, telecommunications, life sciences, marketing agreements, transportation law, government relations, labor relations, marriage/divorce. Member of Legastrat, an alliance of boutique law firms
Sofia Office: Zlatina Ruseva-Savova, LL.M., MBA, managing partner
114 Dimitar Hadjikotsev St. (entry on Slaviste St.), South Park Complex, 1421 Sofia
Tel.: +359 898513629, 2 866 0629
Fax: +359 2 866-0629
E-mail: office@rslaw.eu, lawyers@rslaw.eu
Website: www.rslaw.eu
Offices in Sofia and Russe

Sandoulov's Legal Office
General civil law, real estate law, adoptions, family and probate law, contract and commercial law, company and corporate law, insurance law, foreign investment.
30 Bogatitza Street, 1421 Sofia
Tel.: +359 2 963 3929, 963 5093
Fax: +359 2 963 2058
E-mail: info@sandoulov.com
Web site: www.sandoulov.com

SMT Legal *(Stoyanov, Mittov, Tanev)*
Corporate law, tax services, international transport, customs law, import and export regulations, foreign Investment, antitrust and trade regulation, insurance law, joint ventures, acquisitions, privatization, intellectual property, commercial law, real estate, NGO law, court litigation.
Sofia Office: Ventsislav Tanev and Georgi Stoyanov, Partners
3 Vassil Levski Blvd., Left section, 2nd Floor, 1000 Sofia
Tel./Fax: + 359 2 989 5411
Mobile: + 359 888 702 072, + 359 898 691 670
E-mail: smtlegal@smtlegal.com, vtanev@smtlegal.com
Web site: http://www.smtlegal.com
Plovdiv Office: Ivan Mittov, Partner
3 Tsar Boris III Obedinitel Blvd. 4000 Plovdiv
Tel/Fax: +359 32 622 213
Mobile: + 359 888 312 496
E-mail: smtlegal@smtlegal.com, imittov@smtlegal.com
Website: http://www.smtlegal.com
Offices: Sofia and Plovdiv

Vesselin Tzotchev*, Bulgarian Attorney at Law*
Administrative law, banking/ financial institutions, civil law, business law, collections, commercial law, contracts, corporations, damages, estate and trusts, family (only in relation to tax cases), foreign claims, foreign investments, government relations, immigration, insurance, transportation law and all Bulgarian and U. S. taxes, FATCA, QI, transfer pricing and VAT. Can represent taxpayers before IRS and the state tax authorities. Speaks English, Russian, German and Spanish.
Sofia Office: Vesselin Tzotchev
J. K. Kransno Selo, Bld 200, entr A, Apt 11, 1618 Sofia
FAX: +1 905 248 3316
U.S.: +1 714 881 1019
Mobile: +359 885 589 177
Swiss Office: USCANTAX
Zollerstrasse 14, 8703, Erlenbach, Switzerland
Tel: +41 445 866 155
Mobile +41 789560816
E-mail: vtzochev@uscantax.com
Website: http://www.USCANTAX.com
Offices: Sofia and Erlenbach, Switzerland

VIP Consult Law Firm
Foreign investments, corporate law, real estate & construction, commercial and company law, contract law,

setting up new companies and partnerships, mergers and acquisitions, purchase and sale of businesses, liquidation, tax law, labor law, intellectual property, negotiations and disputes, strategic investment counseling, debt collection, administrative and competition law, litigation, mediation and arbitration, business services, due diligence reports, family and inheritance law, immigration and visas
Varna Office (Headquarters): 20 Omurtag Street, 9000 Varna
Tel/Fax: +359 52 603 183
Mobile: +359 88 755 6632
Bansko Office: 1 Aton Street, Bansko 2770
Tel.: +359 88 655 6631
Sofia Office: 26 Gen. Totleben Blvd, Floor 7, Apt 10, 1606 Sofia
Tel/fax: +359 2 868 4687
Mobile: 08850 77787
E-mail: info@vip-consult.net
Website: http://vip-consult.net/
Offices: Varna, Sofia and Bansko

Wolf Theiss Corporate M&A *(Richard Clegg, Partner since 2008)*
Nuclear, upstream and downstream energy, infrastructure, financial services, banking, private equity, finance, corporate restructuring, mergers and acquisitions, IT, Telecommunications, pharmaceutical, European & International law, antitrust, dispute resolution, arbitration, real estate, tax, intellectual property, commercial contracts, licensing, employment.
Rainbow Plaza, 29 Atanas Dukov Street, 1407 Sofia
Tel: +359 2 861 3735, 861 3700
Fax: +359 2 8620 370
E-mail: Richard.Clegg@wolftheiss.com; stanislava.staneva@wolftheiss.com
Website: http://www.wolftheiss.com

TRADE AND PROJECT FINANCING

METHODS OF PAYMENT

As with any international transactions, the method of payment is determined by the degree of trust in the buyer's ability and willingness to pay. Full payment in advance is recommended for the first delivery and when the importer is still unknown. Most commonly used payment mechanisms are available to facilitate international transactions.

U.S. Exim Bank provides insurance policies and long-term guarantees to U.S. exporters to allow more flexible payment terms. For more information, please visit http://www.exim.gov

BANKING SYSTEM

Although Bulgaria is still predominantly a cash economy, the use of debit and credit cards is increasing. Development of services for consumers, such as credit cards and e-banking, was boosted within the last couple of years, while personal checks are almost unknown and unused as a method of payment for locals. The number of POS terminals in the country and the share of the non-cash transactions grew significantly in the past years.

The Bulgarian National Bank (BNB) operates independently of the government and reports directly to Parliament. The BNB regulates the banking system, however under the Currency Board Arrangement has no discretion in setting monetary or exchange rate policy. The Bulgarian Currency is exchanged at a fixed rate of Euro against the Bulgarian Lev (1 EUR = 1,95583 BGN).

There are 30 commercial banks in Bulgaria; twenty-four are fully licensed and authorized to engage in international transactions and six are branches of foreign banks in Bulgaria. Foreign banking capital is largely predominant on the market. Citibank is the only U.S. bank with an office in Bulgaria.

FOREIGN-EXCHANGE CONTROLS

International financial remittances in payment of imports into Bulgaria are generally allowed. Only bank transfer permits the export of hard currency by commercial entities, including juridical persons and sole traders. Transfers for current international payments (imports of goods and services, transportation, interest and principal payments, insurance, training, medical treatment and other purposes defined in Bulgarian regulations) must be supported by documentation such as invoices, certificates, or transport documents, to the transferring bank.

U.S. BANKS AND LOCAL CORRESPONDENT BANKS

Contact information for all Bulgarian banks may be found on the Bulgarian National Bank

http://www.bnb.bg web site. Some Bulgarian banks may have 100 or more U.S. correspondent banks, and some U.S. banks may have correspondent relations with more than one Bulgarian bank. As banking relationships can change quickly, the best source of current information on correspondent banking arrangements is the banks themselves.

The Business Service Provider is a good place to start when looking for finance and banking services in Bulgaria. Please visit http://www.buyusa.gov/bulgaria/en/serviceproviderlist.html The AmCham web site http://www.amcham.bg is another good resource of information. From the AmCham home page, click on "About us" then "Members list".

PROJECT FINANCING

1.The U.S. Export-Import Bank (Eximbank) is a source of export financing and insurance for U.S. transactions in Bulgaria. Eximbank will guarantee a commercial bank loan up to 85% of the value of the contract. Eximbank will also accept guarantees from the larger municipalities. In 2006, Eximbank concluded a Master Guarantee Agreement with the Bulgarian banks UBB and Postbank, therefore Eximbank financing is available in Bulgaria.

The Small Business Administration (SBA) provides financial and business development assistance to encourage and help small U.S. companies in developing export markets. http://www.sba.gov/

The Overseas Private Investment Corporation's (OPIC) key programs are its loan guarantees, direct loans, and political risk insurance. http://www.opic.gov/

The U.S. Trade and Development Agency (TDA) promotes U.S. exports through funding feasibility studies, technical assistance, training programs, and orientation visits. http://www.ustda.gov/

2.The European Bank for Reconstruction and Development (EBRD), whose largest shareholder is the U.S. Government, has a number of programs available to U.S. investors. The Bank makes loans as well as takes equity stakes in infrastructure projects. The EBRD will increasingly focus on private-sector development in Bulgaria. It also mandates open competitive tenders in procurements, which give U.S. companies opportunities to supply goods and services. For more information, please see http://www.ebrd.com/

The World Bank's procurement procedures enable U.S. exporters to bid on public procurement contracts. To date, approved projects are in the energy, telecommunications, residential heating, railways, health, environmental and public administration sectors. For more information on WB program in Bulgaria, please see http://www.worldbank.bg

The Multilateral Investment Guarantee Agency (MIGA) is part of the World Bank Group. Its purpose is to encourage foreign investment in developing countries by providing investment guarantees (political risk insurance) against the risk of currency transfer, expropriation, war, civil disturbance and breach of contract by the host government. For more information, please see http://www.worldbank.org/

3.Bulgaria's accession to the EU opened access to project financing in the form of EU structural and cohesion funds. EU financial assistance programs provide a wide array of grants, loans, loan guarantees and co-financing for feasibility studies and infrastructure projects in a number of key sectors (e.g., environmental, transportation, energy, telecommunications, tourism, public health). From a commercial perspective, these initiatives create significant market opportunities for U.S. businesses, U.S.-based suppliers, and subcontractors.

The EU supports projects within its member states, as well as EU-wide "economic integration" projects that cross both internal and external EU borders. See http://www.buyusa.gov/europeanunion/eu_funds.html .

Seven EU operational programs are available in Bulgaria, supporting projects in the areas of competitiveness, environment, transport, regional development, technical assistance, capacity building, and human capital development.

The European Union provides project financing through grants from the European Commission and loans from the European Investment Bank. Grants from the Structural Funds are distributed through the member states' national and regional authorities.

The CSEU Tenders Database

The U.S. Commercial Service at the U.S. Mission to the European Union offers a tool on its website to help U.S.-based companies identify European public procurement opportunities. The database features all current public procurement tenders issued by all national and regional public authorities in the 27 Member States of the European Union, plus four other European countries, and that are open to U.S.-based firms under the terms of the Government Procurement Agreement (GPA) implemented in 1995. The database is updated twice weekly and is easy to use with a range of search options, including approximately 20 industry sectors. The database also contains tenders for public procurement contracts relating to structural funds. Readers may access the database at http://www.buyusa.gov/europeanunion/eu_tenders.html .

EU Structural Funds

The EU earmarked EUR 308 billion for projects under the Structural Funds and the Cohesion Fund programs for the 2007-2013 period for the EU-27. In addition to funding economic development projects proposed by Member States or local authorities, EU Structural Funds also support specialized projects promoting EU socioeconomic objectives. For information on approved programs that will result in future project proposals, please visit: http://ec.europa.eu/regional_policy/atlas2007/fiche_index_en.htm .

For projects financed through the Structural Funds, Bulgarian officials are the key decision-makers. They assess the needs of their country; investigate projects; evaluate bids; and award contracts. To become familiar with available financial support programs in Bulgaria, it is advisable for would-be contractors to meet with local officials to discuss local needs.

Tenders issued by Bulgaria's public contracting authorities for projects supported by EU grants are subject to EU public procurement legislation if they meet the EU minimum contract value requirement for the eligible sector. Below this threshold, tender procedures are subject to national procurement legislation. There are no overt prohibitions against the participation of U.S. companies, either as developers or concessionaires of projects supported partially by the Structural Funds, or as bidders on subsequent public tenders related to such projects, but it is advisable to team up with a local partner. All Structural Fund projects are co-financed by national authorities and most may also qualify for a loan from the European Investment Bank. The private sector is also involved in project financing. For more information on these programs, please see the market research section on the website of the US Mission to the EU: http://www.buyusa.gov/europeanunion/mrr.html

The Cohesion Fund

The Cohesion Fund is another instrument of EU structural policy. Its EUR 61.5 billion (2007-2013) budget seeks to improve cohesion within the EU by funding transport infrastructure and environmental projects in Portugal, Spain, Greece and the twelve new (since 2004) EU Member States from Central and Eastern Europe. These projects are generally co-financed by national authorities, the European Investment Bank, and the private sector.

Key Link: http://ec.europa.eu/regional_policy/funds/cf/index_en.htm

Loans from the European Investment Bank

Headquartered in Luxembourg, the European Investment Bank (EIB) is the financing arm of the European Union. As a non-profit banking institution, the EIB offers cost-competitive, long-term lending in Europe. Best known for its project financial and economic analysis, the Bank makes loans to both private and public EU-based borrowers for projects in all sectors of the economy, such as telecommunications, transport, energy infrastructure and environment.

Projects financed by the EIB must contribute to the socioeconomic objectives set out by the European Union, such as fostering the development of less favored regions; improving European transport and telecommunication infrastructure; protecting the environment; supporting the activities of SMEs; assisting urban renewal; and, generally promoting growth, competitiveness and employment in Europe. Last year, the EIB created a list of projects to be considered for approval and posted the list on its website. As such, the EIB website is a source of intelligence on upcoming tenders related to EIB-financed projects: http://www.eib.org/projects/pipeline/index.htm

The EIB presents attractive business opportunities to U.S. businesses. EIB lending rates are lower than most other commercial rates. Like all EIB customers, however, U.S. firms must apply the loan proceeds to a project that contributes to the European objectives cited above.

The EIB's i2i (Innovation 2010 Initiative) is designed to highlight projects that support innovative technology in the European Union, in particular by financing broadband and multimedia networks; the physical or virtual infrastructure providing local access to these networks; and research and development infrastructures, especially in the less developed regions of the European Union. i2i will also finance projects to computerize schools and universities and to provide information technology training in conjunction with public authorities.

Key Link: http://www.eib.org/Attachments/thematic/innovation_2010_initiative_en.pdf

WEB RESOURCES

Export-Import Bank of the United States: http://www.exim.gov

OPIC: http://www.opic.gov

Trade and Development Agency: http://www.tda.gov/

USDA Commodity Credit Corporation: http://www.fsa.usda.gov/ccc/default.htm

European Bank for Reconstruction and Development: http://www.ebrd.bg

World Bank - http://www.worldbank.org/

The European Investment Bank http://www.eib.org/

EIB-financed projects: http://www.eib.org/projects/index.htm?lang=-en

European Union Tenders Database: http://www.buyusa.gov/europeanunion/euopportunities.html

BUSINESS TRAVEL

BUSINESS CUSTOMS

Bulgarians are less formal than Western Europeans from dress to the manner of their business contacts. Meetings, including lunches or dinners, are used as an opportunity to be acquainted and as a basis for developing a relationship of trust. Companies use stand-up evening receptions at hotels, restaurants, trade shows, and even museums and auto showrooms for public relations and to solidify business relationships.

One charming but confusing custom is that head movements indicating agreement or disagreement are reversed in Bulgaria. The rocking of the head from left-to-right, often with a slight smile, means "yes" while nodding up-and-down indicates "no." But with foreign language fluency growing, some Bulgarians will use head movements in typical western fashion. Therefore, it is best to clarify the situation by obtaining a verbal response.

TRAVEL ADVISORY

Bulgarian law requires all travelers entering or leaving EU through Bulgaria with 10 000 Euros (around USD 14,100) or more in cash to declare the sum to customs in order to comply with Regulation (EC) No 1889/2005 of the European Parliament and the Council applicable from June 15, 2007. This initiative has been taken to assist the efforts being made at EU level to tackle crime and improve security by cracking down on money laundering, terrorism and criminality or travelers' checks declare the money/checks upon arrival to customs officials. Travelers entering Bulgaria at Sofia Airport and carrying currency in excess of the above amount should use the red "Something to Declare" line and not the green "Nothing to Declare" line, even if specifically invited into the green line by a customs official.

Travelers who attempt to leave the country with the equivalent of BGN 25,000 or more must complete a customs declaration on which they must state the origin of the money, and present a certificate from the Bulgarian regional internal revenue service proving they do not owe taxes, unless the sum is less than the amount originally reported when initially brought into the country. Please contact the Embassy of Bulgaria in Washington, D.C. or one of Bulgaria's consulates in the United States for specific information regarding customs regulations.

American citizens visiting Bulgaria are encouraged to register at the Consular Section of the U.S. Embassy in Bulgaria and obtain updated information on travel and security within Bulgaria. The Embassy's web site address is http://www.usembassy.bg

Visitors should exchange cash or travelers checks at banks or exchange bureaus. Some exchange bureaus charge commissions on both cash and travelers check transactions, which may be high or not clearly posted. Damaged or much worn U.S. dollar bank notes are often not accepted at banks or exchange bureaus. Major hotels accept credit cards, but most shops and restaurants do not. ATM cash machines are increasing in numbers in Sofia and other major cities, but bankcards, debit cards and credit cards should be used with caution due to the potential for fraud or other criminal activity. Be wary of skimming devices placed on automated tellers. Only use ATMs inside major institutions such as banks or major malls. Limit your use of credit cards to hotel bills or with other major vendors.

If traveling with pets, you must have a certificate of veterinarian examination carried out within one week before departure, as well as a certificate of rabies shot made during the last six months.

For the latest travel and security information, Americans traveling abroad should regularly monitor the Department's Internet web site at http://travel.state.gov Up-to-date information on security can also be obtained by calling 1-888-407-4747 toll free in the

United States, or for callers outside the United States and Canada, a regular toll line at

1-317-472-2328. These numbers are available from 8:00 a.m. to 8:00 p.m. Eastern

Time, Monday through Friday (except U.S. federal holidays).

VISA REQUIREMENTS

A United States passport is required for U.S. citizens who are not also Bulgarian nationals. Bulgarian immigration authorities ask all foreigners to declare the purpose of their visit at the border or upon arrival and to provide their intended address. U.S. citizens who enter the country on regular passports without a Bulgarian visa are authorized to stay for a total of 90 days within a six-month period. Travelers on all types of passports (regular, official or diplomatic) who intend to stay more than 90 days must secure a "D" visa from the Bulgarian Embassy or Consulate. The visa issuance takes about 30 to 40 calendar days. "D" visas may be issued for employment purposes, missionary purposes, or if you are married to a Bulgarian citizen, among other reasons. Travelers using official or diplomatic passports, who intend to stay in Bulgaria for less than 90 days within six months, must secure a Bulgarian visa type "C" from a Bulgarian Embassy or Consulate prior to arrival. As of July 2008, U.S. citizens must apply for a visa at a Bulgarian Embassy/Consulate in the United States or if not residents in the United States, in their country of legal residence. U.S. citizens are also advised that if their purpose of stay in Bulgaria changes (i.e., work or marriage status), they must leave Bulgaria and apply again for a D-visa.

All foreigners receive an entry stamp in their passports. Foreigners who do not have an entry stamp in their passports will encounter difficulties when they try to leave Bulgaria. When entering Bulgaria by car, if the vehicle has been recorded on the passport, the owner may not leave the country without the automobile. Sometimes vehicles are erroneously recorded on the passport of passengers in the car, who then have problems trying to leave the country without the vehicle.

For further information concerning entry requirements, travelers should contact the Embassy of the Republic of Bulgaria at 1621 22nd St. N.W., Washington, D.C. 20008; http://www.bulgaria-embassy.org tel. (202) 483-5885 (main switchboard (202) 387-7969, or the Bulgarian Consulate in New York City.

U.S. Companies that require travel of foreign businesspersons to the United States should be advised that security options be handled via an interagency process. Visa applicants should go to the following links.

State Department Visa Website: http://travel.state.gov/visa/index.html

United States Visas.gov: http://www.unitedstatesvisas.gov/

U.S. Embassy, Sofia, Bulgaria: http://sofia.usembassy.gov/

TELECOMMUNICATIONS

Bulgaria has a good telecommunications infrastructure with three mobile providers and is beginning to launch wireless services for business travelers. Two cellular operators offer BlackBerry service. There are numerous Wi-Fi hotspots in Sofia (mainly at the coffee shops and at the Airport Sofia).

The dialing code for Bulgaria is 359, followed by the appropriate area code: Sofia (2), Plovdiv (32), Varna (52), Bourgas (56), Stara Zagora (42)

TRANSPORTATION

Sofia is served by major European airlines including Air France, Alitalia, Austrian Airlines, British Airways, Czech Airlines, Lauda Air, LOT, Lufthansa, MALEV, Olympic, and Turkish Airlines. Bulgaria Air is also operating international flights as well as domestic service between Sofia and Varna and Bourgas. Hemus Air flies to short-range domestic and regional destinations.

Car rental from Hertz, Avis, Budget and others are available.

Taxis are affordable. It is advisable to call ahead to a reputable taxi company for radio dispatch for personal security as well as to avoid overcharges.

LANGUAGE

Bulgarian is a Slavic language that uses the Cyrillic alphabet. In business, the usage of

English is increasing rapidly. Many Bulgarians have some comprehension of the Russian language. German and French are also widely spoken.

HEALTH

All foreign citizens traveling to Bulgaria may be asked to present valid evidence of health insurance to the Bulgarian border authorities in order to be admitted into the country.

The insurance should be valid for the duration of the traveler's stay in Bulgaria. The

Department of State strongly urges Americans to consult with their medical insurance company prior to traveling abroad to confirm whether their policy applies overseas and if it will cover emergency expenses such as a medical evacuation. U.S. medical insurance plans seldom cover health costs incurred outside the United States unless supplemental coverage is purchased. Further, U.S. Medicare and Medicaid programs do not provide payment for medical services outside the United States. However, many travel agents and private companies offer insurance plans that will cover health care expenses incurred overseas, including emergency services such as medical evacuations. When making a decision regarding health insurance, Americans should consider that many foreign doctors and hospitals require payment in cash prior to providing service and that a medical evacuation to the United States may cost more than 50,000 U.S. Dollars.

Uninsured travelers who require medical care overseas often face extreme difficulties, whereas travelers who have purchased overseas medical insurance have found it to be life saving when a medical emergency has occurred. When consulting with your insurer prior to your trip, please ascertain whether payment will be made to the overseas healthcare provider or if you will be reimbursed later for expenses that you incur.

LOCAL TIME, BUSINESS HOURS, AND HOLIDAYS

Local Time is EST plus 7 hours.
Holidays in Bulgaria include:
January 1 New Year's Day
March 3 National Day
April 2 Orthodox Good Friday
April 5 Orthodox Easter Monday
May 6 St. George's Day, Day of Valor and the Bulgarian Army
May 24 Saints Cyril & Methodius Day
September 6 Unification Day
September 22 Independence Day
December 24 Christmas Eve
December 31 New Year's Day 2011, observed

Work Week

Bulgarians work a 40-hour week with businesses opening between 8:30 and 9:00 a.m. Monday through Friday. During the summer months, scheduling meetings late on

Fridays may be difficult as workers tend to leave early for weekend getaways. As in the rest of Europe, business activity slows considerably during the latter part of July and most of August when many Bulgarians take their extended summer holidays.

TEMPORARY ENTRY OF MATERIALS AND PERSONAL BELONGINGS

In theory, personal items brought in temporarily by travelers such as laptop computers, software, and exhibition materials should be declared upon arrival. Travelers should declare jewelry, cameras, and other valuables upon arrival in order to avoid difficulties when departing. The declaration form should be presented to Customs upon departure.

WEB RESOURCES

Business travelers to Bulgaria seeking appointment with U.S. Embassy Sofia officials should contact the Commercial Section in advance of departure from the United States.

The Commercial Section can be reached by telephone at 359-2-937-5100 and fax at 359-2-937-5320; or e-mail at sofia.office.box@mail.doc.gov. Detailed information on the U.S. Commercial Service Sofia's services and programs are available at: http://www.buyusa.gov/bulgaria and http://www.export.gov

CONTACTS, MARKET TRADE EVENTS

U.S. GOVERNMENT CONTACTS

U.S. Embassy - Sofia http://sofia.usembassy.gov

U.S. Commercial Service – Sofia http://www.buyusa.gov/bulgaria

U.S. Department of State http://www.state.gov

U.S. Department of Commerce http://www.export.gov

U.S. Department of Agriculture http://www.usda.gov

U.S. Agency for International Development http://www.usaid.gov

U.S. Export-Import Bank http://www.exim.gov

Overseas Private Investment Corporation http://www.opic.gov

U.S. Trade and Development Agency http://www.ustda.gov

TRADE AND INDUSTRY ASSOCIATIONS

American Chamber of Commerce in Bulgaria
President: Mr. Anthony Hassiotis
Executive Director: Mr. Valentin Georgiev
Business Park Sofia
Building 2, floor 6
Mladost 4 Area
1715 Sofia
Phone: (359) (2) 974-2743 Fax: (359)(2) 9742 741
E-mail: amcham@amcham.bg Website: http://www.amcham.bg

Bulgarian Chamber of Commerce and Industry
President: Mr. Tzvetan Simeonov
9, Iskar Street
1058 Sofia
Phone: (359) (2) 987-2528, 8117-444, 8117-489; Fax: (359) (2) 8117-490
Business Center Directorate – Mrs. Margarita Damyanova - Director
E-mail: interdept@bcci.bg , office@bcci.bg Website: http://www.bcci.bg/

Confederation of the Employers and Industrialists in Bulgaria
Chairman: Mr. Ivo Prokopiev
Executive Director: Mr. Evgenii Ivanov
55, Alexander Stamboliiski Blvd, 3rd floor
1301 Sofia
Phone: (359) (2) 981-9564, 981-9169 Fax: (359) (2) 988-6776
E-mail: office@ceibg.bg Website: http://www.ceibg.bg/

Bulgarian Industrial Association
Chairman: Mr. Bozhidar Danev
Director, International Organizations and Programs: Mr. Branimir Handjiev
16-20, Alabin Street
1000 Sofia
Phone: (359)(2) 932-0911, 932-0914, 932-0922 Fax: (359)(2) 987-2604
E-mail: office@bia-bg.com; Website: http://www.bia-bg.com/

Bulgarian Construction Chamber
Chairman: Mr. Simeon Peshov
Executive Director: Mr. Ivan Boykov
1, Hristo Smirnenski Blvd.
1164 Sofia
Phone: (359)(2) 806-2910, 806-2911 Fax: (359)(2) 963 2425
E-mail: office@ksb.bg Website: http://www.ksb.bg/

Bulgarian Association for Information Technologies

Chairman: Mr. Theodore Zahov
CEO: Mr. Vesselin Yankov
7 Mizia Street
1124 Sofia
Phone: (359)(2) 946 1513 Fax: (359) (2) 946-1451
E-mail: bait@bait.bg, bait@spnet.net Website: http://www.bait.bg/

BULGARIAN GOVERNMENT CONTACTS

Bulgarian Embassy in Washington, DC http://www.bulgaria-embassy.org/
Bulgarian Government http://www.government.bg/

InvestBulgaria Agency
Executive Director: Mr. Stoyan Stalev
31, Aksakov Street
1000 Sofia
Phone: (359)(2) 980-0918, 985-5500 Fax: (359)(2) 980-1320
E-mail: iba@investbg.government.bg
Website: http://www.investbg.government.bg/

Privatization Agency
Executive Director: Mr. Todor Nikolov
29, Aksakov Street
1000 Sofia
Phone: (359)(2) 987-7579; 987-3249 Fax: (359)(2) 981-6201, 981-1307
E-mail: press@priv.government.bg
Website: http://www.priv.government.bg/

Communications Regulation Commission
Chairperson: Mr. Veselin Bozhkov
6, Gurko St.
1000 Sofia
Phone: (359) (2) 949-2335 Fax: (359) (2) 987-0695
E-mail: info@crc.bg
Website: http://www.crc.bg/

Bulgarian Institute for Standardization
Chairperson: Mr. Ivelin Burov
Executive Director: Mrs. Maya Staneva
13, Lachezar Stanchev Street, Izgrev
1797 Sofia
Phone: (359)(2) 81 74 523 Fax: (359)(2) 873 55 97
E-mail: standards@bds-bg.org
Website: http://www.bds-bg.org/

National Customs Agency
Director General: Mr. Vanyo Tanov
47, G.S. Rakovski Street
1202 Sofia
Phone: (359) (2) 9859-4210, 9859-4213 Fax: (359)(2) 980-4061
E-mail: pr@customs.bg
Website: http://www.customs.bg/

Patent and Trademark Office
President: Mr. Kostadin Manev

52-B G. M. Dimitrov Blvd.
1040 Sofia
Phone: (359)(2) 873 51 71, 9701 321 Fax: (359)(2) 873-52 58, 870 83 25
E-mail: bpo@bpo.bg
Website: http://www.bpo.bg/

BULGARIAN NEWSPAPERS

TRUD daily
47, Tzarigradsko Shousse Blvd., Sofia 1504
Editors in Chief: Mr. Tosho Toshev – (3592) 9214-204 and Mr. Aksel Schindler
Business News Editor: Mr. Plamen Enchev - (3592) 9214-142
Advertisement and announcements: (3592) 942-2130, (3592) 942-2132, (3592) 942-2134, (3592) 942-2133, fax: (3592)-942-2831, 9433940
Website: http://www.trud.bg

24 CHASA daily
47, Tsarigradsko Shosse Blvd., Sofia 1504
Editor in Chief: Mrs. Venelina Gocheva – (3592) 942-25-00
Advertisement: (3592)942-2143, (3592) 942-41-30 (-32,- 33,- 34,- 35) , (3592) 942-21-45 (-46,-47)
Website: http://www.24chasa.bg

STANDART daily
49, Bulgaria Blvd. POB Box 41, Sofia 1404
Editor in Chief: Mrs. Slavka Bozukova – (3592) 8182-303, (359)888-870-455
Advertisement and Marketing: Mrs. Dimitrina Hristova, phone (3592) 81-82-345, 81-82-322; 81-82-311; fax (3592) 81-82-395
Website: http://www.standartnews.com

SEGA daily
1, Bulgaria Square, Sofia 1463
Editor in Chief: Mrs. Teodora Peeva – (3592)4282-300, (3592) 4282-305
Advertisement: phone (3592) 4282-314, (3592) 4282-350
E-mail: adv@segabg.com
Website: http://www.segabg.com

NOVINAR daily
44 Oborishte St., Sofia 1505
Chairman: Mr. Lyuben Dilov-Son – (3592) 943-34-37,
Editor in Chief: Mrs. Desislava Apostolova (3592) 943-45-32
Advertisement: phone (3592) 400-64-27, fax: (3592) 400-6426
E-mail: reklama@novinar.bg
Website: http://www.novinar.net

PARI daily
161, Knyaz Boris I, Str., Sofia 1202
Editor in Chief: Mr. Stefan Nedelchev (3592) 4395802
Editor in Chief pari.bg: Mrs. Maria Veromirova (3592) 4395865
Advertisement: (3592) 8133-451, (3592) 8133-453, (3592) 8133-454
E-mail: office@pari.bg ; reklama@pari.bg
Website: http://www.pari.bg

KAPITAL weekly
20 Ivan Vazov St., Sofia 1000

Editor in Chief: Mrs. Galya Prokopeiva. (3592) 937-6122
Advertisement: phone (3592) 9376-444; fax: (3592) 9376-236, 9376-440
E-mail: reklama@capital.bg
Website: http://www.capital.bg

MONITOR daily
113A, Tsarigradsko Shosse Blvd. Sofia 1784
Chairman of the Editors' Board: Mrs. Irena Krasteva – (3592) 9602-243
Advertisement: Mrs. Natasha Rusenova (3592) 9602-214, fax (3592) 9602-213
E-mail: monitor@monitor.bg
Website: http://www.monitor.bg

DNEVNIK daily
16 Ivan Vazov Street, Sofia 1000
Editor in Chief: Mrs. Velislava Popova: (3592)9376-300, 0888-705-260
Advertisement: (3592) 9376-444, fax: (3592) 9376-236
E-mail: reklama@dnevnik.bg
Website: http://www.dnevnik.bg

DUMA daily
113A Tsarigradsko Shosse, Sofia 1784
Editor in Chief: Mr. Ivelin Nikolov (3592) 9705 200; 9705 203
Advertisement: Mrs. Gabriela Naydenova (3592) 9705-233, fax (3592) 975 2604
E-mail: reklama@duma.bg
Website: http://www.duma.bg

ZEMYA Daily
169, Evlogi Georgiev Blvd. Sofia 1504
Editor in Chief – Mrs. Boryana Kostova, fax (3592) 943-46-64
Advertisement – Mrs. Maria Petrova (3592) 946-12-59 or (3592) 946-19-02(ext.59)
E-mail: reklamenotdel_zemia@abv.bg

KLASSA Daily
49, Bulgaria Blvd. Business Center Vitosha, building 2, Sofia 1404
Editor in Chief – Mrs. Neda Popova (3592) 8088-444, fax (3592) 8088433
Advertisement – Mrs. Lyudmila Peeva (3592) 8088-478
E-mail: web_reklama@klassa.bg , klassa@klassa.bg
Website: http://www.klassa.bg

INTERNATIONAL FINANCIAL INSTITUTIONS

European Bank for Reconstruction and Development
Sofia Resident Office
17, Moskovska Street, 1000 Sofia
Phone: (359) (2) 932-1414 Fax: (359)(2) 932-1441
E-mail: sofiaro@ebrd.com
Website: http://www.ebrd.com/

European Investment Bank
98-100, Boulevard Konrad Adenauer
L-2950 Luxembourg
Phone: (352) 43 79-3122 Fax: (325) 43 79-3191, 43 77 04
E-mail: info@eib.org
Website: http://www.eib.org/

Multilateral Investment Guarantee Agency
World Bank Group
1818 H Street, N.W.
Washington, D.C. 20433
Phone: (202) 473 1000 Fax: (202) 522-2630
Website: http://www.miga.org/

Delegation of the European Commission to Bulgaria
9 Moskovska Str., Sofia 1000
Phone: (359)(2) 933-5252 Fax: (359)(2) 933-5233
E-mail: COMM-REP-SOF@ec.europa.eu ; guest@evropa.bg
Website: http://ec.europa.eu/bulgaria/

World Bank
36, Dragan Tsankov Blvd.
World Trade Center, block A, 5th Fl., 1057 Sofia
Phone: (359)(2) 969-7239; (359 2) 918 14225; Fax: (359)(2) 971-2045
E-mail: itaushanova@worldbank.org
Website: http://www.worldbank.bg/

Bulgarian Banks
Contact information for all Bulgarian banks may be found on the Bulgarian National Bank website http://www.bnb.bg/
http://www.bnb.bg/BankSupervision/BSCreditInstitution/BSCIRegistrers/BS_CI_REG_BANKSLIST_EN

TRADE EVENTS

Bulgarreklama http://www.bulgarreklama.com
Plovdiv Fair http://www.fair.bg
Viaexpo http://www.viaexpo.com
Expoteam http://www.sofia.motorshow.bg
Bulgarian Economic Forum http://www.biforum.org
The Bulgarian Chamber of Commerce and Industry publishes an annual Calendar of the Fairs and Exhibitions in Bulgaria. The BCCI's website is http://www.bcci.bg

BULGARIA CUSTOMS PROCEDURES: IMPORTANT INFORMATION

Most imports are subject only to declaration and registration. However, special licenses are required for imports of tobacco, alcoholic beverages, oils, military hardware, radioactive materials, jewelry, precious metals, pharmaceutical items, and narcotics. The Ministry of Foreign Trade supervises the collection of customs duties. The amount collected is not published.

Goods arriving from foreign points to be unloaded in Bulgaria must have customs manifests and other shipping documents as specified by law. Customs duties are paid ad valorem at a rate of 5% to 40% on industrial products and 5% to 70% on agricultural products. Goods from EU nations receive preferential tariff rates. Duty must be paid on all goods except those specifically exempt, such as many foods products, farm machinery, toiletries, fertilizer and pesticide, mining equipment, and medical and dental supplies. In August 1987, the national assembly adopted a law to establish tariff-free zones to attract foreign investment beginning in January 1988. Taxes on imports include a value-added tax of 20%, a 0.5% customs clearance fee, and a 3% import surcharge.

BULGARIA CUSTOMS OFFICE

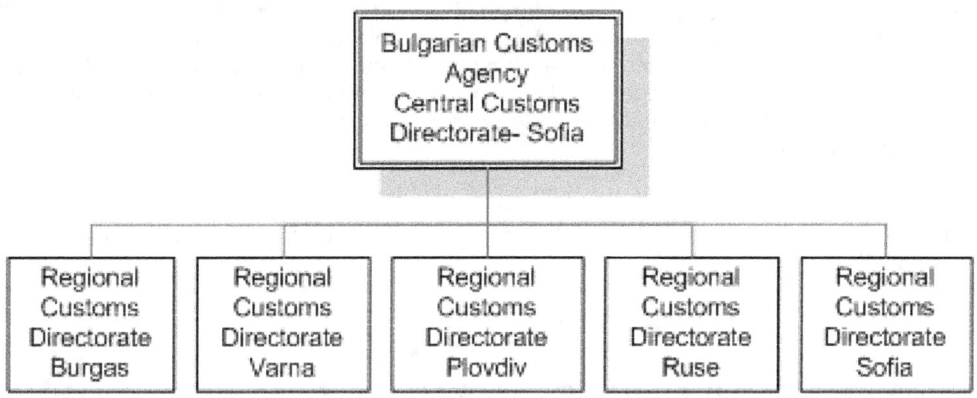

The Bulgarian customs administration is a centralized administrative structure, organized within National Customs Agency (NCA) under the Minister of Finance. NCA is a legal person financed by the state budget. NCA is managed and represented by a Director General who is assisted by four Deputy Directors.

The overall function of NCA is the performance of customs supervision and control of the customs territory of Bulgaria. NCA consists of a four-layer structure:

The Central Customs Directorate (CCD), located in Sofia, currently divided in two physical locations. During 2003, both NCA offices will move to a new Customs Headquarters building.

The Regional Customs Directorates (RCD), currently five (5), located in the main cities of the country.

The Customs Houses (CH), currently seventeen (17), which handle the majority of the clearance processing (approximately 60-70%).

Customs Offices and Border Points, currently hundred two (102).

NCA currently employs 3,826 Customs officers and supporting staff. The functions and structure at each layer are as follows:

CCD - overall functions of CCD are to organize, manage, control and report about the activities of the customs administration. To cover these functions CCD consist of the following Directorates - Customs regimes and procedures, Tariff Policy, Post Clearance Control, Central Customs Laboratory, Customs Intelligence and Investigation, Customs Statistics and Automation, European Integration and International Cooperation, Administrative- legal and Information Service, Finance- economic activities and property management, Inspectorate.

RCD - overall functions of RCD are to organize, manage, control and report about the activities of the customs houses included in RCD structure. To cover this functions RCD consist of departments, which have the same name and functions as CCD directorates, but at the regional level.

Customs Houses - overall functions of CH are to organize, manage, control and report about the activities of the customs offices and border points included in CH structure and together with them to perform customs supervision and control. To cover this functions Customs Houses consist of the following departments: Customs regimes and procedures, Tariff Policy, Customs Statistics and Automation, Customs Intelligence and Investigation, Customs Intelligence and Investigation of Drug Traffic, Administrative- legal and Information Service, Finance- economic activities and property management, Inspectorate.

The Customs Offices and Border Points are operative units performing customs supervision and control.

TRADE REGULATIONS, CUSTOMS AND STANDARDS

Bulgaria became a member of the World Trade Organization in December 1996. This will spur greater market liberalization following a transition period.
Membership in Free Trade Arrangements

In March 1993, Bulgaria signed an Association Agreement with the European Union under which the EU and Bulgaria will eliminate tariffs asymmetrically over a 10-year period with the EU reducing tariffs at an accelerated rate. Agricultural concessions are applied on a reciprocal basis.

The Europe Agreement is also calling for the harmonization of Bulgaria's laws and institutions with those of the European Union in preparation for eventual full membership. Already, Bulgaria is making an effort to take into consideration the requirements of EU directives in drafting new legislation.

In July 1993, Bulgaria joined the European Free Trade Agreement (EFTA). The provisions of the EFTA Agreement mirror those of Bulgaria's Association Agreement with the European Union. Since then, the majority of EFTA member countries have opted to join the EU. Bulgaria joined the World Trade Organizations in December 1996 and the Central European Free Trade Agreement (CEFTA) in January 1999. A free trade agreement between Bulgaria and Turkey took effect in January 1999. A free trade agreement between Bulgaria and Israel is expected to go into effect by the end of 2004.

TARIFF AND NON-TARIFF TRADE BARRIERS

Tariff Barriers

Products imported from the European Union with a Form EUR 1 certificate are subject to reduced customs duties or exempt entirely in accordance with Bulgaria's European Union association agreement. In contrast, U.S. products only receive Most Favored Nation customs tariff rates, which are almost always higher than tariffs applicable to EU products. This has placed some dutiable U.S. products such as soda ash and agricultural machinery at a comparative disadvantage. U.S. Government policy is to urge Bulgaria to reduce its tariffs for non-EU products. One benchmark for reduction would be the level of the European Union's Common External Tariff, which in almost all cases is lower than Bulgaria's tariffs.

Customs duties on agricultural goods and inputs and distilled spirits are also of concern to U.S. exporters. Preferential treatment applies to some tobacco varieties, mainly for those imported from Argentina, Brazil, India and Zimbabwe.

Non-tariff Barriers

Bulgaria's non-tariff barriers are described in the annual National Trade Estimate report issued by the Office of the U.S. Trade Representative each March 31. A major concern is implementation of Bulgaria's customs regulations and policies, which are sometimes reported be cumbersome, arbitrary and inconsistent. Other major concerns are irregular implementation of Bulgaria's 1997 public procurement law and privatization procedures, and protection of U.S. intellectual property rights.

TARIFF RATES

Bulgaria follows the Harmonized System (HS) adopted by the Customs Cooperation Council. Tariffs range between 5 percent and 40 percent on industrial products and 5 percent and 70 percent for agricultural products. Since 1998, average Bulgarian import tariffs have been reduced significantly at the beginning of each year. Following the latest series of reductions in January 2004, the average tariffs were reduced to 12.42 percent. Average levels for industrial and agricultural goods are 10 and 22 percent, respectively. Applying 2004 tariffs to the structure of Bulgarian imports for 2004, the weighted average is 7.04 percent, with industrial and agricultural tariffs at 6.15 and 18.82 percent, respectively. However, tariffs in areas of concern to U.S. exporters - including poultry legs and other agricultural goods and distilled spirits - are still relatively high. Import duties are ad valorem for agricultural products; some products such as meat have minimum import duties in ECU per metric ton.

Bulgaria's tariff schedules consist of two columns of rates. The column 1 rate applies to the 118 countries that qualify for preferential duty rates. Column 2 is equivalent to Most-Favored Nation (MFN) status. Forty-two countries, including the United States, are subject to column 2. Approximately 80 percent by value of Bulgaria's total imports receive column 2 treatment.

PROHIBITED IMPORTS AND U.S.-IMPOSED EXPORT CONTROLS

Prohibited Imports

Bulgaria prohibits imports of ozone-depleting products, ivory, rare birds, and other internationally banned products.

EXPORT CONTROLS

Export Licensing

A limited number of goods are subject to administrative control, stemming from Bulgaria's compliance with international agreements and specific domestic legislation. Registration (automatic license) and permits (administrative license) required by some commodity groups for export are issued by the Ministry of Economy. During 2004, permits are required for export of gold, silver, platinum, opiates, nuclear materials, explosives, arms, endangered species of animals and plants, and some herbicides. Registration of export of five commodities including kerosene and diesel oil is required. Only licensed dealers may export weapons. Bulgaria maintains quotas on the export of textiles and apparel to Canada and the United States; permits for export in these cases are required.

Trade in Arms and Dual-Use Goods and Technologies

Bulgarian Customs supervises control over the export, import, re-export and transit arms and dual-use goods and technologies. Bulgarian regulations follow the EU list of dual-use goods, which integrates the control lists of the Wassenaar Arrangement, missile technology control regime, nuclear suppliers group and the Australian group, and the Wassenaar arrangements munitions list. This list includes goods and technologies in the nuclear weapon, chemical and biological warfare and missile areas.

A permit for each transaction (import, export and re-export) and transit with dual-use goods and arms issued by the Commission for Control and Permission for Foreign Transactions in Arms and Dual-use Goods and Technologies of the Ministry of Trade and Tourism is required regardless of destination. The requirements are as follows:

Export

Bulgarian export control authorities require a completed export permit form, import license, end-user certificate with non-re-export clause issued by the competent authorities of the country of end-user, and end-use and end-user statement for each export. The applicant is obliged to provide a certificate verifying the actual delivery of equivalent document by the end-user confirming customs clearance of goods within 3 months after the date of entry.

Re-export:

In addition to the requirements for export, a permit for re-export by the competent bodies of the state of initial supplier is required.

IMPORT:

The applicant is obliged to submit a completed import permit form, and in case of dual-use goods, an end-use and end-user statement and delivery verification certificate after the customs clearance of goods is also required.

TRANSIT TRANSPORTATION:

Transit of goods such as arms or radioactive, explosive, inflammable, oxidizing, toxic, infectious or corrosive substances, require a transit permit. A completed form shall be presented by the shipper or an authorized party to the Commission no later than 15 days before the entry of goods into Bulgaria. Transit transportation of other dual-use goods requires a transit statement, which must be presented to Customs upon entry into and exit from Bulgaria.

More information on dual use and arms export control is available from the following departments at the Ministry of Trade and Tourism:

Dual-use Goods Export Control: phone/fax: (359) (2) 987-0549
Arms Export Control: phone/fax (359) (2) 989-6794

Customs officials may make on-the-spot checks of goods being exported to ensure compliance with applicable regulations.

U.S. EXPORTS OF SENSITIVE TECHNOLOGY TO BULGARIA

U.S. exporters should consult the U.S. Department of Commerce, Bureau of Export Administration, for specific export licensing requirements concerning exports of sensitive high-technology products to Bulgaria.

IMPORT TAXES AND LICENSE REQUIREMENTS

There are no import taxes. However, all imports are subject to a 20 percent Value Added Tax (VAT) levied at the time of import. Some commodities are also subject to excise duties.

The U.S. Embassy has had no complaints on record from U.S. exporters that Bulgaria's import license regime has negatively affected U.S. exports. As Bulgaria's import licensing regime is subject to frequent change, U.S. companies may wish to consult with CS Sofia for the latest list of affected products.

REGISTRATION

The list of goods subject to registration is changed quite often. For 2004, the list is only five commodities, including kerosene and fuel oil. In principle, the purpose of registration is to monitor the movement of some "sensitive" goods such as textiles and metals, or of food products which have been in short supply on the domestic market for a certain period: some types of meat, dairy products, sunflower and vegetable oils. These products will receive an automatic license within one day of receipt of application in the Ministry of Trade and Tourism and Ministry of Agriculture. Applicants are required to present a certificate from the court in which their incorporation was registered and a certificate of tax registration. Other substantiating documentation may be required: a contract, pro forma invoice, order, tax number, certificate of origin, and/or a certificate of quality.

AUTHORIZATIONS (LICENSES)

Decree Number 307 requires that certain products must receive authorization prior to importation. This is a non-automatic licensing process. Authorization, in the form of an import license, is normally issued within two days of the Ministry's receipt of the application. Applicants are required to present certificates from the court and tax registrations as well as supporting documents (enumerated above). Imports of pharmaceuticals also require a copy of the license for wholesale trade.

Appeals following the Ministry of Trade and Tourism's denial of a license must be made in writing to the Minister of Trade and Tourism within five days after the issuance of the decision. The Minister is required to render a final opinion within five days of receipt of the appeal.

The Decree on Bulgaria's Trade Policies in 2004 provides for licensing of the import of gold, silver, platinum, opiates, nuclear materials, explosives, arms, endangered species of animals and plants, and some herbicides.

IMPORT QUOTAS

Several decrees state that certain goods are subject to quotas where the tariff is reduced or waived completely. The sizes of the quotas are determined by calendar year. Quota allocations are distributed by the Ministry of Trade and Tourism through a tendering process or auction. No single applicant may receive a quota allocation larger than 35 percent of the total. Quota recipients may be required to place a deposit or a performance bond issued by a bank. Quota allocations are not transferable. Goods that are subject to duty-free or reduced tariff-rate-quota regimes require certified, simplified customs declarations for import, or a favorable resolution in writing from the principal ministry or department.

Currently products subject to temporarily duty free quotas are insecticides and fungicides, paper and pulp, wheat and sunflower oil. Products subject to reduced duty quotas are beef, poultry, pork, milk and dairy products, some vegetables and vegetable seeds, barley, corn, rice, canned meat, crude sugar from sugar cane, confections, and some alcoholic beverages.

In 2004, duty free import quotas apply temporarily to some additional commodity groups. The goods covered by this import preference are agricultural insecticides and herbicides. Under a separate list, engines and spare parts for agricultural machines are also covered.

CUSTOMS REGULATIONS AND CONTACT INFORMATION

Bulgaria's customs regulations are based on the 1998 Customs Act, which replaces the former 1960 Customs Act. The new Act generally corresponds to the provisions of the European Community Customs Code.

Customs valuation is based on the transaction value – the price actually paid or payable for the goods when sold for export to Bulgaria, defined in Bulgarian levs. The dutiable value is CIF, consisting of the purchase price, transportation costs, insurance charges, commissions, royalties, license fees and all other expenditures associated with the transport (e.g., loading and unloading) for delivery to the Bulgarian border.

Goods may be declared by a customs declaration, by designated simplified procedures such as a simplified customs declaration, a commercial or other document, or by entry in the records of the declarer, or by data-processing entry or other approved method. The customs authorities may carry out post-clearance examination of relevant documents or data.

The law sets out procedures concerning transit, customs warehousing, inward processing, processing under customs control, temporary import, and outward processing. The law provides for public and private bonded warehouses.

U.S. companies may direct inquiries to the following:

General Customs Directorate
Director: Mr. Zakhari Zakhariev
1, Aksakov Street
1000 Sofia
Phone: (359)(2) 869222/98 591
Fax: (359)(2) 980-6897

TEMPORARY GOODS ENTRY REQUIREMENTS

Products may be imported into Bulgaria on a temporary basis as long as they are not prohibited by law. The rules on temporary imports are contained in the Regulation for Application of the Law on Customs. Article 58 allows entry of samples and products for trade exhibitions. The term of entry cannot exceed six months although a request for extension can be made. Customs duties will not be levied if a letter of guarantee from a Bulgarian organization is presented vouching for eventual return of the goods or payment of duties.

Bulgaria is a party to the Customs Convention on Carnet (ATA) for Temporary Import of Goods. Presentation of an ATA carnet, or TIR carnet, facilitates the process. An entry carnet may be obtained from a local chamber of commerce in the United States. Carnets are usually valid for 1 year and list the products to be imported on a duty-free basis. The carnet must be presented upon entry into Bulgaria. Customs will stamp the carnet thereby validating it. Upon departure, the carnet must again be presented for validation, confirming that the product is being transported out of Bulgaria. Failure to re-export the goods results in application of the duties.

The Regulations also provide for the temporary import of products and equipment. Article 15 lists 15 categories. For example, equipment for repairs, finishing, processing and testing may be imported temporarily duty-free. Any goods intended for re-export, such as textiles and apparel, may also enter duty-free. Article 51 establishes time limits from 3 months to one year for re-export. In practice, Customs requires a deposit equivalent to the assessed duties or a bank guarantee during the temporary import period.

SPECIAL IMPORT/EXPORT REQUIREMENTS AND CERTIFICATIONS

IMPORT REQUIREMENTS

The Regulations for the Application of the Law on Customs require a certificate of origin, commercial invoice, insurance invoice, bill of lading, and packing list for all imported and exported products. In some cases additional information may be required such as receipt of payment of customs processing fees, bill of health (depending upon products), and certificate of import/export (authorization or license). Agricultural products require a certificate of quality and origin, a veterinary or phyto-sanitary certificate, and other applicable health and safety certificates.

If imports are sourced from the European Union, a movement certificate (Form EUR 1) is necessary if the products are to qualify for reduced duties (pursuant to the terms of the Association Agreement). Form EUR 2 should also be included if the shipment is valued below ECU 5,110.

Products sourced from member countries of the European Free Trade Agreement (EFTA) -- Norway, Switzerland and Iceland -- require an exporter's declaration in order to qualify for reduced tariff rates.

Upon arrival, products for human consumption should be analyzed in approved local laboratories in cooperation with local authorities. The State Agency for Standards and Metrology strictly enforces Bulgarian quality standards, which do not always coincide with generally accepted international standards. Foreign certificates may or may not be considered adequate. After approval is issued, the commodities may be sold on the local market.

STANDARDS

The 1964 Law on Standardization and Metrology, as amended, together with the Regulation for Implementation of the Law, sets forth the legal requirements for product standards and quality control in Bulgaria.

The State Agency for Standardization and Metrology is the designated authority for developing national standards. The Committee on Standardization reports to the Council of Ministers. In certain areas, product and sector-specific standards are issued by other ministries or agencies.

The State Agency for Standardization and Metrology is the competent authority for testing and certification of all products except pharmaceuticals, food and telecommunications equipment. The Agency issues approvals attesting to electrical safety and functional characteristics. The Department for Certification and Management Quality Control, within the Committee, handles all testing and certification. In addition to the application, the Department requires a Bulgarian translation as well as certificate(s) of approval from the corresponding home testing authority and a certificate identifying the testing protocol. The fee levied for the testing and certification process is BGN 50-70 per application. The entire testing and certification process requires at least one month. Certificates are valid for two years.

The State Agency for Standardization and Metrology shares responsibilities for food products with the Ministries of Agriculture and Health. The responsible authority for pharmaceuticals is the National Institute for Pharmaceutical Products in the Ministry of Health, which establishes standards and performs testing and certification and is also responsible for drug registration. Approval for any equipment interconnected to Bulgaria's telecommunications network must be obtained from the State Telecommunications Commission.

Bulgaria is making an effort to harmonize its national standards with international standards. Bulgaria is a participant in the International Organization for Standardization (ISO), the International Electrotechnical Commission (IEC) and International Technical Union (ITU). Bulgaria is in the process of harmonizing 1,757 of its standards to European standards, in anticipation of joining the European Union. As of September 18, 2004, all domestic standards on safety, on protection of human life and health and on consumer and environmental protection will no longer be mandatory. The major requirements for the safety of products will be regulated in ordinances to be issued by the separate ministries and will comply with the respective EU directives. By 2004, all current standards are expected to be replaced by adoption of all applicable European Union standards.

LABELING REQUIREMENTS

The 1995 Law on Prices regulates labeling and marking requirements. Labels must contain the following information in Bulgarian: quality, quantity, ingredients, certification authorization number (if any), and manner of storage, transport, use or maintenance. The product must be clearly marked with the date of production, expiration date and the warranty period.

WARRANTY AND NON-WARRANTY REPAIRS

When a product is sent out of Bulgaria for repairs, the value of the repaired or replacement part is dutiable.

FREE TRADE ZONES/WAREHOUSES

Duty Free Trade Zones (FTZ) were established in Bulgaria in 1987 under Decree No. 2242 "On The Duty Free Zones and its Regulations for Application." The new Customs Act, whose provisions do not replace those of Decree No. 2242, renamed the six duty-free zones "free zones." The Customs Act also states that goods located in the free zones and free warehouses are not considered as being in the customs duty of Bulgaria and are not subject to customs duty. Free zones must have access control at fixed entrance and exit points. New construction within the free zones is to be undertaken in conformity with the customs authorities.

Foreign, including U.S., individuals and corporations, and Bulgarian companies with 1 percent or more foreign ownership may set up operations in a free zone. Thus foreign-owned firms have equal or better investment opportunity in the zones as compared to Bulgarian firms.

There are at present six operational "free zones" in Bulgaria: Ruse and Vidin ports on the Danube, Plovdiv, Svilengrad (near the Turkish border), Dragoman (near the Yugoslav border), and Burgas port on the Black Sea. All of them are owned by joint stock companies or a state-owned company owned by the government of Bulgaria. The government provided land and infrastructure for each zone.

Plovdiv, the only inland free zone, is the most profitable, with 24 investment projects. The Burgas FTZ has the largest warehousing and automotive distribution facilities in Bulgaria, and is used by more than 100 foreign and joint venture companies including Samsung and Daewoo. Limited manufacturing is conducted in both the Plovdiv and Ruse FTZs.

All forms of production and trade activities and services may take place in the free zones. Foreign goods delivered to the free zones for production, storage, processing or re-export are VAT and duty exempt. Bulgarian goods may also be stored in free zones with permission from the customs authorities. Convertible foreign currency may be used, and revenues can be transferred abroad freely without any restrictions. Administrative procedures relieve the investor's need to contact local authorities directly. Production and labor costs are low with well-trained and highly qualified labor available. All the zones are located on strategic trade rail, road and/or water trade routes.

The free trade zones in Bulgaria have attracted a number of foreign investors to undertake processing and trade activities - Hyundai Co., Daewoo Co., KIA Motors, CITCO, Schwarzkopf, Henkel, Landmark Chemicals Ltd., Group Schneider, and BINDL Energie Systeme GmbH.

BASIC CUSTOMS RULES AND REGULATIONS FOR TRAVELERS

The Regulations for the Implementation of the Customs Act envision that for each trip an individual traveller makes, they are entitled to an import free of duty, fees, and VAT, a certain amount of goods acquired abroad as well as goods of up to a certain value.

Here is a list of the quantity quotas for duty free import:
Any traveller over the age of 16 is entitled to a duty-free import of:

1 liter of spirits with over 22 per cent volume alcohol content and 2 liters of wine or 2 liters of wine and 2 liters of sparkling or fortified wine;

200 pieces of cigarettes or 100 cigarillos or 50 cigars or 250 grams of tobacco for smoking;

500 grammes of coffee or 200 grammes of coffee extract;

100 grammes of tea or 40 grammes of tea extract;

50 grammes of perfumes and 250 ml of eau de toilette;

medicines in an amount and type corresponding to the personal needs o f the traveller.

Travellers under the age of 16 are not entitled to duty free import of the above-mentioned goods except for medicines.

Travellers, who cross the border more than once within 30 consecutive days, are entitled to 20 per cent of the above quotas.

Value quotas for duty-free import
Apart from being entitled to a duty-free import of goods up to a certain quantity, travellers over the age of 16 are also entitled to a duty–free import of goods acquired abroad and worth up to 100 euros or its equivalent in another currency.
Travellers under the age of 16 are entitled to a duty-free quota for goods acquired abroad and worth up to 50 euros or its equivalent in another currency.

Travellers, who cross the Bulgarian border more than once within 30 consecutive days, are entitled to a lower duty-free import quota for the goods acquired abroad in the amount of 20 euros or its equivalent in another currency.

When a single item is being imported whose value is over 100 euro or its equivalent in another currency, the duty and VAT are paid on the total value of the item. When the total value of two or more items owned by one traveller exceeds 100 euros or its equivalent in another currency, duty-free import is only allowed for those items, the sum of the individual value of which does not exceed 100 euro or its equivalent in a foreign currency.

The duty-free entitlement cannot be distributed between two or more travellers.
For goods that are not intended for sale, whose value is over 100 euros but under 1,500 euros (or its equivalent in another currency), a single Customs rate applies to each traveller in the amount of 5 percent on the individual value of the goods imported. The goods are also taxed with a 20 percent VAT.

The single Customs rate is not applied to goods imported under the above-mentioned requirements if prior to their taxation the declarant proposes that the duties be determined according to the Customs Tariff while also taking into consideration the existing free trade agreements.

Goods that by force of their appearance and amount are not of a commercial nature and for which a declaration is required, if left undeclared by the travellers crossing the state border and are discovered in the usual places during a customs examination are confiscated in favour of the state regardless of whose property they are, and no fine is imposed. If the goods are concealed in unusual places they are confiscated in favour of the state and an act for a customs and/or a currency violation is produced.

The travellers crossing the state border are entitled to importing or exporting without payment of the state receivables also objects for personal use, new and used ones, which a traveller can normally need during his/her travel by taking into account all the circumstances around the travel. These goods are considered placed under the temporary import or temporary export regime respectively. Their declaration is considered made by the traveller's passing through the so-called "green" channel or through a verbal declaration.

The re-export of the personal belongings imported in that manner cannot be carried out later than the moment in which the person who has imported them is leaving the customs territory of Bulgaria.

When objects of a higher value are being imported or exported it is recommendable that the goods customs declaration for travellers be filled out. This declaration is provided at the border point prior to the beginning of the customs examination. The instructions it contains are in Bulgarian, German, English, French, and Russian, and it can be filled out in the language chosen by the tourist. Submitting this declaration will save the eventual trouble which could arise during the subsequent passing through customs and that is why the travellers should keep it until their next crossing of the border. It is evidence that the goods listed in it have actually been imported or exported by the respective person.

Regarding the export and import of levs and foreign currency cash the requirements of the Bulgarian legislation are the following:

1. For import

The local and foreign physical persons can import an unlimited amount of levs and foreign currency cash. When the amount of the imported money is up to 8000 levs or their equivalent in another currency they are not declared in writing and the travellers can walk through the "green channel" which means that the person has nothing to declare. When the amount of the imported money is over 8000 levs one has to fill out a currency customs declaration for the purpose of their being declared to the customs authorities with the travellers obligatorily walking through the "red channel".

2. For export

a. The local and foreign physical persons can export levs and foreign currency cash amounting to up to 8000 levs or their equivalent in a foreign currency without having to declare that in writing, and they can walk through a "green channel". If the amount is from 8000 to 25 000 levs it should be declared in writing in a currency customs declaration. When the amount of the money exceeds 25 000 levs or their equivalent in a foreign currency the manner of acquiring the money is entered and a certificate from the tax administration must be presented that the person does not have any overdue tax liabilities, and its number is entered into the currency customs declaration. For the local physical persons the certificate is issued by the tax subdivision as per the permanent address of the person, and for the foreign physical persons – by the tax subdivision as per the address of the last residence of the person in the country.

b. The foreign physical persons can export Bulgarian levs and foreign currency cash to the amount of over

25 000 levs without a certificate from the tax administration after making a declaration to the customs authorities if the value of the currency or levs being exported does not exceed the value of the imported and declared money during the last entry of the person into the country, for which the traveller presents a previous import currency declaration.

According to the Currency Law of the country there are special requirements regarding the export of precious metals as well.

The local and foreign physical persons can export and import for personal and family use precious metals, precious stones and articles with and from them both unprocessed and processed freely without a declaration in writing up to the following amounts:

gold and platinum, unprocessed and half-processed, (in the form of ingots) and coins up to 37 g in total without regard to the content of the gold or platinum;

jewellery and accessories from alloys of gold and platinum up to 60 g in total without regard to the content of the gold or platinum;

silver, unprocessed or half-processed, and coins, as well as jewellery and accessories from alloys of silver up to 300 g in total without regard to the content of the silver;

precious stones embedded in the items mentioned in p. 2 and 3.

One must declare in writing the precious metals, precious stones, and the articles with and from them over the above-mentioned amounts, as well as the articles from precious metals and precious stones carried in the form of powder or another form which have not been mentioned above.

The declaration of goods, levs and foreign currency cash, precious metals, precious stones and articles with and from them carried by travellers is carried out verbally, in writing, or by means of other actions (for instance by walking through the "red" or the "green" channel).

The undeclared levs, currency, precious metals, and precious stones are confiscated in favour of the state.

In the cases of larger violations fines are imposed as well. When an undeclared goods item or currency in particularly large amounts has been found, apart from them the vehicle which it was transported with is also confiscated in favour of the state.

It is particularly important to know which goods are banned for import and export and which goods can be carried across the border while abiding by a special regime.
Banned for import, export, re-export, and transit are:

narcotic substances and precursors;

explosive substances, firearms, and ammunitions;

quarantine pests regardless of the stage of their development;

dangerous chemical substances and products;

foodstuffs, chemical substances, and other materials and objects harmful or dangerous to people's health;

substances, products, and facilities using, containing, or made with substances which destroy the ozone layer;

Under a special regime after presentation of the respective authorisation the import, export, re-export, and transit of the following is allowed:

specimens of plants and animals or clearly identifiable parts and derivatives of them from the species included in the Convention on International Trade with Endangered Species of the Wild Fauna and Flora;

firearms for hunting, sports, and cultural purposes and the ammunitions for them;

nuclear material, radioactive substances, and other sources of ionising radiations;

medicinal products which are authorised for use in the country and have not expired;

live game and genetic material, hunting trophies, shed game antlers, and game products;

cultural monuments, including those made of precious stones and precious metals;

Banned for export are:

wild protected medicinal plants, fresh or dried;

protected plants and animals and their eggs and nests;

In the case of violation of the set border regime of import, export, or transit the goods are confiscated in favour of the state.

BULGARIAN EXPORT PROMOTION CENTRE

The BULGARIAN EXPORT PROMOTION CENTRE (BEPC) is an institutional system for stimulating the export policy of the Bulgarian companies. BEPC coordinates the interaction between the Government institutions, non-governmental institutions and the private sector in Bulgaria. BEPC assists the Ministry of Economy in elaborating and applying of a strategy for the creation of strong export oriented national economy and provides to the Bulgarian producers and exporters a wide range of qualified services, market's, tender's and business contact's information.

BEPC's activity is made in the following directions:

INFORMATION, RESEARCH AND DEVELOPMENT

Effective business information system- data base, library, web site

Information services in printing and electronic form for the national and world trade statistics, foreign trade regime, trade relations regulation, standardization, packaging, credit and fiscal policy, customs regime.

Disseminating contact and tender information

Market and product studies and analyses of the opportunities of the Bulgarian export potential.

Specialized market services, concerning the organization, regulation and the procedures in the export activity.

Consulting services for the Bulgarian exporters in determining the market strategy and foreign trade practice.

Integrated sector programs for export promotion.

Management of projects of foreign and international organizations; supplying a technical assistance for increasing the compatibility of the Bulgarian export and penetration on new markets.

Analysis of specialized marketing knowledge demands and foreign trade qualification of Bulgarian exporters.

Courses and seminars for specialized education on foreign trade practice.

Projects for professional education and human resources development.

Bilateral and multilateral frame cooperation agreements with trade promotion i.e. export organizations.

INTERNATIONAL EXHIBITIONS AND ADVERTISING"

Programs for international fairs and exhibitions on company, branch and national participation level.

Participation of Bulgarian companies in trade missions and business delegations.

Advertising and publishing activity in favor of Bulgarian exporters.

Bulgarian exporters' directories.

CONTACTS

Managing Director	Tel.: +359 2 980 50 69
Deputy Director	Tel.: +359 2 980 50 69
"Export Marketing" Dept.	Tel.: +359 2 987 99 84
"Information, Research and Development" Dept.	Tel.: +359 2 988 13 44
"International Exhibitions and Advertising" Dept.	Tel.: +359 2 987 21 92
Fax: +359 2 980 58 69	

DUTY FREE ORGANIZATIONS

Public register of organizations and institutions approved by the competent authorities under the Ordinance the Council of Ministers № 75 of April 6, 2007 the application of Articles 51, 59b, 60, 62, 63a, 63c, 65, 71, 72 and 79 of Regulation № 918/83 (EEC) of 28 March 1983 on the Community system of reliefs from customs duty - Zagl. am. - SG. 27 of 2010, in force on 9.04.2010 - Decree № 75 of 6.04.2007 From MS on the application of Articles 43-52, 53, 55, 57, 59, 61, 67, 68 and 74 Regulation (EC) № 1186/2009 of 16 November 2009 establishing a Community system of reliefs from customs duty (codified version) (OJ, L 324 of 10.12.2009 on)

1.
Ministry of Labour and Social Policy
№ 378 / 09.05.2007
Expired
One year from date of issue (up to 09.05.2008 on)
Art. 65 and chl.72
Bulgarian Red Cross
BULSTAT: 000703415

Bull. "James Bourchier" № 76
Gr. Sofia
2
Ministry of Labour and Social Policy
№ 473/13.06.2007 on
Expired
One year from date of issue (until 13.06.2008)

Art. 65 and chl.72
Bulgarian Red Cross
BULSTAT: 000703415

Bull. "James Bourchier" № 76
Gr. Sofia
3.
Ministry of Labour and Social Policy
№ 436/05.06.2007 on expired
Six (6) months from the date of issue (up to 05.12.2007 on)

Art. 65 and chl.72
Foundation Bright Dawn "
BULSTAT: 131324446

Str. "Pirin" № 10
Gr. Sofia
4.
Ministry of Labour and Social Policy
№ 510/27.06.2007 on
Expired
Six (6) months from the date of issuance (until 27.12.2007)
Art. 71
"Association of Lions Clubs, District 130-BULGARIA"
BULSTAT: 112599847
Str. Exarch Joseph "№ 6, Pazardjik
5.
Ministry of Labour and Social Policy
№ 562/17.07.2007 on
Expired
Six (6) months from the date of issue
(By on 01/17/2008)
Art. 65 and Art. 72
ASSOCIATION CARITAS - SOFIA
g. k. "Ilindin, bl. 55, entr. B, floor 1, app. 47
Sofia
6.
Ministry of Labour and Social Policy
№ 566 / 19.07.2007 on
Expired
Six months (6) the date of issuance (until 19.01.2008 on)
Art. 65
ASSOCIATION "Russe Catholic organization - CARITAS"
Str. Bogdan Voyvoda "№ 3, Ruse
7.
Ministry of Labour and Social Policy
№ 537/07.07.2007 on
Expired
Six months (6) the date of issuance (until 05.01.2008 on)
Art. 65 and Art. 72
FOUNDATION WORLD ZORA "
Str. Pirin City, Vitosha, Sofia
8.
Ministry of Labour and Social Policy
№ 629/09.08.2007 on
Expired
Six (6) months from the date of issue (up to 09.02.2008 on)
Art. 65 and Art. 72
HOME FOR OLD PEOPLE
BULSTAT: 000159629114
Str. G. Gradinarov, Vidin, city tower
9.
Ministry of Labour and Social Policy
№ 805 / 29.10.
2007
Expired
Six (6) months from the date of issue (to 29.04.2008g.)
Art. 65 and Art. 72
FOUNDATION "one heart"
BULSTAT:
131074081
Str. George Izmerliev "№ 53 Floor 4, Apt. 8
Plovdiv
10.
Ministry of Labour and Social Policy
903 / 05.12.
2007
Expired
Six (6) months from the date of issuance (until 05.06.2008)
Art. 72
FOUNDATION Adrastus, BULGARIA "
BULSTAT: 121617237
Str. "Thessaloniki" № 10, Sofia
11.
Ministry of Labour and Social Policy
RD01/68/22.01.2008 on
Expired
One (1) year from date of issue (up to 22.01.2009 on)
Art. 65, art. 72
FOUNDATION WORLD ZORA "
BULSTAT:
131324446
Str. "Pirin" № 10, Sofia
12.
Ministry of Health
RD09-11 / 21:01.
2008
For the designated product types
Art. 63a
Hospital St. Nicholas Miracle Worker "
BULSTAT:
130128163
Str. "Kableshkov" № 2, Lom municipality.
Montana
13.
Ministry of Labour and Social Policy
RD01/278 / on 3/21/2008
Expired
One year from date of issue (up to 21.03.2009 on)
Art. 65 and Art. 72
Association Rousse Catholic organization - Caritas "
BULSTAT:
827127955
Str. Bogdan leader "№ 3, Ruse
14.
Ministry of Labour and Social Policy
RD01/402825.04.2008 on
Expired
One year from date of issue
(Up to 25.04.2009 on)
Art. 65 and Art. 72
Bulgarian Red Cross

BULSTAT: 000703415

Bull. "James Bourchier" № 76
Gr. Sofia
15.
Ministry of Health
RD09-184/23.04.2008 on
For certain goods
Art. 63a
Hospital St. Ivan Rilski AD, BULSTAT:
000715054
Bull. Academician Ivan Geshov "№ 15, Sofia -
1431
16.
Ministry of Education and Science
RD 31-02/17.07.2008 on
For certain goods
Art. 51 Art. 59
National Museum of Natural History, BAS, Sofia
BULSTAT:
000665612
Gr. Sofia
17.
Ministry of Health
09-336 RD / on 7/31/2008
One year of service to it (until 31.07.2009 - in the factory)
Art. 63a
Hospital St. Ivan Rilski AD
BULSTAT: 000715054
Bull. Acad Ivan Geshov "№ 15, Sofia;

18.
Ministry of Labour and Social Policy
01/885 RD / 13.10.2008
Expired
One year from date of issue (up to 13.10.2009 on)

Art. 71
National Library for the Blind "Louis Braille"
BULSTAT:
000671177
Square Doe "№ 1B, Sofia
19.
Ministry of Education and Science
RD 31-3/23.10.2008 on
For certain goods
Art. 52
National Astronomical Observatory and Planetarium "Nikolai Kopernik"
"Sea Garden" № 4, Box 120, Varna
20.
Ministry of Education and Science
RD 31-4/14.101.2008 on
For certain goods
Art. 52
Private Language School Prof. Vasil goldsmiths'
Darvenica Blvd University "№ 49, Sofia
21.
Ministry of Labour and Social Policy
RD01 / 7 / 09.01. 2009
Expired
One year on from 23/01/2009 - 01/23/2010 up on
Art. 65 and Art. 72
FOUNDATION WORLD ZORA "
Bulstat:
131324446
Str. "Pirin" № 10 area of Vitosha, Sofia
22.
Ministry of Health
RD 09-54/09.02.2009 on
Expired
One year from its date of service (up to 2.9.2010, the)
Art. 63a
National Center for Public Health
Bulstat: 13135380
Bull. Acad Ivan Geshov "№ 15, Sofia - 1431
23.
Ministry of Labour and Social Policy
RD01/427/07.05.2009 on
Expired
One year from date of issue (up to 07.05.2010 on)
Art. 65 and Art. 72
Bulgarian Red Cross
Bulstat:
000703415
Bull. "James Bourchier" № 76, Sofia
24.
Ministry of Labour and Social Policy
RD01/478/21.05.2009 on
For certain types of goods within one year from date of issue (up to 21.05.2010 on)
Art. 72
Bulgarian Tennis Federation
Bulstat:
000708469
Bull. "Vasil Levski" № 75, Sofia
25.
Ministry of Labour and Social Policy
RD01 / 579 / 19.06. 2009
Expired
One year from date of issue (to 19.06.2010g.)
Art. 65
Association Rousse Catholic organization - Caritas
Bulstat:
827127955
Str. Bogdan leader "№ 3
Gr. Ruse
26.
Ministry of Labour and Social Policy
RD01 / 628 / 13.07. 2009
One year from date of issue (to 13.07.2010g.)
Art. 65 and Art. 72
Association "One Life Bulstat: 131359582
Str. FHT "№ 19
Gr. Sofia 1164
27.
Ministry of Labour and Social Policy

RD01 / 629 / 13.07. 2009
One year from date of issue (to 13.07.2010g.)
Art. 65 and Art. 72
Foundation New Road Bulstat: 175677162
Str. "Pirin" № 10
Gr. Sofia 1618
28.
Ministry of Education, Youth and Science
RD31-2/11.09.2009 on
For specific product
Art. 52
Institute of Electrochemistry and Energy Systems at the Bulgarian Academy of Sciences
BULSTAT:
000662089
Str. Acad G. Bonchev "bl. 10
Gr. Sofia

29.
Ministry of Education, Youth and science
RD 31-03/01.10.2009 on
For the specific product
Art. 52
Chemical Technology and Metallurgy (Metallurgy)
Bulstat: 000670673
Bull. St. University "№ 8
Gr. Sofia 1756
30.
Ministry of Education, Youth and Science
RD 31-06/09.10.2009 on
For specific product
Art. 52
73rd secondary school teaching of foreign languages Vladislav Grammatik "
Bulstat: 000668302
Str. George Izmirliev "№ 2
Gr. Sofia 1604
31.
Ministry of Education, Youth and Science
RD 31-4/06.10.2009 on
For specific product
Art. 52
Faculty of Physics of Sofia University
Bulstat:
000670680
Bull. "James Bourchier" № 5
Gr. Sofia 1164
32.
Ministry of Education, Youth and Science
RD 31-5/06.10.2009 on
For specific product
Art. 52
Faculty of Physics of Sofia University
Bulstat:
000670680
Bull. James Boucher "№ 5
Gr. Sofia 1164
33.
Ministry of Education, Youth and Science
RD 31-07/05.11.2009 on
For specific product
Art. 52
Technical University - Varna
Bulstat: 00083626
Str. "Student" № 1
Gr. 9010 Varna
34.
Ministry of Education, Youth and Science
RD 31-8/03.12.2009 on
For specific product
Art. 52
Institute of Biophysics BULSTAT:
831351304
Acad G. Bonchev "bl.21,
Sofia
35.
Ministry of Labour and Social Policy
RD01-1062/17.12.2009, as amended and supplemented by on RD01-1068/18.12.2009
One year from date of issue (on 12/17/2010)
Art. 65 and Art. 72
"Christian Center - Sofia
BULSTAT:
130088039
Sq. "Sheep font - 1, bl. 418, entr. A, Apt. 1
36.
Ministry of Education, Youth and Science
RD 31-9/22.12.2009 on
For specific product
Art. 52
Scientific Research at University of Rousse "Angel"
BULSTAT:
0005226850014
Str. "Student" № 8, Rousse
37.
Ministry of Education, Youth and Science
RD 31-01/14.01.2010 on
For specific product
Art. 52
Scientific Research at University of Rousse "Angel"
BULSTAT:
0005226850014
Str. "Student" № 8, Rousse
38.
Ministry of Labour and Social Policy
RD01-85 / 28.01. 2010
One year from date of issuance (28.01. 2011)
Art. 65, art. 72

ASSOCIATION CARITAS-SOFIA
BULSTAT:
831189628
Gr. Sofia district Krasna Polyana, hc Ilinden, bl. 55, entr. C, ap. 47, floor 1
39.
Ministry of Labour and Social Policy
RD01/391/20.05.2010 on
One year from date of issue (up to 20.05.2011

on)
Art. 61 and Art. 68

Bulgarian Red Cross
BULSTAT:
000703415
Bull. "James Bourchier" № 76, Sofia
40.

Ministry of Labour and Social Policy

RD01-474 / 23.06. 2010
For specific product
Art. 67

ASSOCIATION NATIONAL ASSOCIATION OF THE DEAF blind-IN BULGARIA
BULSTAT:
115173977
Street Merry "№ 30
Plovdiv

SELECTED LAWS AND REGULATIONS AFFECTING BUSINESS

CUSTOMS LAW

PART ONE KEY PROVISIONS

Chapter One
GENERAL

Art. 1. It governs the structure and organization of the customs administration and carried out by the authorities activities.

Art. 2. (1) (amended and supplemented. - SG. 63 of 2000) The activity of customs authorities include those carried out by the customs territory of the country's customs supervision and control over the import, export and transit of goods to, from and through Republic of Bulgaria, the collection of duties, application of administrative penal provisions and criminal investigations in cases where terms and conditions provided in the Criminal Procedure Code.
(2) Customs supervision is a set of customs actions taken to ensure that customs rules and other provisions applicable to goods under customs supervision.
(3) Customs inspection is carried out by the customs authorities of the specific actions such as examining goods, transport, trade, accounting and other records of individuals and legal persons, vehicles, luggage and other goods transported through the state border, and other such actions to ensure compliance with customs legislation and compliance with other provisions applicable to goods under customs supervision and collection of duties.

Art. 3. Persons and vehicles, and goods to be conveyed or transported by them, crossing the state border at border checkpoints and are subject to customs supervision and control, which takes place in certain places for this purpose. The order in which the customs supervision and control is defined in the Regulations of this Act, hereinafter "the Rules".

Art. 4. (1) (amended and supplemented. - SG. 37, 2003) All persons shall immediately notify the customs authorities left with them, found or seized goods, including vehicles that are known or suspected that have been made without performing the customs formalities. These items should be presented to customs authorities.
(2) (Amended - SG. 37 2003) If the owner left, found or detained goods, including vehicles, is a foreign person, unknown person or a resident of unknown address and seek them within six months from the date of their presentation to customs authorities, the person carried out the formalities for obtaining goods for customs, having paid all costs incurred by the office for them.
(3) left, found or detained goods, including vehicles, shall be deemed abandoned to the State when:
1. (Amended - SG. 37 of 2003) owner is a foreign person, unknown person or a resident of unknown address and the date of their presentation to customs authorities have expired six months;
2. (Amended - SG. 37 of 2003) owner is a resident with a known address in the country and the day of service call for release of goods sent by the office have expired three months. The invitation is sent within one week from the date of presentation of the goods to customs.

Art. 5. (1) (Supplemented - SG. 45 of 2005) All persons, including government bodies within their competence, shall assist the customs authorities in carrying out their activities. They are required within 14 days of receipt of the request by the customs authorities to provide information on those in the facts and circumstances.
(2) No person may dispose of goods under customs supervision without the knowledge and authorization of the customs authorities.

(3) (New - SG. 37 of 2003) Acts done in violation of para. 2, are invalid as against the customs authorities.

Art. 6. All persons who are related to the operations of import, export and transit of goods are required for the purposes of customs supervision and control to provide the customs authorities at their request and within the deadline they set all the information and documentation on specific operations regardless of medium.

Chapter Two CUSTOMS ADMINISTRATION

Section I Structure and organization

Art. 7. (Amended - SG. 83 of 1999 pcs. 63 of 2000) (1) The customs administration is centralized administrative structure organized in the Customs Agency to the Minister of Finance, which is a legal person of the budget with headquarters in Sofia.
(2) The Customs Agency is structured in the central office management and regional customs directorates. General and specialized administration office in central government departments are organized.
(3) Regional Customs Directorate is structured in regional customs control and customs. General and specialized administration in the regional customs office is organized into departments.
(4) The office is structured in office management and territorial customs offices and / or customs posts. General and specialized customs administrations are organized into departments.
(5) The central management office organize, manage, monitor and report the activities of the customs administration and customs work done.
(6) Regional office management organize, manage, monitor and report the activity involved in the structure of the Regional Customs Directorate Customs, Customs carry out activities and provides information services for customs and central office management.
(7) The territorial government office organize, manage, monitor and report on activities included in the structure of customs, customs offices and / or customs offices and with them is a basic implementation of customs supervision and control.
(8) (suppl. - SG. 91 of 2005) general management and operational control of the customs administration is carried out by the Minister of Finance or designated by a deputy minister. Officials of the inspectorate at the Ministry of Finance have access to all information and documents in the customs administration in connection with their inquiries.
(9) Customs Agency may issue specialized publications.

Art. 8. (Amended - SG. 63 of 2000) Regional Customs Directorate, Customs, customs offices and customs posts are created, transformed and closed by the Minister of Finance proposal to the Director of the Customs Agency. Director of Customs Agency determines the structure and size of their staff within the total number of Agency staff.

Art. 9. (Amended - SG. 63 of 2000) (1) Customs Agency is governed and represented by a Director who is appointed and released by the Minister of Finance in consultation with the Prime Minister.
(2) In carrying out its functions, the Director of Customs Agency is assisted by Deputy Directors. The number of deputy directors shall be determined in Regulations of the Agency.
(3) Deputy Directors of the Customs Agency are appointed and released by the Minister of Finance proposal to the Director of the Agency.
(4) The structure of the Customs Agency included inspectorate directly subordinate to the director of the agency, which exercises control over the customs administration.

Art. 10. (1) Customs officers may be capable Bulgarian citizen who has been convicted of a crime of general nature, not the courts denied the right to hold office and qualify for work in the customs administration.
(2) Customs officers may not:
1. are sole proprietors, general partners, or to participate personally or through a brass plate in the management bodies of commercial companies, cooperatives and other organizations with business;
2. to conclude further agreements except as collaborators in research institutes and teachers in schools;
3. (New - SG. 37 of 2003, amend. No.. 95 of 2003) are in hierarchical relationship of command and control with a spouse, relative in direct line without limitation, collateral to the fourth degree or by marriage to the

fourth degree.
(3) (New - SG. 63 of 2000) the Customs officials who hold positions of service contracts must meet the requirements of Art. 7 of the Civil Service Law.
(4) (New - SG. 37 2003) The recruitment customs officials a declaration of the circumstances under para. 1 and 2.
(5) (New - SG. 37 2003 extra. No.. 38 of 2004) In appointing, removing and each year no later than May 31 customs officers are required to declare to the Director of the Agency Customs his fortune and wealth of their husbands (wives) and children under age declaration form approved by the Minister of Finance.
(6) (New - SG. 37 of 2003, amend. No.. 105 of 2005) At the written request of the Director of Agency "Customs authorities of the National Revenue Agency provided data on income and property customs officials.
(7) (New - SG. 37, 2003) On the protection and access to information under par. 5 and 6, processed by the Customs Agency, the provisions of the Protection of personal data.
(8) (New - SG. 37 of 2003) Incompatibility in para. 1 and 2, and failure within a statement under par. 5, is grounds for unilateral termination of employment or service relationship with the customs officer without notice.

Art. 11. (Amended - SG. 63 of 2000) (1) The Council of Ministers upon proposal of the Minister of Finance shall adopt rules of procedure of the Customs Agency and determines the number of employees in the agency and central office management.
(2) In the Rules of the Customs Agency may be certain additional requirements for positions in the customs administration.
(3) The Minister of Finance proposal to the Director of Customs Agency adopt regulations for the organization and operation of regional customs directorates.

Art. 12. The customs authorities shall collect fees for additional services provided and in cases specified in the regulations. These fees are not duties. Their size is determined by the Council of Ministers.

Art. 13. (Amended - SG. 63 of 2000) the Customs Agency collects revenue from contracts with legal entities and individuals authorized by the Minister of Finance activities in the areas of border crossings and elsewhere, whose performance require additional customs control.

Art. 14. (Amended - SG. 83 of 1999) (1) (Amended - SG. 63 of 2000) the Customs Agency is the administrator:
1. Revenue art. 12;
2. Revenue art. 13;
3. ninety percent of the revenues of Art. 240, para. 2;
4. (Amended - SG. 37 of 2003) revenues from exploitation of property - state property and provision of data;
5. (Suppl. - SG. 45 of 2005) twenty percent of collected fines and fines for customs and currency violations;
6. (Amended - SG. 63 of 2000, effective 1.01.2000) the proceeds of print art. Seven, para. 9;
7. Revenue from use of the home base;
8. (New - SG. 63 of 2000, effective 1.01.2000, supplemented. No.. 37 of 2003) revenues of art. 17, item 3 of the Currency Act and art. 251 para. 2 of the Penal Code;
9. (New - SG. 63 of 2000, with effect from 1.01.2000, am. No.. 59 of 2007) revenues of art. 78, para. 6 and 8 of the Code of Civil Procedure.
(2) (Amended - SG. 63 of 2000, with effect from 1.01.2001, the extra. No.. 109 of 2007) Minister of Finance proposal to the Director of Customs Agency defined additional remuneration for employees to participate in the fight against customs and currency violations and crimes, to participate in the detection of breaches of excise rules and incentive.
(3) (New - SG. 63 of 2000 in force on 1.01.2001) The resources under para. 2 is fixed at twenty five per cent of the annual amount of funds for salaries in the budget of the Customs Agency for the year and included in the State Budget Act for that year.
(4) (New - SG. 63 of 2000, effective 1.01.2001) The procedure to determine the individual amount of additional fee under par. 2 is determined by an ordinance issued by the Minister of Finance.

Section II Functions and tasks

Art. 15. (1) The Customs Administration:
1. participate in the development and implementation of customs policy of the state;
2. participate in the development and implementation of international agreements relating to customs activities;
3. Customs carries out international relations;
4. collect, process, analyze, store and provide information on customs and elaborate customs statistics. The arrangements for these activities is determined by an ordinance issued by the Minister of Finance;
5. provide training and retraining of customs officials;
6. (New - SG. 37 of 2003) Customs officials insure against accident and life insurance on behalf of its budget.
(2) The customs authorities:
1. perform customs supervision and control of goods, vehicles and persons in the areas of border crossings and throughout the customs territory of the country;
2. calculate, collect or require the provision of duty on certain imports, exports or transit of goods;
3. apply within their jurisdiction, tariff measures and trade policy of Bulgaria;
4. protecting the economic interests of the country within its jurisdiction;
5. (Amended and supplemented. - SG. 63 of 2000, amended. No.. 37 of 2003) implement a customs intelligence and investigation to combat customs and currency violations;
6. organize and carry out activities to prevent and detect illicit trafficking of narcotic substances and precursors;
7. exchange controls implemented within the given jurisdiction by law;
8. issue a decision on the application of customs regulations;
9. (New - SG. 63 of 2000, OTM. No.. 86 of 2005);
10. (New - SG. 63 of 2000) operate on administrative violations and impose administrative penalties;
11. (New - SG. 63 of 2000) participate in the implementation of operative-search activity in cooperation with the Ministry of Interior under the conditions and procedures of the Ministry of Interior;
12. (New - SG. 37 of 2003) apply for border control measures to protect intellectual property rights.
(3) (New - SG. 63 of 2000) modalities for cooperation between customs authorities and the Ministry of Interior for preventing and detecting customs and currency violations are governed by joint instruction of the Minister of Finance and Minister of Interior.
(4) (former para. 3 - SG. 63 of 2000) the Customs Administration and perform other tasks entrusted to it by law.

Section III Powers of customs authorities

Art. 16. (1) In performing their duties customs authorities:
1. to carry out inspections relating to customs control of goods, vehicles and persons in the areas of border crossings and customs throughout the territory;
2. to take appropriate measures allowed by law to carry out customs control;
3. to require the production or delivery of goods, documents, information and other media related to customs control;
4. require presentation of an identification document;
5. require written or oral explanations;
6. the follow customs control of goods and documents relating to the import, export and transit;
7. to collect amounts: for duty for imported and exported goods, for outstanding obligations and surety, to pay the equivalent of confiscated goods of the country where the missing or alienated, and any other duties and other governmental charges which are collected by customs authorities;
8. impose prescribed by law, seizing and freezing injunctions duties and other governmental charges levied by them;
9. to make personal examination of persons crossing the state border;
10. (Amended - SG. 63 of 2000, amended. And supplemented. No.. 45 of 2005) to conduct searches and seizures of goods that have been or should be subject to customs supervision and control and related documentation in offices and other business premises and personal search of in their persons, subject to the provisions of the Criminal Procedure Code;
11. to carry out controlled deliveries in conjunction with the Ministry of Interior and with the permission of the prosecutors.
(2) (Repealed - SG. 63, 2000).
(3) Customs officials have the right to bear arms and use it in self-defense and absolute necessity.
(4) (New - SG. 76 of 2002) In exercising the powers under para. 1 item 1 specialized control authorities of the Customs Agency are entitled to stop the vehicles within the country in terms and conditions under Art. 15

para. 3.
(5) (New - SG. 37 of 2003, amend. No.. 105 of 2005) At the written request of the Director of Customs Agency, the directors of the regional customs directorates and heads of customs authorities National Revenue Agency provide data on subsequent transactions on the quantity, type, value and origin of goods subject to import-export operations, amounts subject to payment or reimbursement under the Law on Value Added Tax and Excise Act and as established by the authorities of the National Revenue Agency of offenses committed by persons carrying on imports and exports.
(6) (New - SG. 37 of 2003, amend. No.. 105 of 2005) order and the way electronic exchange of information between customs administrations and the National Revenue Agency is determined by joint instruction of the Director Customs Agency and the Executive Director of the National Revenue Agency.
(7) (New - SG. 45 of 2005) When checking in the follow-up or during the investigation to determine the customs duties or on violations where there is evidence of concealment of facts and circumstances which are important for the verification or investigation, as well as prevent their implementation, the customs authorities may conduct searches and seizures under the Criminal Procedure Code. In such cases the customs authorities carrying out the verification or investigation, authorities have the powers of the pre-trial proceedings.
(8) (New - SG. 45 of 2005) provisions of the Criminal Procedure Code shall apply to proceedings and the powers of the customs authorities under par. 1, item 10 in the inspections under para. 7 and the rights and obligations of inspected persons on the grounds and purpose of searches and seizures, authorities it out, and those who attend, and the right to protection of persons tested.

Art. 17. (1) In performing their duties customs officials are required:
1. to observe the organization of work in the office;
2. to protect property rights and freedoms of individuals;
3. to submit and sign a customs official map;
4. (Suppl. - SG. 63 of 2000) to wear uniforms, where provided for the respective positions in the Rules of the Customs Agency;
5. (New - SG. 37 of 2003) to comply with the approved by the Minister of Finance ethical standards of conduct of the customs official;
6. (Amended and supplemented. - SG. 63 2000 prev. 5 pcs. 37 2003 extra. No.. 91 of 2005) not to disclose the circumstances and facts of which they known to or in connection with the execution of their duties defined by this Act as professional secrecy, except upon written request of a public authority, where provided by law, at the request of officials of the Inspectorate to the Minister of Finance or other customs authority in relation to exercising his powers under this Act. The modalities for providing information on the circumstances and facts constituting an official secret, another customs authority shall be determined by the Director of the Customs Agency.
(2) default under par. 1, the customs officers are subject to disciplinary responsibility.
Art. 17a. (New - SG. 45 of 2005) (1) Customs authorities collect and process personal data for purposes of customs supervision and control.
(2) Personal Data Administrator is the Director of Customs Agency, which entrusts the handling of personal information to authorized officials thereof, subject to and in accordance with the Law on protection of personal data.
(3) collected and processed by the customs authorities personal data may be submitted to the authorities of foreign countries and international organizations in the implementation of international agreements to which Bulgaria is a party, under the terms and provisions of the Law on protection of personal data.

Chapter Three RIGHTS AND OBLIGATIONS OF INDIVIDUALS

Section I Representation

Art. 18. (1) Any person may be represented before the customs authorities to perform the actions and procedures provided for in this Act and the regulations for its implementation, including the customs agent.
(2) The manner in which the representation is performed by a customs agent is determined in the rules.
(3) The representative must be resident in addition to those specifically mentioned in this law cases.
(4) The customs authorities shall require any person who declares that acts as an agent to submit written evidence.
Section II
Decisions of the customs authorities
Art. 19. (1) a decision by the customs authorities regarding the application of customs regulations the person

requesting the issuance thereof, shall provide all necessary information and documentation.
(2) The decision under para. 1 must be taken and notified to the applicant within a period specified in the regulations. When the request for a decision is made in writing, the decision must be taken into consideration in the regulation period from the date on which the request is received by the customs authorities. The decision shall be communicated in writing to the applicant.
(3) Where the customs authorities can not decide within the prescribed period because of the need to collect additional information, they must notify the applicant before its expiry, giving their reasons and they need time to take the required decision.
(4) Decisions of the customs authorities, which rejected the claims of persons or harmful to them, must be motivated.

Art. 20. (1) If the decision in favor of the person, based on incorrect or incomplete information, it will be invalidated when:
1. applicant knew or should have known that the information is incorrect or incomplete, and
2. such a decision could be taken on the basis of correct or complete information.
(2) The person must be informed about the cancellation of the decision.
(3) Annulment shall take effect from the date on which the decision was made.

Art. 21. (1) In cases other than art. 20 decision in favor of the person concerned shall be repealed or amended where one or more of its conditions are not met or are no longer running.
(2) Judgement in favor of the person concerned may be revoked and if that person fails to comply with an obligation imposed on him under that decision.
(3) The person to whom the decision relates to the customs office must be notified of its revocation or amendment.
(4) (Amended - SG. 63 of 2000), repeal or amendment shall enter into force on the date of notification under par. 3. Head Office of Customs may, in exceptional cases where the legitimate interests require the person concerned to postpone the date of entry into force of the repeal or amendment of the decision.
Section III
Information

Art. 22. (1) Customs authorities shall provide interested parties information on the application of customs legislation. The customs authority may refuse to answer when the request is not related to actually an import or export operations.
(2) The information under para. 1 is provided free of charge. The costs incurred are paid when they are linked with analysis, of specialized expertise of the goods, returning them to the applicant and others.

Art. 23. (1) (Supplemented - SG. 37 of 2003) Customs authorities shall issue a decision under Art. 19 binding tariff information or binding origin information of the goods at the written request to the terms and conditions set out in regulations.
(2) The information under para. Assume a customs authority and its holder only to the tariff classification or determining the origin of specific goods where the customs formalities are carried out after the date on which the information was issued.
(3) The customs clearance of goods holder of the information received to the customs authorities verify full compliance:
1. between the declared goods and goods specified in the information for the purposes of charging;
2. between the declared goods and the circumstances which determine the origin and acquisition of goods and the circumstances described in the information for the purpose of origin.
(4) Binding information is valid for up to three years from date of issue her shall be annulled where it is based on inaccurate or incomplete data submitted by the applicant, regardless of the conditions under Art. 20, para. 1, items 1 and 2.
(5) The tariff information ceases to be valid:
1. acceptance of new normative act when it does not comply with its provisions;
2. when incompatible with the interpretation of the nomenclatures referred to in Art. 26. Incompatible with the interpretation could be:
a) (amended - State Gazette. 37 of 2003) at national level - following the amendment of national explanatory notes to the Nomenclature of the Customs Tariff, or court decision;
b) at international level - following the issuance of the classification review or amendment of the Explanatory

Notes to the Harmonized System nomenclature Description and Coding System, published by the World Customs Organization;
3. for revocation or amendment under Art. 21 and provided that the holder of the information is notified of the withdrawal of its application, or to change her
(6) Information regarding the origin ceases to be valid:
1. when adopting a new law or upon conclusion of the international agreement by the Republic of Bulgaria, where it corresponds to their provisions;
2. if incompatible:
s) at national level - with explanatory notes and comments, accepted for purposes of interpreting the rules or court decision;
b) at international level - the Agreement on Rules of Origin established in the WTO, or explanatory notes or comments about the origin, adopted the interpretation of the agreement;
3. for cancellation or amendment under Art. 21 and provided that the holder is notified of the withdrawal of its application, or to change her
(7) (Amended - SG. 63 of 2000) holder of binding information which ceases to be valid under par. 5, item 2 or 3 or par. 6, item 2 or 3 can continue using it within a period not exceeding six months from the entry into force of the acts on the terms and conditions set out in regulations.
(8) Where regulations or agreement under par. 5, item 1 and para. 6, paragraph 1 provide for a period other than that paragraph. 7, provided they apply within.
(9) Classification or the origin of the goods it shall be applied only:
1. to determine the import or export duties;
2. (New - SG. 37 of 2003) for calculation of export subsidies and all other grants for the export or import of goods as part of the agricultural policy of the Republic of Bulgaria;
3. (Previous 2 am. - SG. 37 of 2003) for the use of export licenses and certificates for imports or exports are presented for the adoption of the customs declaration of goods, provided that such certificates have been issued on the basis of this binding information.

PART TWO ELEMENTS OF THE BASIS OF WHICH IMPORT OR APPLY EXPORT DUTIES AND OTHER MEASURES PROVIDED BY REGARDING TRADE IN GOODS

(Title amended. - SG. 37 of 2003)
Chapter Four
Customs Tariff. Tariff classification
(Title amended. - SG. 37 of 2003)

Art. 24. (Amended - SG. 63 of 2000 pcs. 37 of 2003) (1) goods transported through the state border of the Republic of Bulgaria, are subject to import or export duties, unless provided otherwise in this or any other law and international treaty to which the country is Bulgaria.
(2) The import or export duties payable on a customs debt is based on the Customs Tariff of the Republic of Bulgaria.

Art. 25. (Amended - SG. 37 of 2003) Other measures to specific areas related to trade in goods provided for in legislation and not referred to in Art. 24, introduced in accordance with the classification of such goods.

Art. 26. (Amended - SG. 63 of 2000 pcs. 37 of 2003) (1) The Customs Tariff includes:
1. Combined Nomenclature of the Republic of Bulgaria;
2. any other nomenclature which is wholly or partly based on the combined nomenclature of the Republic of Bulgaria or further subdivisions to it and which was adopted by a statutory instrument regulating specific areas regarding the application of tariff measures relating to trade in goods;
3. rates and other items of charge applicable to goods falling within combined nomenclature as regards:
a) the duties and
b) levies on imports of goods in accordance with agricultural policy or in accordance with specific provisions applicable to goods produced in the processing of agricultural products;
4. preferential tariff measures contained in agreements to which Bulgaria is a party and provide for the granting of preferential tariff treatment;
5. preferential tariff measures adopted unilaterally by the Republic of Bulgaria for countries, groups of countries or territories;

6. autonomous measures introduced by the Council of Ministers, to temporarily reduce or remove the existing import duties on certain goods (autonomous suspensions) arrangements for the introduction and implementation of autonomous suspensions are determined by decree of the Council of Ministers ;
7. other tariff measures provided for in other regulations.
(2) Subject to the rules on flat duty measures under par. 1, item 4, 5 and 6 shall apply instead of those referred to in item 3 at the request of the declarant if the goods meet the conditions established for these measures. The request can be satisfied, then, if the conditions are met.
(3) When implementing the measures under para. 1, item 4, 5 and 6 is restricted to a certain quantity or value of imports, the application shall be terminated:
1. in quotas - as soon as the quantified limit or a value of imports;
2. in tariff ceilings - from the moment defined by an act.
Art. 26a. (New - SG. 37 of 2003) (1) The Council of Ministers before the end of each calendar year, adopt the Combined Nomenclature of the Republic of Bulgaria and customs duties determined in accordance with the bound rates of duty in the Republic of Bulgaria List of duties and concessions annexed to the General Agreement on Tariffs and Trade 1994 (conventional rates of duty) to be applied from the first day of next year.
(2) CN, conventional rates of duty and autonomous duty rates published in the Official Gazette.

Art. 27. (Amended - SG. 37 of 2003) (1) tariff classification of goods is down in accordance with established rules of enactment:
1. subheading of the nomenclature of art. 26 para. 1, item 1 or any other nomenclature of art. 26 para. 1, item 2, or
2. subheadings from any other nomenclature which is wholly or partly based on the combined nomenclature of the Republic of Bulgaria or further subdivisions to it and which was adopted by a statutory instrument regulating specific areas regarding the application of measures other than tariff measures relating to trade goods.
(2) The Minister of Finance may lay down additional rules on classification of goods in accordance with:
1. Explanatory Notes to the Harmonized System Description and Coding System;
2. Explanatory notes to the combined nomenclature applied in countries - members of the European Union;
3. Reviews of classification of goods adopted by the Harmonised System Committee of WCO;
4. decisions on classification of goods used in the countries - members of the European Union.

Art. 28. (Amended - SG. 63 of 2000) (1) (Amended - SG. 37 of 2003) Conditions under which certain goods can be given favorable tariff treatment by reason of their nature or end Their use is determined by the regulations. When authorization is required, the provisions of Art. 92 and 93.
(2) (Amended - SG. 37 of 2003) According to para. 1, under "favorable tariff treatment" means any temporary reduction or any reduction or elimination (suspension) of import duties, even within the tariff quota.

Chapter Five ORIGIN OF GOODS

Section I
Non-preferential origin

Art. 29. Non-preferential origin of goods specified in Art. 30, 31 and 32 serve the purpose of:
1. (Amended - SG. 37, 2003) applying the Customs Tariff, except for preferential tariff measures referred to in Art. 26 para. 1, item 4 and 5;
2. application of established by the Council of Ministers measures other than tariff;
3. preparation and issue of certificates of origin.

Art. 30. (1) Goods originating in a country are goods wholly obtained or produced in that country.
(2) Wholly obtained goods in a particular country are:
1. mineral products extracted within that country;
2. vegetable products harvested there;
3. live animals born and raised in the country;
4. products from live animals raised there;

5. products from hunting or fishing conducted there;
6. products of sea fishing and other products derived from the sea outside the internal waters and territorial sea of the country by vessels registered in the country and flying its flag;
7. goods obtained or produced on board factory ships from item 6 products originating in the country, provided that such factory ships registered in that country and fly its flag;
8. products extracted from the seabed or subsoil outside the internal waters or territorial sea, provided that it has exclusive rights to exploit that seabed or subsoil;
9. waste and scrap resulting from manufacturing operations in the country, and used articles, provided they were collected and are fit only for the recovery of raw materials;
10. goods produced there exclusively from goods referred to in section 1-9, or their derivatives, at any stage of production.
(3) For the purposes of par. 2 in the customs territory of the country includes its internal waters and territorial sea.

Art. 31. (1) Goods whose production involved more than one country shall be deemed to originate from the country where they underwent their last, substantial, economically justified working or processing in undertaking equipped for that purpose and led to the production of new product or which constitutes an important stage of production.
(2) Working or processing, which is established or there is sufficient evidence that its purpose was solely to circumvent the provisions applicable in the Republic of Bulgaria to products from certain countries are not considered sufficient to give the product resulting from the country , in which the working or processing is carried out.

Art. 32. (1) Document for proof of origin shall be submitted when required by customs or other act.
(2) Notwithstanding the submission of evidence of origin of the goods the customs authorities in cases of reasonable suspicion to request other evidence to confirm that the declared origin corresponds to the non-preferential rules of origin established in Bulgaria.

Section II Preferential origin

Art. 33. (Amended - SG. 37 2003) The conditions for acquiring preferential origin of goods in order to implement the measures under Art. 26 para. 1, item 4 and 5 are covered by:
1. international agreements the Republic of Bulgaria to introduce preferential tariff measures;
2. regulations unilaterally adopted by the Republic of Bulgaria preferential tariff measures.

Chapter Six CUSTOMS VALUE

Art. 34. The customs value is determined for customs purposes of goods worth BGN. The provisions of this chapter governing the determination of customs value for purposes of applying the Customs Tariff of the Republic of Bulgaria, as well as for the implementation of a legislative act established measures other than tariff.
Art. 35. (1) The customs value of imported goods determined under this Article shall be the transaction value, which is actually paid or payable on goods sold for export to Bulgaria, adjusted in accordance with Art. 38, provided that:
1. no restriction on the disposal or use of the goods by the buyer, unless restrictions:
a) are established by legislation of the Republic of Bulgaria;
b) determine the geographical area within which goods may be resold or
c) not adversely affecting the value of the goods;
2. sale or price is not subject to conditions or considerations regarding the value of the goods being valued could not be determined;
3. any part of the proceeds from each sale, ceded the right to use or dispose of goods by the buyer will accrue directly or indirectly to the seller unless the correction is possible under art. 38; and
4. buyer and seller are not related, or when they are connected - if the transaction value is acceptable for customs purposes under par. 2.
(2) Particulars to be recorded in related parties:

1. in determining whether the transaction value is acceptable for purposes of para. 1 fact that the buyer and seller are related persons should not be under contract value to be regarded as unacceptable. If necessary to consider the circumstances of the sale and provided that the relationship did not influence the price, the contract value should be adopted. If, on the basis of information supplied by the buyer or other source information, the customs offices have grounds to believe that the relationship influenced the price, they should communicate their grounds to the declarant and to give him a real opportunity to respond. At the request of the declarant reasons will be communicated in writing;
2. on sales between related parties transaction value should be accepted and the goods be valued in accordance with para. 1, where the declarant demonstrates that this value is very close to one of the following values set in or about the same time:
a) the transaction value in sales of identical or similar goods sold for export to the Republic of Bulgaria between buyers and sellers who are not related;
b) the customs value of identical or similar goods determined under Art. 36, para. 2, item 3;
c) the customs value of identical or similar goods determined under Art. 36, para. 2, item 4.
(3) In applying para. 2, item 2 into account differences in commercial levels, quantity of the elements listed in Art. 38, and costs incurred by the seller in sales when he and the buyer are not related and not made by the seller in sales when he and the buyer are related. Listed in para. 2, item 2 methods are implemented on the initiative of the declarant and only for comparative purposes and not as a basis for determining the customs value.
(4) actually paid or payable is the total amount paid or buyer should pay for imported goods to the seller or for the benefit of the seller and include all payments from the buyer to the seller or the buyer to a third party to meet Seller's obligations which are incurred or to be made as a condition of sale. Payment need not always be in the form of a transfer of money and can be made by credit or negotiable funds and can be made directly or indirectly.
(5) Actions, including marketing undertaken by the buyer's expense, other than those to which adjustment is provided in Art. 38 should not be considered an indirect payment to the seller even when they can be considered to be in favor of the seller or have been taken in agreement with him and their cost should be added to the price actually paid or payable. "Marketing actions" within the meaning of this paragraph, all actions relating to advertising and promoting the sale of the goods being valued and all warranty activities in respect of goods.

Art. 36. (1) Where the customs value can not be determined under Art. 35, it should be determined by a consistent application of the provisions of para. 2, section 1-4, while the terms of the first line provision allowing its implementation. An exception to this order shall be made in the application of paragraphs 3 and 4, if the declarant wishes to exchange the order of these two points. Only where such value can not be determined at a specific point in that sequence, may apply to the next item in the order specified under this paragraph.
(2) The customs value determined under this Article shall be:
1. transaction value of identical goods sold for export to Bulgaria and exported around the same time as the goods being valued;
2. transaction value of similar goods sold for export to Bulgaria and exported around the same time as the goods being valued;
3. value based on the unit price, which is sold in the greatest aggregate quantity of imported goods or identical or similar imported goods to persons not related to the persons from whom they buy such goods;
4. computed value, consisting of the sum of:
a) the cost of materials and production or other operations related to processing of imported goods;
b) the amount for profit and general expenses equal to that usually reflected in sales of goods of the same class or kind as the goods being valued which are made by producers in the exporting country for export to the Republic of Bulgaria;
c) the costs referred to in Art. 38, para. 1, p. 5.
(3) Additional terms and conditions for the application of para. 2 is defined in the Rules.

Art. 37. (1) Where the customs value of imported goods could not be determined under Art. 35 and 36, it should be determined by means consistent with the principles and general provisions of the Agreement on Implementation of Art. VII of the General Agreement on Tariffs and Trade, Art. VII of the General Agreement on Tariffs and Trade and the provisions of this chapter.
(2) The customs value determined under par. 1 can not be based on:
1. selling price in Bulgaria of goods produced in Bulgaria;
2. system provides for the acceptance for customs purposes of the higher of two alternative values;

3. price of goods on the domestic market of the exporting country;
4. cost of production other than computed values which have been determined for identical and similar goods in accordance with Art. 36, para. 2, item 4;
5. prices of goods sold for export, which was not intended to Bulgaria;
6. minimum customs values;
7. arbitrary or fictitious values.

Art. 38. (1) In determining the customs value pursuant to Art. 35 to the price actually paid or payable for the imported goods should be added:
1. (Amended - SG. 63 of 2000) the following costs to the extent that is paid by the buyer but not included in the price actually paid or payable:
a) commissions and brokerage (brokerage), except buying commissions;
b) the cost of containers for customs purposes are treated with the goods being valued;
c) the costs of packaging, including labor and materials;
2. value, apportioned as appropriate, the following goods and services where supplied directly or indirectly by the buyer free of charge or at reduced cost for use in connection with the production and sale for export of imported goods since this value was not included in paid or in payable:
a) materials, components, parts and similar items incorporated in the imported goods;
b) tools, dies, molds and other similar items used in producing the imported goods;
c) materials used in producing the imported goods;
d) engineering, development, artwork, designs, plans and drawings, which are not developed in Bulgaria and were necessary for the production of imported goods;
3. royalties and license fees relating to the goods being valued that the buyer directly or indirectly to pay as a condition of sale of the goods being valued to the extent that such royalties and fees are not included in paid or payable;
4. value of each part of the proceeds from each sale, surrender the right of holding or use of the imported goods to be provided directly or indirectly by the seller;
5. cost:
a) transportation of imported goods to the border point of Bulgaria;
b) cargo handling and operations related to transportation of imported goods to the border point of Bulgaria;
c) insurance of imported goods.
(2) Additions to the price actually paid or payable under this Article shall be made only on the basis of objective and quantifiable data.
(3) In determining the customs value at the price actually paid or payable can not make additions other than those provided in this Article.
(4) (New - SG. 63 of 2000) In this chapter the term 'buying commissions' means fees paid by an importer to his agent for service of representing him in the supply of valued goods.
(5) (former para. 4 - SG. 63 of 2000) Notwithstanding par. 1, item 3:
1. fees for the right to reproduce imported goods in Bulgaria should be added to the price actually paid or payable for imported goods in determining the customs value;
2. payments made by the buyer the right to distribute or resell the imported goods should not be added to the price actually paid or payable for the imported goods if such payments are not a condition of sale of goods for export to Bulgaria.

Art. 39. The customs value of imported goods should include the following expenses, provided that they are distinct from actually paid or payable:
1. costs of transport of goods within the territory of the Republic of Bulgaria after their introduction;
2. costs for construction, erection, installation, maintenance or technical assistance, undertaken for the goods after their importation;
3. fees for the right to reproduce imported goods in Bulgaria;
4. commissions for the purchase;
5. duties, taxes, levies and charges payable in the Republic of Bulgaria on the import or sale of goods;
6. interest on financial arrangements to the purchaser in connection with the purchase of imported goods, regardless of whether the loan is provided by the seller from a bank or a third party, provided that interest shall be segregated from the price actually paid or payable, financing agreement in writing that the purchaser if necessary to prove that:
a) such goods are sold at the time valued at the price declared as actually paid or payable, and
b) the declared interest rate does not exceed the level for the majority of such contracts in the country,

where, and at a time when funding was secured.

Art. 40. The Rules may provide for specific rules for determining the customs value of imported media for use in equipment for electronic data processing, bearing data or instructions.

Art. 41. (Amended - SG. 37 of 2003) procedure for determining the customs value in specific cases is determined by a decree of the Council of Ministers.

Art. 42. (1) The conversion of foreign currency in BGN for calculating the customs value shall be carried out as announced by the Bulgarian National Bank rates of foreign currencies to the euro.
(2) The period in which the relevant exchange rate is determined by the regulations.

Art. 43. (1) The provisions of this chapter shall not affect the specific provisions for determining the customs value of goods imports, which were under a different arrangement.
(2) Notwithstanding the provisions of Art. 35-37 customs value of perishable goods usually delivered on consignment at the request of the declarant can not be determined under simplified rules governed by the regulations.

PART THREE INTRODUCTION OF GOODS INTO THE CUSTOMS TERRITORY OF THE REPUBLIC BULGARIA TO RECEIPT OF CUSTOMS DIRECTION

Chapter Seven INTRODUCTION OF GOODS INTO THE CUSTOMS TERRITORY OF THE REPUBLIC OF BULGARIA

Art. 44. (1) Since the introduction of the customs territory of the country the goods are under customs supervision and may be subject to customs control in accordance with the date of entry provisions.

(2) The goods are under customs supervision to determine the customs status. Except in cases under Art. 88 para. A non-Community goods remain under customs supervision and customs change their status or their entry into a free zone or free warehouse or re-export them or destroy them in accordance with Art. 180.

Art. 45. (1) Goods brought into the customs territory of the country should be immediately transported by the person who establishes, in accordance with their customs to the customs office or other place designated by them. If necessary, the customs authorities determine the route for the transport of goods.
(2) The person who undertakes to transport goods, which were entered into the customs territory of the Republic of Bulgaria, is responsible for fulfilling the obligations under par. 1.
(3) Paragraph 1 shall not preclude the application of provisions in other enactments:
1. mail;
2. travel;
3. shipments of goods of negligible economic importance, provided it does not obstruct the administration of customs supervision and customs control.
(4) Paragraphs 1, 2 and 3 and art. 46-60 do not apply to goods temporarily leave the customs territory of the Republic of Bulgaria, moving between two points in that territory by sea or air, provided that the shipment was made in a direct line from the aircraft or vessel engaged in regular voyage without stop outside the customs territory of Bulgaria.
(5) Paragraph 1 shall not apply to goods on board ships or aircraft crossing the territorial waters or airspace of the Republic of Bulgaria, without having a destination port or airport in the customs territory.

Art. 46. (A) In cases of force majeure or other unforeseeable circumstances where the person can not meet commitments under Art. 45, para. 1, it shall immediately inform the nearest customs authorities. Where the goods are completely destroyed, the customs authorities must be informed of their precise location.
(2) Where a ship or aircraft is forced due to force majeure or other unforeseeable circumstances, to port or to land temporarily in the customs territory of the Republic of Bulgaria, if unable to meet its obligations under

Art. 45, para. 1 person driving the vehicle or any person acting in his place shall immediately notify the customs authorities.
(3) In cases under para. 1 and 2, the customs authorities shall determine the measures to be taken for implementation of customs supervision and, if necessary - to ensure the transport of goods to the customs office or other place designated by them.

Chapter Eight PRESENTATION OF GOODS TO CUSTOMS

Art. 47. Goods are shipped in accordance with Art. 45, para. 1 must be presented to customs by the person who has introduced the customs territory of the Republic of Bulgaria, or the person who has assumed carriage of the goods after their introduction.

Art. 48. For goods carried by passengers or placed under, but not presented to the customs authorities may apply for another order determined by the regulations.

Art. 49. Once submitted, the goods may be subject to analysis or sampling to specify their destination by the customs of the customs authorities.

Chapter Nine Manifest and unloading goods PRESENTED TO CUSTOMS

Art. 50. (1) The goods presented to customs shall be made manifest.
(2) The summary should be submitted immediately after presentation of the goods to customs. The customs authorities may set another date for submission of manifest, but no later than the first working day following the day on which the goods are presented.

Art. 51. (1) The manifest of the goods shall be subject to the terms and conditions set out in regulations. The customs authorities may accept commercial or other document, rather than manifest, if it contains the necessary data for identification of goods.
(2) The summary declaration is lodged by:
1. person who brought the goods into the customs territory of the Republic of Bulgaria, or the person who has assumed carriage of the goods after their introduction;
2. person in whose name the persons referred to in paragraph 1.
Art. 52. Cases in which customs authorities may submit official declaration, and do not require submission of manifest, are determined by the regulations.

Art. 53. (1) Goods shall be unloaded or transhipped from vehicles, which are only authorized by the customs authorities in places designated by them.
(2) Permission is not required in an emergency or other circumstances necessitating the immediate unloading all or part of the goods. In this case, the customs authorities must be informed immediately.
(3) For the purpose of inspecting goods, including vehicles, where they are located, the customs authorities may at any time require unloading and unpacking of goods.

Art. 54. Goods may be removed from that of their original, only with the permission of customs authorities.

Chapter Ten OBLIGATION TO ASSIGN FORMALITIES FOR OBTAINING CUSTOMS DIRECTION OF GOODS PRESENTED TO CUSTOMS

(Title amended. - SG. 37 of 2003)

Art. 55. (Suppl. - SG. 37 of 2003) Foreign goods presented to customs authorities must obtain acceptable arrangement.

Art. 56. (1) (Amended - SG. 37 of 2003) declaring the goods to be carried out the formalities for obtaining customs within:
1. forty-five days from the date of customs declaration for goods carried by sea;
2. twenty days from the date of submission of customs declaration for goods carried otherwise than by sea.
(2) The customs authorities depending on the particular circumstances may determine the periods shorter or longer than those specified in para. 1. The continuation can not be greater than actually necessary.

Chapter Eleven TEMPORARY STORAGE OF GOODS

Art. 57. Pending receipt of customs, goods presented to customs authorities have the status of goods in temporary storage.
Art. 58. (1) Temporarily stored goods may remain only in places where the conditions laid down by the authorities.
(2) (Supplemented - SG. 153 of 1998) the Customs authorities may require the person holding the goods to secure payment of any customs debt which may arise under Art. 199, para. 1, 5, 6 and 7, as well as taxes and excise duties.

Art. 59. Temporarily stored goods may be subject to treatment other than that intended to ensure their preservation in an unaltered state without modifying their appearance or technical characteristics. This provision does not limit the application of Art. 49.

Art. 60. (1) (Amended - SG. 37 of 2003 pcs. 109 of 2007) Notwithstanding the provisions for a customs debt for goods which were not carried out the formalities for obtaining acceptable customs, the customs authorities shall notify in writing the receipt of the goods recipient, within 30 days of receipt of the notice the goods will be deemed abandoned to the state.
(2) (Supplemented - SG. 109 of 2007) After the expiry of para. 1, the goods shall be deemed to be abandoned in favor of the state, unless within that period, the customs debt is extinguished or considered that it was incurred under the customs legislation.
(3) (Amended - SG. 37 of 2003 pcs. 109 of 2007) When the recipient of the goods is a foreign person, unknown person of unknown residence address or the address of undiscovered person notification al. 1 does not send the goods are considered abandoned after three months of their manifest.
(4) (Amended - SG. 37 of 2003 pcs. 109 of 2007) The customs authorities may, at the risk and expense of the holder of the goods to allow removal of any other place under customs supervision.

Chapter Twelve FOREIGN goods in transit

Art. 61. The provisions of Art. 45, except para. 1 and Art. 46-60 does not apply to the introduction of goods into the customs territory of the Republic of Bulgaria placed in transit.

Art. 62. Since foreign goods moved under a transit procedure reach their destination in the customs territory of the Republic of Bulgaria and have been presented to customs authorities under the transit provisions, the provisions of Art. 49-60.

Chapter thirteen MISCELLANEOUS PROVISIONS

Art. 63. Where circumstances require, the customs authorities may stipulate destruction presented to the customs clearance of goods by notifying the holder of the goods. Costs of destroying the goods on his behalf.
Art. 64. Where customs authorities find that the customs territory of the Republic of Bulgaria entered illegally or diverted goods from customs supervision, provided they take legal actions, including their sale.

PART FOUR CUSTOMS

Title I GENERAL

Art. 65. (1) If there are no legal restrictions or prohibitions, the goods may, under certain conditions in this Act, be assigned any customs regardless of their type, quantity, origin, consignment or destination.
(2) Paragraph 1 shall not preclude prohibitions or restrictions relating to the protection of national security, public order and morality, life and health of humans, animals and plants as well as national treasures representing the artistic, historical and archaeological value and the protection of industrial and intellectual property.
(3) (New - SG. 37 2003) When carrying out customs control under par. 2, unless otherwise provided, the customs authorities may defer a reasoned decision within five working days of the authorization requested destination for goods, shall immediately inform the authorities responsible for supervising or monitoring associated with the prohibitions and restrictions.

Title II CUSTOMS PROCEDURES

Chapter Fourteen
Placing goods under a customs procedure
Art. 66. (1) Any goods intended to be placed under a customs procedure must be declared for the procedure.
(2) Local goods declared for export, temporary export, outward processing, transit or customs warehousing, under customs supervision from the time of declaring them to customs by leaving the customs territory of the Republic of Bulgaria or destruction, or cancellation the customs declaration.

Art. 66a. (New - SG. 63 of 2000) (1) The Director of Customs Agency by order may determine individual offices carrying out customs activity in respect of certain goods and / or according to customs procedures under which they will be placed.
(2) The order under para. 1 is published in the Official Gazette.

Art. 67. (Amended - SG. 63 of 2000) (1) The customs declaration shall be made:
1. writing;
2. electronically;
3. oral;
4. by any other act whereby the holder of goods expresses its desire to place them under the arrangements.
(2) The procedure for declaring the cases under para. 1, 2, 3 and 4 are defined in the Rules.

Section I Written declaration of the normal procedure

Art. 68. (1) The written declaration shall be made by a customs declaration form and manner determined by the Minister of Finance.
(2) (New - SG. 37 of 2003) the Customs declaration must be signed and contain all data necessary to implement the provisions of the customs procedure for which the goods are declared.
(3) (former para. 2 - SG. 37 2003) The declaration shall be accompanied by all documents legally authorizing certain customs procedure for which the goods are declared.

Art. 69. Declarations formed under Art. 68 be adopted immediately by the customs authorities, provided that the goods are presented to them.

Art. 70. (1) (Amended - SG. 63 of 2000) The declaration may be made by anyone, including his representative who may submit or cause to be submitted to the competent customs authorities goods and documents necessary to deal with the customs procedure for which the goods are declared.
(2) (Amended - SG. 63 of 2000) When the adoption of a customs declaration imposes particular obligations on a specific person, the declaration must be made by him or on his behalf.
(3) The declarant must be a resident. This condition is not required for persons who:
1. (Amended - SG. 63 of 2000) make a declaration for transit or temporary import, or
2. declare goods occasionally, and if the customs authorities consider the declaration to be admissible.

Art. 71. (1) After adoption of the declaration at the request of the declarant, the customs authorities may authorize the performance of one or more amendments to the declaration. The amendment may not include goods other than those originally declared.
(2) may not be repairable, when the request is made after the customs authorities:
1. informed the declarant of their intention to examine the goods;
2. established that the inaccuracy of data in the declaration;
3. have released the goods.

Art. 72. (1) Customs authorities at the request of the declarant, invalidate the adopted declaration, the declarant proves that the goods have been declared for the wrong procedure or because of special circumstances, keeping it under the declared customs regime is unwarranted.
(2) Where the customs authorities have informed the declarant of their intention to examine the goods, the request for invalidation of the declaration may be accepted after that examination.
(3) The declaration may be invalidated after the authorization for release of goods, except in cases provided for in the Rules.
(4) Invalidation of the declaration does not preclude the application of penal provisions.

Art. 73. The date of the application of customs procedure under which goods are declared shall be the date of the declaration by the customs authorities, unless a provision of law provides otherwise.

Art. 74. Verification of declarations adopted the customs authorities may:
1. documentary review of the declaration and accompanying documents. The customs authorities may require the declarant presentation of other documents verifying the accuracy of the declaration;
2. inspection of goods and take samples for analysis or review.

Art. 75. (1) Transport of goods to the places of inspection and sampling, and all operations necessary to carry out inspections and sampling are carried out by the declarant and his responsibility. The costs incurred are borne by the declarant.
(2) The declarant shall be entitled to participate in the inspection of goods and sampling. The customs authorities may require the presence of the declarant or his representative in the inspection and sampling to facilitate the commission of investigation.
(3) When samples are taken under current regulations, the customs authorities due benefits, but pay the cost of analysis or review.

Art. 76. (1) When a checklist is part of the goods in a statement, the findings are valid for all the goods in this declaration.
(2) The declarant may ask for additional verification of the goods if he considers that the results of the partial examination are not valid for the rest of the goods declared.
(3) For the purposes of par. 1 where the declaration included several items for each type of data is considered a separate declaration.
Art. 77. (1) The results of verifying the declaration shall be used for the implementation of customs procedure under which goods are placed.
(2) If not checked the statement, justification for the application of the customs procedure is data in the declaration.

Art. 78. (1) Customs authorities shall take the necessary steps to identify the goods where it is necessary to ensure compliance with the conditions governing the customs procedure under which goods are declared.
(2) Means of identification affixed to the goods or cargo holds of vehicles can be removed or destroyed only by customs authorities or with their permission. This provision shall not apply in cases of force majeure or other unforeseeable circumstances to protect the goods and vehicles.

Art. 78a. (New - SG. 37 of 2003) (1) Customs authorities postponed a reasoned decision granting permission for removal of declared for import goods and immediately inform the competent authorities under the supervision of the market when the inspection when they find that:
1. products show certain characteristics that give rise to reasonable doubts that a serious and immediate

risk to health and safety in the event of their use in normal and foreseeable conditions, or
2. goods not accompanied by documents required under the safety rules or are not marked in accordance with these rules.
(2) In cases under para. 1, the competent authorities under the supervision of the market consider that the goods do not pose a serious and immediate risk to health and safety, customs authorities shall release the goods, provided that they fulfill all other requirements and formalities for placing under import.
(3) If within three working days from the day following the action under par. 1, the customs authorities have not informed by the competent authorities for market surveillance measures taken by them, the goods shall be permitted, provided they have met all other requirements and formalities for placing under import under current legislation.
(4) The customs authorities do not authorize release of the goods and their placing under import, when informed by the competent authorities under the supervision of market goods that pose a serious and immediate risk to health and safety and they have taken measures to prohibit the placing on the market. In such cases the customs authorities have called on the invoice and accompanying text documents "Dangerous product - import regime is not allowed.
(5) Customs authorities shall release the goods and their placing under import and when informed by the competent authority supervising the market, the goods do not conform to current safety rules and they are taken to ban the placing on the market. In such cases the customs authorities have called on the invoice and the accompanying text document "Product conformity - mode import is not permitted."
(6) The provisions of this Article shall apply to goods for which customs authorities have been notified in advance by supervisors on the market that are subject to review for compliance with safety rules. Notification is carried out in line agreed between Customs authorities and market surveillance.
(7) The provisions of this Article shall apply, since the enactment otherwise the organization of border controls on specific goods.

Art. 78b. (New - SG. 37 of 2003) provisions of Art. 78a do not apply when a legislative act are regulated veterinary and zootechnical checks and controls concerning the protection of plant and animal protection.

Art. 79. (1) (Amended - SG. 37 of 2003) Subject to the provisions of Art. 80, where the conditions for placing goods under the procedure if they are not subject to bans or restrictions, customs authorities shall release them after the declaration data have been verified or accepted without verification. Permission for release of goods is given where verification can not be completed within a reasonable time and availability of goods is no longer necessary to carry out her
(2) Removal of goods allowed for all the goods declared in a statement. When the declaration included several items, the data pertaining to each species are considered a separate declaration.

Art. 80. (1) Where acceptance of a customs declaration gives rise to a customs debt, the goods included in this Declaration are permitted only if the debt is paid or secured. This paragraph does not apply to temporary admission with partial relief from import duties in compliance with par. 2.
(2) Where the customs procedure under which goods are declared, required collateral, the customs authorities shall release the goods only after its establishment.
(3) hazardous to health and environment, fire, perishable and other goods can be removed with the written permission of the customs authorities before setting up their security.

Art. 81. Customs authorities take legal action envisaged, including the withdrawal to the State and sale of goods:
1. which can not be released for the following reasons:
a) examination of the goods could not be initiated or conducted within the limits of the customs authorities for reasons attributable to the declarant;
b) not submitted the documents necessary for placing the goods under the customs procedure requested;
c) are not paid or secured within the prescribed period the import or export duties;
d) the goods are subject to bans or restrictions;
2. (Amended - SG. 153 of 1998) are not removed within a reasonable period after the authorization.

Section II Written declaration under a simplified procedure

Art. 82. (1) facilitation of customs formalities in accordance with the procedures for declaring and conditions specified in the rules customs authorities:
1. submission of simplified customs declaration, which is the declaration under Art. 68, containing some of the requested data or to which they are not implemented some of the requested documents;
2. declaration instead of art. 68 is a commercial or other document, accompanied by a request for placing the goods under the customs procedure;
3. declaration of goods under the customs procedure to be performed by entering them in the records of the declarant. In this case, the customs authorities may exempt the declarant of the obligation to produce goods.
(2) simplified declaration, commercial or other document or entry in the accounting records should contain the data necessary to identify the goods. Entry in the records must be included and the date on which it is made.
(3) Except as specified in the Rules, the declarant shall furnish a supplementary declaration which may be a general, periodic or recapitulative nature.
(4) additional statement under par. 3 is considered a single, unitary document with the documents referred to in para. 1, item 1, 2 and 3 which shall enter into force upon adoption by the authorities. In the cases under para. 1, item 3 entry in the records have the same legal effect as the declaration under Art. 68.
(5) simplified procedures for transit are defined in the Rules.

Section III Other declarations

Art. 83. (1) (Supplemented - SG. 63 of 2000, the previous text of Art. 83 pcs. 37 2003) Where the customs declaration is made electronically, orally or by other action under Article . 67 provisions of Art. 68-82 is applied, mutatis mutandis, without prejudice to the principles set out therein.
(2) (New - SG. 37 2003) When the declaration is made electronically, the customs authorities may require the application of the documents under Art. 68 para. 3. In these cases the documents must be available to the customs authorities for the purposes of customs control.
(3) (New - SG. 37 of 2003) Minister of Finance shall determine the procedures for customs declarations by electronic means, mutatis mutandis.

Section IV Follow-up to the declaration

Art. 84. (1) Following authorization for release of goods, customs authorities may, ex officio or at the request of the declarant to re-check the declaration.
(2) The customs authorities after releasing the goods to verify the details of the declaration, inspect the commercial documents and data for import or export operations in respect of goods or to subsequent commercial transactions with them. This control takes place when the declarant, if any person directly or indirectly with the above operations, as well as any other person holding such documents and data. The customs authorities may inspect the goods if they can be presented.
(3) Where a re-examination of the declaration or follow-up is found that the arrangement is implemented on the basis of incorrect or incomplete information, the customs authorities take the necessary measures, taking into account new circumstances.
(4) Any person directly or indirectly related to the operations of import, export and transit of goods is required to retain a 5-year period all documentation in specific operations, regardless of the medium. This period starts from the end of the calendar year in which:
1. for goods imported under shaped other than those specified in item 2, or goods declared for export have adopted the customs declarations;
2. for goods imported under formed with reduced or zero duty because of their use for specific purposes they cease to be under customs supervision;
3. goods placed under another customs procedure, customs procedure ends;
4. goods placed in free zone or free warehouse, the goods leave a free zone or free warehouse.
Art. 84a. (New - SG. 45 of 2005) (1) Follow-up of the declaration is made on all persons who exercise or are related to the activity which has control over the customs authorities by law.
(2) The follow-up to check the legality of the inspected person in the implementation of the regimes, procedures and measures of trade policy and to implement its obligations to pay public state receivables collected by customs authorities.
(3) Customs authorities shall establish impartial facts and circumstances under par. 2 as detrimental, and in favor of the inspected person. During the review, the review is entitled to receive information on established facts and circumstances to the extent it does not hinder her performance
(4) The verification includes products, stocks, accounts, marketing, accounting and other records of the

inspected person, which is relevant to the case.
(5) (Amended - SG. 105 of 2005) the Customs authorities are obliged to explain to the checked person and the other participants in proceedings under this Act, their procedural rights provided in the Tax Procedure Code, the criminal- Procedure Code and provide an opportunity to exercise them.

Art. 84b. (New - SG. 45 of 2005) (1) The subsequent review carried out by customs officers in specialized units for follow-up in the central office management and regional customs offices. If necessary, further control units may be created and territorial customs offices in accordance with Art. 11, para. 3.
(2) The jurisdiction of the unit follow-up is determined by the address of, respectively, the permanent address of the inspected person. Jurisdiction of the unit follow-up in central office administration is a national.
(3) If necessary to establish the facts and circumstances concerning the operation of the inspected person in his unit, facility, business or property located within the jurisdiction of another unit for further review, the Director of Customs Agency can allow performing all checks or separate action the Unit for follow-up.
(4) The need for specific knowledge and expertise in the examination may be involved and other customs officers to possess them, or they may be required expertise.

Art. 84v. (New - SG. 45 of 2005) (1) check in the follow-up is based on an order for the award.
(2) The order under para. 1 is issued by:
1. Director of Customs Agency or its authorized officials of the Customs Agency;
2. Director of Regional Customs Directorate and Head of the office to which notify the Director of the Customs Agency.
(3) The order under para. 1 shall be issued in writing and include:
1. legal and factual grounds for the inspection;
2. names and position of the customs officers to carry out the inspection;
3. data inspected person;
4. RIP;
5. the type and scope of inspection;
6. date of commencement of examination and duration of her performance
(4) The order under para. 1 is given to the person examined by the customs authorities at the beginning of the investigation. Inspected person can be informed prior to beginning the examination, if they do not jeopardize the purpose of her
(5) The order under para. 1 may be amended by a new order driven by the body entrusted with the inspection. The amendment shall be deemed made by the date of issuance of new notes to be handed to the inspected person.
(6) The period of inspection within the follow-up could not be more than two months.
(7) In the period reasonably necessary under par. 6 can be extended by no more than four months with a new order driven by the body entrusted with the inspection.
(8) The authority delegated examination, proceedings:
1. in case of force majeure - the day of the event;
2. when instituted judicial or administrative proceedings relevant to the outcome of the check - after presenting a certificate to that fact issued by the authority before which proceedings are opened;
3. otherwise provided by law.
(9) The authority delegated inspection may order suspending it for a specified period not exceeding 30 days, at the reasoned request of the inspected person, after checking the facts.
(10) The period of inspection is not on the date of occurrence of the circumstance to stop it until the date of resuming her
(11) The investigation shall be resumed by order of the authority which is entrusted, in case of the reason for her suspension order shall be served on the resumption inspected person.
(12) award orders, modification, suspension or resumption of examination is not subject to appeal.

Art. 84g. (New - SG. 45 of 2005) (1) person shall be inspected to assist customs authorities in clarifying the facts and circumstances which are important for verification, such as:
1. provides business, accounting and other records;
2. provide explanations requested by the customs authorities;
3. prepare reports;
4. authenticated by customs authorities requested information and copies of documents;
5. provide access to offices, warehouses and boxes;
6. conditions and provides a place for the inspection;

7. determine the persons to assist in carrying out the inspection.
(2) The person shall be inspected in by the customs authorities a reasonable time but not less than 24 hours to submit all data, information, documents, papers, articles, media and other evidence of the facts and circumstances, subject to establishment during the inspection and identify all persons, state and municipal authorities in which they are located. This period may be extended if this important reasons.
(3) The person shall be inspected to ensure that the customs authorities access to its automated information system, where the collection, storage and processing of information under par. 2 is effected by such a system.
(4) Failing to carry out the inspection in person checked it out in the office. In this case, the authorities compile a record and inventory of documents, property and other evidence submitted to them.

Art. 84d. (New - SG. 45 of 2005) (1) Evidence in proceedings under this section may be factual data relating to the circumstances of importance for verification purposes, contribute to their clarification and were collected and verified procedure provided for in this Law.
(2) The evidence is collected and verified by written explanations, reports and declarations of the inspected persons or their representatives, minutes of explanations third participating in the administrative process persons reports for the actions of the customs authorities, expertise, and official documents obtained by exchanging information with governments of other countries through international cooperation and other means provided by law.
(3) All persons, state and municipal authorities are required within 7 days of receipt of a request by the customs authorities to provide data, information, documents, papers, articles, media and other evidence mentioned in the request on the facts and circumstances. This period may be extended by the authority entrusted with the inspection.
(4) Upon verification in writing the customs authorities may request assistance from other authorities to carry out work to establish the responsibilities or obligations of the inspected person.
(5) Where to clarify arising from the checks, circumstances and issues needed special knowledge, such as the customs authorities have, on their own initiative or at the request of the person examined, the body entrusted with the inspection, an expert. When the expert was appointed at the request of the inspected person, the cost of making it are on his behalf.

Art. 84e. (New - SG. 45 of 2005) (1) During the checks, customs authorities may take action to secure evidence through inventory or through a search and seizure under Art. 16, para. 7 and 8 of the documents, papers and other media, goods and means of information processing as well as copying information from the technical media that enable her to play by taking the necessary measures to preserve its authenticity .
(2) Where no other option for securing evidence, the customs authorities can seal the offices, funds, stocks and other commercial premises within 72 hours.
(3) action under par. 1 and 2 are drawn, a copy of which shall be served on the inspected person.
(4) Within the period under para. 2 authority assigned inspection may require the district court at the location of the object extension of the sealing. Court ruling on the date of receipt of the request in closed session with the order, setting a time period of the closure. The definition is not subject to appeal.
(5) The customs authorities shall suspend sealing, if by the deadline under par. 2nd District Court has not resolved his extension.
(6) Actions to ensure that evidence may be appealed within three days before the body entrusted with the inspection, which give a reasoned decision later in the day following receipt of the complaint. In its decision the authority entrusted with the inspection, may confirm or partially or annul the contested action.
(7) (Amended - SG. 30, 2006, effective 1.03.2007) The Omission of the authority under par. 6 in the prescribed period or dismiss the appeal action to ensure the evidence can be challenged as to their legality within 7 days of the deadline for a decision under para. 6, respectively, of receiving the decision before the administrative court at the location of the body entrusted with the inspection. The court shall rule within 14 days an order can not be appealed.
(8) The appeal does not suspend action to secure evidence.
(9) The decision under para. 6 or definition under par. 7, ordering the suspension of action to ensure that evidence is implemented by the customs authority which has taken them.

Art. 84zh. (New - SG. 45 of 2005, amended. No.. 105 of 2005) For all matters concerning the collection, verification and provision of evidence and production of means of proof, the relevant provisions of the Tax Procedure Code .

Art. 84z. (New - SG. 45 of 2005) In the inspection, the customs authorities may impose provisional protective measures under Chapter twenty-sixth, Section Ia to prevent the commission to act on the property of the person examined, due to that the collection of customs duties and other public state receivables will be impossible or would greatly hamper.
Art. 84i. (New - SG. 45 of 2005) (1) Customs authorities conducting an examination under the follow-up, may find out their designated items for taxation and to adopt a set of measures to avoid trade policy when there is one of the following circumstances:
1. missing or not provided accounting under the Accounting Act or doing the bookkeeping does not allow for establishing or determining the amount of public state receivables, and where the documents necessary to establish public state receivables due to the application of commercial policy measures, are destroyed not by the established order;
2. required documents are missing or damaged so that they are unfit for use;
3. necessary additional data and information can be obtained, as checked person is not found at the registered office or its permanent address after thorough and documented search by customs authorities;
4. in the inspection inspected person did not submit evidence relevant term of art. 84g, para. 2.
(2) In cases under para. 1, the customs authorities shall take account of any relevant person to verify the circumstances on:
1. type and nature of actual activity carried out;
2. paid customs duties and other public state receivables;
3. movement and remains in bank accounts;
4. official and private documents;
5. contracts made by the inspected person in connection with the performance of its activities;
6. difference between delivered and raw materials and supplies;
7. aggregated data for profit, revenue or income, respectively, from other members of the same or similar activities under the same or similar conditions;
8. price and other terms of transactions, including data on such transactions between persons related to the inspected person;
9. received and carried supplies and exercised a right of deduction;
10. other evidence relevant to the case.
(3) The circumstances under par. 1 and 2 shall be reported for investigation.
(4) Where the circumstances under para. 1, item 1, 2 and 4, the customs authorities shall inform the inspected person that finds their designated items for taxation and finds that the avoidance of commercial policy measures, and set a deadline for submission of documents and advice.

Art. 84k. (New - SG. 45 of 2005) (1) When in the course of in term of art. 84v, para. 3, item 6 were collected evidence of committed customs violations or for a different amount of customs duties and other public state receivables, the customs authorities performing inspection conducted by the inspected person final discussion of the circumstances identified in the inspection and possible legal consequences of , unless the inspected person renounces in writing by the discussion. Within 7 days of the final discussion inspected person may submit written observations on the preliminary findings and new evidence.
(2) held a final discussion is drawn up, signed by customs officials, verified, and inspected person.
(3) If the person refuses checked final discussion or not signing the Protocol under par. 2, this fact is attested by two witnesses.

Art. 84l. (New - SG. 45 of 2005) (1) Within 14 days after the expiry of art. 84v, para. 3, item 6 shall prepare a written report of findings which shall include:
1. number and date;
2. names and position of the customs officers verified;
3. factual and legal grounds for the inspection;
4. data inspected person;
5. the type and scope of inspection;
6. underlying action and established facts and circumstances;
7. findings;
8. measures taken to secure the evidence and the public to the state;
9. proposals for determining the amount of customs duties and other public state receivables and instituting the administrative penal proceedings;
10. Inventory of attached evidence;
11. signatures of customs officials, drew up the report and the head of the department for follow-up.
(2) evidence attached to the report are an integral part thereof. The originals of documentary evidence

collected is attached to the report, for the customs authority delegated inspection and certified copies thereof shall apply to copies intended for the inspected person.
(3) The factual findings of the report must be supported by evidence and are considered true until proven otherwise.
(4) Within 7 days of its establishment inspection report and the evidence attached thereto, shall be served on the person checked against the signature and forwarded to the authority delegated inspection follow-up. Failing this report to be served personally inspected person the customs authorities sent him a registered letter with acknowledgment of receipt.
(5) inspected person may submit written objections and to present additional evidence to the authority delegated inspection within 14 days of receipt of the report.
Art. 84 meters. (New - SG. 45 of 2005) for service of notices and documents with checks in the post-control provisions of Art. 211g.
Chapter fifteen
IMPORTS

Art. 85. (1) The formation of the import regime attaches of foreign goods duty status of goods.
(2) Imports involves the application of commercial policy measures, completion of formalities for the import of goods, taxation and customs duties.

Art. 86. (1) If after the date of declaration of imports, but before release of goods, reduce the rates of customs duties and charges having equivalent effect, the declarant may request application of more favorable rates or fees. In these cases the provisions of art. 73.
(2) Paragraph 1 shall not apply where the goods have not been released by the fault of the declarant.

Art. 87. Where a consignment of goods with different classification, which leads to a separate declaration and processing costs, inconsistent with the amount of import duties, customs authorities at the request of the declarant, agree on the whole consignment tax under the classification of goods with highest duty.

Art. 88. (1) (Amended - SG. 37 of 2003) Goods which by their specific use have been placed under import at reduced or zero rates of duty or relief shall remain under customs supervision . Customs supervision ends when:
1. defined conditions for taxation at reduced rates of duty or exemption from import duties cease to apply;
2. goods are exported or destroyed or
3. permit the use of goods for purposes other than those specified for the application of reduced or zero duty or relief after payment of customs duties.
(2) The provisions of Art. 94, para. 2 and 3 and art. 96 apply to goods referred to in para. 1, mutatis mutandis.

Art. 89. Imports lose their customs status of goods when:
1. import declaration is invalidated after release, or
2. import duties on those goods are repaid or remitted under the terms and conditions set out in regulations.
Chapter sixteen
Suspensive arrangements and customs ECONOMIC IMPACT
Section I
General provisions

Art. 90. (1) For purposes of applying the provisions of Art. 91-96:
1. the term "suspension" refers to foreign goods, the following arrangements:
a) transit;
b) warehousing;
c) the inward processing suspension system;
d) processing under customs control;
e) the temporary admission;
2. the term 'customs procedure with economic impact "refers to goods placed under the following modes:
a) customs warehousing;

b) inward processing;
c) processing under customs control;
d) temporary admission;
e) OPT.
(2) Goods placed under suspension, as well as goods under the inward processing drawback system, have been subject to import formalities and formalities provided for in art. 128, para. 4 are considered imports.
(3) Imported goods under the inward processing and processing under customs control, have undergone no processing or processing are considered goods in unaltered state.

Art. 91. Implementation of any economic customs procedure is allowed with a permit issued by the customs authorities.

Art. 92. Authorisations under Art. 91 and art. 106, para. 1 is issued subject to the conditions laid down for the procedure:
1. (Amended and supplemented. - SG. 63 of 2000) to persons who are able to ensure the proper conduct of operations, and
2. (Amended - SG. 63 of 2000) where the customs authorities are able to provide supervision and control system without having to introduce administrative arrangements disproportionate to the economic needs of the system.

Art. 93. (1) The conditions under which the relevant arrangements shall be specified in the permit.
(Second) the permit holder is required to notify the customs authorities of any change after it is issued, which may influence its content and the conditions for its implementation.

Art. 94. (1) The rules set out in cases where goods manufactured from goods under suspension shall not be considered for local goods produced are considered to be placed under the same regime.
(2) placing the goods under a suspensive customs authorities may require provision of the debt.
(3) any suspension in the rules may provide for special provisions concerning the provision of security.

Art. 95. (1) (amended and supplemented. - SG. 63 of 2000) Customs economically suspension is discharged when the goods placed under the arrangement or to compensating or processed products derived from new permitted customs.
(2nd) The customs authorities shall take all necessary measures defined in the Rules for the goods to which the procedure has not been discharged under the conditions.

Art. 96. Rights and obligations of the holder of the arrangements may, under certain conditions by the customs authorities, be transferred successively to other persons eligible to benefit from the scheme.

Section IITransit

Art. 97. (1) (Amended - SG. 37 of 2003, effective 1.11.2003) The transit procedure allows transport from one point to another within the customs territory of the Republic of Bulgaria:
1. foreign goods without being subject to import duties and without being subject to commercial policy measures;
2. (Amended - SG. 63 of 2000 pcs. 37 of 2003, with effect from 1.11.2003) circulation in cases and under conditions determined by the regulations for which such products are provided restrictions or incentives for exports to these measures should not be avoided or used improperly.
(2) (Amended - SG. 37 of 2003, effective 1.11.2003) The transport of para. 1st place:
1. under the provisions for transit in the Republic of Bulgaria;
2. under cover of TIR Carnet used as a transit guarantee document under the Customs Convention on International Transport of Goods under Cover of TIR Carnets (TIR Convention 1975), where:
a) (amended - SG. 37 of 2003, effective 1.11.2003) the shipment has commenced or is to end outside the country, or
b) (amended - SG. 37 of 2003, with effect from 1.11.2003) carriage applies to consignments of goods to be

unloaded in the country, and which are conveyed with goods landing abroad;
3. under the ATA carnet used as a transit guarantee document under the Customs Convention on Temporary Admission of Goods (ATA Convention 1961) and other conventions to which Bulgaria is a party;
4. (New - SG. 37 of 2003, with effect from 1.11.2003) under cover of form 302 (NATO Manifesto 302) under ratified, promulgated and entered into treaties of the Republic of Bulgaria with North Atlantic Treaty Organisation , countries - NATO members and partner countries participating in the Partnership for Peace ";
5. (Prev. 4 - SG. 37 of 2003, with effect from 1.11.2003) by mail, including parcels.
(3) Transit shall be without prejudice to any special provisions relating to the movement of goods placed under the economic regime.

Art. 98. (Amended - SG. 37 of 2003, effective 1.11.2003) (1) The transit ends and obligations of the principal is satisfied where goods placed under the procedure and required documents are presented at the office, in accordance with the rules.
(2) The customs authorities closed transit when established on the basis of a comparison of available departure data available at the office is evidence that the procedure has ended correctly.

Art. 99. (Amended - SG. 37 of 2003, effective 1.11.2003) The transit to goods in the territory of another state applies when:
1. this possibility is provided in an international agreement or
2. transport of goods in another country is based on a single transport document issued to the customs territory of the Republic of Bulgaria, in which case the arrangements shall be suspended in the territory of another state.

Bulgarian to English translation

Art. 100. (Amended - SG. 37 of 2003, effective 1.11.2003) (1) The principal of transit is required to provide collateral to secure payment of customs duty and other public state receivables that may arise with the goods.
(2) A guarantee may be:
1. once covering a transit operation, or
2. generally covering several transit operations when customs authorities have allowed the principal to use such a comprehensive guarantee.
(3) A permit under par. 2, item 2 shall be given to residents who:
1. regularly use transit or for which customs authorities know that they are able to fulfill their obligations to the scheme and
2. have not committed serious or repeated breaches of customs or tax legislation.
(4) Persons who demonstrate to customs authorities to meet the higher requirements for reliability, can obtain permission to use a comprehensive guarantee for a reduced amount or dispensation from the obligation of a guarantor. Additional criteria for this permit include:
1. proper use of transit for a certain period;
2. cooperation with customs authorities and
3. to permit exemption for collateral - good enough financial position to cover the liabilities of individuals.
(5) Detailed rules for applying the criteria and procedure for granting permission under par. 4 is determined by the regulations.
(6) A permit for exemption from submission of security under par. 4 does not apply to transit operations involving goods as defined in regulations as an increased risk.
(7) Subject to the principles in para. 4, may temporarily prohibit the use of a comprehensive guarantee for a reduced amount for transit as an exceptional measure in special circumstances.
(8) Taking into account the principles in para. 4, may temporarily prohibit the use of general security for the transit of goods in general use of collateral have been identified as a wide range of fraud.
(9) The measures under par. 7 and 8 are introduced by order of the Director of Customs Agency, to be published in the Official Gazette.

Art. 101. (Amended - SG. 37 of 2003, with effect from 1.11.2003) is not required to furnish a guarantee for:
1. transport by sea and air;
2. transfer of power and pipelines;
3. carriage by rail from licensed railway carriers and postal services including parcel;
4. services defined by an act of the Council of Ministers.

Art. 102. (Amended and supplemented. - SG. 63 of 2000, amended. No.. 37 of 2003, effective 1.11.2003)
(1) The responsible person is the holder of transit. The responsible person must:
1. to produce the goods intact at the customs office within the prescribed period and subject to the measures taken by the customs authorities to identify them;
2. comply with the provisions for transit.
(2) Notwithstanding the obligations of the responsible person under par. A carrier or consignee who accepts goods and know that they are placed in transit, is also required to submit them intact at the office of destination within the prescribed period and subject to the measures taken by customs authorities for their identification.

Art. 103. (1) (Prev. text of art. 103 - SG. 37 of 2003, effective 1.11.2003) The terms, conditions and exceptions in the implementation of transit are defined in the Rules.
(2) (New - SG. 37 of 2003, with effect from 1.11.2003) Subject to the measures provided for the goods shall be allowed:
1. implementation through bilateral or multilateral agreements on soft formalities applicable to certain goods or activities under the agreements mentioned criteria;
2. introduction by the Council of Ministers of the formalities for soft goods under certain conditions.

Section III Warehousing

Art. 104. (1) The customs warehousing procedure permit the placement and storage in a customs warehouse:
1. foreign goods are not subject to import duties and not subject to commercial policy measures;
2. circulation, which under current regulations when they are in a bonded warehouse provided application of measures such as export.
(2) Customs warehouse means any place approved by the customs authorities and under the supervision of a place where you can store the goods under certain conditions.
(3) Cases in which the goods under para. 1 may be placed under the customs warehousing procedure without being located in a customs warehouse shall be determined by the regulations.

Art. 105. (1) The customs warehouse may be public or private, is a public warehouse, which can be used for storage of goods of all persons is a private customs warehouse can be used for storage of goods by the storer.
(2) warehousekeeper is the person authorized to operate a customs warehouse.
(3) Depositor in a store is the person responsible for the declaration placing the goods under customs warehousing or person to whom those rights and obligations are transferred.

Art. 106. (1) opening and operation of the warehouse is permitted after authorization by the customs authorities, except where the warehouse is operated by these bodies.
(2) Any person who wishes to open and operate a customs warehouse shall submit a written request to the customs authorities, containing the information required for authorization and demonstrating economic need for warehousing. The authorization shall specify the conditions under which a customs warehouse shall be opened and managed.
(3) The permit shall be issued only to residents.

Art. 107. Storekeeper shall:
1. to ensure no diversion of goods from customs supervision during their storage in a customs warehouse;
2. (Amended - SG. 37 of 2003, effective 1.11.2003) to fulfill the obligations arising from the storage of goods;
3. comply with the conditions specified in the authorization.

Art. 108. (1) (Amended - SG. 63 of 2000) Where the authorization concerns a public warehouse, the obligations under Art. 107, item 1 and / or 2 may be assigned only to depositors in the store.
(2) The depositor is always responsible for meeting obligations arising from the placing of goods under the customs warehousing.

Art. 109. Rights and duties of storekeeper can be transferred to another person authorized by the customs authorities.
Art. 110. Customs authorities subject to the provisions of art. 94 entitled to require the storekeeper to provide a guarantee of its obligations under Art. 107.

Art. 111. (1) stock records of goods placed under the customs warehousing procedure is conducted by a person approved by the authorities, approved by those terms and conditions, except in cases where public warehouse is operated by the customs authorities.
(2) Goods under the customs warehousing procedure shall be entered in the documents immediately after their introduction in the store.
(3) Subject to the provisions of Art. 92 customs authorities may not require stock records when:
1. (Amended - SG. 63 of 2000 extra. No.. 37 of 2003, effective 1.11.2003) the obligations under Art. 107, item 1 and / or 2 are assigned only to the depositor and
2. goods are placed under the customs warehousing with a written declaration of the normal procedure or a commercial or other document, together with an application for placing them under this scheme.

Art. 112. (1) Where an economic need exists and not to hamper customs control, customs authorities may allow:
1. a customs warehouse of goods except goods mentioned in Art. 104 para. 1, p. 2;
2. processing in a customs warehouse of foreign goods admitted for inward processing, subject to the requirements of the regime;
3. processing in the warehouse as non-admitted under the procedure for processing under customs control, subject to the requirements of the regime;
4. formalities can not be performed in a customs warehouse under items 2 and 3 according to the rules.
(2) In cases under para. 1, the goods shall not be placed under the customs warehousing.
(3) The customs authorities may require goods under par. To bring a report pursuant to Art. 111.

Art. 113. (1) time spent on the goods under the customs warehousing procedure is limited.
(2) Rules may be certain cases where the customs authorities may set a time limit by which the depositor is obliged to seek a new arrangement.
Art. 114. (1) During the customs warehousing to import goods may be carried out routine operations under rules designed to preserve them, improve their appearance or marketable quality or prepare them for distribution or resale.
(2) Operations under par. First be agreed in advance with customs authorities to determine the conditions for them.

Art. 115. (1) Goods placed under the customs warehousing procedure may be temporarily removed from the customs warehouse, where required by circumstances. Removal must be authorized in advance by the customs authorities, which stipulate the conditions for its fulfillment.
(2) During the stay outside the customs warehouse the goods may be subject to the operations of art. 114 under the conditions specified therein.

Art. 116. Goods under the customs warehousing may be transferred from one customs warehouse to another with the permission of customs authorities.

Art. 117. (Amended - SG. 63 of 2000 pcs. 37 of 2003, effective 1.11.2003) (1) Where a customs debt on importation of goods and the customs value of such goods is based on the price actually paid or payable which includes the cost of storage and preservation of goods during their stay in the warehouse, those costs should be included in the customs value, provided they are separated from the actually paid or payable payment price of the goods.
(2) Where imported goods have undergone routine operations within the meaning of art. 114, at the request of the declarant for fixing the import duties are applied to the data type, quantity and customs value, when the customs debt incurred would be invoked for this product if they had not undergone such handling. Exceptions to these provisions are provided in the Rules.
(3) When foreign goods are placed under the import of art. 82, para. 1, item 3 without submitting to customs authorities in determining the amount of import duties are valid species, customs value and quantity of such goods at the time they were placed under the customs warehousing procedure, provided that these elements of taxation have been adopted or released by the customs authorities in placing the goods under the customs warehousing procedure and the person concerned has not submitted a request for application of the taxation elements valid at the time when the customs debt. Done clearance does not preclude application of the follow-up.

Section IV Inward

Art. 118. (1) Subject to the requirements of Art. 119 inward processing allowed to be carried out one or more transactions in the customs territory of the Republic of Bulgaria on the improvement of:

1. foreign goods intended for re-export of compensating products, without being subject to import duties and without being subject to commercial policy measures;
2. (Suppl. - SG. 63 of 2000) imported goods that will be repaid or remitted import duty if exported as compensating products outside the customs territory of Bulgaria.
(2) For the purpose of inward processing:
1. suspension system means the inward processing procedure under par. 1, p. 1;
2. drawback system means inward processing under par. 1, p. 2;
3. processing operations:
a) processing of goods, including installation and acquisition of other goods;
b) processing of goods;
c) repair of goods, including restoring them;
d) use of certain goods in the rules that are not found in the compensating products, but which allow or facilitate their production even if they are wholly or partly in the production process;
4. compensating products means products resulting from processing operations of the goods;
5. equivalent goods are domestic products over imported goods used for manufacture of compensating products;
6. yield is the amount or percentage of compensating products obtained from processing of a given quantity of imported goods.

Art. 119. (1) The customs authorities:
1. compensating products to be obtained from equivalent goods;
2. compensating products obtained from equivalent goods to be exported outside the customs territory of the Republic of Bulgaria before the introduction of imported goods.
(2nd) Equivalent goods must be of the same quality and have the same characteristics as the imported goods. In certain cases, the regulations may allow goods to be equivalent in the advanced stage of manufacture than the import goods.
(3) For customs purposes in the application of para. 1, imported goods shall be considered equivalent, and equivalent - for import.
(4) (amended and supplemented. - SG. 37 of 2003, effective 1.11.2003) The application of the provision of para. 1 may be prohibited, restricted or relaxed in the terms and conditions set out in regulations.
(5) In cases under para. 1, item 2, where the compensating products subject to export duties and those products not be exported or re-exported under the inward processing procedure, the holder of the permit provides for the duties within the prescribed period if the imported goods are not imported.

Art. 120. The authorization shall be issued at the request of the person who carries out or arranges for the implementation of processing operations.

Art. 121. The permit is issued to residents by allowing the issuance of permit and non-residents, if imports of a commercial nature:
1. (Suppl. - SG. 37 of 2003, effective 1.11.2003) the possible identification of imported goods in the compensating products, except products of art. 118, para. 2, item 3, letter "d" and for goods under Art. 119 - where it is possible to verify compliance with the conditions provided for equivalent goods and
2. (Suppl. - SG. 37 of 2003, with effect from 1.11.2003) where the inward processing helps create more favorable conditions for export or re-export of compensating products and do not affect basic economic interests producers in Bulgaria (Economic conditions). Cases where economic conditions are deemed to be fulfilled are defined in the Rules.

Art. 122. (1) The customs authorities shall specify the period within which the compensating products must be exported or re-exported or assigned another customs. That period is determined according to the length of processing operations and dispose of compensating products.
(2) (Supplemented - SG. 63 of 2000) period starts from the date on which foreign goods are placed under the inward processing. The customs authorities may extend this period, a duly substantiated request by the holder of the permit. The customs authorities may allow a period starting in the month or quarter shall expire on the last day of the subsequent month, quarter respectively.
(3) In applying the provisions of art. 119, para. 1, item 2, the customs authorities shall specify the deadline for foreign goods and declared for the procedure. This period starts from the date of declaration of export of compensating products obtained from equivalent goods.
(4) for certain import goods processing operations or in the rules can be set specific deadlines.

Art. 123. (1) Customs authorities approved yield for the processing operations of the goods or the method of fixing. Yield is determined based on actual conditions in which place or should be done processing

operation.
(2) In the case of normally carry out processing of goods with constant characteristics in identical technological conditions conducive to the manufacture of compensating products of uniform quality, based on accumulated data, the regulations may set standard rates of yield.
Art. 124. Cases and conditions under which goods in the unaltered state or compensating products are to be placed under import, shall be determined by the regulations.

Art. 125. (1) Where a customs debt, its amount is determined on the basis of the taxation elements appropriate to the import goods at the time of adoption of the declaration placing them under the inward processing, taking into account the provisions of Art. 126.
(2) (Amended - SG. 63 of 2000) If the adoption of import declaration, there is preferential tariff treatment within tariff quotas or ceilings on identical goods declared, these goods can enjoy preferences provided under provided that at the time of adoption of the declaration for inward processing imported goods are eligible for preferential tariff treatment.

Art. 126. Apart from art. 125 compensating products:
1. (Amended - SG. 63 of 2000) shall be subject to import duties for these products when they are placed under the import and included in the list annexed to these Regulations, and if they are in amounts corresponding to a yield part of the exported compensating products not included in the list. The authorization holder may request taxation of these products in the art. 125;
2. be subject to import duties under certain provisions of suspension or free zone or free warehouse if they are placed under the procedure or in a free zone or free warehouse by:
a) request that person's charge may be made under the provisions of Art. 125;
b) where the compensating products have been one of those customs lines, except for processing under customs control, the amount of import duties shall be not less than the amount determined under the provisions of Art. 125;
3. may be taxed under the regime of processing under customs control where the imported goods may be placed under the procedure;
4. (Suppl. - SG. 63 of 2000) may benefit from a more favorable tariff treatment by reason of their purpose, if such treatment is provided for identical goods imported;
5. (Suppl. - SG. 63 of 2000) shall be exempt from import duties if such release is scheduled for identical goods imported in the cases. 181, para. 1.

Art. 127. (1) The compensating products and goods intact, or parts thereof may be temporarily exported for further processing outside the customs territory of the Republic of Bulgaria in terms of outward processing.
(2) Where in respect of reimported products and goods referred to in para. A customs debt arises, subject to:
1. (Suppl. - SG. 63 of 2000) compensating products or goods intact under par. 1, whose import duties shall be determined in accordance with Art. 125 and 126, and
2. products reimported after processing outside the customs territory of the Republic of Bulgaria, the amount of import duty is calculated under outward processing under the same conditions which would have applied had the products exported under this regime would be allowed for import before export.

Art. 128. (1) (Amended - SG. 37 of 2003, with effect from 1.11.2003) Application of drawback is for all goods, except when at the time of declaration of admission:
1. imported goods are quantitative restrictions on imports;
2. imported goods applied tariff measures within quotas;
3. for imported goods is required to import or export licenses or certificates under the CAP;
4. compensating products are provided export subsidies or taxes.
(2) (Amended - SG. 37 of 2003, with effect from 1.11.2003) There shall be no refund if at the time of declaration of export of compensating products are required for submission of import or export licenses or certificates under the CAP or they provide export subsidies or taxes.
(3) (Amended - SG. 37 of 2003, with effect from 1.11.2003) Exceptions to par. 1 and 2 can be defined in the Rules.
(4) import declaration shall indicate that the system is being used in recovery, and the number and date of the authorization application.
Art. 129. When the drawback system shall apply the provisions of Art. 119, para. 1, item 2 and para. 3 and

5, Art. 122, para. 3, Art. 124, art. 125, art. 126, item 3 and art. 132.

Art. 130. Temporary exportation of compensating products carried out in accordance with Art. 127, para. 1 is not considered for export within the meaning of art. 131, unless these products are not reimported into the Republic of Bulgaria within the prescribed period.

Art. 131. (1) The authorization holder is entitled to demand repayment or remission of import duties where evidence presented to customs authorities that goods imported under the drawback system or compensating products obtained from them are:
1. exported, or
2. for subsequent re-exported, placed under transit, customs warehousing, temporary import for inward processing suspension system or a free zone or free warehouse.
(2) The provisions of para. 1 applies if the conditions are satisfied to benefit from the procedure.
(3) receipt of customs under par. 1, item 2 imported goods and compensating products are considered foreign goods.
(4) An application for refund is filed within a period determined by the regulations.
(5) (Supplemented - SG. 153 of 1998 pcs. 63 2000) compensating products or goods in the unaltered state placed under a free zone or free warehouse or under par. 1 may be placed under the import authorized by the customs authorities. In this case, subject to the requirements of Art. 126, item 2, the amount reimbursed or remitted import duties to the amount of the debt.
(6) In determining the amount of import duties to be repaid or remitted, the provisions of Art. 126, section 1, mutatis mutandis.

Art. 132. The inward processing procedure under the suspension system compensating products shall be exempt from export duties to be levied on such products of domestic products instead of imported.

Section VProcessing under customs control

Art. 133. Procedure for processing under customs control shall allow the customs territory of the Republic of Bulgaria of foreign goods for processing in order to change the type or state, without charge import duties or be subject to commercial policy measures. The resulting processing products (processed products) are formed for import into the country after the payment due to import duties.

Art. 134. (Suppl. - SG. 37 of 2003, effective on 11/01/2003) case and the specific conditions under which it can be used for processing under customs control shall be determined in the rules.

Art. 135. (1) Authorisation for processing under customs control at the request of the person who carries out or arranges for the implementation of the processing.
(2) The permit shall be issued to residents where:
1. (Amended - SG. 63 of 2000) imported goods can be identified in the processed products;
2. after processing of goods is economically justified to recover the species and their condition, they were placed under the procedure;
3. application of the system will not lead to circumvention of the rules of origin and quantitative restrictions provided for imported goods;
4. (Suppl. - SG. 37 of 2003, effective 1.11.2003) the implementation of the system stimulate the activity in the country, without adversely affecting the essential economic interests of local producers of similar goods (economic conditions) . Cases where economic conditions are deemed to be fulfilled are defined in the Rules.

Art. 136. The provisions of Art. 122, para. 1 and 2 and art. 123 shall apply for processing under customs control, taking appropriate account of the specifics of this arrangement.

Art. 137. Where a customs debt for goods in an unaltered state or products are at an intermediate stage of processing with regard to the authorization provided in the amount of this obligation is determined based on the elements of the charge to the import goods in the declaration of processing of goods under customs control.

Art. 138. (1) (Amended - SG. 153 of 1998) in allowing a procedure for processing under customs control where the imported goods were eligible for the use of preferential tariff treatment if it is applicable to products identical to grooming import processed products for calculation of import duties on processed products are the preferential duty rates.
(2) The provisions of para. 1 apply to tariff quotas or ceilings. In such cases of tariff quotas or ceilings applicable to acceptance of the customs import declaration will be deducted the amount of import goods used for the processed product.
Section VI
Temporary importation

Art. 139. The temporary import permit use of the customs territory of the Republic of Bulgaria, with full or partial exemption from import duties and without the application of commercial policy measures on foreign goods to be re-exported without having undergone any change except normal depreciation due to use.

Art. 140. Authorization for temporary importation shall be granted at the request of the person who uses or orders the use of these products.

Art. 141. (1) Customs authorities do not permit the temporary import where import goods is impossible to identify.
(2) The customs authorities may authorize the temporary importation of goods without identifying where the nature or operations to be undertaken will lead to abuse of the procedure.

Art. 142. (1) The period within which import goods must be re-exported or assigned a new customs are determined by customs authorities. This period should be sufficient to implement the authorized use.
(2) (Supplemented - SG. 63 of 2000) The maximum period during which goods may remain under temporary importation is 24 months, subject to the provisions on the specific terms of art. 143. The customs authorities may set a shorter period with the consent of the person concerned.
(3) (Supplemented - SG. 63 of 2000) In exceptional circumstances, customs authorities may extend the periods referred to in para. 1 and 2 at the request of the person concerned, within reasonable limits, to make the authorized use.

Art. 143. Cases, the terms and conditions under which it may be allowed temporary importation procedure with full exemption from import duties shall be determined by the regulations.

Art. 144. (1) (Amended - SG. 37 of 2003, with effect from 1.11.2003) Use of temporary admission with partial relief from import duties shall be granted for goods which are not indicated in cases Art. 143 or referred to, but do not meet all the conditions to the granting of temporary admission with full exemption from import duties.
(2) (Amended - SG. 37 of 2003, effective 1.11.2003) The conditions for the use of temporary admission with partial relief from import duties and goods to which this regime can be used are defined in the Rules.

Art. 145. (1) (Amended - SG. 153 of 1998) the amount of import duties on goods placed under temporary admission with partial relief, for each calendar month or part month during which a this scheme is 3 per cent of the amount of duty payable on those goods if they were admitted under the admission of the date on which they were placed under temporary importation.
(2) The total amount of partial import duties payable shall not exceed the amount of duty that would be payable if the goods are placed under the import of the date on which they were placed under temporary importation, without added interest due.

(3) The transfer of rights and obligations arising from the temporary importation procedure under Art. 96 does not require application of the same relief for any period of use.
(4) If a transfer of the rights and obligations is made with partial relief for both the principal during the same month, the first holder due to the amount of import duties on the entire month.

Art. 146. (1) (Amended - SG. 63 of 2000) When a customs duty for imported goods, its size is determined on the basis of the taxation elements appropriate to the goods at the time of adoption of the declaration placing them under temporary admission. In cases under Art. 143 down in the Rules, the amount of liability is determined on the basis of the taxation elements appropriate to the goods at the time of occurrence of the customs duty.
(2) Where by reason other than the placing of goods under temporary admission with partial relief from import duties, a customs duty for these goods, the amount of that debt is equal to the difference between the duties specified under par. 1, and duties established under Art. 145.

Section VII OPT

Art. 147. (1) Subject to the provisions of Art. 156-161 and Art. 127 applied to the standard exchange system, outward processing permit to export goods temporarily resident outside the Republic of Bulgaria to undergo operations on their improvement and the resulting products of these operations have been placed under imports full or partial exemption from import duties.
(2) Temporary export of goods to include their tax duties, application of commercial policy measures and other formalities for the export of goods outside the customs territory of Bulgaria.
(3) For the purpose of outward processing:
1. temporarily exported goods are goods placed under outward processing;
2. processing operations are the operations of art. 118, para. 2, item 3, points "a" "b" and "c";
3. compensating products means products resulting from processing operations of the goods;
4. yield is the amount or percentage of compensating products obtained from processing of a given quantity of temporary export goods.

Art. 148. (1) can not be placed under the outward processing of goods:
1. whose export gives rise to repayment or remission of import duties;
2. (Amended - SG. 37 of 2003, with effect from 1.11.2003) which were pre-export import under a full exemption from import duties on account of their specific purposes, while the conditions set for granting such relief are in force;
3. export gives entitlement to subsidy.
(2) Exceptions to the rule of par. 1 item 2 can be defined in the Rules.

Art. 149. (1) outward processing permit shall be issued at the request of the person who ordered the execution of the processing operations.
(2) Use of outward processing may be granted to another person of Bulgarian origin goods under this Act, where the processing operation consists in incorporating those goods into goods obtained outside the Republic of Bulgaria and imported as compensating products . Application of the system is permitted if facilitating the sale of exported goods, without prejudice to the fundamental interests of domestic producers of goods identical or similar to the imported compensating products.
(3) case and the specific conditions of application of para. 2 is defined in the Rules.

Art. 150. The permit is issued to residents where:
1. it is possible to establish that the compensating products resulting from the processing of temporary export goods. Exceptions to this provision may be specified in the regulations;
2. Authorisation to use outward processing will not materially affect the economic interests of local producers.

Art. 151. (1) The period within which the compensating products must be reimported into the customs territory of the Republic of Bulgaria is determined by the customs authorities. That period may be extended at the reasoned request of the holder of the permit.

(2) The yield of the processing operation of the goods shall be determined by the customs authorities, where necessary, the method for its determination.

Art. 152. (1) Full or partial exemption from import duties under Art. 153, para. 1 is permitted provided that the compensating products are declared for importation by or on behalf of:
1. holder of the permit; or
2. any other resident, if it has obtained the consent of the holder of the permit if the permit conditions are met.
(2) shall not be granted full or partial exemption from import duties under Art. 153, para. 1, where one or more of the conditions or obligations under the outward processing procedure have not been met, except where the failure has not contravened the proper functioning of the system.

Art. 153. (1) Total or partial exemption from import duties under Art. 147 para. 1 is done by deducting the amount of import duties due on imported compensating products, the amount of import duties that would be caused by the same date for the temporary export goods if they are introduced into the customs territory of the Republic of Bulgaria the country where have undergone surgery or last processing operation.
(2) (Supplemented - SG. 37 of 2003, effective 1.11.2003) The amount to be deducted under par. 1 is calculated based on the amount and type of temporary export goods on the date of adoption of the declaration placing them under the outward processing and based on other elements of taxation applicable to those goods on the date of declaration of imports compensating products. In applying paragraph. 1 the temporary export goods that is to be taken into account for those goods in determining the customs value of compensating products in accordance with Art. 38, para. 1, item 2, letter "a" or if the value can not be determined in this way - the difference between the customs value of compensating products and the processing costs determined by any other suitable method.
(3) (Amended - SG. 37 of 2003, with effect from 1.11.2003) For purposes of applying para. 2:
1. the regulations define the costs are not taken into account when calculating the amount to be deducted;
2. where the temporary export goods placed under outward processing have been placed under the import duties reduced on account of their specific objectives and long as the conditions for the reduced duties remain in force, the amount to deduct the amount of import duties actually collected on their shape under imports.
(4) (New - SG. 37 of 2003, effective 1.11.2003) If the temporary export goods could be placed under in imports would benefit from reduced or zero duties on account of their specific objectives that amount of duty is taken into account, provided that these goods were subject to the same operations provided for such specific purpose in a country where they were undergoing surgery or last processing operation.
(5) (New - SG. 37 of 2003, with effect from 1.11.2003) Where compensating products qualify for preferential tariff measure within the meaning of art. 26 para. 1, item 4 or 5 and if such measure is in force for the commodities of the same tariff number as the temporary export, the amount of import duties to be taken into account when calculating the amount to be deducted under par. 1 is that which would apply if the temporary export goods eligible under which this preferential tariff measure may be applied.
(6) (former para. 4 - SG. 37 of 2003, effective 1.11.2003) If, in the context of trade between Bulgaria and other countries provided free of import duties on certain compensation products, the provisions of this Article shall not apply.

Art. 154. (1) When the processing operation is the repair of temporary export goods, their last imports made under full exemption from import duties if it is proved that the amendment was made free because of warranty obligation or manufacturing defect.
(2) Paragraph 1 shall not apply when the product defect is discovered and taken into account at the time of initial importation of this product.

Art. 155. (1) (Prev. text of art. 155 - SG. 37 of 2003, effective 1.11.2003) If the processing operation is the repair of the temporary exported goods against payment partial exemption from import duties is determining the amount of customs duties on the basis of the taxation elements compensating products on the date of declaration of their imports, the customs value is equal to the cost of repairs, if these costs are only paid to the holder of the permit and are not affected by links between it and the ongoing repair person.
(2) (New - SG. 37 of 2003, with effect from 1.11.2003) Notwithstanding the provisions of Art. 153 in the Rules can be defined in which cases and under what conditions specific goods may be placed under the import after outward processing by the processing costs are taken as the basis for determining the customs

value for purposes of applying the Customs Tariff of the Republic of Bulgaria .

Art. 156. (1) compensating products may be replaced with imported goods - a substitute product in the application of the standard exchange system and subject to the provisions of Art. 156-161.
(2) Application of the standard exchange system is authorized by the customs authorities, where the processing operation involves the repair of goods.
(3) The provisions applicable to compensating products shall apply to replacement products, except those in the art. 149, para. 2 and 3 and art. 150.
(4) The customs authorities may, under certain conditions they, prior importation of replacement products prior to export of temporarily exported goods.
(5) prior import substitute product shall provide a guarantee of import duties.

Art. 157. (1) Replacement products shall have the same classification, commercial quality and technical features designed for the repair temporarily exported goods.
(2) Where the temporary export goods have been used before export, the replacement products must also be used. The customs authorities may authorize the replacement product not be used if it is supplied free of charge due to warranty obligations or manufacturing defect.

Art. 158. Standard exchange is allowed if it is possible to verify compliance with the conditions of art. 157.

Art. 159. (1) The preliminary import export of temporarily exported goods must be made within two months from the date of the declaration of import replacement products.
(2) The customs authorities may extend the deadline under par. A reasoned request of the holder.

Art. 160. In prior importation and application of art. 153 the amount of deduction is determined by the taxation elements of the temporary export goods to the adoption of the declaration placing them under the outward processing.
Art. 161. Standard exchange does not apply to art. 149, para. 2 and 3 and art. 150.

Art. 162. The procedures provided for outward processing shall also apply to goods qualifying commercial policy measures other than tariff.

Chapter seventeenth EXPORTS

Art. 163. (1) The export procedure is the removal of goods from the customs territory of the Republic of Bulgaria and includes application of the formalities provided for the export of goods, including commercial policy measures and, where provided for - liable to export duties.
(2) Local goods intended for export shall be placed under the export. This provision does not apply to goods placed under outward processing or temporary export.
(3) The export declaration is presented to the customs office near you to prepare shipment and loading of goods for export. Exceptions to this provision may be specified in the regulations.
(4) circulation, which by law are provided as fiscal incentives for exports, export scheme may be applied if the goods do not leave the customs territory of the Republic of Bulgaria to the terms and conditions set out in regulations.

Art. 164. Exports are permitted if the goods leave the customs territory of the Republic of Bulgaria in the same condition as they were when the declaration for export.
Chapter Eighteen
Temporary exportation

Art. 165. (1) The temporary export of goods permitted to temporarily exported outside the customs territory of the Republic of Bulgaria provided to be reimported, without having undergone any change except normal

depreciation due to use.
(2) (Amended - SG. 63 of 2000) terms, conditions and deadlines for the temporary export are defined in the Rules.

Title III OTHER CUSTOMS directions

Chapter nineteenth Free zones and free warehouses

Section I General

Art. 166. Free zones and free warehouses are separate parts of the customs territory of the Republic of Bulgaria or on its premises, in which:
1. foreign goods for customs duties and commercial policy measures on imports are considered outside the customs territory of the Republic of Bulgaria, if they are placed under the import or under another customs procedure and are not consumed or used in violation of customs regulations ;
2. local goods can use the measures applied to exports of goods, if ordered by another law or the Council of Ministers.

Art. 167. (1) (Amended - SG. 37 of 2003, with effect from 1.11.2003) Free zones must be fenced, except for those under Art. 168a. Free zones and free warehouses must have defined entry and exit checkpoints.
(2) The performance of new works in the free zone shall be coordinated with customs authorities on the possibility of customs control and supervision. Coordination is carried out in 30 days. If the authorities do not decide within this period, it is assumed that coordination has taken place.

Art. 168. (1) (Supplemented - SG. 37 of 2003, effective 1.11.2003) The boundaries, entry and exit checkpoints of free zones and warehouses are subject to customs supervision, except for free zones referred to in Art. 168a.
(2) The customs authorities may exercise customs control on persons and vehicles carried their goods entering or leaving a free zone or free warehouse.
(3) Access to a free zone or free warehouse may be denied to persons not complying with this law.
(4) The importation of goods into a free zone or warehouse their stay and the removal of those goods from a free zone or warehouse can be controlled by customs authorities. In furtherance of that review all the documents accompanying the goods upon their importation into or exportation from the zone or free warehouse shall be submitted to the customs authorities or designated by them, who keeps them at their disposal. The customs authorities may require the submission of other documents. Where such checks goods must be available to the customs authorities.
Art. 168a. (New - SG. 37 of 2003, in force from 11.01.2003) (1) The Council of Ministers may designate free zones in which customs checks and formalities are carried out under the provisions for warehousing by apply for the scheme envisaged provisions on debt. In respect of these free zones do not apply Art. 170, 176 and 179.
(2) The provisions of Art. 44, para. 2, Art. 199, para. 1 pt 8 and para. 3, item 6 and art. 202, para. 1, item 5 shall not apply to free zones under par. 1.

Section II Import of goods in free zones or free warehouses

Art. 169. (1) free zone or free warehouse can be stored for both foreign and domestic products.
(2) The customs authorities may require goods presenting a hazard that can damage other goods requiring special storage conditions should be placed in such goods equipped rooms or locations.

Art. 170. (1) Subject to the provisions of Art. 168, para. 4 goods entering a free zone or free warehouse need not be presented to customs authorities or to lodge a customs declaration.
(2) In carrying out the formalities with the customs authorities shall be submitted where:
1. placed under a customs procedure which enter a free zone or free warehouse leads to the conclusion of this regime. Presentation of the goods is not necessary unless required by the provisions of the customs procedure;

2. subject to authorization for repayment or remission of import duties, provided that it allowed the entry of those goods in a free zone or free warehouse;
3. benefit from the measures under Art. 166, item 2.
(3) The customs authorities must be notified of the goods subject to export duties or other regulations governing exports.
(4) At the request of the persons concerned customs authorities certify the foreign or domestic status of goods placed in free zone or a free warehouse.

Section III Operation of free zones and free warehouses

Art. 171. (1) The length of time goods in free zones or in free warehouses.
(2) Rules can be defined terms of stay of certain goods in free zones or free warehouses.

Art. 172. (1) free zones and free warehouses are permitted Any industrial or commercial character, as well as performing services in compliance with the provisions of this Act. In pursuing these activities shall notify the customs authorities in advance.
(2) The customs authorities may prohibit or restrict the activities of para. 1 according to:
1. nature of the goods - the subject of such activities;
2. requirements of customs supervision.
(3) The customs authorities may prohibit the exercise of activity in free zones and free warehouses to persons who do not comply with the provisions of this Act.
Art. 173. (1) Foreign goods in a free zone or free warehouse may be:
1. placed under the import requirements under this scheme and the provisions of Art. 178;
2. subject to normal operations referred to in Art. 114, para. 1 without authorization;
3. placed under the inward processing under the requirements of that system;
4. placed under the processing under customs control in accordance with that procedure;
5. placed under temporary importation requirements under this scheme;
6. abandoned in accordance with Art. 180;
7. destroyed, provided that the person concerned to provide customs authorities with the necessary information.
(2) Where goods are placed under the arrangements referred to in para. 1, item 3, 4 and 5, how to control comply with the terms of the functioning of free zones or free warehouses and customs supervision in them.

Art. 174. (1) Local goods under Art. 166, item 2 may be subject only to operations aimed at their conservation. These operations can be performed without the permission of customs authorities.
(2) Local goods under Art. 166, item 2 can be subjected to operations other than those aimed at keeping them under the control of customs authorities, provided that after these operations will leave the territory of Bulgaria.
(3) Local goods which have not benefited from the measures provided for in art. 166, item 2 may be subject to other operations other than those aimed at keeping them under the control of customs authorities.

Art. 175. (1) Goods are in free zones and free warehouses, except for foreign, which is attached article. 173, and local, have not benefited from the measures provided for in art. 166, item 2, can not be consumed or used.
(2) Except as provided for supplying products to vessels, aircraft and trains, on international routes, and to an extent which allows the arrangements, para. 1 does not apply to the use or consumption of goods the system or temporary importation shall not be subject to import duties and not subject to commercial policy measures.

Art. 176. (1) Every person engaged in activity involving the storage, handling, processing or sale of goods in free zone or free warehouse shall keep stock records in a form approved by the customs authorities of the goods in the free zone or free warehouse. The stock records must enable the customs authorities to identify the goods and to track their movements.
(2) In case of transhipment of goods in free zone associated with this transaction documents must be available to the customs authorities. Short-term storage of goods under congestion is considered part of the

operation.

Section IV Removal of goods from free zones and free warehouses

Art. 177. (1) Subject to specific provisions goods in a free zone or free warehouse may be:
1. or re-exported outside the customs territory of the Republic of Bulgaria or
2. introduced the rest of the customs territory of the Republic of Bulgaria.
(2) Except as provided in Art. 55-60 in terms of local goods provisions of Part Three apply for entry of goods from free zones or free warehouses in the rest of the customs territory of the country. These provisions do not apply to goods exported from the zone by sea or air without being placed under a transit or other customs procedure.

Art. 178. (1) Where a customs duty on foreign goods whose customs value is formed on the basis of actually paid or payable, including the cost of storage of goods while they remain in the free zone or free warehouse, such costs are not included in the customs value, provided they are separated from the actually paid or payable for the goods.
(2) When the foreign goods have undergone in the free zone or free warehouse routine operations under Art. 114, para. 1, data type, quantity and customs value of goods used to determine the amount of import duties are those which, when a customs debt would be invoked for this product if they had not undergone such handling. This provision shall apply at the declarant and provided that operations are aligned under Art. 114, para. 2.
(3) The rules may provide exemptions from the cases under par. 2.

Art. 179. (1) The introduction or reintroduction of goods from free zone or free warehouse with the rest of the customs territory of the Republic of Bulgaria or their placing under customs regime of art authentication. 170, par. 4 can be used to demonstrate local or foreign status of such goods.
(2) If not determined the specific status of the goods, they shall be considered:
1. goods - for the purpose of levying export duties and application of commercial policy measures on export;
2. foreign goods - in other cases.

Chapter twenty RE, destruction and abandonment to the Exchequer and Leaving the customs territory

(Title addl. - SG. 37 of 2003)

Art. 180. (1) Foreign goods can be:
1. re-exported outside the customs territory of the Republic of Bulgaria;
2. destroyed or abandoned in favor of the state authorized by the customs authorities.
(2) (Amended - SG. 37 of 2003) In re-apply exit formalities of goods and commercial policy measures.
(3) (Amended - SG. 37, 2003) Council of Ministers may determine cases in which foreign goods may be placed under suspension in view of non-application of commercial policy measures on exports.
(4) (New - SG. 37 of 2003) the Customs authorities must be notified in advance of re-export or destruction of goods. The customs authorities shall prohibit re-exportation should the formalities or measures referred to in para. 2 require.
(5) (New - SG. 37 2003) When re-goods during their stay in the customs territory of the Republic of Bulgaria under an economic customs procedure, customs declaration is submitted in accordance with the provisions of Art. 66-84 and art. 163, para. 3 and 4.
(6) (former para. 4, Suppl. - SG. 37 2003) The destruction and abandonment of goods to the State shall be under the provisions of these Regulations. Destruction or abandonment of goods to the State should not cause any costs for it.
(7) (former para. 5 - SG. 37 of 2003) Waste and scrap resulting from destruction of goods, receive their own customs provided for foreign goods. They remain under customs supervision until the time specified in Art. 44, para. 2.
Art. 180a is inserted. (New - SG. 37 of 2003) Goods leaving the customs territory are under customs supervision. They may be subject to inspection by customs authorities in accordance with current

regulations. The goods must leave the customs territory of the country designated by the competent authorities ways and means.

PART FIVE LIGHTEN CUSTOMS

Chapter twenty-first EXEMPTION FROM DUTIES

Art. 181. (1) cases in which exemptions from duties on imports or exports, shall be determined by the regulations.
(2) The exemption from fees provided for in other legislation does not include exemption from fees under Art. 12 of this law except where explicitly regulated.
(3) There shall be no exemption from customs duties for goods sold in the areas of customs controls at border crossings, except:
1. normal ship and aircraft fuel supply and products;
2. sale of retail goods at ports and airports after customs control;
3. retailing on board aircraft on international routes, and ships on international voyages;
4. sale in specialized stores of the Diplomatic Service.

Chapter twenty-second PRODUCTS sea fishing and other products derived from SEA

Art. 182. Without prejudice to the requirements of Art. 30, para. 2, item 6, where they were placed under import relief from import duties:
1. products of sea fishing and other products taken outside the territorial waters of Bulgaria by vessels registered in Bulgaria and flying its flag;
2. products obtained from products of item 1, on board factory ships registered in the Republic of Bulgaria and flying its flag.

Chapter twenty-third RETURNED GOODS

Art. 183. (1) (Amended - SG. 63 of 2000) Local goods exported outside the customs territory of the Republic of Bulgaria, should be reintroduced in its import within three years are exempt from import duties at the request of person concerned.
(2) (amended and supplemented. - SG. 63 of 2000) in special circumstances, three-year period may be extended by the Director of Customs Agency or his authorized representative.
(3) (Amended - SG. 63 of 2000) When returning goods before export from the customs territory of the Republic of Bulgaria was formed to import regime with reduced or zero duties because of their use for specific purposes, an exemption under al. 1 shall be permitted if they are to be used again for the same purpose. If these goods have the same purpose, the amount of import duties shall be reduced by the amount of duties paid on initial import. When the amount to be deducted is greater than the amount due for returned goods is not allowed recovery.
(4) Exemption from import duties under par. 1 shall not be granted for goods exported outside the customs territory of the Republic of Bulgaria under the outward processing procedure, except when the goods are in a state in which they were exported.

Art. 184. Exemption from import duties under Art. 183 is authorized for goods that are reimported in the state in which they were exported. Cases and circumstances in which derogations from this provision may be specified in the regulations.

Art. 185. (1) (Amended - SG. 63 of 2000) provisions of Art. 183 and 184 apply, taking into account relevant specificity and returned compensating products which are exported or re-exported after having been under the inward processing.
(2) The amount of import duties payable is determined according to the rules for inward processing, with the date of re-export is considered as the date of importation.

PART SIX CUSTOMS DEBT

Chapter twenty-fourth Secure the amount of duty

Art. 186. (1) Where the application of customs law customs authorities require a guarantee for the customs debt, such security must be submitted by the debtor or the person may become a debtor.
(2) The customs authorities may require only a single guarantee for a customs debt.
(3) The customs authorities may allow security to be provided by a person other than the person who is required.
(4) (Amended - SG. 63 of 2000) Where the debtor or the person may become a debtor is a public body or local authority, the Director of Customs Agency is entitled to free him completely or partly from a security.
(5) The customs authorities may require the provision of security for the minor amount to be determined by the regulations.

Art. 187. (1) Where the customs rules make no provision of a guarantee, such guarantee may be required at the discretion of the customs authorities in the event that payment of the prescribed period due to a customs debt or one which may occur is uncertain.
(2) Where the collateral under par. 1 is not required, the customs authorities may ask the person under Art. 186, para. 1 to assume responsibility for writing the existing obligations.
(3) A guarantee under par. 1 may be required:
1. at the time of application of the provisions providing for the possibility of requiring such security, or
2. at any subsequent time when the customs authorities find that the deadlines in the payment of customs debt or one which might occur is uncertain.

Art. 188. At the request of the person under Art. 186, para. 1 or 3 customs authorities may authorize the establishment of a comprehensive guarantee to cover several transactions, of which arises or may arise customs debt.

Art. 189. (1) (Supplemented - SG. 37 2003) When the customs rules provide for the provision of security, the customs authorities in the light of specific provisions for transit as defined in the regulations, determine the amount that is equal to:
1. specific amount of the debt or obligations, if that amount can be determined in a secure manner at the time the security is required, or
2. highest by the customs authorities the amount of the debt or obligations that have arisen or which may arise for other cases.
(2) In a comprehensive guarantee of customs duties, which amount is changing over time, the amount of that security must be set so that at any moment to cover the full amount of the customs duties.
(3) Where the customs rules provide optional and a guarantee to the customs authorities so require, they determine its size so that it can not exceed those referred to in para. 1 and 2 sizes.
(4) The conditions and in cases specified in the regulations, the customs authorities have the right to negotiate with the debtor in collateral other than those mentioned in this article sizes.

Art. 190. The security may be provided with a cash deposit with a bank guarantee, in the cases determined by the regulations, and other ways to ensure payment of the debt.

Art. 191. A cash deposit must be made in the forms and means of payment established under the law.

Art. 192. For collateral accepted customs authorities do not owe interest.

Art. 193. (1) The bank guarantee shall be given in writing by the guarantor undertakes to pay jointly and severally liable with the debtor the secured amount of the debt falls to be paid.
(2) The customs authorities may refuse to accept the proposed bank guarantee if it does not provide payment of the debt within the prescribed period.

Art. 194. (1) The person is required to provide security, be free to choose the types of provided for in art. 190.
(2) Customs authorities in the manner specified in the rules to refuse acceptance of collateral offered, and ways of its formation when they are incompatible with the proper functioning of the arrangements. The customs authorities may set a time when the selected method of freezing can not be changed.

Art. 195. The customs authorities may refuse to guarantee proposed by the debtor when it secures the payment of the debt.

Art. 196. Where customs authorities find that the guarantee does not guarantee or is no longer disputed or provide full payment of the debt within the prescribed period, they require the person under Art. 186, para. An additional security or collateral to replace the original with new.

Art. 197. (1) (Amended - SG. 63 of 2000) security is not released until the debt for which it was given is extinguished or can arise. The security shall be released immediately after the debt is extinguished or can no longer occur.
(2) Where the customs debt is extinguished in part or may not occur as part of the amount which has been secured, the part of the collateral is released at the request of the person concerned.

Art. 198. Exceptions to the application of the provisions of this chapter shall be allowed in the implementation of international treaties to which Bulgaria is a party.
Chapter twenty fifth
The customs debt

Art. 199. (1) Customs debt for goods liable to import duties incurred through:
1. clearance of import regime;
2. placed under temporary admission with partial relief from import duties;
3. unlawful introduction into the customs territory of the Republic of Bulgaria in violation of Art. 45-48;
4. unlawful introduction of a free zone or free warehouse in the rest of the customs territory of the country in breach of Art. 177, para. 1, p. 2;
5. removal from customs supervision;
6. failure to comply with a requirement for temporary storage or for use of the arrangements;
7. (Amended - SG. 37 of 2003) compliance with a condition set to be placed under the customs procedure and the application of reduced or zero import duties or exemption from import duties due to the use of the goods for specific purposes;
8. consumed or used in a free zone or free warehouse under conditions other than those specified in current regulations. In the case of the disappearance of the product and if this disappearance is not submitted to the customs authorities is credible evidence to believe that goods are consumed or used in a free zone or free warehouse;
9. Release of documents necessary to obtain preferential treatment for products of Bulgarian origin in other countries concluded between Bulgaria and those agreements provide for payment of customs duties on foreign goods deposited.
(2) The provisions of para. 1, item 6 and 7 shall apply in cases other than those mentioned in paragraph 5 of that subparagraph if the deficiencies have led to real consequences for the proper functioning of the temporary storage or customs procedure.
(3) The customs debt is incurred in:
1. time of acceptance of customs declaration for the cases under para. 1, items 1 and 2;
2. time of unlawful entry for the cases under para. 1, item 3 and 4;
3. time of removal from customs supervision cases under para. 1, p. 5;
4. when no longer required to be fulfilled, which creates a customs debt default in cases under para. 1, p. 6;
5. time of placing the goods under the procedure in cases under para. 1, p. 7;
6. time of initial usage or consumption of the product under conditions other than those provided under existing legislation for the cases under para. 1, p. 8;
7. time of acceptance of customs declaration for export goods, which shall be issued for the use of preferential tariff treatment to the cases under para. 1 pt 9.
(4) Specific event of a customs debt outstanding at par. 1, and where no customs debt is incurred shall be

determined by the regulations.

Art. 200. (1) Customs debt on exportation occurs when:
1. export declaration from the customs territory of the Republic of Bulgaria of goods liable to export duties;
2. removal without a customs declaration the customs territory of the Republic of Bulgaria of goods liable to export duties;
3. the conditions for dispatch outside of customs territory of the Republic of Bulgaria with total or partial relief from export duties.
(2) export customs debt is incurred in:
1. time the export declaration in cases under para. 1, p. 1;
2. when the goods actually exported outside the country for the cases under para. 1, p. 2;
3. when the product has reached destination other than what is allowed to leave with full or partial exemption from duties or, failing that customs authorities to determine this moment - the moment at which the deadline for the submission of evidence to fulfill the prescribed conditions for the cases under para. 1, p. 3.

Art. 200. (1) Customs debt on exportation occurs when:
1. export declaration from the customs territory of the Republic of Bulgaria of goods liable to export duties;
2. removal without a customs declaration the customs territory of the Republic of Bulgaria of goods liable to export duties;
3. the conditions for dispatch outside of customs territory of the Republic of Bulgaria with total or partial relief from export duties.
(2) export customs debt is incurred in:
1. time the export declaration in cases under para. 1, p. 1;
2. when the goods actually exported outside the country for the cases under para. 1, p. 2;
3. when the product has reached destination other than what is allowed to leave with full or partial exemption from duties or, failing that customs authorities to determine this moment - the moment at which the deadline for the submission of evidence to fulfill the prescribed conditions for the cases under para. 1, p. 3.

Art. 201. (1) Customs duties under Art. 199, para. 1 and Art. 200, para. Occur when a concern for good - the subject of a prohibition or restriction on imports or exports.
(2) (Amended - SG. 30 of 1999) Customs duty does not arise in the unlawful introduction into the customs territory of the Republic of Bulgaria forged or counterfeit currency, drugs which are liable under the Penal Code.
(3) (New - SG. 37 2003) Where customs legislation provides a favorable tariff treatment of goods by their nature or end-use or partial or total exemption from import or export duties pursuant to Art. 28, 88, 147, 181 and 183-185, such a favorable tariff treatment or full or partial exemption from import duties applied in the occurrence of import duties under art. 199, 200 and 201, provided that that person's actions are not related to bad faith or with gross negligence and the person proves that the other conditions for favorable tariff treatment or for full or partial exemption are met.

Art. 202. (1) A debtor for payment of the debt is:
1. (Suppl. - SG. 37 of 2003) in the cases. 199, para. 1, item 1, 2 and 9 and art. 200, para. 1, items 1 and 3 - the declarant, if the debtor is indirect representation, the person on whose behalf the declaration is made. Where the customs declaration for the procedure has been prepared based on information that leads to partial or full he or she fails any import duties liable for payment of the debt is the person who provided the information necessary to make the declaration and who knew or should reasonably have known that the information is not accurate;
2. in the cases. 199, para. 1, item 3 and 4:
a) the person committing the unlawful introduction of goods or participated in it;
b) the person bought or accepted goods which they knew or ought reasonably to suspect that illegally introduced;
3. in the cases. 199, para. 1, p. 5:
a) the person or persons diverted goods from customs supervision or participated in a diversion;
b) the person bought or accepted goods which they knew or ought reasonably to suspect that they are removed from customs supervision;
c) (new - SG. 63 of 2000, amended. No.. 45 of 2005) the person to fulfill the obligations arising from

temporary storage of goods or use of the customs procedure under which they were placed;
4. in the cases. 199, para. 1, item 6 and 7 - person outstanding requirements arising from the temporary storage of goods or use a customs procedure, or the failure of one of the conditions provided the arrangements;
5. (Amended - SG. 45 of 2005) in the cases. 199, para. 1, item 8 - the person used the goods or spent, and any person who had participated in this action knew or reasonably should have known that the goods are used or consumed under conditions other than those specified in the legislation , where the customs authorities can not establish with certainty the person spent or used the goods to the debtor believes the person is known to authorities as the last holder of the goods;
6. in the cases. 200, para. 1 pt 2 - the person who removed without a customs declaration of goods subject to excise duties and the person or persons involved in export and knew or reasonably should have known that the goods must be submitted to Customs declaration.
(2) Where a customs debt has more than one debtor, they are jointly liable for its payment.

Art. 203. (1) Unless otherwise provided in this Act, the amount of import or export duties payable for the goods shall be determined on the basis of the taxation elements of this product at the time of occurrence of the customs duty.
(2) Exceptions to the provisions of para. 1 for individual specific cases may be determined by the regulations.
(3) (New - SG. 63 of 2000) In cases defined in the rules in case of import duties related to the suspensive procedures, the debtor shall pay interest at the rate of statutory interest on the amount of import duties duties due to postponement of the date of occurrence or taking it into account.
Art. 204. (1) The customs debt incurred at the place where the acts that led to its occurrence.
(2) Where it is not possible to determine the place, the debt shall be deemed to arise in the place where the customs authorities establish that the goods are due to customs duties.
(3) (amended and supplemented. - SG. 37 2003) Where the customs regime for goods is not completed and the site of the customs debt can not be determined under par. 1 and 2, the debt shall be deemed to arise in the place where the goods have been placed under this regime.
(4) (New - SG. 37 2003) When the information available to the customs authorities to establish that the customs debt was already incurred when the goods were in another place at an earlier date, it is believed was incurred at that location, which can be defined as the location of goods at the earliest time when it can be established that it was incurred.
(5) (former para. 4 - SG. 37 of 2003) exempted from provisions of par. 1 for individual specific cases may be determined by the regulations.

Chapter twenty-sixth PAYMENT OF CUSTOMS DUTY

Section I Taking into account the debtor for the amount of duty

Art. 205. (1) Customs authorities calculate the amount of duty resulting from a customs debt as soon as they have the elements necessary and enter them in the accounting records or any other form of accounting information to the accounts.
(2) cases in which para. 1 shall not apply and the procedures and time limits for the accounts are defined in the Rules.
(3) (New - SG. 63 of 2000) Where the customs debt is incurred, except in art. 199, para. 1, item 1 and art. 200, para. 1, item 1, and missing the type of goods, it is considered that the debt was incurred:
1. where there is evidence of a certain group of goods - goods for the highest duty of all goods that are covered in this group;
2. where there are no data on the type of goods - the most visokooblagaemata product, taking into account all collected by the customs authorities state claims.

Art. 206. (1) (Supplemented - SG. 45 of 2005) the debtor must be notified in writing of the amount of duty as soon as they are taken into account. Notification of the debtor shall be made pursuant to Art. 211g.
(2) Where the amount of duty entered in the customs declaration is only informative and not yet accepted by the customs authorities, the notification made under para. 1 only if the amount of those duties does not comply by themselves. When the amount of informative those duties to the amount specified by the Customs authorities and subject to the relevant provisions specified in the rules, authorization of release of goods shall be the debtor.

(3) (Amended - SG. 37 of 2003) Notification of the debtor can not be made after the expiration of 3 years from the date of the customs debt. This period can be suspended from the time of filing a complaint under Art. 220 for time on appeal.

Section Ia Interim measures by the customs authorities

Art. 206a. (1) When payment of customs duties and other governmental charges levied by the customs authorities is not guaranteed under chapter twenty-fourth, the customs authorities may impose the following precautionary measures:
1. attachment of movable property and claims of the debtor, including accounts in banks;
2. seizure of goods in turnover;
3. lien on the property.
(2) The security measures are imposed where without them it would be impossible or difficult will be the collection of customs duties and other governmental charges levied by customs authorities.
(3) The security measures imposed in accordance with the amount of customs duties and other governmental charges levied by customs authorities.
(4) (Amended - SG. 105 of 2005) Measures under par. 1 may not be imposed on the assets, which could not be directed enforcement, except with the consent of the debtor, as well as remuneration for work to the dimensions specified in the Tax Procedure Code.

Art. 206b. (1) (Prev. text of art. 206b - SG. 45 of 2005) The security measures imposed by the decree of the head of the office area in which it is established that the amount of customs debt provision or other public state-making .
(2) (New - SG. 45 of 2005) Order at para. 1 may be appealed under review the stipulations for enforcement of public state receivables.

Art. 206v. (Amended - SG. 105 of 2005) For outstanding questions in this section, the provisions of chapter twenty-fourth of the Tax Procedure Code.
Section II
Terms and Returns
Art. 207. Duties for which notification is made under Art. 206 must be paid by the debtor in the period stipulated in the rules.

Art. 208. (1) Payment must be made in the frame of the office or non-cash.
(2) At the request of the debtor's payment may be made by offsetting the customs authorities of unduly paid amounts for its duties.

Art. 209. (1) Upon request of the person concerned customs authorities may defer payment of duty under conditions and terms specified in the regulations.
(2) Deferral of payment shall ensure the following duties of the debtor.
(3) additional services performed in connection with the settlement of deferred payment of customs authorities collect expenses.

Art. 210. Duties may be paid by another person other than the debtor.

Art. 211. (1) Where the amount of duty is not paid within the prescribed period, the customs authorities:
1. (Amended - SG. 63 of 2000) used all possibilities to ensure payment of duties provided for in this Law and other regulations, including issuance of administrative acts for enforcement;
2. (Amended - SG. 63 of 2000) collect statutory interest on the amount of customs duties.
(2) (Amended - SG. 63 of 2000) In accordance with para. 1 is provided along with the payment of interest and other state receivables collected by the customs authorities are not paid within the prescribed period.

Section III Orders for compulsory collection of public state receivables issued by the customs authorities

Art. 211a. Orders for compulsory collection of public state receivables are individual administrative acts issued by the chief of customs in whose area has occurred within the outstanding debt, which establishes customs duties and other public debts.

Art. 211b. (Amended and supplemented. - SG. 110 of 2001 pcs. 105 of 2005) the Order is issued in four originals - the debtor for the office of the competent territorial directorate of the National Revenue Agency and State Receivables Collection Agency.

Art. 211v. (1) Order is issued in writing and include:
1. name of the authority issuing it;
2. name and number;
3. factual and legal grounds for the issue;
4. data for the debtor;
5. amount of duties and other public debts;
6. the occurrence of the public revenue;
7. (Revoked - SG. 37 of 2003);
8. possible measures to safeguard and advance its implementation;
9. to which authority and timeframe can be appealed;
10. date of issue and signature of the respective head of office.
(2) (Amended - SG. 45 of 2005) the Order is sent by the chief of customs with a receipt to the State Receivables Agency for enforcement, except in the cases. 211zh, para. 2.
(3) (New - SG. 45 of 2005) Getting enforceable decree shall be confirmed in writing by the public executor at customs, which oversees the receipt account and amounts of customs duties and other state claims.

Art. 211g. (Amended - SG. 45 of 2005) (1) service of the order of individuals is certified by the signature of the person or his representative. When vrachitelyat not find the person he gives the order to an adult family member if he agreed to surrender. The person thus becomes a service, is in receipt signed, taking note of his three names, the UCC and how the adopted decree, and his obligation to deliver it.
(2) Service of the decree of legal persons shall be certified by the signature of the official who received the order to show the full name, the UCC and the position of the recipient.
(3) Service of the decree of employment shall be made by an official of the administration. The service is regular, if there are three names, UCC and position of the recipient.
(4) Vrachitelyat attested by his signature the date and manner of service. Failure to accept the decree shall be attested by the signature of vrachitelya and at least one witness, as noted vrachitelyat names, personal identification number and address and make note on the receipt. In this case the order is considered delivered.
(5) Where it can not be assured a witness, the decree is sent with a receipt. Order sent by registered mail shall be deemed as delivered on the date on which the acknowledgment was signed or the date on which the refusal was made to obtain a ruling that refused to certify the postal employee. If the person fails to report and certify receipt in postal communication instructions in time, the decree and post documents to the file and the order is considered delivered.
(6) Individuals who began to manufacture, which are informed and who reside for more than 30 consecutive days abroad are required to designate a person in the country, to represent them before the customs authorities and thereby served notices and other acts of customs administration.
(7) Service of the decree sentenced to imprisonment and detention carried out by the administration of the offices.
(8) The service of soldiers of the decree of actual military service shall be made by the commander of the unit.
(9) Service of the order by applying to the case shall be made after 14 days of putting a message to appear in person where:
1. address of the person is unknown;
2. person, his agent or attorney can not be found or the address of their permanent address after thorough and documented search by customs authorities.
(10) Communication under par. 9 is placed on a defined place in the customs office which issued the decree. Communication is published on the Internet page of the customs administration.
(11) The circumstances under par. 9, item 1 shall be certified to the case, but al. 9, item 2 - a document

coming from the mail, or by the signature of vrachitelya and at least one witness, as noted vrachitelyat full name, personal number and address and make note on the receipt.
(12) Where the person fails to appear before the deadline under par. 9, the ruling applies to the case and is considered delivered.

Art. 211d. (Amended - SG. 45 of 2005) Where, after issuance of the decree debtor pay duties and other governmental charges, together with interest or any part thereof, the head of customs shall inform the public implementation of such circumstances.

Art. 211e. Order may be appealed by the chief of the office which issued it, the director of the Regional Customs Directorate within fourteen days of service thereof.

Art. 211zh. (1) The appeal of the ruling will not stop its execution.
(2) Implementation of the decree be suspended at the request of the debtor, if the provision of security in the amount of principal and interest. Security may be in cash deposit or bank guarantee.
(3) The application for stay of execution made simultaneously with the filing of the complaint and apply it to proof of collateral.
(4) For the period of suspension due to legal interest on the principal.
(5) (New - SG. 45 of 2005) Paragraph 1 shall not apply in cases where a decree for the enforcement of public state claims are established obligations arising from the application of international conventions to which the Republic of Bulgaria joined, and debtors are guaranteeing organizations designated by the Council of Ministers.

Art. 211z. The head of the office through an appeal is required within seven days of its receipt to send it together with an opinion and fitted case concerned Regional Director of Customs Office in whose area the office is concerned. When the request for suspension, it also is used together with relevant evidence. If filed within appeal was improperly addressed, it is automatically forwarded to the competent authority, the deadline is met.
Art. 211i. (1) The Director of Regional Customs Directorate shall consider the appeal on the merits and consider all the circumstances of the decree.
(2) The Director shall act within thirty days of receipt of the application by reasoned decision confirming or canceling all or part of the decree, in its reasons set out the positions of the parties and the reasons for its decision. It shall also rule on the request for stay of execution when such was done.
(3) Where it is established that an order is unlawful for him to be another issue, Director of Regional Customs Directorate and the decree annulled the contested case back to the respective head of office by any mandatory instructions.
(4) The decision shall be issued in four original counterparts - the debtor for the office of Regional Customs Directorate and State Receivables Agency, which sent no later than seven days following the expiry al. 2.
(5) (Amended - SG. 45 of 2005 pcs. 30 of 2006, in force since 1.03.2007) Order, confirmed by decision of the Director of Regional Customs Directorate, subject to appeal to administrative court in its location within fourteen days of receipt of the decision under para. 4. Complaint is filed by the respective head of office.
(6) Order can be appealed before the courts in so far that has not been contested by administrative order, or in part, the complaint is wholly or partially upheld.

Art. 211k. (1) (Amended - SG. 105 of 2005 pcs. 59 of 2007) In judicial proceedings on appeal and cassation proceedings, the relevant provisions of the seventeenth and nineteenth chapters of the Tax Procedure Code a cancellation of final decisions can be requested by the Party under the conditions and terms of art. 303 of the Code of Civil Procedure.
(2) (Amended - SG. 105 of 2005) When complaints are called in court the authority which issued the contested decision, the applicant and the National Revenue Agency, as interested party.

Art. 211l. Order shall enter into force when:
1. was not appealed within the relevant Regional Director of Customs Directorate;
2. was appealed to the Director of Regional Customs Directorate, he has not upheld the appeal and the ruling was not appealed in court;

3. was confirmed by the court.

Art. 211 meters. (Repealed - SG. 45 of 2005).

Chapter twenty-seventh EXTINCTION OF CUSTOMS DEBT

Art. 212. (1) The customs debt is extinguished:
1. by payment of customs duties;
2. by remission of duty;
3. provided the goods declared for a customs procedure requiring the payment of duties:
a) customs declaration is invalidated;
b) (amended - SG. 153 of 1998) before their release granted, the goods are seized and simultaneously or subsequently: confiscated country, destroyed by order of the customs authorities, destroyed or abandoned under Art. 180; destroyed or irretrievably lost for reasons relating to the nature of the goods or due to force majeure or other unforeseen circumstances;
4. when goods for which customs debt is incurred under Art. 199, para. 1, item 3 and 4 are seized upon their unlawful introduction and are simultaneously or subsequently confiscated state.
(2) (Amended - SG. 63 of 2000) The right to collect customs duties shall be terminated upon the expiration of five years from 1 January of the year following the year in which occurred the customs duties and other State public debts established by a decree of enforcement.
(3) Paragraph. 1 does not apply when opening a court of bankruptcy of the debtor.

Art. 212a. (New - SG. 45 of 2005) The customs debt incurred under Art. 199, para. 1, item 9 is extinguished when the formalities for settlement of preferential tariff treatment to be repealed.

Art. 213. Ways of discharging the obligations arising in specific cases, be determined by the regulations.

Chapter twenty-eighth REFUND AND REMISSION OF DUTIES

Art. 214. (1) drawback is a return to full or partial refund of paid import or export duties.
(2) Recovery occurs when it is found that at the time of payment of duties were not owed or reason for their payment has dropped.

Art. 215. (1) Remission of duty is:
1. solution for full or partial she fails to import or export duties, or
2. solution for full or partial cancellation of the accounts the amount of import or export duties when they were paid.
(2) Remission occurs when it is found that when taken into account the duties were not owed or reason for them in the accounts no longer exist.

Art. 216. (1) Recovery or remission may be granted when the action led to the payment or the accounts of undue duties resulting from the deception of the person concerned.
(2) Repayment or remission of import or export duties shall be granted upon written request to the appropriate office before the expiration of three years from the date on which the debtor has been notified of these duties.
(3) (New - SG. 45 of 2005) period under par. 2 may be extended if the person concerned provides evidence that it was prevented from submitting such a request due to unforeseeable circumstances or force majeure.

Art. 216a. (New - SG. 45 of 2005) Recovery of import or export duties be performed if the customs declaration is invalidated and the duties were paid. Repayment shall be granted upon written request of the person who made the deadline for submission of application for cancellation of the declaration.

Art. 217. The Rules may be certain cases and conditions other than those of previous members, who may grant a refund or remission of import or export duties.

Art. 218. The Rules can be a minimum amount of import or export duties, under which no repayment or remission.

Art. 219. When mistakes because debt has been remitted or the corresponding amount of duty was reinstated the original debt is reinstated.

Art. 219a. (New - SG. 37 of 2003) recovered duties are not due interest. In cases where duties are defined by an unlawful act of the customs authorities wrongly paid shall be repaid with the interest rate.

PART SEVEN APPEALS AGAINST DECISIONS

Art. 220. Any person may appeal decisions affecting him to the customs authorities pursuant to the Administrative Code.
Art. 221. Where the contested decision relates to the taxation of import or export duties on stopping its implementation requires the provision of their size.
Art. 222. The provisions of the seventh part do not apply to cases relating to the repeal or modify regulations issued by the customs authorities on the basis of administrative penal provisions of this Act.

PART EIGHT ADMINISTRATIVE PROVISIONS

Chapter twenty-ninth GENERAL PROVISIONS

Art. 223. The customs authorities investigate, detect and punish any breach or attempted breach of customs legislation, as far as the act does not constitute a crime.
Art. 224. Acts which constitute the customs violations, the penalties imposed on them, and the responsibilities thereof shall be determined by this law.
Art. 225. (1) establishment of violations, issue criminal warrants and their appeal is made under the Law on Administrative Offences and penalties.
(2) implementation of the enacted criminal rulings and the court is made under the Law on Administrative Offences and penalties to the extent that law provides otherwise.
Art. 226. (1) (Amended - SG. 63 of 2000, amended. And supplemented. No.. 37 of 2003) administrative penal responsibility are those who have committed a customs violation of the customs territory of the Republic of Bulgaria and instigators, accessories, and concealers dopustitelite.
(2) (Amended - SG. 63 of 2000) Persons under par. Jointly responsible for a resulting from the breach duties and other public state receivables, except the penalty fine.
(3) (Repealed - SG. 37 of 2003).
(4) (Repealed - SG. 37 of 2003).
Art. 226a. (New - SG. 37 of 2003) (1) Customs authorities shall prescribe the Forfeiture of the State of goods subject to customs offense, and the motor and transmission means serve to transport or transfer of goods in cases when this measure is provided in this or any other Act, except in cases of art. 229b, para. 1, p. 3.
(2) Before the completion of administrative penal proceedings, the customs authorities may dispose of in accordance with Art. 239 with goods subject to rapid deterioration, as well as goods whose storage entails significant costs for the customs administration.
(3) Where the withdrawal to the State is impossible in the cases under para. 2 persons of art. 226, para. Two jointly pay an amount equal to the customs value of the subject of infringement, as well as vehicles and transport vehicles which used to transport or transfer of goods.

Chapter thirtieth ADMINISTRATIVE PENALTIES

Art. 227. (1) customs violations provides the following penalties:
1. fine;
2. suspension of the right to import and export of goods to legal persons and sole traders;

3. (Amended - SG. 45 of 2005) fines for legal persons and sole traders.
(2) Deprivation of the right to import and export of goods is a temporary ban on the offender to carry out such activity for six months to two years. This penalty shall be imposed when a heavy customs smuggling case or repeated violations of this law.

Art. 228. For minor cases of customs violations identified in their execution, the customs authorities may impose fines where violations of law and in the amounts set out in Art. 39 of the Law on Administrative Offences and penalties.

Art. 229. (1) The customs authorities may seize and detain goods - subject to a customs violation, transmission, transport and other means, led to their concealment, importation or exportation of the country, material evidence necessary or related to the procedure of investigation and goods and amounts to cover potential claims drawn up act.
(2) (Amended - SG. 63 of 2000) pending the completion of administrative penal and criminal procedure seized and detained goods held by customs.
(3) (New - SG. 63 of 2000) the Customs authorities detained and kept under customs supervision goods subject or vehicle or evidence of a crime, until completion of customs formalities in respect of them under current legislation .
(4) (Amended - SG. 30 of 1999, the previous paragraph. 3 pcs. 63 of 2000) for the customs authorities seized narcotics, the provisions of the Law on control of narcotic substances and precursors.
(5) (former para. 4 - SG. 63 of 2000) the Customs authorities immediately transmitted to the Ministry of Interior arrested and seized weapons, ammunition and explosives.
(6) (former para. 5 am. - SG. 63 of 2000) Where the goods - the subject of customs offense, shall not be withdrawn in favor of the state, including the award of equivalence, duties and other public government claims they are due on a general basis.
(7) (New - SG. 37 of 2003) the Customs authorities may impose measures under Chapter twenty-sixth, Section Ia to ensure claims act drawn up to establish a customs violation.

Art. 229a. (New - SG. 37 of 2003, with effect from 1.07.2003, amend. No.. 105 of 2006) To the issue of penal provision, but not later than 30 days from the establishment of order to establish the breach between administrativnonakazvashtiya customs authority and the offender may be agreed to terminate the administrative penal proceedings for violations of art. 233, para. 1, 2 and 3, Art. 234 and Art. 234a, except where the act constitutes a crime.

Art. 229b. (New - SG. 37 of 2003, effective 1.07.2003) (1) The Agreement shall be in written form and reflects the authority and the offender administrativnonakazvashtiya the following questions:
1. I have committed an offense committed there, it is committed and the offender is guilty of it, the act constitutes a breach of customs;
2. how to type and amount of punishment;
3. (Amended - SG. 45 of 2005) take you to the State goods - the subject of infringement and motor and transmission means serve to transport or transfer of goods, or they pay an amount not less than 25 percent of their equivalence.
(2) The Agreement can not be determined:
1. punishment of a kind different from that provided by law for the particular customs offense;
2. amount of fine or penalty of less than the minimum prescribed for the particular customs offense;
3. (Amended - SG. 45 of 2005) an amount less than 25 percent of the monetary value of the subject of infringement and monetary value of the vehicle and transmission medium representing the customs value.
(3) the Agreement signed by administrativnonakazvashtiya authority and the offender or his representative expressly authorized settlement.
(4) Within 14 days of signing the Agreement on cessation of administrative penal proceedings, the Director of Customs Agency or his authorized officer shall issue a decision approving or refusing to approve the agreement. Decisions to approve the agreement on cessation of administrative penal proceedings shall be forwarded to the appropriate prosecutor within 7 days of their issuance.
(5) The termination of the administrative penal proceedings shall be approved if the requirements of the law and if set forth in the public state receivables are paid or secured by deposit account of the customs office.
(6) The decision under para. 4 not subject to appeal, except a decision approving the agreement on cessation of administrative penal proceedings against whom the prosecutor may file a protest regarding the

legality of the court under the Administrative Code. In this case, the prosecutor's protest does not stop execution of the decision.
(7) The deadlines for issuance of a penal provision should be suspended from the initiation of legal proceedings in protest of the prosecutor until its conclusion.
(8) In cases where the agreement to terminate the administrative penal proceedings shall not be approved or the decision is approved, be annulled by the court administrativnonakazvashtiyat authority issued a decree of the general criminal law.

Art. 229v. (New - SG. 37 of 2003, with effect from 1.07.2003, amend. No.. 105 of 2005) The termination of the administrative penal proceedings shall enter into force upon its approval. Agreement has the effect of enacted penal provision and enforceable under the Tax Procedure Code.

Chapter thirty-first PRODUCTION in infringement of the customs procedure

Art. 230. For every case of violations of the customs regime shall be established by decision of the customs authorities.

Art. 231. (Amended - SG, issue. 63 of 2000) Penalty decrees issued by the Director of Customs Agency, or any of its officials.

Art. 232. (1) (New - SG. 63 of 2000, amended. No.. 37 2003) When the offender is unknown, the act is signed by aktosastavitelya and one witness and not be served. In this case, issue a penal provision, which shall enter into force upon its issuance.
(2) (Prev. text of art. 232 amended. - SG. 63 of 2000) When the offender is known but not found at the address indicated in the service of the order for an administrative violation, or has left the country or designates only address abroad penal provision is not given. Order shall be deemed to come into legal force two months after its release.

Chapter thirty-second CUSTOMS VIOLATIONS AND DETERMINATION OF ADMINISTRATIVE PENALTIES

Art. 233. (1) (Amended - SG. 45 of 2005) who carry or transport goods across state borders or attempt thereof without the knowledge and permission of the customs authorities so far not committed an offense shall be punished for smuggling Customs fine of 100 to 200 percent of the customs value of goods.
(2) (New - SG. 105 of 2006) for customs contraband and punishing those who carry or transport goods across the external borders of the European Union without the knowledge and permission of the customs authorities and the goods were found as a result of the inspection the territory of Bulgaria.
(3) (Amended - SG. 45 of 2005, the previous paragraph. 2 pcs. 105 of 2006) When the subject of Customs are smuggling goods on which excise is due, or banned for import or export goods is a fine of 150 to 250 percent of the customs value of goods.
(4) (former para. 3 - SG. 105 of 2006) goods - subject to customs smuggling are withdrawn in favor of the state regardless of whose property is, if missing or alienated, its equivalent shall be awarded representing the customs value.
(5) (former para. 4 - SG. 105 of 2006) goods - subject to customs smuggling are withdrawn in favor of the state in cases where the offender is unknown.
(6) (former para. 5 - SG. 105 of 2006) Vehicles and transport equipment, which were used for transportation or carriage of goods - subject to customs smuggling are withdrawn in favor of the state regardless of whose property are value unless they clearly do not correspond to the value of the subject of customs smuggling.

Art. 234. (Amended - SG. 63 of 2000 pcs. 37 of 2003 pcs. 45 of 2005) (1) Those who avoid or try to avoid:
1. full or partial payment or provision of customs duties or other public state receivables collected by the customs authorities, or
2. prohibitions or restrictions on imports or exports, or the application of commercial policy measures, be liable for customs fraud.
(2) customs fraud penalty is fine - for individuals or penalty - for legal persons and sole traders from 100 to

200 percent of:
1. amount of avoided public state claims - for breach of para. 1, p. 1;
2. customs value of goods subject to infringement under par. 1, p. 2.
(3) Where a customs fraud are goods on which excise is due, the penalty is fine - for individuals or penalty - for legal persons and sole traders from 150 to 250 percent of:
1. amount of avoided public state claims - for breach of para. 1, p. 1;
2. customs value of goods subject to infringement under par. 1, p. 2.
(4) (Amended - SG. 105 of 2006) In the cases under para. 1 and 3 shall apply the provisions of Article. 233, para. 4 and 5.

Art. 234a. (New - SG. 63 of 2000, amended. No.. 45 of 2005) (1) who depart temporarily stored goods or goods which are given customs regime or customs, it does not meet established in or the regulations prescribed by the customs authorities, be fined - for individuals or penalty - for legal persons and sole traders from 100 to 200 per cent of customs value of goods - the subject of infringement.
(2) Where a violation under par. 1 are goods on which excise is due, the penalty is fine - for individuals or penalty - for legal persons and sole traders from 150 to 250 per cent of customs value of goods - the subject of infringement.
(3) (Amended - SG. 105 of 2006) In the cases under para. 1 and 2 shall apply the provisions of Article. 233, para. 4, 5 and 6.

Art. 235. (1) (Amended - SG. 63 of 2000 extra. No.. 45 of 2005) who sell, buy or try this, give or take a gift for safekeeping, for use rent or a pledge of goods for which it knew or should reasonably have suspected of being imported in violation of customs laws or in violation of normativnoopredelenite restrictions and conditions for duty-free goods or goods imported at reduced or zero duties because their specific purpose, shall be fined - for individuals or penalty - for legal persons and sole traders up to 1000 leva
(2) Where the order under par. 1 out of goods - subject to customs violations of art. 233 and 234, these goods are withdrawn in favor of the state regardless of whose property is.
(3) The sentence does not exempt persons from payment of customs duties and other governmental charges levied by the customs authorities, except under par. 2.

Art. 236. In the penalty under Art. 235, para. 1 and punish those who do not fulfill their obligations under Art. 4 para. 1.

Art. 237. Goods by type and quantity of non-commercial nature and for which a declaration, if not declared by passengers crossing the state border, and be found in the usual places for customs examination shall be forfeited in favor of the state regardless of whose property is without be fined.

Art. 238. (1) (Supplemented - SG. 45 of 2005) Any breach of regulations applicable to goods under customs supervision established by the customs authorities, unless otherwise provided, be punished by a fine or penalty in Art. 235, para. 1.
(2) The same punishment shall be punished and who is opposed to the customs authorities in the performance of their duties and who is required under this Act to provide goods to those authorities, documents and information, but refuse to do so.
Art. 238a. (New - SG. 63 of 2000 extra. No.. 45 of 2005) who fails to comply with the regulations established or designated by the customs authorities deadlines, be fined - for individuals or penalty - for legal persons and sole traders to 2000 levs
Art. 238b. (New - SG. 45 of 2005) who did not fulfill an obligation under Art. 10, para. 5 shall be punished by a fine of up to BGN 1000

PART NINE DISPOSAL OF GOODS, WITHDRAWN OR ABANDONED TO STATE AND DISTRIBUTION OF AMOUNTS INCOMING

Art. 239. The customs administration is withdrawn and dispose of abandoned goods of the country in terms and conditions set out in regulations.
Art. 240. (1) The amounts received from the conversion of abandoned and confiscated goods of the state,

paid the costs incurred by the customs offices, finding, transportation and storage, and cost evaluation and performance of their sales.
(2) (Amended - SG. 83 of 1999) After deduction of costs, the amounts under par. 1 and amounts representing the equivalent of confiscated goods of the country where they are missing or alienated, shall be entered as income under Art. 14.

EXCISE DUTIES AND TAX WAREHOUSES ACT

Excise Duties and Tax Warehouses Act

Promulgated State Gazette No. 91/15.11.2005, effective 1.01.2006, amended SG No. 105/29.12.2005, effective 1.01.2006, SG No. 30/11.04.2006, effective 12.07.2006, amended, SG No. 34/25.04.2006, effective 1.01.2008 (*)(**), amended and upplemented, SG No. 63/4.08.2006, effective 4.08.2006, SG No. 81/6.10.2006, amended and supplemented, SG No. 105/22.12.2006, effective 1.01.2007, amended, SG No. 108/29.12.2006, effective 1.01.2007, SG No. 31/13.04.2007, effective 13.04.2007, SG No. 108/19.12.2007, effective 19.12.2007, amended and supplemented, SG No. 109/20.12.2007, effective 1.01.2008

(*) effective 1.07.2007 - amended, SG No. 80/3.10.2006, effective 3.10.2006

(**) effective 1.01.2008 - amended, SG No. 53/30.06.2007, effective 30.06.2007

Text in Bulgarian: Закон за акцизите и данъчните складове

CHAPTER ONE GENERAL PROVISIONS

Section I

Scope of Application

Article 1. (Effective 1.07.2006) This Act shall govern excise duty taxation as well as control on production, use, storage, movement and securing of goods subject to excise tax.

Section II

Object of Excise Taxation and Persons Subject to Excise Duty

Article 2. (Effective 1.07.2006) Subject to excise tax shall be:

1. alcohol and alcoholic beverages;

2. tobacco products;

3. (supplemented, SG No. 105/2006) energy products and electricity;

4. (repealed, SG No. 109/2007)

5. automobiles.

Article 3. (Effective 1.07.2006) Persons subject to excise duty shall be:

1. (amended, SG No. 105/2006) licensed warehouse keepers and persons registered under this Act;

2. (amended, SG No. 105/2006) persons for whom a liability has arisen under the customs legislation in respect of excisable goods;

3. persons who have produced excisable goods outside a tax warehouse in violation of this Act or have disposed with excisable goods for which no excise duty has been paid;

4. (supplemented, SG No. 105/2006) excise-exempt end users and non-registered traders;

5. (new, SG No. 105/2006) tax representatives of VAT-registered persons in another Member State who supply excisable goods under the terms of distant selling within the Value Added Tax Act;

6. (new, SG No. 105/2006) the persons who receive on the territory of the country excisable goods released for consumption in another Member State, except for the cases of item 5 where the tax representative shall be obliged to pay the exise duty.

7. (new, SG No. 109/2007) the persons who introduce into the territory of this country automobiles from another Member State.

Section III

Terms

Article 4. (Effective 1.07.2006) For the purposes of this Act:

1. "Excisable goods" shall be the goods specified in Article 2.

2. "Licensed warehouse keeper" shall be a trader within the meaning of the Commerce Act , who has been granted a license to produce, store, receive or dispatch excisable goods under excise duty suspension arrangement.

3. "Tax warehouse" shall be the place where excisable goods under excise duty suspension arrangement are produced, stored, received or dispatched by a licensed warehouse keeper in accordance with the provisions of this Act.

4. " Excise duty suspension arrangement" shall be a set of rules applicable to production, storage and movement of goods under excise duty suspension arrangement.

5. (Amended, SG No. 105/2006) "CN code" shall be tariff codes according to the Combined Nomenclature as per Appendix I of Council Regulation No. 2658/87 (EEC) on the Tariff and Statistical Nomenclature and the Common Customs Tariff. For alcohol and alcoholic beverages the CN codes are according to the Combined Nomenclature applied at 31 December 1992, and for energy products and electricity according to the Combined Nomenclature applied at 1 January 2002.

6. "Selling price" shall be the price written on the excise label at which tobacco products are sold to end users, including production and distribution costs of the producer (importer), customs charges due, payments, fees, excise duty and value added tax.

7. "Excise label" shall be a government security proving payment of excise duty due, which shall be purchased from the Ministry of Finance and may not be subject to further transaction.

8. (Supplemented, SG No. 63/2006, amended, SG No. 81/2006) "Specialised small distillery" shall be a distillation unit where ethyl alcohol (rakiya) is produced from grapes and fruits - own production of natural persons, for their personal and family consumption up to 30 litres of ethyl alcohol (rakiya) per annum per family.

9. "Small producer of wine" shall be a unit where no more than 1,000 hectolitres are produced per annum.

10. (Amended, SG No. 63/2006) "Dual use energy product" shall be a product which is used both as heating fuel and for purposes other than as motor fuel and heating fuel; the use of energy products for chemical reduction and in electrolytic and metallurgical processes shall be regarded as dual use.

11. "Marking" shall be an action where a marker is added to gas oil and kerosene, which satisfies the requirements set down in the implementing regulation to this Act.

12. "Denaturation" shall be an action where poisonous substances or substances of unpleasant taste and flavour (mixtures) are added to ethyl alcohol, thereby making it dangerous for health or unfit for drinking.

13. "Technical specification" shall be a document of the producer containing a description of the product regarding the production technology and its intended use, technical requirements, rated values of particular indicators and methods of their testing, packaging and designation, storage and transportation.

14. (Amended, SG No. 105/2006) "Excise-exempt end user" shall be a sole trader or legal entity entitled to receive energy products which are used for purposes exempt from excise duty based on a certificate of excise exemption.

15. "Private pleasure flying and sailing" shall be the use of a vessel or aircraft by its owner or by a natural person or legal entity for purposes other than transportation of passengers or goods or provision of goods against consideration or for the needs of government authorities.

16. (Amended, SG No. 105/2006) "New automobile" shall be an automobile for which one of the following conditions obtain at the date of importation, the date of filing the declaration under Article 76d to the customs authorities respectively:

a) no more than 6 months have expired from the date of its initial registration (including registration abroad); or

b) has run not more than 6,000 km.

17. "Repeated" violation shall be a violation committed within one year from entry into force of a penalty enactment by virtue of which the person had been penalized for the same type of violation.

18. (Amended, SG No. 63/2006) "Grave" violation shall be a violation for which a penalty enactment has been enforced with imposed property sanction exceeding BGN 15,000.

19. "Actual alcoholic strength by volume (alcoholic content)" shall be the volumes of pure ethyl alcohol contained at temperature of 20 °C in 100 volumes of product at the same temperature.

20. (Amended, SG No. 105/2006) "% vol" and "% mas" are designations of the alcoholic strength by volume and mass.

21. "Pure alcohol" is ethyl alcohol with actual alcoholic strength by volume 100 % vol (absolute alcohol).

22. "Biodiesel" is methyl ester derived from vegetable oils or animal fats, having the quality of diesel fuel used as motor fuel for diesel engines, derived from biodegradable fractions of products, waste and residues (including vegetable or animal substances) from agriculture, forestry, as well as biodegradable fractions from industrial or household waste.

23 (New, SG No. 81/2006) "Bioethanol" is ethanol, derived from biomass and/or from the biodegradable part of the waste, intended for use as biofuel.

24. (New, SG No. 105/2006) "Territory of the country" is the geographic territory of the Republic of Bulgaria, the continental shelf and the exlusive economic zone.

25. (New, SG No. 105/2006) "Territory of a Member State" is the territory of every Member State wherein the Treaty establishing the European Community applies, specified for every Member State in Article 299 of said Treaty where:

a) excluded from said territory shall be:

aa) for Federal Republic of Germany: Isle of Heligoland and the Busingen territory;

bb) for Kingdom of Spain: Ceuta, Melilla and Canary Islands;

cc) for Republic of Italy: Livigno, Campione d'Italia and the Italian waters of Lugano Lake;

dd) (repealed, SG No. 108/2007);

ee) for United Kingdom of Great Britain and Northern Ireland: Anglo-Normand Isles and Gibraltar;

ff) for Republic of France: French Overseas Departments;

b) movement of excisable goods to or from:

aa) Principality of Monako - will be treated as movement to or from the Republic of France;

bb) Isle of Man - will be treated as movement to or from the United Kingdom of Great Britain and Northern Ireland;

cc) Jungholz and Mittelberg (Kleines Walsertal) - will be treated as movement to or from the Federal Republic of Germany;

dd) San Marino - will be treated as movement to or from the Republic of Italy.

26. (New, SG No. 105/2006) "Community" and "Community territory" is the territory of the Member States.

27. (New, SG No. 105/2006) "Third country" or "third territory" is any territory other than the territory of Member States.

28. (New, SG No. 105/2006) "Registered trader" is a person other than a licensed warehouse keeper who is entitled to receive under certain conditions excisable goods from another Member State under excise duty suspension arrangement. The registered trader may not store or send excisable goods under excise duty suspension arrangement.

29. (New, SG No. 105/2006) "Non-registered trader" is a person other than a licensed warehouse keeper who is entitled to receive under certain conditions a specific

quantity of excisable goods from another Member State under excise duty suspension arrangement. A non-registered trader may not store or send excisable goods under excise duty suspension arrangement.

30. (New, SG No. 105/2006) "Importer" is the person owing payment of import customs charges as well as the person who has received goods on the teritory of the country from third territories which are part of the Community customs territory.

31. (New, SG No. 105/2006) "Standard tanks" (normal tank) shall mean:

a) the tanks permanently fixed by the manufacturer to all motor vehicles and whose permanent fitting enables fuel to be used directly, both for the purpose of propulsion and, where appropriate, for the operation, during transport, of refrigeration systems and other systems; gas tanks fitted to motor vehicles designed for the direct use of gas as fuel and tanks fitted to the other systems with which the vehicle may be equipped shall also be considered to be standard tanks;

b) the tanks permanently fixed by the manufacturer to all containers and whose permanent fitting enables fuel to be used directly for the operation, during transport, of refrigeration systems and the other systems with which special containers are equipped.

32. (New, SG No. 105/2006) "Special container" shall mean any container fitted with specially designed apparatus for refrigeration systems, oxygenation systems, thermal insulation systems or other systems.

33. (New, SG No. 105/2006) "Mineralogical processes" shall mean the processes classified in the NACE (General Industrial Classification of Economic Activities within the European Community) nomenclature under code DI 26 "manufacture of other non-metallic mineral products" in Council Regulation (EEC) No. 3037/90 on the statistical classification of economic activities in the European Community.

34. (New, SG No. 105/2006) "Cost of a product" shall be the value of the product within the meaning of the accountancy legislation. This cost shall be calculated per unit on average.

35. (New, SG No. 105/2006) "Cost of electricity" shall mean the actual purchase value of electricity or the cost of production of electricity if it is generated in the business.

36. (New, SG No. 105/2006) "Export" shall mean movement of excisable goods from the territory of the country to the territory of a third country or third territory.

37. (New, SG No. 109/2007) "Energy product for heating" shall mean a product involved in a process, related to release of heat, to be used directly or via a transmission medium in its principal function.

CHAPTER TWO EXCISABLE GOODS

Section I

Alcohol and Alcoholic Beverages

Article 5. (Effective 1.07.2006) "Beer" shall be any product falling within CN code 2203 or any product which is a mixture of beer and soft drinks falling within CN code 2206, in both cases with actual alcoholic strength by volume exceeding 0.5 % vol.

Article 6. (Effective as of 1.07.2006) (1) "Still wines" shall be products falling within CN codes 2204 and 2205, but outside the scope of paragraph 2, which have:

1. actual alcoholic strength by volume exceeding 1.2 % vol, but not exceeding 15 % vol, provided that the alcohol contained in the finished product is entirely of fermented origin, or

2. actual alcoholic strength by volume exceeding 15 % vol but not exceeding 18 % vol, provided that they have been produced without any enrichment and provided that the alcohol contained in the finished product is entirely of fermented origin.

(2) (Amended, SG No. 105/2006) "Sparkling wines" shall be all products falling within CN codes 2204 10, 2204 21 10, 2204 29 10 and 2205, which are:

1. in bottles with 'mushroom stoppers' held in place by ties or fastenings, or they have an excess pressure due to carbon dioxide in solution of three bar or more, and

2. actual alcoholic strength by volume exceeding 1.2 % vol, but not exceeding 15 % vol, provided that the alcohol contained in the finished product is entirely of fermented origin.

Article 7. (Effective 1.07.2006) "Other fermented beverages" other than beer and wine shall be:

1. still fermented beverages falling within CN codes 2204 and 2205, but outside the scope of Article 6, as well as the products falling within CN code 2206, but outside the scope of item 2, which have:

a) actual alcoholic strength by volume exceeding 1.2 % vol but not exceeding 10 % vol, or

b) actual alcoholic strength by volume exceeding 10 % vol, but not exceeding 15 % vol, provided that the alcohol contained in the finished product is entirely of fermented origin;

2. (amended, SG No. 105/2006) sparkling fermented beverages falling within CN code 2206 00 91, as well as products falling within CN codes 2204 10, 2204 21 10, 2204 29 10 and 2205, but outside the scope of Article 6, which are:

a) in bottles with 'mushroom stoppers' held in place by ties or fastenings, or they have an excess pressure due to carbon dioxide in solution of three bar or more, and

b) with actual alcoholic strength by volume exceeding 1.2 % vol, but not exceeding 13 % vol, or with actual alcoholic strength by volume exceeding 13% but not exceeding 15% vol, provided that the alcohol contained in the finished product is entirely of fermented origin.

Article 8. (Effective 1.07.2006) "Intermediate products" shall be all products with actual alcoholic strength by volume exceeding 1.2 % vol, but not exceeding 22 % vol, falling within CN codes 2204, 2205 and 2206, but outside the scope of Articles 5, 6 and 7.

Article 9. (Effective as of 1.07.2006) "Ethyl alcohol (alcohol)" shall be any product:

1. falling within CN codes 2207 and 2208, with actual alcoholic strength by volume exceeding 1.2 % vol, even when such product is part of another product falling within another chapter of the Combined Nomenclature of the Republic of Bulgaria;

2. falling within CN codes 2204, 2205 and 2206, with actual alcoholic strength by volume exceeding 22 % vol.

3. (new, SG No. 63/2006) obtained from distillation and potable, containing other products, whether in solution or not.

Section II

Tobacco Products

Article 10. (Effective 1.07.2006) (1) "Cigars and cigarillos" shall be fit for smoking rolls of tobacco which:

1. are made entirely of natural tobacco, or

2. have an outer wrapper of natural tobacco, or

3. contain fine-cut tobacco and have an outer wrapper and a binder, both of reconstituted tobacco, and the outer wrapper is of the normal colour of a cigar and binds entirely the roll, including the filter but not the mouth-piece, if any, provided that the unit weight of the item not including the filter and the mouth-piece is equal to or does not exceed 1.2 g and the outer wrapper is fitted in spiral form with an acute angle of at least 30 ° to the longitudinal axis of the item, or

4. contain fine-cut tobacco and an outer wrapper of the normal colour of a cigar, of reconstituted tobacco, where the outer wrapper binds entirely the roll, including the filter but not the mouth-piece, if any, provided that the unit weight of the item not including the filter and the mouth-piece is equal to or exceeds 2.3 g and the circumference over at least one third of the length is not less than 34 mm.

(2) "Cigars and cigarillos" are furthermore deemed to be products made partially of substances other than tobacco but meeting the requirements of Paragraph 1, provided that they have:

1. one outer wrapper of natural tobacco;

2. one outer wrapper and one binder, both of restituted tobacco;

3. one outer wrapper of restituted tobacco.

(3) (New, SG No. 105/2006) Items which do not contain tobacco and are used exclusively for medical purposes shall not be considered to be "cigars and cigarillos".

Article 11. (Effective 1.07.2006) (1) "Cigarettes" shall be:

1. rolls of tobacco capable of being smoked which do not meet the requirements of for cigars and cigarillos under Article 10;

2. rolls of tobacco which, by simple non-industrial handling, are inserted into cigarette-paper tubes;

3. rolls of tobacco which, by simple non-industrial handling, are wrapped in cigarette paper.

(2) "Cigarettes" shall furthermore be considered to be products made partially or entirely of substances other than tobacco but meeting the requirements of Paragraph 1.

(3) The smoking products referred to in Paragraphs 1 and 2 shall, for excise duty purposes, be considered as two cigarettes where, excluding filter or mouth piece, it is longer

than 90 mm cm but not longer than 180 mm, as three cigarettes where, excluding filter or mouthpiece, it is longer than 180 mm but not longer than 270 mm, and so on.

(4) Products which do not contain tobacco and are used exclusively for medical purposes shall not be considered to be "cigarettes".

Article 12. (Effective 1.07.2006) (1) "Smoking tobacco (for pipe and cigarettes)" shall be:

1. tobacco which has been cut or otherwise split, twisted or pressed into blocks and is capable of being smoked without further industrial processing;

2. tobacco refuse capable of being smoked and put up for retail sale, provided that it does not meet the requirements of Article 10 and Article 11;

3. fine-cut tobacco for the rolling of cigarettes meeting the requirements of items and 2 in which more than 25 % by weight of the tobacco particles have a cut width of less than 1 mm.

(2) "Smoking tobacco" shall furthermore be items made entirely or partially of substances other than tobacco but meeting the requirements of the definition of smoking tobacco under Article 1.

(3) Items which do not contain tobacco and are used exclusively for medical purposes shall not be considered "smoking tobacco".

Section III Energy Products and Electricity

(Title supplemented, SG No. 105/2006)

Article 13. (Effective 1.07.2006, amended, SG No. 105/2006) (1) "Energy products" shall be products falling within:

1. CN codes 1507 through 1518, provided that they are intended for use as fuel for heating purposes or motor fuel;

2. CN codes 2701, 2702 and from 2704 through 2715;

3. CN codes 2901 and 2902;

4. CN code 2905 11 00, which are not of synthetic origin, if intended for use as fuel for heating purposes or motor fuel;

5. CN code 3403;

6. CN code 3811;

7. CN code 3817;

8. CN code 3824 90 99, including biodiesel, if intended for use as fuel for heating purposes or motor fuel.

(2) "Electricity" is a product falling within CN code 2716.

Article 14. (Effective 1.07.2006 - SG No. 91/2005, amended, SG No. 63/2006, No. 105/2006) (1) The provisions of Chapter Four shall apply in respect of the following energy products:

1. falling within CN codes 1507 through 1518, if intended for use as fuel for heating purposes or motor fuel;

2. falling within CN codes 2707 10, 2707 20; 2707 30 and 2707 50;

3. falling within CN codes 2710 11 through 2710 19 69; for energy products with CN codes 2710 11 21, 2710 11 25 and 2710 19 29 the provisions of the law regarding movement of excisable goods under excise duty suspension arrangement and supervision on them shall apply only where these are in draft condition;

4. falling within CN codes 2711, excluding CN codes 2711 11, 2711 21 and 2711 29;

5. falling within CN codes 2901 10;

6. falling within CN codes 2902 20, 2902 30, 2902 41, 2902 42, 2902 43 and 2902 44;

7. falling within CN code 2905 11 00, which are not of synthetic origin, if intended for use as fuel for heating purposes or motor fuel;

8. falling within CN code 3824 90 99, if intended for use as fuel for heating purposes or motor fuel, including biodiesel.

(2) (Amended, SG No. 109/2007) The provisions of Chapter Four shall also apply on the territory of this country in respect of energy products for which an excise duty rate is specified and which are intended for:

1. use, for sale as motor fuel, as heating fuel, or as an additive for or extender in motor fuel;

2. supply to end-users, exempted from excise duty.

(3) (New, SG No. 109/2007) Any energy product, falling within CN codes 2710 11 21, 2710 11 25 and 2710 19 29, shall be deemed in "draft condition" if it is unpackaged, transported in vessels, forming integral part of the means of transportation, as well as in cases, if its unpackaged, transported in vessels of a volume in excess of 210 lt.

Section IV (Repealed, SG No. 109/2007)

Coffee

Article 15. (Effective 1.07.2006, SG No. 91/2005, repealed, SG No. 109/2007).

Article 16. (Effective 1.07.2006, SG No. 91/2005, repealed, SG No. 109/2007).

Article 17. (Effective 1.07.2006, SG No. 91/2005, repealed, SG No. 109/2007).

Section V

Automobiles

Article 18. (Effective 1.07.2006) "Automobiles" shall be new and used passenger automobiles, cargo and passenger automobiles and racing automobiles, capable of carrying not more than 9 persons, including the driver, with engine power over 120 kilowatt (kW) according to the DIN system, respectively 126 kilowatt (kW) according to the SAE system, falling within CN code 8703.

CHAPTER THREE TAX LIABILITY

Section I

Incurrence of Excise Duty Liability

Article 19. (Effective 1.07.2006, amended, SG No. 105/2006) (1) The goods under Article 2 shall be subject to excise duty taxation, unless they are subject to excise duty suspension arrangement:

1. at their manufacturing on the territory of the country;

2. at their bringing into the territory of the country from the territory of another Member State;

3. at their importation on the territory of the country.

(2) Import of excisable goods shall mean their bringing into the territory of the country of non-Community excisable goods, as well as bringing into the territory of the country of Community excisable goods from third territories which are part of the customs territory of the Community.

(3) Notwithstanding Paragraph 2, where the goods are placed under customs regime at their bringing into the territory of the country, their import shall be considered to have been accomplished when they are released for free circulation.

Article 20. (Effective 1.07.2006) (1) The liability for excise duty payment shall arise from the date of release of excisable goods for consumption.

(2) Release for consumption shall be:

1. bringing out excisable goods from a tax warehouse, unless the goods move under excise duty suspension arrangement from the moment of bringing them out in compliance with the terms and procedures of this Act;

2. failure to meet the conditions for movement of excisable goods under excise duty suspension arrangement;

3. cons7umption of excisable goods in a warehouse, unless they have been input as raw materials for the production of excisable goods;

4. production of excisable goods not subject to excise duty suspension arrangement;

5. importation, including in violation of customs legislation, unless excisable goods are placed under excise duty suspension arrangement;

6. bringing out from a tax warehouse of excisable goods affixed with an excise label;

7. expiry of 60 days from receipt of excise labels for goods for which the excise duty has not become due on another ground;

8. (supplemented, SG No. 105/2006) establishing shortage of goods for which excise duty is due, including shortage of coal, coke, electricity or natural gas established in respect of the persons under Article 57a, Paragraph 1, items 1 and 2;

9. termination of the validity of a license for tax warehouse management - for all goods which at the time of termination are subject to excise duty suspension arrangement.

10. (new, SG No. 105/2006) deregistration of the persons - for the stock of goods on which no excise duty has been charged;

11. (new, SG No. 105/2006) receipt of excisable goods from a registered trader under excise duty suspension arrangement;

12. (new, SG No. 105/2006) receipt of excisable goods from a non- registered trader under excise duty suspension arrangement;

13. (new, SG No. 105/2006, supplemented, SG No. 109/2007) receipt of excisable goods released for consumption in another Member State, except where such goods are deposited in a tax warehouse on the territory of this country;

14. (new, SG No. 105/2006) receipt of excisable goods under conditions of distant selling within the meaning of the Value Added Tax Act;

15. (new, SG No. 105/2006) the sale of coal and coke to persons other than those registered under Article 57a, Paragraph 1, item 1, except for sale to natural persons other than sole traders;

16. (new, SG No. 105/2006) consumption of coke and coal by the persons under Article 57a Paragraph 1, item 1 for their own needs;

17. (new, SG No. 105/2006) the sale of electricity or natural gas to consumers of electricity and natural gas for household and business purposes within the meaning of the Energy Act;

18. (new, SG No. 105/2006) consumption of electricity or natural gas by the persons under Article 57a, Paragraph 1, item 1 for their own purposes, except for the cases of electricity used to produce electricity and electricity used to maintain the ability to produce electricity;

19. (new, SG No. 105/2006) consumption of energy products by excise- exempt end users other than those specified in the certificate.

20. (new, SG No. 109/2007) introduction into the territory of this country of automobiles from the territory of another Member State.

(3) Where the moment of release for consumption cannot be established, such date shall be the date on which supervisory authorities establish the actions, facts and circumstances under Paragraph 2.

Section II

Exemption and Refunding

Article 21. (Effective 1.07.2006) (1) Exempt from payment of excise duty shall be:

1. excisable goods designated for diplomatic missions and consulates and representations of international organizations and members of their staff;

2. (amended, SG No. 63/2006) excisable goods for which a duly ratified, promulgated and enacted international treaty provides for exemption from any tax, levy and other charges (payments, deductions) having the effect of indirect tax;

3. excisable goods designated for the armed forces of any other country which is a party to the North Atlantic Treaty Organisation, for use by such armed forces; for the needs of the civil staff accompanying them or for supply of relevant officer canteens or mess-rooms;

4. (amended, SG No. 105/2006) excisable goods imported by means of international postal and other parcels as well as in the personal luggage of passengers within the authorized duty-free import limits under the customs legislation;

5. (new, SG No. 105/2006, amended, SG No. 109/2007) tobacco products, alcohol and alcoholic beverages, purchased in another Member State by natural persons for personal purposes and transported by them in quantities laid down in the implementing regulation to this Act;

6. (new, SG No. 105/2006) excisable goods intended for the institutions of the European Community;

7. (new, SG No. 105/2006) import of or bringing from another Member State of electricity and natural gas;

8. (new, SG No. 105/2006) ethyl alcohol contained in products imported or brought into the territory of the country, which by their characteristics are not intended for consumption as food or drinks or which are not intended as additives in the production of food or drinks;

9. (new, SG No. 105/2006) import of or bringing from another Member State of coke or coal by persons under Article 57a Paragraph 1, item 1.

(2) (New, SG No. 63/2006, supplemented, SG No. 109/2007) Where excise duty has been paid on the goods referred to in Items 1 and 3 of Paragraph (1), exemption shall be granted by a refund. The refund procedure shall be specified, as follows:

1. for those under Item 1 of Paragraph (1) - by ordinance of the Minsiter of Finance and the Minister of Foreign Affairs;

2. for those under Item 3 of Paragraph (1) - by ordinance of the Minsiter of Finance and the Minister of Defence.

(3) (Renumbered from Paragraph 2, SG No. 63/2006, amended, SG No. 109/2007) The procedure for implementation of Paragraph (1) shall be determined by the implementing regulation to this Act.

(4) (Renumbered from Paragraph 3, SG No. 63/2006, amended, SG No. 105/2006) No excise duty shall be due or the excise duty paid shall be refunded for motor vehicles which have been deforced or stolen and import customs charges on them are refunded or released under the customs legislation.

Article 22. (Effective 1.07.2006 - SG No. 91/2005) (1) (Amended, SG No. 63/2006) Completely denatured ethyl alcohol shall be exempted from levy of excise duty.

(2) (New, SG No. 63/2006) The excise duty paid on ethyl alcohol, which is both expressly denatured and used for the manufacture of products not for human consumption, shall be refunded.

(3) (Renumbered from Paragraph 2, SG No. 63/2006) Refunded shall be the excise duty paid on alcohol and alcoholic beverages where used for production of:

1. vinegar falling within CN code 2209;

2. (supplemented, SG No. 105/2006, amended, SG No. 31/2007) medicines within the meaning of the Medicinal Products in Human Medicine Act and veterinary medical products within the Veterinary Practices Act;

3. (amended, SG No. 105/2006) flavours with alcoholic strength not exceeding 1.2 % vol used as additives to foodstuffs and soft drinks;

4. (amended, SG No. 109/2007) foodstuffs (with filling or otherwise prepared), where the alcohol and alcohoilic beverages were input directly of as ingredients in semi-finished products, provided that the alcoholic strength does not exceed 8.5 litres of pure alcohol per 100 kg of the chocolates, and 5 litres of pure alcohol per 100 kg of the other foodstuffs.

(4) (Renumbered from Paragraph 3, SG No. 63/2006) Refunded shall be the excise duty paid on alcohol and alcoholic beverages where used:

1. for medical treatment purposes in medical establishments and pharmacies;

2. as samples for analysis, for necessary production tests, or for scientific purposes;

3. for scientific research;

4. in a manufacturing process provided that the finished product does not contain alcohol.

(5) (New, SG No. 105/2006) Refunded shall be the excise duty paid on flavours with alcoholic strength exceeding 1.2% vol used as additives in the production of foodstuffs and soft drinks with alcoholic strength not exceeding 1.2 % vol.

(6) (Renumbered from Paragraph 4, amended, SG No. 63/2006, renumbered from Paragraph 5, amended, SG No. 105/2006) The excise duty paid under Paragraphs 2 to 5 shall be refunded after the sale of the manufactured products referred to in Paragraphs 2, 3 and 5 or, respectively, after the use thereof under Paragraph 4.

Article 23. (Effective 1.07.2006, amended, SG No. 105/2006) (1) The excise duty paid by the persons under Article 76a, Paragraph 4 shall be refunded where the following conditions obtain simultaneously:

1. the persons have fulfilled their obligations under Article 76b;

2. the persons have the third copy of the simplified accompanying document, certified by the recipient in the other Member State;

3. (repealed, SG No. 109/2007).

(2) Refund under Paragraph 1 shall be carried out by filing a written request for excise duty refund to the competent customs authority under Article 76b, Paragraph 1, item 1.

(3) Attached to the request under Paragraph 2 shall be documents set out in the implementing regulation to this Act.

(4) The head of the competent customs authority shall, within 30 days from receipt of the request and the required documents, issue a motivated decision granting or refusing to grant the request, in whole or in part.

(5) The decision under Paragraph 4 may be appealed under the procedure of the Tax and Social-Insurance Procedure Code.

Article 24. (Effective 1.07.2006) (1) Exempt from excise duty shall be the energy products:

1. for aircraft and vessels, unless used for private pleasure flying and sailing;

2. (amended, SG, No. 105/2006) in standard tanks of motor vehicles and in containers for special use - upon the entry of the vehicles in the territory of the country;

3. (new, SG No. 105/2006) with CN codes 2710 11 21, 2710 11 25 and 2710 19 29 - in consumer packages of up to 3 litres within the meaning of the Consumer Protection and Rules of Trade Act;

4. (new, SG No. 105/2006) with CN codes 2705, 2707 40, 2707 60, from 2707 99 30 to 2708 20, from 2710 19 81 to 2710 19 99, 2712, 2713, 2714, 2715 from 2902 50 to 2902 90, 3403, 3811 21, 3811 29 where used for purposes other than as motor fuel or heating fuel.

(2) Exempt from excise duty shall be energy products:

1. (amended, SG No. 63/2006) with dual use for purposes;

2. used for injection into blast-furnaces for the purposes of chemical reduction as additive to carbonates used as basic fuel;

3. (amended, SG, No. 105/2006) used in production of electricity;

4. (new, SG No. 63/2006) used for purposes other than as motor fuel and heating fuel.

5. (new, SG No. 105/2006) used in mineralogical processes;

6. (new, SG No. 105/2006) used in a tax warehouse for production of energy products provided that the energy products used are produced in the same tax warehouse.

(3) Exemption under Paragraph 1, item 1, and Paragraph 2 shall apply only to excise-exempt end users.

(4) The procedure for exemption and issuance of certificates to end users shall be determined by implementing regulation to this Act.

(5) The Customs Agency shall keep a register of the certificates issued under Paragraph 4.

(6) The form and content of the register under Paragraph 5 shall be determined by the implementing regulation to this Act.

Article 24a. (New, SG, No. 105/2006) (1) Excise duty paid on electricity shall be refunded:

1. to persons using electricity for chemical reduction or in electrolytic, metallurgical or mineralogical processes;

2. to persons using electricity in the manufacture of products, provided that the cost of the electricity accounts for more than 50 per cent of the cost of the product;

3. to licensed railway carriers and railway infrastructure managers - for traction and non-traction electricity used by them in the conduct of their business.

(2) The refund under Paragraph 1 shall be made on the basis of a written request, to be submitted by 30 April in the year following the use of electricity under Paragraph 1.

(3) The request under Paragraph 2 shall be filed to the head of the customs authority by domicile of the persons under Paragraph 1.

(4) Enclosed to the request shall be documents set out in the implementing regulation to this Act.

(5) The head of the competent customs authority shall, within 30 days from receipt of the request and the required documents, issue a motivated decision granting or refusing to grant the request, in whole or in part.

(6) The decision under Paragraph 5 may be appealed under the procedure of the Tax and Social-Insurance Procedure Code.

(7) The excise duty shall be refunded within 14 days from the date of issue of the decision under Paragraph 5.

Article 25. (Effective 1.07.2006) (1) (Amended, SG No. 105/2006) Licensed warehouse keepers and registered persons shall be exempt from excise duty or excise duty paid shall be refunded upon:

1. (amended, SG No. 109/2007) destruction of excisable goods under the control of customs bodies, including where said goods are affixed with excise label, as well as upon retirement or destruction of excise labels under the terms of Article 27, Paragraphs 7, 8 and 10;

2. shortages and irrecoverable loss of excisable goods as a result of force majeure, including where said goods are affixed with excise label;

3. losses from natural wastage resulting from changes in the physical and chemical properties during storage and transportation of excisable goods, within normal limits, corresponding to established allowances for maximum natural wastage according to the regulation under Paragraph 2;

4. (supplemented, SG No. 109/2007) technological rejects of excisable goods within the admissible norms laid down in the technological documentation for the relevant production or activity.

(2) The norms for maximum natural wastage of excisable goods shall be determined by an ordinance of the Minister of Finance.

Article 26. (Effective 1.07.2006) (1) (Renumbered from Article 26, amended, SG No. 105/2006) In the cases of export of excisable goods the excise duty paid to the republican budget shall be refunded.

(2) (New, SG No. 105/2006) Except for the cases of Article 24, Paragraph 1, item 1, supply of energy products for feeding of vessels and aircraft shall be considered export and the excise duty secured/paid on the goods shall be released/refunded according to a procedure and within time limits set out in the implementing regulation to this Act. This shall not apply to vessels and aircraft used for sports, pleasure or private purposes.

Article 27. (Effective 1.07.2006) (1) Undue but paid excise duty or excise duty subject to refunding shall be refunded or offset against excise duty due on the basis of a written request filed to the head of the customs authority by domicile of the person or by location of the tax warehouse in the cases where the person is a licensed warehouse keeper.

(2) Enclosed to the request shall be the documents laid down in the implementing regulation to this Act.

(3) The authority under Paragraph 1, within 30 days from receipt of the request, removal of irregularities respectively, shall make a motivated decision on granting or refusing to grant the request - in whole or in pArticle The time limit for making a decision in the cases of

Article 26 shall be 14 days. Where no decision has been issued, this shall be deemed as a silent refusal of the request in whole.

(4) (Amended, SG No. 105/2006) The decision or refusal under Paragraph 3 may be appealed before the director of the regional customs directorate, who shall issue a decision on the claim within 14 days. If no decision is issued within the said time limit, this shall be deemed as confirmation in whole of the decision in the appealed Article The decision or absence of a decision of the director of the regional customs directorate may be appealed under the Tax and Social-Insurance Procedure Code.

(5) The excise duty shall be refunded within 14 days from entry into force of the statement of refunding.

(6) (Amended, SG No. 105/2006) Excise labels ordered and received by the persons under Article 64, Paragraphs 1, 2 and 3 may be returned to the competent customs authority, provided that said excise labels have not been affixed on bottled beverages or tobacco products, and a written statement of ascertainment shall be executed, indicating the type, issue or serial number, total number, consecutive numbering as well as other specific features typical of respective excise labels.

(7) (New, SG No. 105/2006) Excise labels that have become defective in the process of production of tobacco products and bottled alcoholic beverages shall be retired by a bilaterally signed protocol between the persons under Article 64 and the competent customs authority and shall be handed over to the latter.

(8) (New, SG No. 105/2006) Where owing to objective reasons excisable goods or consumer packages do not meet normative requirements or technical or quality standards of the manufacturer and thus cannot be sold on the market, excise labels affixed on the packages shall be retired and destroyed in the presence of a customs authority under the procedure and in the manner set out in the implementing regulation to this Act.

(9) (Renumbered from Paragraph 7, amended, SG No. 105/2006) The excise duty under Paragraph 6 shall be refunded or offset under the procedure of this Article on the basis of a request for refund, which shall be filed not later than 30 days from the date of executing the written statement of ascertainment under Paragraph 6.

(10) (New, SG No. 105/2006) In the cases of Paragraphs 7 and 8 the excise duty shall be offset or refunded under the procedure of this Article on the basis of a request for refund, which shall be filed not later than 30 days from the date of executing the protocol under Paragraphs 7 and 8 provided that the visible requisites and securities ascertain incontestably the authenticity of the excise label.

Section III Tax Base

Article 28. (Effective 1.07.2006) The tax base for excise duty purposes shall be as follows:

1. for beer - the number of hectoliters for Plato degrees;

2. for wine - the number of hectoliters per finished product;

3. for other fermented beverages - the number of hectoliters per finished product;

4. for intermediate products - the number of hectoliters per finished product;

5. for ethyl alcohol - the number of hectoliters of pure alcohol measured at a temperature of 20 °C;

6. for petrol, gas oil and kerosene - the number of litres recalculated to a comparative temperature of 15°C;

7. for fuel oils and liquefied petroleum gas (LPG) - the quantity of fuel oils and liquefied petroleum gas (LPG) measured in tons;

8. for natural gas - calorific capacity measured in gigajoules;

9. (repealed, SG No. 109/2007);

10. for cigars and cigarillos - the quantity of units per product;

11. (supplemented, SG No. 81/2006) for biodiesel and bioethanol - the quantity of litres recalculated to a comparative temperature of 15 °C;

12. (new, SG No. 105/2006, amended, SG No 109/2007) for coke and coal Ц the highest calorific capacity measured in gigajoules;

13. (new, SG No. 105/2006) for electricity - the quantity measured in megawatthours.

Article 29. (Effective 1.07.2006) (1) Excise duty on tobacco shall be calculated as a sum of a specific excise duty and a proportional excise duty. The tax base for calculating the specific excise duty on cigarettes shall be the quantity of units per product and of the proportional excise duty, the selling price.

(2) The excise duty on smoking tobacco (for pipe and cigarettes) shall be calculated as a sum of a specific excise duty and a proportional excise duty. The tax base for calculating the specific excise duty shall be the quantity of kilograms, and of the proportional excise duty, the selling price.

(3) The selling price under Paragraphs 1 and 2 shall be:

1. (amended, SG No. 105/2006) the price registered according to the prevailing established procedure under Article 20, Paragraph 2, items 1 - 5, 8 and 9;

2. the price written on the excise label - in the cases under Article 20, Paragraph 2, items 6 and 7;

3. (amended, SG No. 105/2006) the price registered according to the established procedure at the time of placing the goods under excise duty suspension arrangement respectively, except for the cases under Item 4;

4. (amended, SG No. 105/2006) the price registered according to the established procedure at the time of placing the goods under excise duty suspension arrangement or temporary storage respectively;

5. (amended, SG No. 105/2006) the price fixed in the implementing regulation to this Act - in the cases where no selling price for the respective cigarette brand under Paragraphs 1 and 2 has been registered according to the established procedure;

6. (amended, SG No. 105/2006) the price registered or laid down in the regulation at the time of supervisory authorities establishing violations under Chapter Nine.

Article 30. (Effective 1.07.2006) The tax base for automobiles shall be as follows:

1. for used automobiles - number of kilowatts depending on the engine power;

2. for new automobiles - number of kilowatts depending on the engine power for the excess over 120 kilowatts 120 (kW) under DIN system and for the excess over 126 kilowatts (kW) under SAE system.

Section IV Excise Rate

Article 31. (Effective 1.07.2006) Excise rates on alcohol and alcoholic beverages shall be:

1. for beer - BGN 1.50 per 1 hectolitre of Plato degree;

2. for wine - BGN 0 per 1 hectolitre;

3. for other fermented beverages - BGN 0 per 1 hectolitre of finished product;

4. for intermediate products - BGN 90 per 1 hectolitre of finished product;

5. for ethyl alcohol - BGN 1,100 per 1 hectolitre of pure alcohol;

6. (amended, SG No. 105/2006) for ethyl alcohol (rakiya) produced in a specialized small distillery - BGN 550 per 1 hectolitre of pure alcohol.

Article 32. (Effective 1.07.2006) (1) (Amended, SG No. 105/2006) Excise rates on motor fuels shall be as follows:

1. for leaded petrol falling within CN codes 2710 11 31, 2710 11 51, and 2710 11 59 - BGN 830 per 1,000 litres;

2. (amended, SG No. 109/2007) for unleaded petrol falling within CN codes 2710 11 31, 2710 11 41, 2710 11 45, and 2710 11 49 - BGN 685 per 1,000 litres;

3. (amended, SG No. 109/2007) for gas oil falling within CN codes 2710 19 41 through 2710 19 49 - BGN 600 per 1,000 litres;

4. (amended, SG No. 109/2007) for kerosene falling within CN codes 2710 19 21,and 2710 19 25 - BGN 535 per 1,000 litres;

5. for liquefied petroleum gas (LPG) falling within CN codes 2711 12 11 through 2711 19 00, including energy products falling within CN codes 2901, 2711 29, from 2902 11 through 2902 44 - BGN 340 per 1,000 kilograms;

6. for natural gas falling within CN codes 2711 11 00, and 2711 21 00 - BGN 0 per 1 gigajoule;

7. (supplemented, SG No. 109/2007) for biodiesel falling within CN code 3824 90 99 and bioethanol falling within CN code 2207 20 00, which conform to the requirements of Article 26 of the Renewable aand Alternative Energy Sources and Biofuels Act - BGN 0 per 1,000 litres.

8. (new, SG No. 109/2007, effective upon issuance of positive decision by the European Commission) for lead free petrol falling within CN codes 2710 11 31, 2710 11 41, 2710 11 45 and 2710 11 49, where the content of bioethanol falling within CN code 2207 20 00 and conforming to the requirements of Article 26 of the Renewable and Alternative Energy Sources and Biofuels Act is from 4 to 5 percent inclusive - BGN 664 per 1,000 litres.

9. (new, SG No. 109/2007, effective upon issuance of positive decision by the European Commission) for gas oil falling within CN codes from 2710 19 41 to 2710 19 49, where the content of biodiesel falling within CN code 3824 90 99 and conforming to the

requirements of Article 26 of the Renewable and Alternative Energy Sources and Biofuels Act is from 4 to 5 percent inclusive - BGN 582 per 1,000 litres.

(2) (Amended, SG No. 63/2006, No. 81/2006, No. 105/2006) The excise rates on motor fuel used for tillage of agricultural land by agricultural producers approved for financial assistance under the Agricultural Producers Support Act,shall be as follows:

1. for gas oil falling within CN codes 2710 19 41 through 2710 19 49 - BGN 50 per 1,000 litres;

2. for kerosene falling within CN codes 2710 19 21 and 2710 19 25 - BGN 50 per 1,000 litres;

3. for natural gas falling within CN codes 2711 11 00 and 2711 21 00 - BGN 0 per gigajoule;

4. (supplemented, SG No. 109/2007) for biodiesel falling within CN code 3824 90 99 and bioethanol falling within CN code 2207 20 00, which conform to the requirements of Article 26 of the Renewable and Alternative Energy Sources and Biofuels Act - BGN 0 per 1,000 litres.

(3) (New, SG No. 63/2006) The rates of excise duty referred to in Items 1 and 2 of Paragraph (2) shall be applied by means of reimbursement of the difference between the relevant rate under Paragraph (1) and the rate under Paragraph (2) for a quantity calculated on the basis of an annual fuel consumption rate of 73 litres per hectare of registered arable agricultural land.

(4) (New, SG No. 63/2006) Not later than the 1st day of July of each year, the Minister of Agriculture and Forestry shall provide the Director of the National Customs Agency with the following information from the Register of Agricultural Producers:

1. identification particulars of the agricultural producer;

2. legal form of business organization, name (business name), permanent address (registered office and address of the place of management), telephone, fax, electronic mail address;

3. data on the agricultural land farmed (in hectares) according to the agricultural land parcel identification.

(5) (New, SG No. 63/2006, amended, SG No 109/2007) The right to reimbursement shall be exercised by the agricultural producers on two occasions in respect of the motor fuel purchased thereby during the current year, based on an approval annual consumption rate of 7.3 litres per decare of registered cultivated agricultural land. The requests for reimbursement shall be submitted once from the 1st day of July until the 15th day of August in respect to the quantities, consumed up to that period and from the 15th day of August until the 31st day of December in the current year Ц for the balance of the consumption rate amount.

(6) (New, SG No. 63/2006) Reimbursement under Paragraph (3) shall be effected within two months after submission of the request according to a procedure established the Regulations for Application of this Act .

(7) (New, SG No. 105/2006, amended, SG No 109/2007) The excise rate on energy products falling within CN codes 2710 11, other than those under Paragraphs 1 and 2, as well as for energy products falling within CN codes 2707 10, 2707 20, 2707 30, 2707 50, 2709 shall be BGN 685 per 1,000 litres.

(8) (New, SG No. 105/2006, amended, SG No 109/2007) The excise rate for energy products falling within CN codes 2710 19, other than those under Paragraphs 1 and 2, shall be BGN 600 per 1,000 litres.

(9) (New, SG No. 105/2006, amended, SG No 109/2007) The excise rate on energy products intended for use as additives or extenders to motor fuels shall be the rate under Items 2 - 5 of Paragraph 1 depending on the type of the fuel to which they refer. Where the type of fuel for which they are intended cannot be determined, the rate for them shall be BGN 685 per 1,000 litres.

Article 33. (1) (Amended, SG No. 63/2006, No. 105/2006) Excise rates on energy products for heating shall be as follows:

1. (effective 1.01.2009 - SG, No. 109/2007) for gas oil falling within CN codes 2710 19 41 through 2710 19 49 - BGN 50 per 1,000 litres;

2. for fuel oils falling within CN codes 2710 19 61 through 2710 19 69 and for energy products falling within CN codes 2706, 2707 91, 2707 99 11, 2707 99 19, 2710 91, and 2710 99 - BGN 30 per 1,000 kg;

3. (effective 1.01.2009 - SG, No. 109/2007) for kerosene falling within CN codes 2710 19 21 0 and 2710 19 25 - BGN 50 per 1,000 litres;

4. for liquefied petroleum gas (LPG) falling within CN codes 2711 12 11 through 2711 19 00 - BGN 0 per 1,000 kg;

5. for natural gas falling within CN codes 2711 11 00 and 2711 21 00 - BGN 0 per gigajoule;

6. for biodiesel falling within CN code 3824 90 99 - BGN 0 per 1,000 litres;

7. (amended, SG No. 109/2007) for coal and coke falling within CN codes 2701, 2702 and 2704 Ц BGN 0.40 per gigajoule.

(2) The rate under Paragraph 1, item 4 shall apply to liquefied petroleum gas (LPG) in containers used for heating and household purposes and meeting the requirements laid down in the implementing regulation to this Act.

Article 34. (Effective 1.07.2006 - SG No. 91/2005, amended, SG No. 63/2006) The rates on gas oil and kerosene under Article 33 shall apply only to marked fuel.

Article 34a. (New, SG No. 105/2006) (1) (Amended, SG No. 109/2007) The excise rate for electricity falling within CN code 2716, except for the cases of Paragraph 2, shall be BGN 1.20 per megawatthour.

(2) The excise rate for electricity falling within CN code 2716 for consumers of electricity for household purposes within the meaning of the Energy Act shall be BGN 0 per megawatthour.

Article 35. (Effective 1.07.2006) (1) The energy products under Article 13 intended for use, offered for sale or used as heating fuel or motor fuel and for which no excise rate is fixed in Article 32, Paragraph 1 and Article 33, Paragraph 1 shall be charged at the rate set for the equivalent heating fuel or motor fuel.

(2) (Supplemented, SG No. 105/2006) Apart from the energy products under Article 13 and bioethanol, all other products intended for use, offered for sale or used as motor fuel, as additive or as extender of motor fuel shall be charged at the rate set for the equivalent motor fuel in Article 32, Paragraph 1.

(3) In addition to the energy products under Article 13 all other hydrocarbons, except peat, which are intended for use, offered for sale or used as heating fuel, shall be charged at the rate set for the equivalent heating fuel under Article 33, Paragraph 1.

Article 36. (Effective 1.07.2006, SG No. 91/2005, repealed, SG No 109/2007).

Article 37. (Effective 1.07.2006) The excise rate on cigars and cigarillos shall be BGN 270 per 1,000 pieces.

Article 38. (Effective 1.07.2006) The excise rate on smoking tobacco (for pipe and cigarettes) shall be:

1. of the specific excise duty - BGN 4.50 per 100 g;

2. of the proportional excise duty - 10 per cent of the selling price.

Article 39. (Effective 1.07.2006) The excise rate on cigarettes shall be:

1. (amended, SG No. 105/2006, SG No 109/2007) of the specific excise duty - BGN 37 per 1,000 pieces;

2. (amended, SG No. 105/2006, SG No 109/2007) of the proportional excise duty - 35 per cent of the selling price.

Article 40. (Effective 1.07.2006) (1) The excise duty on used automobiles shall be:

1. for automobiles with engine power exceeding 120 kW to 150 kW under DIN system - BGN 35 per 1 kW;

2. for automobiles with engine power exceeding 150 kW under DIN system - BGN 60 per 1 kW;

3. for automobiles with engine power exceeding 126 kW to 157.5 kW under SAE system - BGN 33.33 per 1 kW;

4. for automobiles with engine power exceeding 157.5 kW under SAE system - BGN 57.14 per 1 kW.

(2) The excise duty on new automobiles shall be:

1. seven hundred lev + BGN 90 per 1 kW for the excess over 120 kW under DIN system;

2. seven hundred lev + BGN 85.71 per 1 kW for the excess over 126 kW under SAE system.

Section V Calculation and Payment of Excise Duty

Article 41. (Effective 1.07.2006) The amount of the excise duty due shall be calculated by multiplying the tax base by the excise rate.

Article 42. (Effective 1.07.2006) In the cases under Article 20, Paragraph 2, item 5 the excise duty shall be determined and accounted for in accordance with the procedure laid down for the customs liability.

Article 43. (Effective 1.07.2006) (1) (Amended, SG No. 105/2006) Outside the cases under Article 42 the excise duty shall be charged by:

1. (amended, SG No. 109/2007) the licensed warehouse keeper, the persons under Article 3, points 4 and 6 and the registered persons under Article 57, Article 57b, Paragraph 3, and Article 57c on the date it becomes due - by issuing a tax document under Article 84, Paragraph 1;

2. the registered person under Article 57a, Paragraph 1, items 1, 2 and 3 - by issuing a tax document under Article 84, Paragraph 1 under the terms of Article 84, Paragraph 3 for the goods on which the excise duty becomes due as per Article 20, Paragraph 2, items 15, 16, 17 and 18;

3. the registered person under Article 57a, Paragraph 1, items 1 and 2 - on the date of establishing the shortage under Article 20, Paragraph 2, item 8 by issuing a tax document under Article 84, Paragraph 1.

(2) The persons under Paragraph 1 shall declare the excise duty charged for the tax period by filing an excise declaration.

(3) The tax period shall cover one month and shall coincide with the calendar month.

(4) The first tax period shall cover the time from the date of submitting the license or the certificate of registration under this Act until the last day of the calendar month in which licensing or registration is made.

(5) The last tax period shall cover the time from the beginning of the calendar month in which the license was terminated until the date of termination thereof.

Article 44. (Effective 1.07.2006) (1) The excise duty due shall be paid to the republican budget as follows:

1. (amended, SG No. 105/2006) in the cases under Article 20, Paragraph 2, item 5 - to the account or in cash at the tills of the competent customs authority by the importer within the time limits for payment of the customs liability laid down in the Customs Act where the debtor is a natural person other than a sole trader;

2. (amended, SG No. 105/2006) in the cases under Article 20, Paragraph 2, item 5 - to the account of the competent customs authority by the importer within the time limits for payment of the customs liability laid down in the Customs Act;

3. (new, SG No. 105/2006) in the cases under Article 20, Paragraph 2, items 12 and 13 - to the account of the competent customs authority by permanent address, domicile respectively, by the person who is the recipient of the goods, within 14 days from their receipt;

4. (new, SG No. 105/2006) in the cases under Article 20, Paragraph 2, item 19 - to the account of the competent customs authority by the excise- exempt end user within 14 days from use of the energy products for purposes other than those specified in the certificate;

5. (new, SG No. 105/2006) in the cases under Article 76d - to the account of the competent customs authority by permanent address, domicile respectively, by the person within 14 days from the date of his being notified about the amount of the excise duty;

6. (renumbered from item 3, SG No. 105/2006) in all other cases - to the account of the competent customs authority by the licensed warehouse keeper or the registered person within the time limit for filing the excise declaration.

(2) The excise duty may furthermore be paid by a person other than the person under Paragraph 1 with the written consent of the debtor.

(3) The excise duty shall be deemed to have been paid to the republican budget as from the date on which the amount is received on the account or at the tills of the competent customs authority under Paragraph 1.

(4) Where the excise duty has not been paid to the republican budget within the time limits set forth under this Article, the person obligated to pay it shall be the person under Paragraph 1.

(5) The customs authorities shall authorize release of the goods after payment or securing of the excise duty due according to the procedure laid down for the customs liability.

(6) (New, SG No. 109/2007) In the cases under Article 64, Paragraph 2 the competent customs authority under Paragraph1, item 2 shall be the customs authority, where the persons have applied for excise labels. This customs authority shall confirm payment of the excise duty due to the customs authority, where import clearance is performed, with the view of authorizing release of the goods.

Article 45. (Effective 1.07.2006) (1) (Amended, SG No. 109/2007) Upon entry into force of a new amount of the excise rate the persons under Article 64, Paragraphs 1, 2 and 3 shall declare available stocks of tobacco products and alcoholic beverages falling within CN code 2208, affixed with excise labels, before the competent customs authority by location of the warehouse according to the procedure laid down in the implementing regulation to this Act.

(2) Available stocks under Paragraph 1 shall be charged additionally and the additional excise duty due shall be paid within the time limits under Article 44.

CHAPTER FOUR EXCISE DUTY SUSPENSION ARRANGEMENT

Section I General Provisions

Article 46. (Effective 1.07.2006) (1) (Amended, SG No. 105/2006) Under excise duty suspension arrangement within the meaning of this Act excise taxation of goods shall be suspended temporarily on their production, bringing or importation into the territory of the country.

(2) Excise duty suspension arrangement shall be applied by a licensed warehouse keeper for:

1. production of excisable goods in a tax warehouse;

2. storage of excisable goods in a tax warehouse;

3. movement of excisable goods.

(3) Excise duty suspension arrangement shall not apply to the other tax liabilities of the person subject to taxation.

Section II Licensing

Article 47. (1) (Renumbered from Article 47, SG No. 105/2006) A licensed warehouse keeper may be a person who:

1. (amended, SG No. 105/2006) is a trader within the meaning of the Commerce Act or the legislation of another Member State or a country which is a signatory to the European Economic Area Agreement as well as a legal person set up on the grounds of a normative act - where the person is a producer of excisable goods, or is an equity commercial company with

registered and fully paid-in capital of not less than BGN 500,000 - in the cases where the person is not a producer of excisable goods;

2. is not undergoing bankruptcy proceedings or liquidation;

3. is represented by persons who:

a) have not been convicted of a crime of general nature;

b) have not been members of a managing or controlling body or unlimited liability partners in a company dissolved by insolvency, if unsatisfied creditors have remained;

4. has no due and payable customs liabilities, tax liabilities and compulsory social security liabilities;

5. (amended, SG No. 63/2006) has not committed a grave or repeated violation under this Act;

6. has been granted a license or permit or have been registered to conduct the activity where this is provided for by another law;

7. has own or rented premises for carrying out the activities under Article 46, Paragraph 2, which meet the security and control requirements laid down in the implementing regulation to this Act;

8. uses automated reporting systems, allowing real-time control on raw materials, excisable goods produced or stored and ensuring that the person is capable of meeting the requirements of the arrangement.

(2) (New, SG No. 105/2006) Traders within the meaning of the legislation of another Member State or a country which is a signatory to the European Economic Area Agreement shall carry out activity as a licensed warehouse keeper through a branch in the Republic of Bulgaria.

Article 48. (1) To obtain a license for management of a tax warehouse a written application shall be filed to the Director of the Customs Agency, which shall contain:

1. description of the operations to be performed in the tax warehouse;

2. the type of excisable goods to be produced or stored;

3. annual projected volume of excisable goods produced and/or stored under excise duty suspension arrangement according to the business plan under Paragraph 2, item 13;

4. annual projected volume of movement of excisable goods under excise duty suspension arrangement;

5. (supplemented, SG No. 105/2006) description of the systems under Article 47, Paragraph 1, item 8;

6. exact location, description and intended use of the tax warehouse premises;

7. type of security to be provided;

8. names of employees authorized to sign accompanying administrative documents.

(2) The following documents shall be attached to the application under Paragraph 1:

1. (amended, SG, No. 34/2006) a current certificate of registration in the Commercial Register;

2. (supplemented, SG No. 105/2006) a conviction certificate of the circumstances under Article 47, Paragraph 1, item 3, littera "a", and where the persons are non-residents - a declaration;

3. (supplemented, SG No. 105/2006) a declaration of the circumstances under Article 47, Paragraph 1, item 3, littera "b";

4. a certificate of presence or absence of tax liabilities on compulsory social security payments;

5. (supplemented, SG No. 105/2006) a declaration of the circumstances under Article 47, Paragraph 1, item 5;

6. a license, permit or registration for conducting business where this is required by law;

7. a deed of ownership or rent contract for the tax warehouse premises;

8. (supplemented, SG No. 109/2007) a current sketch of the real estate;

9. a layout of the tax warehouse premises;

10. annual financial statements for the previous years audited by a registered auditor or a specialised audit enterprise within the meaning of the Independent Financial Audit Act where the person has operated more than two years and interim financial statements prepared at the end of the month preceding the month of filing the application;

11. technical documentation for the automated reporting systems;

12. a technological scheme of the production process, input norms, maximum values of technological losses, technical specification;

13. a business plan including information about:

a) the type of excisable goods to be produced or stored in the tax warehouse;

b) the monthly average quantity of excisable goods to be stored - by type of goods and excise rates;

c) the maximum projected quantity of excisable goods that will move simultaneously under excise duty suspension arrangement - by type of goods and excise rates;

d) the production capacity for excisable goods and the maximum warehouse capacity for storage of excisable goods - by type of goods and excise rates;

e) the monthly average projected amount of the excise duty due - by type of goods and excise rates;

14. specimen of the persons under paragraph 1, item 8;

15. (new, SG No. 105/2006) a certified copy of a document verifying the uniform identification code of the person.

(3) One application may be filed to apply for licenses for management of more than one tax warehouse.

Article 49. (1) (New, SG No. 105/2006) Where the conditions for granting a license for management of tax warehouse are fulfilled and the documents submitted meet the requirements, the authority under Article 48, Paragraph 1 shall issue a decision on the application within one month from filing thereof.

(2) (Renumbered from Paragraph 1, SG No. 105/2006) Where the documents submitted under Article 48, Paragraph 2 do not meet the requirements or the information provided is insufficient, the authority under Article 48, Paragraph 1 shall notify the applicant within 14 days from receipt of the application and shall set a time limit to remove irregularities or provide additional information within 14 days from receipt of the notification.

(3) (Renumbered from Paragraph 2, amended SG No. 105/2006) Within the time limit under Paragraph 1 the applicant shall remove any irregularities or submit additional required information and upon failure to fulfill this obligation the authority under Article 48, Paragraph 2 shall refuse granting the requested license.

(4) (Renumbered from Paragraph 3, amended SG No. 105/2006) After removal of the irregularities or provision of the required additional information the authority under Article 48, Paragraph 1 shall consider the application and the documents attached thereto and shall issue a decision on the application.

Article 50. (1) (Amended, SG No. 105/2006) Within the time limits under Article 49 the Director of the Customs Agency shall issue a license for management of a tax warehouse for production and/or storage of excisable goods or a motivated refusal.

(2) A separate license shall be issued for every individual tax warehouse.

(3) The license issued or the refusal for issuing a license may be appealed under the Administrative Procedure Code . The absence of a decision within the time limit set shall be deemed to be a refusal for issuing a license.

Article 51. (1) The license shall contain:

1. the name of the issuing body;

2. the identification number of the licensed warehouse keeper;

3. the identification number of the tax warehouse;

4. factual and legal grounds for its issuance;

5. (amended, SG, No. 34/2006, SG No. 63/2006) the company name, seat and registered address, the single identification code of the licensed warehouse keeper;

6. the address of the tax warehouse;

7. description of the activities to be performed in the tax warehouse and the type of excisable goods;

8. the type and amount of security;

9. the full name and the personal identification number of the persons representing the licensed warehouse keeper as well as other persons authorized to sign accompanying administrative documents;

10. the date of issue and signature of the person issuing the license.

(2) (Amended, SG No. 105/2006) The license for management of a tax warehouse shall be delivered upon presentation of the security.

(3) The right to apply excise duty suspension arrangement shall arise from the date of the license delivery.

Article 52. (1) (Renumbered from Article 52, SG No. 105/2006) The licensed warehouse keeper shall be obliged:

1. not to allow the full amount of the excise duty that has arisen or could arise upon application of the excise duty suspension arrangement to exceed the amount of the security provided;

2. notify customs authorities of any changes in the circumstances under which the license for management of the tax warehouse has been issued within 14 days of their occurrence by submitting the necessary documents;

3. ensure free access of customs authorities to all premises and the entire territory of the tax warehouse and shall ensure premises for conduct of the inspections;

4. observe all specific requirements for the production, storage and movement of excisable goods;

5. keep separate documentary records by type of activity and by type of excisable goods.

(2) (New, SG No. 105/2006) In the event of a change of the circumstances subject to recording in the license granted, the Director of the Customs Agency shall issue a decision, which shall form an integral part of the license granted and delivered.

Article 53. (1) The validity of the license for management of a tax warehouse shall be terminated:

1. on dissolution of the legal entity or death of the natural person - sole trader;

2. at a written request of the licensed warehouse keeper;

3. on revocation of the license.

(2) The license for management of a tax warehouse shall be revoked where:

1. the licensed warehouse keeper no longer meets the requirements under Article 47, or

2. if within the time limits set no new security has been provided, required in the cases where a new amount of the security has been fixed or where the security is no longer valid.

(3) The license shall be terminated by a decision of the Director of the Customs Agency, which may be appealed under the Administrative Procedure Code.

Article 54. (1) A register of the licensed warehouse keepers and tax warehouses shall be kept by the Customs Agency.

(2) The register shall contain:

1. the identification number of the licensed warehouse keeper;

2. the identification number of the tax warehouse;

3. (amended, SG, No. 34/2006, SG No. 63/2006) the company name, seat and registered address, the single identification code of the licensed warehouse keeper;

4. the address of the tax warehouse;

5. the type of excisable goods that may be produced and/or stored in the tax warehouse;

6. the date of issue of the license;

7. the date of termination of the validity of the license.

(3) Subject to entry in the register shall be any subsequent changes in the circumstances under Paragraph 2.

(4) The format of the register under Paragraph 1 shall be laid down in the implementing regulation to this Act.

Article 55. Any licensed warehouse keeper shall be entitled to receive information from the registers under Article 24, Paragraph 5 and Article 54 according to a procedure laid down in the implementing regulation to this Act.

Section III Registration of Specialised Small Distilleries and Small Producers of Wine

Article 56. (1) Subject to compulsory registration under this Act shall be:

1. specialized small distilleries;

2. small producers of wine.

(2) The Customs Agency shall keep a register of the registered units under Paragraph 1, which shall contain the following information:

1. identification number of the unit;

2. (amended, SG, No. 34/2006, SG No. 63/2006) name, seat and registered address, the single identification code of the person;

3. address of the unit;

4. the type of excisable goods that may be produced;

5. date of registration;

6. date of termination of the registration.

(3) The format of the register under Paragraph 2 shall be laid down in the implementing regulation to this Act.

Article 57. (1) (Amended, SG No. 105/2006) The owners or tenants of a unit under Article 56, Paragraph 1 may be only persons under Article 40c of the Wine and Spirit Drinks Act.

(2) The persons under Paragraph 1 may file an application for registration of the unit to the head of the customs authority by location of the unit before commencing activity.

(3) The following shall be attached to the application under paragraph 2:

1. (amended, SG, No. 34/2006) current certificate of registration in the Commercial Register - in original or a notary certified copy;

2. (amended, SG, No. 81/2006) technical information on the opened and closed production units or warehouses, specifying the area and their location, full description of the technological equipment, including containers and their volume;

3. the original or a notary certified copy of a document certifying the unit's commissioning, issued in accordance with the Spatial Development Act;

4. (repealed, SG No. 105/2006);

5. (amended, SG, No. 34/2006, SG No. 63/2006) a copy of BULSTAT Register identification card, certified by the person;

6. a license, permit or registration, where this is required by law;

7. a declaration that the unit meets the requirements of Article 4, items 8 and 9;

8. a list of the full names and personal identification numbers of the persons that manage the production process (in charge of the units) and comply with the requirements of the Wine and Spirit Drinks Act and the by-laws for its implementation.

(4) Based on the application and documents attached thereto under paragraph 3, the head of the customs authority, within 14 days from submission of the documents, removal of irregularities respectively, shall issue a certificate of registration or shall refuse to issue said certificate with a motivated decision. Absence of a decision within the time limit set shall be deemed to be a refusal for issuing the act.

(5) The registered person shall notify in writing the head of the customs authority of any change in the data contained in the application within 14 days from occurrence thereof.

Section IIIa (New, SG No. 105/2006)

Compulsory Registration

Article 57a. (New, SG No. 105/2006) Subject to compulsory registration shall be the persons:

1. who produce, import or bring into the territory of the country coke or coal, as well as the persons who initiate transactions in coke or coal;

2. licensed under the Energy Act, who sell electricity or natural gas to consumers of electricity or natural gas for household or industrial purposes within the meaning of the Energy Act;

3. licensed under the Energy Act to produce electricity, for transfer or distribution of electricity or natural gas, for trade in electricity, for public supply of electricity or natural gas or supply of end suppliers of electricity or natural gas which use own electricity or natural gas for their own needs;

4. registered for VAT purposes in another Member State, who bring into the territory of the country excisable goods for supply under the terms of distant selling within the meaning of the Value Added Tax Act.

(2) The Customs Agency shall keep a register of the registered persons under Paragraph 1, which shall contain the following information:

1. name, registered address and registered office, uniform identification code of the person;

2. types of excisable goods subject to excise duty taxation by the person;

3. date of registration and number of the certificate of registration;

4. date of deregistration and number of the decision on deregistration;

5. the competent customs authority.

Article 57b. (New, SG No. 105/2006) (1) The persons under Article 57a, Paragraph 1, items 1 - 3 shall file an application for registration to the head of the customs authority by registered address and registered office before start up of activity.

(2) The persons under Article 57a, Paragraph 1, item 4 shall file an application for registration to the head of the customs authority by permanent address, registered address and registered office of the tax representative respectively.

(3) A tax representative of a non-resident person registered for VAT purposes in another Member State may be only a capable natural person with permanent address in the country or permanently residing therein or a resident legal person which is not undergoing liquidation or is not declared in bankruptcy and has no payable and unpaid tax liabilities and liabilities for insurance contributions collected by the National Revenue Agency.

(4) The tax representative shall represent the non-resident person in all its/his tax legal relations which have arisen hereunder and shall be responsible jointly and severally and unlimitedly for the obligations of the registered non-resident person under this Act.

(5) The application under Paragraphs 1 and 2 shall contain:

1. a current certificate of registration with the commercial register - the original or a notary certified copy if the person is subject to such registration;

2. a copy of a document certified by the person, certifying its/his uniform identification code;

3. a license, permit or registration, where this is required by law;

4. type of excisable goods;

5. average monthly quantity of excisable goods supplied under the terms of distant selling;

6. the type of the security provided - for the persons under Paragraph 3.

(6) On the grounds of the application and the documents enclosed thereto under Paragraph 5 the head of the customs authority shall, within 14 days from receipt of the documents, removal of inconsistencies therein respectively, issue a certificate of registration or

shall refuse to issue it by a motivated decision. Failing to issue said certificate shall be considered an express refusal of registration.

(7) Refusal of registration may be appealed under the Administrative Procedure Code.

(8) The certificate of registration under Paragraph 6 shall be delivered to the tax representative upon submission of the security under Article 83a.

(9) The registered person shall:

1. notify in writing the head of the competent customs authority of any change of the data in the application within 14 days of their occurrence;

2. keep documentation and accounting in accordance with the requirements set out in the implementing regulation to this Act.

Section IIIb Registered Traders

Article 57c. (New, SG No. 105/2006) (1) An equity company under the Commerce Act , with registered and fully paid in capital of not less than BGN 500,000 shall have the right to register as a registered trader.

(2) The person under Paragraph 1 shall file an application for registration to the head of the customs authority by registered address and registered office before start up of activity, which shall contain:

1. a current certificate of registration with the commercial register - the original or a notary certified copy;

2. a copy of a document certified by the person, certifying its uniform identification code;

3. a license, permit or registration, where this is required by law;

4. location and layout of the premises where the goods are received as well as a document of ownership or a rent contract for such premises;

5. type of excisable goods received;

6. average monthly quantity of excisable goods supplied under excise duty suspension arrangement;

7. a list with the full name and the personal identification number of the persons who are authorised to sign accompanying administrative documents and specimens of their signatures;

8. the type of the security provided.

(3) Where the conditions for registration are fulfilled and the documents submitted meet the requirements, the authority under Paragraph 2 shall issue a decision on the application within one month from its receipt.

(4) Where the documents submitted under Paragraph 2 do not meet the requirements or the information provided is insufficient, the authority under Paragraph 2 shall, within 14 days from receipt of the application, notify the applicant and set a 14-day time limit for

removal of inconsistencies or provision of additional information effective as from receipt of the notification.

(5) Within the time limit set under Paragraph 4, the applicant shall remove inconsistencies or provide the required additional information and should it fail to do so the authority under Paragraph 2 shall refuse to grant registration.

(6) Within one month from removal of inconsistencies or provision of the required additional information the authority under Paragraph 2 shall examine the application and the documents attached thereto and shall issue a decision.

Article 57d. (New, SG No. 105/2006) (1) In the time limits under Article 57c the head of the competent customs authority shall issue a certificate of registration to the registered trader or shall refuse to issue it by a motivated decision. Failing to issue said certificate shall be considered a refusal of registration.

(2) Refusal of registration may be appealed under the Administrative Procedure Code.

(3) The certificate of registration shall be delivered to the person upon submission of the security under Article 83a.

(4) The right of the registered person to receive goods under excise duty suspension arrangement shall arise on the date of delivery of the certificate of registration.

Article 57e. (New, SG No. 105/2006) The registered trader shall:

1. keep separate document reporting by type of excisable goods and store separately from other goods the goods received under excise duty suspension arrangement;

2. notify in writing the head of the customs authority of any change in the data in the application for registration within 14 days from its occurrence;

3. (amended, SG No. 109/2007) ensure free access of customs authorities to all premises and the entire territory of the facilityand ensure them premises for conducting the checks;

4. not allow the full amount of the excise duty which has arisen or could arise upon application of the excise duty suspension arrangement exceed the amount of the security provided.

Article 58. (Amended, SG No. 105/2006) The authority under Article 57, Paragraph 2, Article 57b, Paragraphs 1 and 2, and Article 57c, Paragraph 2 shall terminate the registration:

1. at a request of the registered person, where the grounds for compulsory registration do not exist;

2. on dissolution or liquidation of the registered person;

3. at its initiative, where:

a) the registered person does not meet the requirements of this Act, or

b) the registered trader or tax representative fails to provide a new security within the time limits set, required where a new amount of the security is stipulated or where the security is no longer valid.

Section IIIc Non-registered Traders

Article 58a. (New, SG No. 105/2006) (1) A right to receive a specific quantity of excisable goods under ecvise duty suspension arrangement from a licensed warehouse keeper in another Member State shall have a person who is a trader within the meaning of the Commerce Act, who is registered under the Value Added Tax Act and who has obtained a permit under the procedure of this Section for every specific supply of excisable goods.

(2) To obtain a permit the person under Paragraph 1 shall file an application to the head of the customs authority by registered address and registered office not later than 30 days before the date of receipt of the goods, which shall contain:

1. a current certificate of registration with the commercial register - the original or a notary certified copy;

2. a copy of a document certified by the person, certifying its uniform identification code;

3. a license, permit or registration, where this is required by law;

4. location and layout of the premises where the goods are received as well as a document of ownership or a rent contract for such premises;

5. type and quantity of excisable goods received;

5. contract for supply of the excisable goods;

6. a company name/name and identification number of the licensed warehouse keeper - sender;

8. a list with the full name and the personal identification number of the persons who are authorised to sign the accompanying administrative document and specimens of their signatures.

(3) Where the conditions for registration are fulfilled and the documents submitted meet the requirements, the authority under Paragraph 2 shall determine the amount of the excise duty due and shall notify the person thereof within 7 days from their receipt.

(4) Where the documents submitted under Paragraph 2 do not meet the requirements or the information provided is insufficient, the authority under Paragraph 2 shall refuse to grant a permit within 7 days from receipt of the application. Failing to issue a decision shall be considered a refusal to issue a permit.

(5) The refusal under Paragraph 4 may be appealed under the terms of the Administrative Procedure Code.

Article 58b. (New, SG No. 105/2006) (1) Within 7 days from provision of the collateral or payment of the excise duty due the head of the competent customs authority shall issue a permit to the non-registered trader authorising the non-registered trader to receive the specific quantity of excisable goods under excise duty suspension arrangement.

(2) The right of the non-registered trader to receive excisable goods under excise duty suspension arrangement shall arise after the date of delivery of the permit.

Section IV Production of Excisable goods

Article 59. (Effective 1.07.2006 - SG No. 91/2005) (1) (Supplemented, SG No. 63/2006) Production of excisable goods shall be any processing and reprocessing, including extraction, recovery and mixing, of raw materials, materials and/or products as a result of which excisable goods are produced or packaged.

(2) (Amended, SG No. 105/2006) Production of excisable goods shall furthermore be considered the production of goods which contain ethyl alcohol exceeding 1.2% vol (1% mas), intended by their characteristics for consumption as food and drinks or as additives in the production of food or drinks.

(3) (Amended, SG No. 109/2007) The activities and operations under Paragraph 1 with the goods under Article 2, item 5 for which excise duty has been paid, shall not be considered production of excisable goods.

Article 60. (Effective 1.07.2006) (1) (Amended, SG No. 105/2006, supplemented, SG No. 109/2007) Production of goods under Article 2, items 1 and 2 and under Article 14 shall be carried out only in a tax warehouse for manufacture and storage.

(2) Alcoholic beverages falling within CN code 2208 (rakiya) may be produced in registered specialized small distilleries as well.

(3) Wine may be produced in registered units of small producers of wine as well.

(4) (Amended, SG No. 105/2006) Paragraphs 1 and 3 shall not apply to the production of wine and other fermented beverages from fruits and grapes - own production - intended only for personal consumption of the natural person or his family.

(5) (Repealed, SG No. 63/2006) .

(6) (Repealed, SG No. 63/2006) .

(7) (New, SG No. 109/2007) Processing and manufacture operations, permitted to be conducted also in tax warehouses for storage, may be specified by the implementing regulation to this Act.

Article 61. (Effective 1.07.2006) (1) Producers of goods under Article 2 shall use in production measuring instruments meeting the requirements of the Measurements Act and the implementing regulations thereof.

(2) Specific requirements and control on measuring instruments under Paragraph 1 shall be determined by the Minister of Finance.

Article 62. (Effective 1.07.2006) (1) (Amended, SG No. 109/2007) For every batch produced the producers of petrol, gas oil, kerosene, biodiesel and bioethanol shall:

1. determine the volume in litres;

2. issue analysis certificate, containing the indicator of density (in kg/m3) at 15°C.

(2) In case of import of goods under Paragraph 1 the analysis certificate under Paragraph 1, item 2 shall be submitted for each batch.

(3) The volume shall be recalculated to a comparative temperature of 15 °C by measuring the weight in kilograms and recalculating it in litres based on the density at a temperature of 15 °C.

(4) The density at 15 °C shall be determined in accordance with the methods BDS EN ISO 3675 or BDS EN ISO 12185 and the tables under BDS ISO 91-1.

(5) The values of the initial extract content expressed in Plato degrees of bottled and draft beer shall be certified by an analysis certificate.

Article 63. (Effective 1.07.2006, SG No. 91/2005, repealed, SG No. 109/2007).

Article 64. (Effective 1.07.2006) (1) Producers of tobacco products and bottled alcoholic beverages falling within CN code 2208 with alcoholic content exceeding 15 % vol, intended for sale on the domestic market, shall affix excise labels on the consumer package. The excise label shall be affixed in the tax warehouse of the producer.

(2) The persons importing goods under paragraph 1 into the territory of the country shall ensure affixing of excise labels on the consumer package in the following manner:

1. with the producer - outside the country's territory, or

2. in a tax warehouse, or

3. (amended, SG No. 109/2007) in a bonded or customs warehouse within the meaning of the customs legislation.

(3) (New, SG No. 105/2006) The persons bringing into the territory of the country goods under Paragraph 1 from another Member State shall ensure that excise labels are affixed on the consumer package under the terms of Paragraph 2.

(4) (Renumbered from Paragraph 3, SG No. 105/2006) The excise label shall be affixed on the consumer package in a manner that ensures that it is impossible to use the good without destroying the excise label by tearing it off.

(5) (Renumbered from Paragraph 4, SG No. 105/2006, amended, SG No. 109/2007) The excise label shall contain the series, number, other durable signs and symbols. The selling price shall also be indicated on the excise label of tobacco products. The excise labels of consumer packages of manually rolled cigars shall also indicate the number of pieces in the package, as well as their unit prices.

(6) (Renumbered from Paragraph 5, SG No. 105/2006) The samples of excise labels shall be approved by an order of the Minister of Finance, to be promulgated in the State Gazette.

(7) (Renumbered from Paragraph 6, SG No. 105/2006) The excise labels shall be ordered, printed, purchased, distributed and placed according to a procedure and manner determined by the Minister of Finance.

(8) (Renumbered from Paragraph 7, amended, SG No. 105/2006) The persons under paragraphs 1, 2 and 3 shall order the necessary number of excise labels to the competent customs authority which shall deliver the excise labels to the applicants within 30 days from their ordering.

(9) (Renumbered from Paragraph 8, amended, SG No. 105/2006) Excise labels for tobacco products shall be ordered at the latest registered price according to the established procedure.

(10) (New, SG No. 109/2007) The provisions of this article shall not apply in the cases under Article 21, Paragraph 1, items 1 - 6.

Section V Storage of Excisable goods

Article 65. (Effective 1.07.2006) (1) (Amended, SG No. 109/2007) Warehousing of excisable goods under excise duty suspension arrangement involves placing and storage of excisable goods in a tax warehouse for storage or in a tax warehouse for manufacture and storage.

(2) In a tax warehouse may be stored excisable goods, which:

1. have been produced in the same tax warehouse;

2. (amended, SG No. 63/2006) have been released for free circulation with simultaneous placing under an excise duty suspension arrangement;

3. (supplemented, SG No. 105/2006) have been transported under excise duty suspension arrangement from another tax warehouse to the teritory of the country or from a tax warehouse on the territory of another Member State.

4. (new, SG No. 109/2007) introduced into this countryTs territory under the procedure of Article 76c.

(3) Storage is permitted only for excisable goods owned by:

1. a licensed warehouse keeper, or

2. a person - depositor, registered under the Value Added Tax Act.

Article 66. (Effective 1.07.2006 (1) The licensed warehouse keeper shall store the goods, separating them by type and depositor, including separation of the goods for which excise duty has or has not been paid.

(2) Storage in a tax warehouse of excisable goods which are not subject to excise tax is not allowed except for goods produced from energy products.

(3) (New, SG No. 63/2006) Authorized warehousekeepers shall be obligated to use measuring instruments complying with the requirements of the Measurements Act and the statutory instruments on the application thereof.

(4) (New, SG No. 63/2006) The specific requirements and the control over the measuring instruments referred to in Paragraph (3) shall be determined according to the procedure established by Article 61 (2) herein.

Section VI Movement of Excisable Goods

Article 67. (Effective 1.07.2006, amended, SG No. 63/2006, No. 105/2006) Movement of excisable goods under excise duty suspension arrangement shall be:

1. transportation of excisable goods from a tax warehouse on the territory of the counrry to another tax warehouse on the territory of the country, to another tax warehouse on the territory of another Member State, to a registered or non-registered trader in another Member State or to the persons under Article 21, Paragraph 1, items 1 and 3;

2. transportation of excisable goods from a tax warehouse on the territory of the country to an exit border customs office or to third territories - in cases of export;

3. transportation of excisable goods, released for free circulation with simultaneous placing under an excise duty suspension arrangement, to a tax warehouse on the territory of the country;

4. transportation of excisable goods from a tax warehouse on the territory of another Member State to a tax warehouse on the territory of the country, to a registered or non-registered trader on the territory of the country or to the persons under Aticle 21, Paragraph 1, items 1, 3 and 6.

Article 68. (Effective 1.07.2006) (1) During movement of excisable goods under excise duty suspension arrangement the goods shall be accompanied by an accompanying administrative document.

(2) (Amend, SG No. 105/2006) The accompanying administrative document shall be issued in 5 copies as follows:

1. by the licensed warehouse keeper sender - upon transfer of the goods from the tax warehouse on the territory of the country to:

a) another tax warehouse on the territory of the country, or

b) another tax warehouse on the territory of another Member State, or

c) a registered trader in another Member State, or

d) a non-registered trader in another Member State, or

e) the persons under Article 21, Paragraph 1, items 1 and 3;

2. by the licensed warehouse keeper sender - upon transfer of the goods from the tax warehouse on the territory of the country for the purposes of export to an exit border customs office or to third territories;

3. by the licensed warehouse keeper in whose tax warehouse the goods owned by the holder of the free circulation admission regime will be received - upon placing the goods under free circulation admission customs arrangement.

(3) (New, SG No. 105/2006) Upon transfer of excisable goods under excise duty suspension arrangement to a non-registered trader in another Member State the goods shall be also accompanied by a document issued by the competent administration of the Member State of the recipient, certifying that the excise duty on the goods in the Member State of receipt is paid or secured.

(4) (New, SG, No. 105/2006) The mandatory requisites of the document under Paragraph 3 shall be determined by the implementing regulation to this Act.

(5) (New, SG No. 105/2006, amended, SG No. 109/2007) Upon transfer of excisable goods under excise duty suspension arrangement to the persons under Article 21, Paragraph 1, items 1 and 3 the goods shall also be accompanied by a certificate of exemption from f excise duty according to a standard form set out in the implementing regulation to this Act.

(6) (New, SG No. 105/2006) Where the transfer of the excisable goods is related to leaving the territory of the country before bringing them out from a tax warehouse, the licensed warehouse keeper shall submit for certification to the competent customs authority the copies of the accompanying administrative document issued.

Article 69. (Effective 1.07.2006) (1) In the cases under Article 68, Paragraph 2, item 1 the first copy of the accompanying administrative document shall be kept by the sender, the second, third and fourth copies shall accompany the goods and the fifth copy shall be sent to the competent customs authority by location of the sender's warehouse.

(2) (Amended, SG No. 105/2006) The second, third and fourth copies of the accompanying administrative document shall be certified upon receipt of the goods by the licensed warehouse keeper - recipient, by the registered or non-registered trader in another Member State or by the persons under Article 21, Paragraph 1, items 1 and 3.

(3) (Amended, SG No. 105/2006) The second copy shall be kept by the person under Paragraph 2, the third copy shall be returned to the sender, and the fourth copy shall be sent to the competent customs authority by location of the tax warehouse, the competent customs authority by registered address of the recipient respectively.

(4) (New, SG No. 105/2006) Where the recipient of the goods is established in another Member State, the third copy of the accompanying administrative document under Paragraph 3 shall be certified by the competent administration of said Member State.

Article 70. (Effective 1.07.2006) (1) In the cases under Article 68, Paragraph 2, item 2 the first copy of the accompanying administrative document shall be kept by the sender, the second, third and fourth copies shall accompany the goods and the fifth copy shall be returned to the competent customs authority by location of the warehouse.

(2) (Amended, SG No. 105/2006) The second, third and fourth copies of the accompanying administrative document shall be certified by the exit border customs office, which shall keep the fourth copy.

(3) (Amended, SG No. 105/2006) The second copy shall be kept by the person specified in cell 7 of the accompanying administrative document, and the third copy shall be returned to the sender and kept by it.

Article 71. (Effective 1.07.2006) (1) In the cases under Article 68, Paragraph 2, item 3 the first copy of the accompanying administrative document shall be kept by the person - holder of the free circulation admission arrangement, and the second, third and fourth copies shall accompany the goods. The fifth copy shall be kept by the customs authority that has administered the arrangement.

(2) The second, third and fourth copies of the accompanying administrative document shall be certified by the licensed warehouse keeper upon receipt of the goods in the warehouse.

(3) (Amended, SG No. 105/2006) The second copies shall be kept by the person under Paragraph 2. The third copy shall be sent to the customs authority that has administered the arrangement and the fourth copy shall be sent to the competent customs authority by location of the warehouse.

Article 71a. (New, SG No. 105/2006) (1) In the cases of movement of excisable goods under excise duty suspension arrangement under Article 67, item 4 the second, third and fourth copies issued by the licensed warehouse keeper in another Member State shall accompany the goods.

(2) The second, third and fourth copies of the accompanying administrative document shall be certified by the recipient of the goods under Article 67, item 4.

(3) The second copy shall be kept by the recipient, and the fourth copy shall be sent to the competent customs authority by location of the tax warehouse, the competent customs authority by registered address of the registered trader, non-registered trader or the person under Article 21, Paragraph 1, items 1 and 2 respectively.

(4) The third copy shall be returned to the sender, certified also by the competent customs authority of the recipient.

Article 72. (Effective 1.07.2006) (1) Amendments and supplements to the accompanying administrative document shall be prohibited. An incorrectly drawn up accompanying administrative document shall be cancelled and a new one shall be drawn up.

(2) The sample, format and requisites of the accompanying administrative document shall be determined by the implementing regulation to this Act.

(3) The accompanying administrative document shall be recorded in the register "Warehouse Stocks Log" in the tax period for which it is issued, received, respectively.

(4) The accompanying administrative document shall be kept by the issuer and the receiver and shall be made available to supervisory authorities for a term of 5 years.

Article 73. (Effective 1.07.2006) The copies of the accompanying administrative document shall be submitted to the competent customs authority of the sender, the receiver respectively, within 15 days from dispatch of the goods, receipt of the goods respectively.

Article 74. (Effective 1.07.2006, SG No. 91/2005, amended, No. 105/2006) The licensed warehouse keeper - sender or the licensed warehouse keeper in whose warehouse the goods owned by the holder of the free circulation admission arrangement will be received shall owe excise duty on the goods sent or imported as specified in the accompanying administrative document, except in the following cases:

1. (amended, SG No. 109/2007) upon movement of the goods under Article 67, item 1 - where up to 45 days following the bringing out of the goods from the warehouse the warehouse keeper has received the third copy of the accompanying administrative document certified by the recipient;

2. (amended, SG No. 109/2007) upon movement of the goods under Article 67, item 2 - where up to 45 days following the bringing out of the goods from the warehouse the warehouse keeper has received the third copy of the accompanying administrative document, certified by the customs authority of departure;

3. (amended, SG No. 109/2007) upon movement of the goods under Article 67, item 3 - where up to 45 days following the release of the goods for free circulation, the customs authority that has administered the regime has received the third copy.

Article 75. (Effective 1.07.2006, SG No. 91/2005, amended, No. 105/2006) The recipients under Article 67, item 4, except for the persons under Article 21, Paragraph 1, items 1 and 3 shall owe excise duty due on the received goods as specified in the accompanying administrative document.

Article 76. (Effective 1.07.2006, SG No. 91/2005, amended, No. 105/2006) Where the copies of the accompanying administrative document are received after the time limits under Article 74, the licensed warehouse keeper - sender or the licensed warehouse keeper in whose warehouse the goods owned by the holder of the free circulation admission arrangement will be received shall adjust the amount of the excise duty due, which has arisen as a result of the application of Article 75 during the tax period in which he received the accompanying administrative document, in the manner and form as laid down in the implementing regulation to this Act.

CHAPTER FOUR "A" MOVEMENT OF EXCISABLE GOODS RELEASED FOR CONSUMPTION ON

THE COMMUNITY TERRITORY

Section I

Movement of Excisable Goods Released for Consumption on the Territory

of the Country

Article 76a. (New, SG No. 105/2006) (1) Upon movement of excisable goods under Article 2, items 1, 2 and 3 from the territory of the country to the territory of another Member State, which are released for consumption on the territory of the country, the goods shall be accompanied by a simplified accompanying document.

(2) Upon movement of fully denatured ethyl alcohol in accordance with European Commission Regulation No. 3199/93 from the territory of the country to the territory of another Member State the goods shall be accompanied by a simplified accompanying document.

(3) (Repealed, SG No. 109/2007).

(4) The simplified accompanying document under Paragraphs 1 and 2 shall be issued in three copies by the sender of the goods.

(5) The first copy shall be kept by the person under Parahraph 4, and the second and third copies shall accompany the goods.

(6) The person under Paragraph 4 shall have the right to refund the excise duty paid on the goods under Article 23.

(7) The standard form, the format and requisites of the simplified administrative document shall be determined by the implementing regulation to this Act.

(8) A simplified accompanying document may be issued when the goods are accompanied by a commercial document (invoice, document of delivery, transport dicument etc.) provided that said commercial document contains the requisites of the simplified accompanying document and said requisites correspond by content and number of the requisites in the simplified accompanying document.

(9) (Repealed, SG No. 109/2007).

Article 76b. (New, SG No. 105/2006) The person under Article 76a, Paragraph 4 shall be entitled to refund the excise duty paid on the goods where the following conditions obtain:

1. the person has notified in writing the competent customs authority by permanent address, registered address respectively, of its intention to send the excisable goods under Article 76a to another Member State before sending the excisable goods from the territory of the country;

2. the person has ensured free access of the customs authorities for possible examination;

3. the person has submitted to the competent customs authority a copy of a document certifying the payment or the securing of an excise duty in the Member State where the goods are sent.

(2) The written notification under Paragraph 1 shall contain:

1. name/company name, address, personal identification code of the person under Paragraph 1;

2. date of sending the excisable goods from the territory of the country;

3. description of the route from the territory of the country to the territory of the recipient Member State;

4. description of the types of excisable goods and their quantity;

5. name/company name and address of the recipient and the carrier;

6. place of receipt of excisable goods on the territory of another Member State;

7. the time limit in which the excisable goods are to be received on the territory of the other Member State.

Section II

Movement of Excisable Goods Released for Consumption on the Territory of Another Member State

Article 76c. (New, SG No. 105/2006) (1) Upon movement of excisable goods under Article 2, items 1, 2 and 3 from the territory of another Member State to the territory of the country, which have been released for consumption on the territory of the other Member State, the goods shall be accompanied by a simplified accompanying document issued by the sender in the other Member State.

(2) Upon movement of fully denatured ethyl alcohol in accordance with European Commission Regulation No. 3199/93 from the territory of another Member State to the territory of the country, which has been released for consumption on the territory of the other Member State, the goods shall be accompanied by a simplified accompanying document issued by the sender in the other Member State.

(3) Upon movement under Paragraph 1 the excisable goods shall be also accompanied by the document under Article 83h, Paragraph 1.

(4) The person under Article 3, item 6, which receives goods under items 1 and 2, shall:

1. before sending the excisable goods from the other Member State, notify in writing the competent customs authority by permanent address, registered address respectively, that the said person intends to receive excisable goods;

2. before sending the excisable goods from the other Member State, provide security or pay the amount of the excise duty due to the competent customs authority, except for the cases of exemption from excise duty under this Act;

3. receive the excisable goods within the time limits specified in the notification under item 1;

4. submit to the competent customs authority a copy of the third copy of the simplified accompanying document, certified by the recipient, not later than 7 days from receipt of the goods on the territory of the country, including the date of receipt;

5. inform immediately the competent customs authority if it does not receive the goods within the time limits specified in the notification, as well as of the reasons for the delay or non-receipt.

(5) The written notification under Paragraph 4, item 1 shall contain:

1. name/company name, address, uniform identification code of the person under Paragraph 2;

2. date of sending the excisable goods from the other Member State;

3. description of the route from the sending Member State to the Republic of Bulgaria;

4. description of the types of goods and their quantity;

5. name/company name and address of the sender and the carrier;

6. place of receipt of the excisable goods on the territory of the country;

7. the time limit by which the excisable goods shall be received on the territory of the country.

(6) Within 7 days from receipt of the notification under Article 4, item 1, 7 days from removal of inconsistencies in it respectively, the head of the competent customs authority shall determine the excise duty due and notify the person of its amount.

(7) (New, SG No. 109/2007) The provisions of Paragraph 1 shall not apply in the cases of introduction of excisable goods into the territory of this country, which are not excisable on the territory of the respective Member State.

Article 76d. (New, SG. No. 105/2006) (1) (Amended, SG No. 109/2007) Any person who brings into the territory of the country excisable goods under Article 2, item 5 from the territory of another Member State shall file a declaration according to a standard form set out in the implementing regulation to this Act.

(2) (Amended, SG No. 109/2007) The declaration under Paragraph 1 shall be filed to the competent customs authority by permanent address, by registered address respectively, of the person within 14 days from bringing of the goods. The declaration shall be submitted prior to the original registration of the automobile in the Republic of Bulgaria.

(3) The customs authorities shall have the right to require submission of the goods together with the declaration under Paragraph 2.

(4) On the grounds of the declaration filed the competent customs authority shall determine the amount of the excise duty due and shall notify it to the person.

CHAPTER FIVE SECURITY

Section I

Security under Excise Duty Suspension Arrangement Payment Regime

Article 77. (Effective 1.07.2006) (1) (Supplemented, SG No. 109/2007) The licensed warehouse keeper shall provide security to the customs authorities to ensure payment of the excise duty that may arise for the goods under excise duty suspension arrangement, including for the excise labels provided.

(2) (Supplemented, SG No. 63/2006) The amount of the security shall be determined in such manner as to cover at any time the full amount of the excise duty which has arisen or

may arise during implementation of the excise duty suspension arrangement, with the exception of the cases referred to in Article 78 (3) herein.

Article 78. (Effective 1.07.2006) (1) The amount of the security under Article 77 shall be calculated as a sum of:

1. thirty per cent of the amount of excise duty on the monthly average quantity of stored goods - by type of goods;

2. ten per cent of the of the amount of excise duty on the monthly average quantity of stored goods:

a) (amended, SG No. 105/2006, SG No. 109/2007) for quantities of stored raw distillate, or

b) for mandatory quantities under the Mandatory Stocks of Crude Oil and Petroleum Products Act stored in a licensed tax warehouse;

3. one hundred fifty per cent of the amount of excise duty due on the monthly average quantity of goods released for consumption;

4. twenty per cent of the amount of excise duty on the monthly average quantity of goods moving under excise duty suspension arrangement.

(2) The indicators "monthly average quantity of stored goods", "monthly average quantity of goods released for consumption", and "monthly average quantity of goods moving under excise duty suspension arrangement" shall be calculated according to a procedure laid down in the implementing regulation to this Act.

(3) (New, SG No. 63/2006) The amount of the security for a tax warehouse for production and storage of excisable goods may not exceed BGN 30 million.

(4) (Renumbered from Paragraph 3, SG No. 63/2006) At the request of the licensed warehouse keeper the amount of the security may be fixed at a higher amount than the one under Paragraph 1.

Article 79. (Effective 1.07.2006) In the event of a change in the circumstances which materially affects the calculation of the amount of the security a new amount of the security may be determined.

Article 80. (Effective 1.07.2006) (1) (Amended, SG No. 105/2006, supplemented, SG No 109/2007) The security under Article 77 may be created by cash deposit or bank guarantee under the customs legislation. The form of the bank guarantee shall be determined in the implementing regulation to this Act.

(2) The security shall be accepted in Bulgarian lev.

(3) No interest shall accrue on the security created by cash deposit.

Article 81. (Effective 1.07.2006) (1) A change of the type or amount of security shall be made by a decision of the Director of the Customs Agency, which shall form an integral part of the license for the warehouse management.

(2) (Supplemented, SG No. 105/2006) The licensed warehouse keeper shall provide the new security within 30 days from delivery of the decision under Paragraph 1, but not later than the expiry of the validity of the previous security.

(3) (Amended, SG No. 105/2006) The previous security shall be realeased by a decision of the Director of the Customs Agency within 30 days, effective from the date of provision of the new security under Paragraph 2.

(4) (Amended, SG No. 105/2006) In cases of withdrawal of the license the security shall be released by a decision of the authority under Paragraph 1 after the liability for payment of excise duty has been discharged.

Section II

Security Provided upon Customs Arrangements or upon Receipt of Excise Labels

(Title amended, SG No. 105/2006)

Article 82. (Effective 1.07.2006) (1) (Amended, SG No. 105/2006) Where goods are placed under excise duty suspension arrangement or temporarily stored the full amount of the excise duty payable shall be secured by cash deposit or bank guarantee according to the procedure for securing customs charges laid down in the customs legislation.

(2) Transit of goods shall be furthermore secured in the amounts and according to the procedure for securing customs charges.

(3) (Amended, SG No. 105/2006) A person licensed to open and manage a bonded warehouse (warehouse keeper) within the meaning of the customs legislation shall be liable jointly and severally with the depositor of the goods for the excise duty due in the event of deviation of the goods from the customs regime during their storage in the warehouse.

Article 83. (Effective 1.07.2006) (1) The persons that have ordered excise labels for foreign goods shall provide a security to the customs authorities to the full amount of the excise duty before receipt of excise labels.

(2) The provision of Paragraph 1 shall not apply to licensed warehouse keepers.

(3) The security under Paragraph 1 may be created as cash deposit or bank guarantee. The security shall be accepted in Bulgarian lev.

(4) Where the security under Paragraph 1 is created by bank guarantee, the latter shall have validity of not less than 90 days effective from the date of receipt of excise labels.

(5) No interest shall accrue on the security provided in the form of cash deposit.

(6) After expiry of 60 days from the date of receipt of the excise labels under Paragraph 1 the customs authorities shall take actions for utilization of the security provided in the amount of the due excise duty.

(7) Within 30 days the security under Paragraph 1 shall be released upon payment of the full amount of the excise duty for the excise labels received.

(8) (New, SG No. 105/2006) The persons under Paragraph 1 shall have the right to pay the full amount of the excise duty due for the excise labels ordered before their receipt.

Section III

(New, SG No. 105/2006)

Security Provided by Registered Traders or Tax Representatives

Article 83a. (New, SG No. 105/2006) (1) Tax representatives under Article 57b, Paragraph 3 and registered traders under Article 57c shall provide security to the customs authorities to secure the payment of the excise duty which may arise for the goods received by the non-resident person under Article 57a, Paragraph 1, item 4, the goods received under excise duty suspension arrangement respectively, from a tax warehouse on the teritory of another Member State.

(2) The amount of the security shall be determined in a way so as to cover at any time the full amount of the excise duty on the goods received, which has arisen or might arise.

Article 83b. (New, SG No. 105/2006) (1) The amount of the security under Article 83a shall be 150 per cent of the amount of the excise duty due for the average monthly quantity of received goods.

(2) The indicator "average monthly quantity" shall be calculated under a procedure laid down in the implementing regulation to this Act.

(3) At the person's request a higher amount of the security than the one referred to in Paragraph 1 may be determined.

Article 83c. (New, SG No. 105/2006) In the event of a change in the circumstances instrumental to determining the amount of the security a new amount of the security may be determined.

Article 83d. (New, SG No. 105/2006) (1) The security under Article 83a may be created by cash deposit or bank guarantee in accordance with the customs legislation.

(2) The security shall be accepted in Bulgarian lev.

(3) No interest shall accrue on the security created by cash deposit.

Article 83e. (New, SG No. 105/2006) (1) The amount of the security shall be determined by a decision of the head of the competent customs authority by registration of the person.

(2) A change of the type or amount of the security shall be made by a decision of the authority under Paragraph 1.

(3) The decisions under Paragraphs 1 and 2 shall be issued within the time limits under Article 57b, Paragraph 6, Article 57c, Paragraphs 3 and 4 respectively, and shall be delivered to the persons.

(4) The decisions under Paragraphs 1 and 2 shall be an integral part of the issued certificate of registration.

(5) Within 30 days from delivery of the decision under Paragraph 2 the person shall provide the new security but not later than expiry of the validity of the previous security.

(6) The previous security shall be released by a decision of the head of the competent customs authority within 30 days, effective from the date of provision of the new security under Paragraph 5.

(7) In the cases of deregistration the security shall be released by a decision of the head of the competent customs authority after the liability for payment of excise duty has been discharged.

Section IV

(New, SG No. 105/2006)

Security Provided by Non-registered Traders or by Persons Receiving Excisable Goods on the Territory of the Country, Released for Consumption on the Territory of Another Member State

Article 83f. (New, SG No. 105/2006) (1) Non-registered traders under Article 58a and the persons under Article 76c, Paragraph 4 shall provide security to the customs authorities or shall pay the full amount of the excise duty due for the goods which are released for consumption on the teritory of another Member State and which will be received on the territory of the country.

(2) The security under Paragraph 1 shall be created by cash deposit in accordance with customs legislation.

(3) The security shall be accepted in Bulgarian lev and no interest shall be due on it.

Article 83g. (New, SG No. 105/2006) (1) The amount of the security as well as the amount of the excise duty that shall be paid shall be determined by a decision of the head of the competent customs authority within the time limits of Article 58a, Paragraph 3, Article 76c, Paragraph 6.

(2) The decisions under Paragraph 1 may be appealed under the Administrative Procedure Code.

Article 83h. (New, SG No. 105/2006) (1) After provision of the security or payment of the excise duty the head of the competent customs authority shall issue a document to the person, certifying that the excise duty on the goods to be received has been paid, secured or that the goods are exempt from payment of excise duty.

(2) The mandatory requisites of the document under Paragraph 1 shall be laid down in the implementing regulation to this Act.

Article 83i. (New, SG No. 105/2006) (1) The security shall be released by a decision of the head of the competent customs authority within 30 days, effective from the date on which the liability for payment of excise duty has been discharged.

(2) Where the amount of the excise duty for the goods received is lower than the amount of the excise duty paid under Article 83h, the unduly paid excise duty shall be refunded under the terms of Article 27.

Chapter Six

DOCUMENTATION AND REPORTING

Section I

Tax Documents

Article 84. (Effective 1.07.2006) (1) Tax documents within the meaning of this Act shall be:

1. an excise tax document;

2. a note of an excise tax document.

(2) (Supplemented, SG No. 105/2006, amended,SG No 109/2007) An excise tax document shall be issued on the date on which the excise duty becomes due within the

meaning of Article 20, Paragraph 2, except in the cases under Article 20, Paragraph 2, items 5, 15 - 18 and 20.

(3) (New, SG No. 105/2006) In the cases of release for consumption under Article 20, items 15 - 18 an excise tax document shall be issued for total sales effected, total quantity of coke, coal, electricity or natural gas used respectively, on the 10th day of the month following the month in which the sales/use is effected.

(4) (Renumbered from 3, SG No. 105/2006) Tax documents shall be issued in at least two copies.

(5) (Renumbered from 4, SG No. 105/2006) Tax documents issued shall be recorded in the accounting system and the register of the issuer for the tax period in which they have been issued.

(6) (Renumbered from 5, SG No. 105/2006) Tax documents may not be amended or supplemented. Incorrectly drawn up or corrected tax documents shall be cancelled. Said documents shall not be destroyed and all copies of them shall be kept by the person that has issued the document.

(7) (Renumbered from 6, amended, SG No. 105/2006) In the cases under Paragraph 6 new documents shall be issued.

(8) (Renumbered from 7, SG No. 105/2006) Tax documents issued under the procedure of this Act shall be stored for a period of 5 years after expiry of the tax period for which they refer.

(9) (Renumbered from 8, SG No. 105/2006) In the event of stolen, lost, damaged or destroyed tax documents, the person shall notify forthwith in writing the relevant competent customs authority of the circumstances.

(10) (Renumbered from 9, SG No. 105/2006) Issuance of tax documents may be manual and automated.

Article 85. (Effective 1.07.2006) (1) Tax documents shall be private written documents issued by a licensed warehouse keeper or a person registered under this Act for certifying incurrence of an obligation for payment and charge of excise duty.

(2) In addition to the requisites under Article 7 of the Accountancy Act the tax documents shall contain:

1. a ten-digit number of the document including only Arabic figures;

2. the stamp "original" on the first copy;

3. the type of the excisable goods, quantity, excise tax base and excise rate;

4. the amount of excise duty charged - on a separate line;

5. grounds for incurrence of the liability for excise duty charge.

Article 86. (Effective 1.07.2006) (1) Modification of the amount of excise duty charged in an excise tax document issued shall be documented by a note to the document, specifying the grounds for modification. A note shall be given only to an excise tax document issued.

(2) The note shall be:

1. excise debit note - a tax document reflecting the increase of the excise duty charged in an excise tax document issued;

2. excise credit note - a tax document reflecting the decrease of the excise duty charged in an excise tax document issued.

(3) The requisites of the tax note shall be:

1. all mandatory requisites for the excise tax document;

2. additional indication "excise debit note" or "excise credit note";

3. grounds for modification as well as the number and date of the excise tax document for which the note is issued.

Section II

Other Documents

Article 87. (Effective 1.07.2006) (1) The excise declaration is a document in which the licensed warehouse keeper or the registered person declares for every tax period specific information relating to his business, which is a ground for incurrence of rights and obligations.

(2) The declaration under Paragraph 1 shall be submitted for every tax warehouse, specialized small distillery or a small producer of wine to the competent customs authority by location of the warehouse or unit within 14 days from expiry of the tax period for which it refers.

(3) (New, SG No. 105/2006) The declaration under Paragraph 1 for the registered persons under Article 57a and Article 57c shall be filed to the competent customs authority by registration of the persons within 14 days from expiry of the tax period for which it refers.

(4) (Renumbered from Paragraph 3, SG No. 105/2006) Licensed warehouse keepers and registered persons shall file furthermore an excise declaration in the cases where no excise duty has been charged for the tax period.

(5) (Renumbered from Paragraph 4, SG No. 105/2006) In the presence of force majeure or at the request of the licensed warehouse keeper or registered person the competent customs authority may extend the term for filing the excise declaration until expiry of the next tax period.

(6) (New, SG No. 109/2007) In the cases under Article 20, Paragraph 2, items 12, 13 and 19, the excise declaration shall be filed within 14 days of receipt of excisable goods, respectively of consumption of energy products for purposes, other than those, indicated in the certificate.

Article 88. (Effective 1.07.2006) (1) (Amended, SG No. 105/2006) The licensed warehouse keeper shall keep a "Warehouse Stocks Log" register.

(2) In the register under Paragraph 1 shall be recorded excisable goods produced and/or stored, goods moving under excise duty suspension arrangement and goods released for consumption.

(3) Together with the excise declaration for the tax period the licensed warehouse keeper shall submit the information from the register under Paragraph 2 on a magnetic carrier according to parameters set out in the implementing regulation to this Act as well as a copy of

the register under Paragraph 1, except in the cases provided for in the implementing regulation to this Act.

(4) (Amended, SG No. 63/2006) The licensed warehouse keeper may furthermore submit electronically the excise declaration and the information under Paragraph 2 under the terms and according to the procedure laid down in the Tax and Social-Insurance Procedure Code . In this case Paragraph 3 shall not apply.

(5) Data from the Warehouse Stocks Log shall be accounted for in accordance with the established procedure in the accounting system of the persons under Paragraph 1.

(6) New, SG No. 105/2006) The persons registered under this Act shall keep reporting for the excisable goods, as laid down in the implementing regulation to this Act.

Article 89. (1) (Effective 1.07.2006, SG No. 91/2005, renumbered from Article 89, No. 105/2006) The certificate of excise exemption is a document issued by the competent customs authority, certifying that a particular person is an excise-exempt end user.

(2) (New, SG No. 105/2006) The certificate of registration is a document issued by the competent customs authority, certifying that a specific person is registered under this Act.

(3) (New, SG No. 105/2006) The permit for incindental receipt of excisable goods under excise duty suspension arrangement shall be a document issued by the competent customs authority, certifying that a non-registered trader has the right to receive incidentally a specific type and quantity of excisable goods under excise duty suspension arrangement from a licensed warehouse keeper in another Member State.

Article 90. (Effective 1.07.2006) The sample, format and requisites under this Chapter shall be set out in the implementing regulation to this Act.

Chapter Seven

RESTRICTIONS AND PROHIBITIONS

Article 91. (Effective 1.07.2006) Production of excisable goods under Article 2, items 1, 2 and 3 outside a tax warehouse shall be prohibited, unless otherwise provided for by this Act.

Article 91a. (New, SG No. 109/2007) Production and storage in a tax warehouse of excisable goods, not included within the scope of the tax warehouse operation license, shall be prohibited.

Article 92. (Effective 1.07.2006) (1) Retail sale of excisable goods from a tax warehouse shall be prohibited.

(2) (Amended, SG No. 105/2006) Paragraph 1 shall not apply to licensed warehouse keepers which feed in liquefied petroleum gas (LPG) in bottles other than bottles for gas equipment of automobiles, nor to licensed warehouse keepers which feed in liquefied petroleum gas (LPG) in gas equipment and heating systems and facilities in public, administrative, residential and office buildings fed in by containers of liquefied hydrocarbon gases with volume of up to 10m3.

(3) (New, SG No. 105/2006) Paragraph 1 shall not apply to licensed warehouse keepers who provide wine and/or ethyl alcohol (rakiya) to persons registered as producers of wine grapes, wine and grape products and wine for family consumption, who have provided the grapes for processing to the licensed warehouse keeper.

Article 93. (Effective 1.07.2006) (1) Licensed warehouse keepers of energy products shall mark all types of gas oil falling within CN codes 2710 19 41 0 through 2710 19 49 0 and kerosene falling within CN codes 2710 19 21 0 and 2710 19 25 0, which shall be charged at a lower excise rate than the excise rate on motor fuel.

(2) Marking under Paragraph 1 on the customs territory of the country shall be carried out only in a tax warehouse in the presence of a customs authority under the terms and procedure laid down in the implementing regulation to this Act.

Article 94. (Effective 1.07.2006) (1) Fuel oils and marked gas oil and kerosene shall not be fed in:

1. the fuel tank of motor vehicles, private vessels and private aircrafts;

2. tanks of fuel filling stations, pumps for filling motor vehicles or private vessels and private aircrafts.

(2) (Repealed, SG No. 63/2006) .

Article 95. (Effective 1.07.2006) (1) Feeding liquefied petroleum gas (LPG) in bottles other than liquefied petroleum gas bottles in motor vehicle petrol stations shall be prohibited.

(2) Sale and storage of liquefied petroleum gas (LPG) in bottles other than the liquefied petroleum gas bottles in motor vehicle petrol stations shall be allowed only where the bottles have been fed in the relevant bottle filling plants and/or in independent authorized outlets for feeding liquefied petroleum gas (LPG) bottles outside the territory of motor vehicle petrol stations. The bottles shall be secured by thermo-shrinkable caps which shall be destroyed before use and shall have the brand name of the producer.

Article 96. (Effective 1.07.2006) Any actions resulting in reduction or destruction of the effect of the marker shall be prohibited.

Article 97. (Effective 1.07.2006 - SG No. 91/2005) (1) (Amended, SG No. 63/2006) Complete denaturing of ethyl alcohol on the customs territory of the country shall be carried out only in a tax warehouse.

(2) Denaturing under Paragraph 1 shall be carried out in the presence of customs authorities under the terms and procedure set out in the implementing regulation to this Act.

(3) The type and quantity of the substances for denaturing shall be laid down in the implementing regulation to this Act.

Article 98. (Effective 1.07.2006) Extraction in whole or in part of denaturing substances as well as any other actions resulting in reduction or destruction of the effect of denaturing substances shall be prohibited.

Article 99. (Effective 1.07.2006) (1) (Supplemented, SG No. 109/2007) Excise labels may not be affixed on bottled alcoholic beverages falling within CN 2208 and such beverages may not be stored, transported and sold, if the indicated volume of hectoliters of pure alcohol measured at a temperature of 20 °C is lower than the actual volume of hectoliters of pure alcohol measured at a temperature of 20 °C in the respective bottle.

(2) Sale of tobacco products at a price other than the selling price written on the excise label shall be prohibited.

(3) Labeling of beer with labels indicating lower initial extract content measured in Plato degrees than the actual one shall be prohibited.

Article 100. (Effective 1.07.2006) (1) Bottled alcoholic beverages falling under CN code 2208 and with alcoholic strength by volume exceeding 15% vol and tobacco products intended for the domestic market shall be sold only with excise label affixed.

(2) The procedure and manner of introducing excise labels shall be established by the Council of Ministers.

Article 101. (Effective 1.07.2006) (1) Sale of draft (unbottled) alcoholic beverages falling within CN code 2208 and with alcoholic strength by volume exceeding 15% vol shall be prohibited.

(2) The provision of Paragraph 1 shall not apply to sale of alcoholic beverages among licensed warehouse keepers.

(3) Sale of alcoholic beverages falling within CN code 2208 and with alcoholic strength by volume exceeding 15% vol in plastic packages (bottles) shall be prohibited.

(4) (Supplemented, SG No. 109/2007) The provision of Paragraph 3 shall not apply to sale of alcoholic beverages in packages (bottles) of up to 0.5 liters inclusive.

Chapter Eight

CONTROL

Article 102. (Effective 1.07.2006) (1) Control on excisable goods, including goods under excise duty suspension arrangement, shall be exercised by customs authorities.

(2) Control shall include inspections of licensed warehouse keepers, persons registered under this Act, excise-exempt end users as well as all other persons dealing with excisable goods.

(3) Customs authorities may install technical devices to control movement and use of excisable goods.

(4) Customs authorities may take fuel samples from fuel tanks of motor vehicles.

(5) (New, SG No. 109/2007, effective 24.12.2007) Control over mandatory stocks of crude oil and petroleum products in tax warehouses shall be performed by the persons referred to in Article 30, paragraph 1 of the Mandatory Stocks of Crude Oil and Petroleum Products Act.

Article 103. (Effective 1.07.2006) Control shall be exercised by means of physical inspection of the quantity and other data and indicators concerning excise taxation as well as the accounting and commercial documentation of the inspected persons.

Article 104. (Effective 1.07.2006, amended, SG No. 105/2005) (1) The proceedings for establishing, securing and collecting excise duty liabilities shall be governed by the Tax and Social Insurance Procedure Code unless provided otherwise in this Act. Customs authorities shall have the powers of revenue authorities and in the cases of Article 121 of the Tax and Social Insurance Procedure Code , of public enforcement authority.

(2) For the purposes of Paragraph 1 customs authorities stipulated in the Customs Act shall have the competencies of territorial directorates of the National Revenue Agency, the Director of the Customs Agency shall have the powers of executive director of the National Revenue Agency and heads of customs offices shall have the powers of territorial directors.

(3) The powers under Article 112, Paragraph 2, item 1 of the Tax and Social Insurance Code shall be exercised by the head of the competent territorial customs agency.

(4) The powers of a decision-making body within the meaning of Article 152, Paragraph 2 of the Tax and Social Insurance Code shall be exercised by the director of the relevant regional customs directorate.

Article 105. (Effective 1.07.2006) Government and local authorities shall, at the request of a customs administration authority, provide timely assistance in the inspection and investigation of circumstances or establishing of facts directly related to the rights and obligations of the persons subject to tax duty under this Act.

Article 106. (Effective 1.07.2006 - SG No. 91/2005) (1) (Amended, SG No. 63/2006) The customs administration may use information from a revenue or customs administration of another country received in response to an official enquiry in determining the liabilities of persons dealing with excise goods as well as use this information as evidence in administrative and court proceedings.

(2) (Amended, SG 105/2005) The information collected under Paragraph 1 shall be considered a new circumstance in determining the rights and obligations of persons subject to excise duty under this Act and may be used in revising effective excise tax liabilities where the time limits for initiation of proceedings for issuance of a certificate of audit have not expired, provided for in the Tax and Social Insurance Code .

Article 106a. (New, SG No. 109/2007) Excisable goods which have not been claimed within 20 days of drawing up the protocol of their finding by the customs bodies in the course of control exercised, nor documents concerning their ownership have been provided, shall be deemed abandoned in favor of the state.

Article 107. (Effective 1.07.2006) The Minister of Finance shall issue an ordinance on sampling and analysis methods for the purposes of control on excisable goods.

Chapter Nine

ADMINISTRATIVE PENAL PROVISIONS

Article 108. (Effective 1.07.2006) (1) Where a person subject to excise duty fails to register under this Act, he shall be subject to property sanction ranging from BGN 500 to BGN 3,000.

(2) In the cases under Paragraph 1 in addition to the penalty the person shall owe the amount of the uncharged excise duty on the excisable goods produced until the date of establishing the violation.

Article 109. (Effective 1.07.2006) (1) A person who violates the provision of Article 60 shall be subject to a fine ranging from BGN 1,000 to BGN 3,000 - for natural persons, and a property sanction ranging from BGN 2,000 to BGN 6,000 - for legal entities and sole traders.

(2) In the event of a repeated violation the fine shall range from BGN 2,000 to BGN 6,000 and the property sanction, from BGN 4,000 to BGN 12,000.

(3) In the cases of Paragraphs 1 and 2 in addition to the penalty the person shall owe the amount of the uncharged excise duty on the excisable goods produced until the date of establishing the violation.

Article 109a. (New, SG No. 109/2007) (1) A person who violates the provision of Article 91a shall be subject to a fine ranging from BGN 500 to BGN 2,000 - for natural persons, and a property sanction ranging from BGN 1,000 to BGN 3,000 - for legal entities and sole traders.

(2) In the event of a repeated violation under Paragraph 1 the fine shall range from BGN 1,000 to BGN 4,000 and the property sanction, from BGN 2,000 to BGN 6,000.

Article 110. (Effective 1.07.2006) (1) (Amended, SG No. 109/2007) A person who fails to file an excise declaration within the time limit under Article 76d or under Article 87, shall be subject to a property sanction ranging from BGN 500 to BGN 2,500.

(2) In the event of a repeated violation under Paragraph 1 the property sanction shall range from BGN 1,000 to BGN 5,000.

(3) (Repealed, SG No. 109/2007).

(4) (Repealed, SG No. 109/2007).

Article 111. (Effective 1.07.2006) (1) (Amended, SG No. 105/2006, supplemented, SG No 109/2007) A person who fails to observe the time limit for notification in the event of changes in the circumstances, under which the tax warehouse operation license or the certificate of registration under this Act were issued, shall be subject to a property sanction ranging from BGN 500 to BGN 2,500.

(2) A person who fails to observe the time limit under Article 73 shall be subject to a property sanction ranging from BGN 500 to BGN 2,500.

(3) In the event of a repeated violation under Paragraphs 1 and 2 the property sanction shall range from BGN 1,000 to BGN 5,000.

Article 112. (Effective 1.07.2006) (1) Where a person subject to excise duty fails to charge it, he shall be subject to a property sanction to the double amount of the uncharged excise duty but not less than BGN 500.

(2) In the event of a repeated violation under Paragraph 1 the property sanction shall be to the double amount of the uncharged excise duty but not less than BGN 1,000.

(3) In the event of violation under Paragraphs 1 and 2, where the person has charged the excise duty in the period following the period in which the excise duty should have been charged, the property sanction shall be 25 per cent of the excise duty but not less than BGN 200.

Article 112a. (New, SG No. 105/2006) (1) Where a person subject to excise duty fails to issue a simplified accompanying document, he shall be subject to a fine, property sanction, respectively, in the amount of BGN 100.

(2) Upon a repeated violation under Paragraph 1 the amount of the fine/sanction shall be BGN 300.

Article 113. (Effective 1.07.2006) (1) A person who fails to account for or record a tax document or an accompanying administrative document in his books or in the Warehouse Stocks Log or in the excise declaration for the relevant tax period, or uses documents with incorrect content, forged or false documents in his accounting which result in determination of a lower excise duty due or higher refundable excise duty, shall be subject to a property sanction ranging from BGN 200 to BGN 10,000.

(2) In the event of a repeated violation under Paragraph 1 the property sanction shall range from BGN 500 to BGN 20,000.

Article 114. (Effective 1.07.2006) A person who violates the provision of Article 61 shall be subject to a property sanction ranging from BGN 5,000 to BGN 10,000 and in the event of a repeated violation, from BGN 10,000 to BGN 50,000.

Article 115. (Effective 1.07.2006) A person who violates the provision of Article 92 shall be subject to a property sanction ranging from BGN 2,000 to BGN 5,000 and in the event of a repeated violation, from BGN 4,000 to BGN 10,000.

Article 116. (Effective 1.07.2006) A person who violates the provision of Article 93 shall be subject to a property sanction ranging from BGN 5,000 to BGN 10,000 and in the event of a repeated violation, from BGN 10,000 to BGN 50,000.

Article 117. (Effective 1.07.2006) (1) A person who violates the provision of Article 94 shall be subject to a fine ranging from BGN 100 to BGN 300 - for natural persons, and a property sanction ranging from BGN 3,000 to BGN 10,000 - for legal entities and sole traders.

(2) In the event of a repeated violation under Paragraph 1 the fine shall range from BGN 200 to BGN 600, and the property sanction, from BGN 6,000 to BGN 20,000.

Article 118. (Effective 1.07.2006) (1) A person who violates the provision of Article 95 shall be subject to a fine ranging from BGN 1,000 to BGN 3,000 - for natural persons, and a property sanction ranging from BGN 3,000 to BGN 10,000 - for legal entities and sole traders.

(2) In the event of a repeated violation under Paragraph 1 the fine shall range from BGN 2,000 to BGN 6,000, and the property sanction, from BGN 6,000 to BGN 20,000.

Article 119. (Effective 1.07.2006) (1) A person who violates the provisions of Articles 96, 97 and 98 shall be subject to a fine ranging from BGN 100 to BGN 300 - for natural persons, and a property sanction ranging from BGN 3,000 to BGN 10,000 - for legal entities and sole traders.

(2) In the event of a repeated violation under Paragraph 1 the fine shall range from BGN 200 to BGN 600, and the property sanction, from BGN 6,000 to BGN 20,000.

Article 120. (Effective 1.07.2006) (1) A person who violates the provision of Article 99, Paragraph 1 shall be subject to a property sanction ranging from BGN 5,000 to BGN 10,000, and in the event of a repeated violation - from BGN 10,000 to BGN 20,000.

(2) A person who violates the provision of Article 99, Paragraph 2 shall be subject to a fine ranging from BGN 100 to BGN 300 - for natural persons, and a property sanction ranging from BGN 3,000 to BGN 10,000 - for legal entities and sole traders.

(3) (New, SG No. 105/2006) A person who violates the provision of Article 99, Paragraph 3 shall be subject to a property sanction ranging from BGN 2,000 to BGN 5,000, and in the event of a repeated violation - from BGN 5,000 to BGN 10,000.

(4) (Renumbered from Paragraph 3, SG No. 105/2006) In the event of a repeated violation under Paragraph 2 the fine shall range from BGN 200 to BGN 600, and the property sanction, from BGN 6,000 to BGN 20,000.

Article 121. (Effective 1.07.2006) (1) (Amended, SG No. 105/2006, amended, SG No 109/2007) A person who violates the provision of Article 64, Paragraphs 1 - 4, shall be subject to a fine ranging from BGN 1,000 to BGN 3,000 - for natural persons, and a property sanction ranging from BGN 2,000 to BGN 6,000 - for legal entities and sole traders.

(2) In the event of a repeated violation under Paragraph 1 the fine shall range from BGN 2,000 to BGN 6,000, and the property sanction, from BGN 4,000 to BGN 12,000.

(3) A person who produces or imports excisable goods and affixes on them false or forged excise labels or excise labels with expired validity shall be subject to a property sanction to the double amount of the excise duty due, but not less than BGN 5,000, and in the event of a repeated violation - not less than BGN 10,000.

(4) A person who violates the procedure and manner of introducing excise labels shall be subject to a property sanction of BGN 2,000 and in the event of a repeated violation - BGN 4,000.

(5) (New, SG No. 109/2007) A person which affixes, stores, carries or transports used excise labels in violation of the requirements of this Act and of the normative acts on its implementation, shall be subject to a fine ranging from BGN 1,000 to BGN 3,000 - for natural persons, and a property sanction ranging from BGN 2,000 to BGN 6,000 - for legal entities and sole traders.

Article 122. (Effective 1.07.2006) (1) A person who violates the provision of Article 101 shall be subject to a fine ranging from BGN 100 to BGN 300 - for natural persons, and a property sanction ranging from BGN 3,000 to BGN 10,000 - for legal entities and sole traders.

(2) In the event of a repeated violation under Paragraph 1 the fine shall range from BGN 200 to BGN 600, and the property sanction, from BGN 6,000 to BGN 20,000.

Article 123. (Effective 1.07.2006) (1) (Amended, SG No. 109/2007) A natural person who keeps in a warehouse or a retail outlet or in a vehicle, offers, sells, transports or carries excisable goods without excise label where such excise label is mandatory, or excisable goods with affixed false or forged excise labels or excise labels with expired validity shall be subject to a fine to the double amount of the excise duty due but not less than BGN 1,000, and in the event of a repeated violation - not less than BGN 2,000.

(2) A legal entity or a sole trader who keeps in a warehouse or a retail outlet or in a vehicle, offers, sells or transports excisable goods without excise label where such excise label is mandatory, or excisable goods with affixed false or forged excise labels or excise labels with expired validity shall be subject to a property sanction to the double amount of the excise duty due but not less than BGN 2,000, and in the event of a repeated violation - not less than BGN 4,000.

(3) Paragraphs 1 and 2 shall not apply to excisable goods without affixed excise labels or with affixed excise labels with expired validity moving under excise duty suspension arrangement.

(4) Where a legal entity or a sole trader keeping, offering, selling or transporting excisable goods establishes upon receipt of the delivery excisable goods without excise label where such excise label is mandatory, or excisable goods with affixed false or forged excise labels or excise labels with expired validity, he shall take inventory of the goods according to a sample approved by the Minister of Finance and shall notify in writing within three days from the day of acceptance or receipt of the goods the competent customs authority by location of the unit. In this case no sanction under Paragraph 2 shall be imposed on the person who has notified the customs authority.

(5) The sanctions under Paragraphs 1 and 2 shall be imposed on the person who keeps in a warehouse or transports excisable goods without excise labels where such are mandatory, or excisable goods with affixed false or forged excise labels or excise labels with expired validity in the cases where the owner cannot be found.

(6) A person who sells or stores in retail premises other than duty-free retail outlets alcoholic beverages and tobacco products affixed with the excise label DUTY FREE, with an inscription which obligatorily contains the words DUTY FREE respectively, shall be subject to a fine - for natural persons other than traders, or a property sanction - for legal entities and sole traders, to the double amount of the excise duty due but not less than BGN 1,000 and in the event of a repeated violation - not less than BGN 2,000.

(7) (New, SG No. 109/2007) Paragraph 6 shall not apply, if the excisable goods are under customs warehousing regime or are under a deferred payment of excise duty regime in a tax warehouse

(8) (Renumbered from Paragraph 7, SG No. 109/2007) Upon establishing tobacco products without excise labels or with affixed false or forged excise labels or with excise labels with expired validity or with excise labels with the inscription under Paragraph 6 in vending machines for sale of tobacco products, the sanctions under Paragraphs 1 and 2 shall be imposed on the person who has been licensed for trade in tobacco products from such vending machines in accordance with the Bulgarian legislation.

Article 123a. (New, SG No. 105/2006) (1) A person who evades full or partial payment or security of the excise duty due under this Act shall be subject to a fine in the double amount of the evaded excise duty but not less than BGN 1,000, and a property sanction shall be imposed on legal persons and sole traders in the double amount of the evaded excise duty, but not less than BGN 2,000.

(2) Upon a repeated violation under Paragraph 1 the fine shall be in the triple amount of the evaded excise duty but not less than BGN 2,000 and the property sanction shall be in the triple amount of the evaded excise duty but not less than BGN 4,000.

Article 124. (Effective 1.07.2006) (1) (Amended, SG No. 105/2006, SG No 109/2007) In the event of violations under Articles 115, 116, 117, 118 and Article 120, Paragraph 1, Article 121, Paragraphs 1, 2 and 3, Articles 122, 123 and 126, the goods subject of the breach shall be confiscated in favour of the State, regardless of their ownership.

(2) (New, SG No. 105/2006, amended, SG No 109/2007) The funds owned by the perpetrator, which have been used for violation of this Act, shall be confiscated in favour of the State unless their value does not correspond visibly to the gravity of the violation.

(3) (New, SG No. 109/2007) All facilities employed in committing a breach under Article 109, Paragraph 1, shall be confiscated in favour of the State, regardless of their ownership.

(4) (Renumbered from 2, SG No. 105/2006, renumbered from Paragraph 3, SG No. 109/2007) The Minister of Finance shall issue an ordinance stipulating the terms and procedure for disposal with excisable goods confiscated in favour of the State.

Article 125. (Effective 1.07.2006) (1) (Supplemented, SG No. 105/2006) An excise-exempt end user who has received energy products and has used them for purposes other than those stipulated in the certificate of excise exemption and who has not paid the excise duty due under this Act shall be subject to a property sanction to the double amount of the excise duty due on motor fuels of the relevant type, but not less than BGN 5,000.

(2) In the event of a repeated violation, the certificate shall be revoked and the property sanction under Paragraph 1 shall not be less than BGN 10,000.

(3) In the cases under Paragraph 2 the person shall pay the amount of the excise duty due on motor fuel of the respective type for the quantities available at the time of revocation of the certificate.

(4) (New, SG No. 63/2006) The sanctions referred to in Paragraphs (1), (2) and (3) shall furthermore be imposed on any agricultural producer which uses motor fuel at reduced rates in violation of Article 32 herein.

Article 126. (Effective 1.07.2006, SG No. 91/2005, supplemented, SG No. 109/2007) A person who produces, keeps in a warehouse or a retail outlet or in a vehicle, offers, sells or transports excisable goods without an excise document under this Act, or an invoice, or a customs declaration, or an accompanying administrative document, or other document, certifying the payment, charge or security of the excise duty, shall be subject to a fine - for natural persons, or to a property sanction - for legal entities and sole proprietors, in the double amount of the excise duty due but not less than BGN 1,000, and in the event of a repeated violation - not less than BGN 2,000.

Article 126a. (New, SG No. 105/2006) Any violation of the provisions of this Act established by the customs authorities, unless provided otherwise, shall be subject to a fine ranging from BGN 200 to BGN 1,000 or to a property sanction ranging from BGN 500 to BGN 2,000.

Article 126b. (New, SG No. 105/2006, amended, SG No 109/2007) For minor cases of violation of articles 118, 122, 123, 126 and 126a, established upon their commitment, the customs authorities may impose a fine by issuing a ticket under the procedure and in the amounts set out in Article 39, Paragraph 2 of the Administrative Violations and Sanctions Act.

Article 127. (Effective 1.07.2006) (1) A customs authority that fails to issue within 7 days a certificate of presence or absence of liabilities under this Act, shall be subject to a fine of up to BGN 250, and in the event of a repeated violation - up to BGN 500.

(2) Statements of violations shall be drawn up by officials in the inspectorate to the Minister of Finance and penalty enactments shall be issued by the Minister of Finance.

Article 128. (Effective 1.07.2006) (1) Establishment of violations, issuance, appeal and enforcement of penalty enactments shall be subject to the terms and procedures of the Administrative Violations and Sanctions Act.

(2) The statements of violations shall be drawn up by the customs authorities and the penalty enactments shall be issued by the Director of the Customs Agency or an official authorized by him.

TRANSITIONAL AND CONCLUDING PROVISIONS

§ 1. (1) (Effective 1.07.2006) This Act shall repeal the Excise Tax Act (promulgated State Gazette No. 19/1994.; amended SG Nos. 58/1995 and 70/1995, Nos. 21, 56 and 107/1996, No. 51/1997, Nos.15, 89 and 153/1998, No. 103/1999, No. 102/2000, No. 110/2001, Nos. 45 and 118/2002; corrected, No. 9/2003; amended, Nos. 37, 103 and 112/2003, Nos. 53 and 113/2004), except for Article 11 , Paragraphs 9 and 10, Article 12c , Article 17a, Paragraph 10 , § 2, item 25 of the additional provisions, § 26 of the transitional and concluding provisions of the Act Amending and Supplementing the Excise Tax Act (SG, No. 110/2001) and § 20 of the transitional and concluding provisions of the Act Amending and Supplementing the Excise Tax Act (SG, No. 118/2002) which shall apply until adoption of a duty-free trade act.

(2) (Effective 15.11.2005) The persons under § 20, Paragraph 2 of the transitional and concluding provisions of the Act Amending and Supplementing the Excise Tax Act (SG, No. 118/2002) the validity of whose permits has expired after 31 July 2005 shall continue to operate as duty-free operators until adoption of a duty-free trade act.

(3) (Effective 1.07.2006, - SG, No. 91/2005, repealed, SG No. 105/2006, effective as from the date of entry into force of the Treaty of Accession of the Republic of Bulgaria to the European Union - 1.01.2007).

§ 2. (1) (Amended, SG No. 63/2006) Any proceedings for the establishment and collection of excise duty liabilities, initiated on or before the 30th day of June 2006, as well any proceedings for reimbursement of excise duty initiated until the said date, shall be completed by the National Revenue Agency authorities.

(2) (Amended, SG, No. 105/2005, SG No. 63/2006) The excise duty charged on or before the 30th day of June 2006 shall be declared and remitted according to the procedure and within the time limits established by the Excise Tax Act and the Regulations for Application thereof.

(3) (New, SG No. 63/2006) The provisions of the Excise Tax Act shall apply to any excise duty liabilities which have arisen on or before the 30th day of June 2006, and the said liabilities shall be established, secured and collected by the National Revenue Agency

authorities according to the procedure established by the Tax and Social-Insurance Procedure Code .

(4) (New, SG No. 63/2006) The security furnished under the Excise Tax Act, furnished on or before the 30th day of June 2006, shall be released or utilized by the National Revenue Agency according to the procedure and under the terms established by the Excise Tax Act and the Regulations for Application thereof.

§ 2a. (New, SG No. 63/2006) (1) Authorized warehousekeepers shall have the right to reimbursement of the excise duty paid until the 30th day of June 2006 on:

1. ethyl alcohol (alcohol-containing raw materials) used in the production of alcoholic beverages;

2. gases intended for processing, falling within CN codes 2901 24 100, 2711 14 000, 2901 22 000 and 2901 21 000, which have undergone specific or chemical processing into excisable finished products;

3. heavy oils intended for processing, falling within CN codes 2710 19 710 and 2710 19 750, and for heavy fuel oils, falling within CN codes 2710 19 510 and 2710 19 550, which have under undergone specific or chemical processing into excisable finished products;

4. naphtha used in the production of ethylene;

5. ethylene used in the production of ethylene dichloride.

(2) Reimbursement shall be effected after release for consumption of the excisable goods in which the goods covered under Paragraph (1) are used or, respectively, after the sale of the ethylene dichloride, but not later than the 1st day of July 2007.

(3) (New, SG No. 109/2007) The term under Paragraph 2 shall not apply to excisable goods under Paragraph 1, item 1.

§ 2b. (New, SG No. 63/2006) The annual fuel consumption rate, referred to in Article 32 (3) herein, for 2006, shall be 44 litres per hectare of registered arable agricultural land.

§ 3. The documents in respect of which a sample is required under this Act shall be laid down in the implementing regulation to this Act.

§ 4. (Effective 15.11.2005) The Minister of Finance shall issue an implementing regulation to this Act within 6 months from its promulgation in the State Gazette.

§ 5. (Amended, SG No. 63/2006) The ordinances under Article 21, Paragraph 3, Article 25, Paragraph 2, Article 107 and Article 124, Paragraph 2 shall be issued within three months from entry into force of this Act.

§ 6. The Minister of Finance:

1. shall determine by an order the information in the registers under Article 24, Paragraph 5, Article 54, Paragraph 1 and Article 56, Paragraph 2, which shall be public;

2. may determine jointly with the Governor of the Bulgarian National Bank a special procedure for the tax payment.

§ 7. The Corporate Income Tax Act (promulgated SG, No. 115/1997; amended, No. 19/1998; amended, Nos. 21 and 153/1998, Nos. 12, 50, 51, 64, 81, 103, 110 and 111/1999, Nos. 105 and 108/2000, Nos. 34 and 110/2001, Nos. 45, 61, 62 and 119/2002, Nos. 42 and 109/2003, Nos. 18, 53 and 107/2004, No. 39/2005) shall be supplemented as follows:

1. Article 2d shall be created:

"Article 2d. (1) Persons organizing games of chance with gambling slot machines, bookmaking facilities for betting on horse or dog-racing results, rulette and other gaming equipment in gaming casinos, instead of the corporate profit tax and/or final tax under Article 2a on games of chance with gaming slot machines, bookmaking facilities for betting on horse or dog-racing results, rulette and other gaming equipment in gaming casinos, shall be charged with a final tax on the respective facility.

(2) The persons under Paragraph 1 shall accrue and pay the tax in the respective territorial tax directorate by place of its tax registration in advance quarterly installments and shall send a copy of the payment order to the territorial tax directorate by location of the gambling hall, bookmaking facilities or the casino and to the gambling supervision authority. The installments shall be paid for every object of gambling with a separate payment order specifying the location and address of the object. The persons under Paragraph 1 shall file a declaration for the respective quarter according to a sample approved by the Minister of Finance within the time limits for payment of the tax.

(3) The tax under Paragraph 1 shall be paid by 3 January for the first quarter of the calendar year, by 1 April - for the second quarter, by 1 July - for the third quarter, and by 1 October - for the fourth quarter of the calendar year.

(4) For any other activities taxation of the persons under Paragraph 1 shall be in accordance with the general procedure."

2. Article 46d shall be created:

"Article 46d. The amount of the tax under Article 2d shall be as follows:

1. for gambling slot machines or bookmaking facilities for betting on horse or dog-racing results -BGN 300 per quarter per facility;

2. for rulette in a casino for gaming table - BGN 18,000 per quarter per facility;

3. for other gaming facility in a casino - BGN 3,000 per quarter per facility."

3. Paragraphs 7, 8 and 9 are created in Article 67a:

"(7) A person who runs games of chance or uses gaming slot machines and gaming facilities under Article 2d without having paid the tax due shall be subject to a fine - for natural persons other than traders or to a property sanction - for legal persons and sole traders, to the double amount of the tax due but not less than BGN 3,000.

(8) In the event of a repeated violation under Paragraph 7 the amount of the fine or the property sanction shall be to the amount of the double tax due but not less than BGN 5,000.

(9) The sanctions under Paragraphs 7 and 8 shall apply regardless of the sanctions provided for in other acts and the gambling supervision authorities under the Gambling Act shall be notified within three days of establishing the violation."

§ 8. The Customs Act (promulgated SG, No. 15/1998; amended, Nos. 89 and 153/1998, Nos. 30 and 83/1999, No. 63/2000, No. 110/2001, No. 76/2002, Nos. 37 and 95/2003, No. 38/2004, Nos. 45 and 86/2005) shall be amended and supplemented as follows:

1. In Article 7 , Paragraph 8 a second sentence shall be inserted: "Officials from the inspectorate to the Minister of Finance shall be entitled to access to any data and documents in the customs administration in connection with the inspections conducted by them."

2. In Article 17 , Paragraph 1, item 6, first sentence, after the wording "provided for by law" shall be added "at the request of the officials from the inspectorate to the Minister of Finance ".

§ 9. Until entry into force of the statement of issuance of a license for management of a tax warehouse or refusal for its issuance existing producers of excisable goods at 1 January 2006 who file an application for license by 1 March 2006 shall continue their activity as licensed warehouse keepers under the procedure of this Act.

§ 10. The Tobacco and Tobacco Products Act (promulgated SG, No. 101/1993; amended, No. 19/1994, No. 110/1996, No. 153/1998, No. 113/1999, Nos. 33 and 102/2000, No. 110/2001, No. 20/2003, Nos. 57 and 70/2004) shall be amended and supplemented as follows:

1. Article 29 shall be amended as follows:

"Article 29. (1) Domestically produced or imported cigarettes shall be sold on the domestic market at prices, under terms and according to a procedure as laid down by the Council of Ministers.

(2) The terms and procedure for registration of prices of tobacco products, except those under Paragraph 1, domestically produced and imported, the trade in tobacco products and control on them shall be stipulated in a regulation of the Council of Ministers."

2. (Effective 15.11.2005) § 3a shall be created in the transitional and concluding provisions:

"§ 3a. By 1 January 2006 the Council of Ministers shall adopt the necessary amendments and supplements to the implementing regulations to this Act."

§ 11. Enforcement of this Act is assigned to the Minister of Finance.

§ 12. The Act enters into force on 1 January 2006 except for:

1. (amended, SG No. 63/2006) the provisions of Articles 1 to 31, Article 32, Items 2, 4, 5 and 6 of Article 33 (1) and Article 33 (2), Articles 34 to 46, Articles 59 to 128, § 1 (1) regarding the repeal of the Excise Tax Act , as well as § 1 (3), which shall enter into force as from the 1st day of July 2006;

2. the provisions of § 1, Paragraph 2 , § 4 and § 10, item 2, which shall enter into force on the date of promulgation of this Act in the State Gazette.

3. (new, SG No. 63/2006, amended, SG No. 108/2006, SG No. 109/2007) the provisions of Items 1 and 3 of Article 33 (1), which shall enter into force as from the 1st day of January 2009.

The Act was passed by the 40th National Assembly on 2 November 2005 and the Official Seal of the National Assembly has been affixed to it.

TRANSITIONAL AND FINAL PROVISIONS

of the Administrative Procedure Code

(SG, No. 30/2006, effective 12.07.2006)

. . . .

§ 21. Everywhere in the Excise Duties and Tax Warehouses Act (Promulgated State Gazette No. 91/2005, amended SG No. 105/2005) the words "the Administrative Procedure Act" and shall be replaced by "the Administrative Procedure Code".

(*) Act to Amend the Commercial Register Act

(SG No. 80/2006, effective 3.10.2006)

§ 1. In § 56 of the Transitional and Final Provisions the words "1 October 2006" shall be replased by "1 July 2007"

TRANSITIONAL AND FINAL PROVISIONS

to the Act to Amend the Excise Duties and Tax Warehouses Act

(SG No. 105/2006, effective 1.01.2007)

§ 77. (1) The persons under Article 57a, Paragraph 1, items 1, 2 and 3 who carry out activity at the date of entry into force of this Act shall file an application for registration within 14 days from its entry into force.

(2) Until delivery of the certificate of registration the persons under Paragraph 1 shall have all the rights and obligations of registered persons under this Act.

§ 78. For goods to which the circumstances under Appendix V, Chapter IV "Customs Union" of the Protocol to the Treaty of Accession of the Republic of Bulgaria to the European Union the provision of Article 19, Paragraph 1, item 3 shall apply at the date of completion of customs formalities.

§ 79. State aids referred to in Article 32, Paragraph 1, item 7, Paragraph 2, item 4, and Article 33, Paragraph 1, item 6 shall be provided after the European Commission issues a positive decision on their compatibility with the Common Market.

....

FINAL PROVISION

to the Act to Amend the Excise Duties and Tax Warehouses Act

(SG No. 109/2007, effective 1.01.2008)

§ 56. This Act shall enter into force as from 1 January 2008, except for the tax reliefs uder § 12, Item 1, letter "e", constituting state aid, which shall enter into force upon issuance of positive decision by the European Commission.

THE TOBACCO AND TOBACCO PRODUCTS ACT

LAW ON THE CONTROL OF FOREIGN TRADE ACTIVITY IN ARMS AND IN DUAL - USE GOODS AND TECHNOLOGIES

CHAPTER ONE GENERAL PROVISIONS

Article 1

1. The present Law regulates the terms and procedure for the conducting of foreign trade activity in arms and in goods and technologies of potential dual use and state control over these activities.

2. Goods and technologies are deemed to be of potential dual-use when they can be used for both civil and military purposes.

Article 2

The conducting of foreign trade activity pursuant to Art 1 is subject to state control in order to ensure that national security and the foreign political interests of the state will be protected, international credibility and stability - strengthened and the international obligations of the Republic of Bulgaria-fulfilled.

Article 3

In order to ensure the attainment of the purposes referred to in Art 2 the government bodies, within the scope of their competence, may directly co-operate and exchange information with the corresponding competent authorities of other states, the signing of Cooperation Agreements included.

Article 4

1. The state may introduce restrictions and impose bans on the execution of foreign trade activity in arms and in dual-use goods and technologies when:

1) the activity contravenes the purposes referred to in Art 2;

2) the goods and technologies are intended or may be used for the development, production, operation, handling, maintenance, storage and dissemination of mass destruction weapons;

3) the Republic of Bulgaria has acceded to international conventions on non-proliferation of the weapons or by virtue of membership in international organizations has undertaken such obligations, as well as in the event of sanctions in respect of a certain state, introduced by the Security Council of the UN.

2. The list of the arms and of the dual-use goods and technologies in respect whereof the regime to Para 1 is applied, shall be established by the Council of Ministers and shall be published in the State Gazette.

CHAPTER TWO FOREIGN TRADE ACTIVITY IN ARMS REGIME

Article 5

1. Foreign trade activity in arms may be solely effected by trade companies where Bulgarian equity participation exceeds 50 % under observance of the provisions of the present Law.

2. Foreign trade activity in arms is effected on the basis of a license granted for the execution of the respective activity and a permit for every individual transaction, issued by government bodies designated by the Council of Ministers and headed by Ministers.

3. The license and permit have a certain period of validity. The scope of the license is laid down by the body referred to in Para 2.

Article 6

The requirements to be satisfied by the trade companies applying for a license and a permit and the terms for the revocation thereof are established in the Regulation on the Implementation of the present Law in accordance with the purposes referred to in Art 2.

Article 7

1. Where necessary the government bodies to Art 5, Para 2 may request the opinion of other government bodies.

2. For the issue of licenses and permits and the performance of inspections the competent government bodies may designate experts who shall give their opinion on matters requiring specialist knowledge.

3. For the issue of the licenses and permits state fees shall be paid in amounts established by the Council of Ministers.

Article 8

Transit transportation of arms through the territory of the Republic of Bulgaria shall be effected on the basis of a transit transportation license wherein the customs posts, route and time of transit shall be indicated. The license shall be issued on a case-by-case basis under the terms and procedure established in the Regulation on the Implementation of the present Law.

CHAPTER THREE FOREIGN TRADE ACTIVITY IN DUAL-USE GOODS AND TECHNOLOGIES REGIME

Article 9

1. Any person may carry out foreign trade activity in dual-use goods and technologies on observing the provisions of the present Law and in accordance with the Laws and Regulations in force.

2. Foreign trade activity in dual-use goods and technologies whereon restrictions have been introduced under Art 4, shall be effected on the basis of an individual transaction permit, issued by a government body designated by the Council of Ministers and headed by a Minister.

3. Foreign trade activity in a certain type of goods and technologies, referred to in the List to Art 4, Para 2, shall be effected on the basis of a license granted by the body to Para 2. A transaction permit for this type of goods and technologies shall be issued to the licensee.

4. The licenses and permits to this Chapter are issued with a certain period of validity according to the terms and procedure established in the Regulation on the Implementation of the present Law.

Article 10

1. For the issue of an individual transaction permit a declaration of confirmation is required from the end-user in respect of the end-use of the dual-use goods and technology.

2. For the issue of licenses and permits and the performance of inspections the competent bodies may designate experts who shall give their opinion on matters requiring specialist knowledge.

3. For the issue of the licenses and permits state fees shall be paid in amounts established by the Council of Ministers.

Article 11

The body pursuant to Art 9, Para 2 shall deny the issue of or revoke a granted license or permit when:

1) the information relevant to the issuance thereof has not been submitted or the information submitted is false or incomplete;

2) the Applicant has not complied with the terms under which the license and permit have been granted within the established time-limit;

3) circumstances contravene the purposes referred to in Art 2;

4) circumstances, envisaged by the present Law, arise.

Article 12

Transit transporation of dual-use goods and technologies through the territory of the Republic of Bulgaria shall be effected on the basis of a transit transportation license wherein the customs posts, route and time of transit shall be indicated. The permit shall be issued on a case-by-case basis according to the terms and procedure established in the Regulation on the Implementation of the present Law.

Article 13

The issue of a permit for foreign trade activity in dual-use goods and technologies not listed in Art 4 shall be required when the exporter or importer is aware of, could have been aware of or has been informed in writing by the relevant bodies that:

1) the dual-use goods and technologies may be intended, in their entirety or in part, for the development, production, handling, operation, maintenance, storage, detection or dissemination of chemical, biological or nuclear weapons or for the development, production, maintenance or storage of missiles capable of delivering chemical, biological or nuclear weapons, covered by the international agreements for the prohibition or non-proliferation of such weapons;

2) dual-use goods and technologies are intended for a country in respect of which the Security Council of the UN has undertaken measures for the maintenance or re-establishment of international peace and security, or in respect of a country, in whose territory military operations are being conducted or which participates in a military conflict.

CHAPTER FOUR OBLIGATIONS OF THE PARTIES TO FOREIGN TRADE ACTIVITY

Article 14

The persons engaged in foreign trade activity in arms and in goods and technologies subject to control as stipulated in the present Law, are under the obligation to:

1) keep a separate register of the transactions effected as per the present Law, and retain transaction and transportation documents and the information related to the execution of the transaction for at least five years;

2) observe the terms and conditions under which this activity has been licensed, and immediately notify in writing the control bodies of any change thereof;

3) indicate the name, position and address of the representatives of the party to the transaction and of the end-user, in charge of the performance of the obligations to the transaction, and immediately notify of any replacement or change thereof;

4) inform the respective government bodies should a probability become apparent that the goods and technologies subject of foreign trade activity may be used in the way envisaged in Art 13.

Article 15

Importers and exporters of arms are under the obligation to incorporate a provision in the foreign commercial contract ensuring guarantees on the part of the buyer that the purchased arms may not be transferred to third natural or juridical persons without the express consent of the importer or exporter.

Article 16

The license and permit obtained under the present Law may be used solely by the grantee thereof. The transference of the license and permit or of rights thereof to a third party shall invalidate the said license and permit whereas the transferor shall thereby forfeit any rights arising from them.

CHAPTER FIVE CONTROL ON THE OBSERVANCE OF THE FOREIGN TRADE ACTIVITY IN ARMS AND IN DUAL-USE GOODS AND TECHNOLOGIES REGIME

Article 17

1. The control on the performance of the obligations and terms related to the issued license or permit under the present Law is enforced by the bodies issuing the license or permit and by other government bodies in accordance with their competence.

2. The enforcement of control includes inspections prior to and after the issue of the license and permit for foreign trade activity under the present Law.

3. In the enforcement of control the control bodies pursuant to Para 1 may:

1) request information necessary to the enforcement of control;

2) apply to the competent organs of other states for their submission of information necessary to the enforcement of control;

3) perform inspections on the observance of the obligations of the parties to the transaction and of the end-user in the event of import.

4. The control bodies are under the obligation to keep in confidence any official, production or commercial secrets of the persons undergoing inspection.

5. In the presence of information about a committed crime the government body designated by the Council of Ministers shall refer the matter to the prosecution authorities.

6. Representatives of a foreign state may participate in the enforcement of control in accordance with the international obligations of the Republic of Bulgaria assumed under international agreements or by virtue of participation in international organizations.

Article 18

A written protocol on the results of the inspection shall be prepared. On the establishment of evidence of a committed crime, the official preparing the protocol shall forward a copy thereof to the prosecution authorities.

CHAPTER SIX ADMINISTRATIVE-PENAL PROVISIONS AND PROPERTY SANCTIONS

Article 19

The natural persons engaged in foreign trade activity, the representatives of the parties to the transaction and of the end-user of arms or dual-use goods and technologies shall be penalized with a fine in amounts ranging from 50 000 to 500 000 leva on failure to perform their obligations referred to in Arts 14 and 15 if the perpetrated act is not a crime.

Article 20

The juridical persons engaged in foreign trade activity shall be penalized with property sanctions on failure to perform their obligations referred to in Arts 14 and 15, amounting to double the total transaction value, determined on the basis of the foreign commercial transaction data.

Article 21

On non-performance of other obligations arising from the present Law natural persons shall be penalized with a fine in amounts ranging from 25 000 to 250 000 leva unless they are subject to a heavier punishment, whereas juridical persons shall be penalized with a property sanction in amounts of up to 500 000 leva.

Article 22

1. The protocol on the establishment of violations is prepared by officials of the organs of control to Art 17, Para 1.

2. Penal decrees shall be issued by the Minister in charge of the respective body to Art 5, Para 2 and Art 9, Para 2.

3. The drawing up of the protocol on the establishment of administrative violations, the imposition of administrative penalties, the appeal against and the enactment of the penal decrees shall take place as prescribed by the Law on Administrative Violations and Penalties.

ADDITIONAL PROVISION

§1. In exceptional events, should the state's national security or the performance of international obligations assumed by the state be jeopardized, or should the state's foreign political interests be infringed, the Council of Ministers may ban the carrying out of import, export, re-export or transit transportation of arms and dual-use goods and technologies, regardless of the issued license and permit.

TRANSITIONAL AND FINAL PROVISIONS

§2. In Art 5, Subpara 3 of the Law on Economic Activity of Foreign Persons and on the Protection of Foreign Investment (publ. in the State Gazette, issue 8, 1992; amended issue 92, 1992) the words "and trade in" are replaced by the word "of".

§3.In the Criminal Code (publ. SG, issue 26, 1968; amended issue 29, 1968; mod. and add. issue 92, 1969, issues 26 and 27,1973, issue 89, 1974, issue 95, 1975, issue 3, 1977, issue 54, 1978, issue 89, 1979, issue 28, 1982; amended issue 31, 1982; mod. and add. issue 44, 1984, issues 41 and 79, 1985; amended issue 80, 1985; mod. and add. issue 89, 1986; amended issue 90, 1986; amended issues 37, 91 and 99, 1989, issues 10,31 and 81, 1990, issues 1 and 86, 1991; amended issue 90, 1991; mod. issue 105, 1991, issue 54, 1992, issue 10, 1993 and issue 50, 1995) a new Article 233 is incorporated:

Article 233

1. Anyone engaged in foreign trade activity in dual-use goods and technologies without respective authorization shall be penalized with imprisonment of up to 6 years and with a fine to the amount of up to 500 000 leva.

2. For particularly serious offenses, referred to in Para 1, the penalty shall be imprisonment from 3 to 8 years and a fine to the amount of up to 1 million leva.

3. For minor offenses, referred to in Para 1, the penalty shall be a fine to the amount of up to 50 000 leva.

4. The dual-use goods constituting the subject of the crime shall be seized on behalf of the state irrespective of the fact whose property they are, or in the event of a lack or alienation thereof their equal value determined as per the foreign commercial contract shall be adjudged.

§4. The present Law shall enter into force two months after its publication in the State Gazette.

§5. The implementation of the present Law is assigned to the Council of Ministers that adopts a Regulation on its implementation within one month of its entry into force.

This Law was passed by the XXXVII National Assembly this 8-th day of November, in the year 1995 and the State Seal was affixed thereto.

DECREE FOR ADOPTION OF REGULATION ON IMPLEMENTATION OF THE LAW ON CONTROL OF THE FOREIGN TRADE ACTIVITY IN ARMS AND DUAL-USE GOODS AND TECHNOLOGIES AND FOR AMENDMENT OF LEGAL ACTS OF THE COUNCIL OF MINISTERS

REPUBLIC OF BULGARIA

COUNCIL OF MINISTERS
DECREE No 38
of March 6, 1996

Decree for Adoption of Regulation on Implementation of the Law on Control of the Foreign Trade Activity in Arms and Dual-Use Goods and Technologies and for Amendment of Legal Acts of the Council of Ministers

THE COUNCIL OF MINISTERS

DECREED:

Art.1. Adopted shall be the Regulation on implementation of the Law for control of the foreign trade activity in arms and dual-use goods and technologies according to appendix No 1.

Art.2.(1) Established shall be a Commission for control and permission of the foreign trade transactions with arms and with dual-use goods and technologies at the Ministry of Commerce and Foreign Economic Co-operation according to appendix No 2.

(2) The names of the members of the commission shall be approved by the Minister of Commerce and Foreign Economic Co-operation at a proposal by the corresponding heads of Ministries or Departments.

(3) The chairman of the commission shall determine the proceedings of its work.

Art.3. The commission for control and permission of foreign trade transactions with arms and with dual-use goods and technologies shall:

1. issue permits for foreign trade transactions with arms and with dual-use goods and technologies;

2. permit the participation of the trade companies in international tenders for export or re-export of arms;

3. submit to the Interdepartmental council on the issues of the military industrial complex and the mobilisation convenience of the country regular information about the conducted sessions and the decisions taken by it.

TRANSITIONAL AND FINAL PROVISIONS

§ 1. Repealed shall be the Ordinance for control on the regime of the foreign trade activity in military and special production, adopted by Decree No 51 of the Council of Ministers of 1994 (promulgated SG 29/94, amended SG 57/95) except appendix No 8 of §1 of the additional provision of the ordinance - List of the military and special production, technical assistance and services in the field of defense industry and defense, subject to control at foreign trade with them".

§ 2. Repealed shall be the Ordinance for control on the foreign trade activity in goods and technologies with potential double (civil and military) use, adopted by Decree No 224 of the Council of Ministers of 1992 (promulgated SG 92/92, amended SG 54/94), except: appendix No 1 of the ordinance - List of the nuclear equipment, materials and the technologies connected with them with potential application in the field of nuclear weapons (INFCIRC 254 Rev.1 Part 1 INFCIRC 254 Rev.1 Part 2, Cocom International Atomic Energy List); appendix No 2 - List of the internationally controlled goods and technologies (Cocom Industrial List); appendix No 3 - List of the goods and technologies with potential application in the field of chemical and biological weapons (Chemical and Biological weapons non-proliferation list) and appendix No 4 - List of the goods and technologies with potential application in the field of missile carriers for chemical, biological and nuclear weapons (Missile Technology Control Regime), promulgated as a publication of the Ministry of Commerce.

§ 3. The decree is issued pursuant to art.105, para 2 of the Constitution of the Republic of Bulgaria and § 5 of the transitional and final provisions of the Law on control of the foreign trade activity in arms and dual-use goods and technologies.

§ 4. In Decree No 193 of the Council of Ministers of 1993 for closing of the Government commission for regulation of and control on the regime for production and trade with military and special production and the Interdepartmental council for defense-mobilisation preparation of the country and for establishing of Interdepartmental council on the issues of military-industrial complex and mobilisation convenience of the country (promulgated SG 89/93, amended SG 24/94, SG 31, 97/95) the following changes shall be made:

1. In art.3:

a) item 2 of para 1 shall be changed as follows:

"2. in the field of trade with arms and with dual-use goods and technologies:

a) proposes to the Council of Ministers drafts for acts on the state policy in the field of trade with arms and with dual-use goods and technologies;

b) co-ordinates and controls the conduct of market and price policy in the field of trade with arms and with dual-use goods and technologies;

c) issues licenses for execution of foreign trade activity in arms and in dual-use goods and technologies;

d) issues licenses for the rights to transport arms and dual-use goods and technologies;

e) keeps a register of the companies, licensed for foreign trade activity or for transportation of arms and dual-use goods and technologies;

f) considers information by the Commission for control and permission of foreign trade transactions with arms and with dual-use goods and technologies about all submitted applications for permits for import, export, as well as about all permitted, postponed or revoked applications for foreign trade transactions with arms and with dual-use goods and technologies. On the basis of the submitted information and documents the Interdepartmental council shall decide ultimately about problem issues, raised by members of the council or by the commission, about particular deals with arms and with dual-use goods and technologies;

g) approves annual account about the activity of the commission of item "f" in the field of foreign trade activity in arms and with dual-use goods and technologies."

b) in item 4 of para 1 shall be created items "d" and "e":

"d) co-ordinates the activity of the Ministries, other departments and trade companies at implementing the industrial and scientific -research co-operation in the field of defense industry;

e) co-ordinates the activity of the Ministries and other departments about the integration of the Republic of Bulgaria in the international organisations, controlling the trade with arms and with dual-use goods and technologies."

2. Para 2 of art.4 shall be changed to:

"(2) Chairman of the council shall be a member of the Council of Ministers, appointed by a decision of the Council of Ministers."

3. Para 3 of art.5 shall be changed to:

"(3) The Service shall work under the rule of the chairman of the Interdepartmental council."

§ 5. In the Regulation on the activity of the Interdepartmental council in the issues of military-industrial complex and the mobilisation convenience of the country, approved by Decree No 51 of the Council of Ministers of 1994 (promulgated SG 29/94, amended SG57/95) the following changes shall be made:

1. In art.3 the following amendments shall be made:

a) item 2 shall be changed to:

"2. issues licenses for execution of foreign trade activity in arms and in dual-use goods and technologies;"

b) item 3 shall created:

"3. issues licenses for the rights to transport arms and dual-use goods and technologies."

3. In item 1 of art.5 after the word "co-operation" shall be added "in the defense industry".

§ 6. The decree shall enter into force on the day of its promulgation in "State Gazette".

REGULATION on implementation of the Law for foreign trade activity in arms and in dual-use goods and technologies(SG 102/95)

CHAPTER ONE FOREIGN TRADE ACTIVITY IN ARMS

Section I

General provisions

Art.1.(1) Foreign trade activity in arms shall be effected by trade companies where Bulgarian equity participation exceeds 50% and which have been granted a license for such activity by the Interdepartmental council on the issues of the military-industrial complex and the mobilisation convenience of the country, called hereinafter "The Interdepartmental council".

(2) The license for foreign trade activity in arms shall be issued with a term of validity up to 1 year.

(3) The license of para 1 shall be possible to be full and limited with regard to the implemented activities and the country - end-user.

Art.2. The companies which have been granted a license referred to in art.1, shall carry out transactions with arms on the basis of a permit issued by the Commission for control and permission of foreign trade transactions with arms and with dual-use goods and technologies at the Ministry of Commerce and Foreign Economic Co-operation, called hereinafter "the commission". The permit shall be issued for a definite term.

Art.3. To acquire a license for foreign trade activity in arms and of a permit for a transaction fees shall be paid in extent determined by the Council of Ministers. At revocation of the license and/or the permit the fees paid shall not be subject to redeeming.

SECTION II LICENSE FOR FOREIGN TRADE ACTIVITY IN ARMS

Art.4. The trade companies referred to in art.1 applying for a license, shall present at the Interdepartmental council:

1. application (explanatory note);

2. court certificate about the circumstances entered into the trade register, containing all the changes of these circumstances following the entering;

3. a document from the Ministry of Internal Affairs that the applicant has created conditions and the necessary organisation for:

a) foreign trade activity in arms according to the requirements of the Law for control on the explosive substances, arms and ammunitions;

b) work with secret documents and protection of state secret according to the requirements of the legal acts in effect;

4. a list of the individuals who are directly involved in this activity, accompanied with biography and CV information, a certificate about the court record and a sample of the signature;

5. a document for fees paid;

6. a copy of the documents certifying the tax registration and the registration at the National Statistics Institute (code BULSTAT).

Art.5. The Interdepartmental council shall consider the submitted applications in 30 days term after the date of applying. The decision to grant a licence or the refusal shall be announced to the applicant in 7 days term after the date of taking the decision.

Art.6. The Interdepartmental council shall notify within 5 working days the Ministry of Internal Affairs, the Ministry of Finance - General Customs Directorate and the commission for the issued and renewed licenses.

Section III Permit for foreign trade transaction with arms

Art.7.(1) A permit for foreign trade transaction with arms shall only be given to the trade companies referred to in art.1 that have been granted a license for such activity.

(2) The commission shall consider the submitted applications for permit of particular foreign trade transactions in 15 days term after the date of applying. The permit or the refusal shall be announced to the applicant in 7 days term after the date of taking the decision.

(3) If a transaction permitted under the regulations of this chapter is not implemented in term, the applicant shall be able to appeal by a motivated written claim an extension of the term 15 days before its expiry, pointing out the part of the unrealised quantities.

Art.8.(1) The participation of trade companies in international tenders for export or re-export shall be permitted by the commission.

(2) The trade companies shall submit a written application, accompanied with an invitation for participation in the tender.

Art.9. Within 5 working days the commission shall inform the bodies of the Ministry of Finance - General Customs Directorate, and the Ministry of Internal Affairs about the permits which term has been extended or has expired.

A. Import

Art.10.(1) The import of arms shall be carried out on the basis of a permit for import, issued by the commission.

(2) The permit for import shall be valid 180 days from the date of issuing or for the pointed out in the contract term of delivery which cannot be longer than the term of the issued license to art.1

Art.11.(1) For import of arm the licensed company shall submit to the commission the following documents:

1. a letter-application about the transaction for import where the terms and the prices of the deal are pointed out;

2. a filled-in form permit for import according to appendix No 1 in 4 copies;

3. a copy and a Bulgarian translation of a document, issued by a competent body of the country where the selling company is registered, that the said company has a permit to trade with arms;

4. a written declaration by the importer and a written declaration by the end-user that the imported arms will not be re-exported or transferred to third individuals or corporate bodies without the permit of the competent Bulgarian bodies and that it would be used observing the Bulgarian laws in effect.

(2) To acquire a permit for: temporary import of arms in the Republic of Bulgaria with a reverse export abroad in a changed status (TI) - code 7 (according to Instruction No 2 of the Ministry of Finance of 1992); temporary import of arms in the Republic of Bulgaria with reverse export abroad in an unchanged status (TI) - code 8, and for reverse export of arms (RE) - code 4, shall be filled-in a permit for temporary import according to appendix No 2 and a permit for reverse export according to appendix No 2a.

(3) The permit for import shall be presented by the importer at the corresponding customs department together with the bill of entry, filled-in according to the instructions in appendix No 3.

(4) The import shall be verified by a copy of the bill of entry, certified by the customs department, filled-in according to the instructions in appendix No 3, and a permit for import according to appendix No 1 where under each separate shipment are filled-in the number and the date of the customs manifest and the number and the date of the bill of entry.

(5) The commission shall be able to refuse issuing a permit for import of arms in case that a Bulgarian producer is able to produce arms of the same or similar technical characteristics, quality and price.

Art.12. In case the seller requires from the Bulgarian buyer a certificate for end-user, the buyer shall present a certificate, filled-in according to the requirements contracted between the two parties, signed and stamped by the buyer (user) and certified as follows:

1. by the Ministry of Defense - in case that the goods are designated for the same Ministry or for the forces of the other departments;

2. by the Ministry of Industry - in case that the goods are designated for the production activity of the trade companies;

3. by the Ministry of Internal Affairs - in case that the goods are designated for the same Ministry or for security needs of banks, companies and other departments.

B. EXPORT AND RE-EXPORT

Art.13. The export or the re-export of arms shall be executed on the basis of permits issued by the commission.

Art.14.(1) To acquire of permit for export the exporter shall present at the commission for each transaction the following documents:

1. a filled-in sample permit according to appendix No 4;

2. a copy and a Bulgarian translation of a document, issued by a competent body from the country of the foreign contractor importer that the same contractor has a permit to trade with arms;

3. a copy and a Bulgarian translation of the certificate for end-user, issued by the competent bodies of the country user.

(2) The original of the certificate shall be safe-kept by the exporter till the end of the transaction after which it shall be sent to the commission for safe-keeping.

(3) To acquire a permit for: temporary export of arms abroad with its reversion in the Republic of Bulgaria in changed status (THE) - code 2 (according to Instruction No 2 of the Ministry of Finance of 1992); temporary export of arms abroad with its reversion in the Republic of Bulgaria in unchanged status (THE) - code 3, and reverse import (RI) - code 9, shall be filled-in a permit for temporary export according to appendix No 5 and a permit for reverse import according to appendix No 5a.

Art.15.(1) The exporter shall be obliged to include in the foreign trade contract a clause ensuring guarantees on behalf of the buyer that the bought arms will not be re-exported.

(2) In case that the contract for export is not concluded directly with the Ministry of Defense or with the Ministry of Internal Affairs of the corresponding country - importer but through a middleman, the clause of para 1 in the sale contract shall also be included in the certificate for end-user, issued by the competent body of the country user.

(3) After receiving of permit for a particular transaction changes of the conditions of the transaction shall be possible to be made with the consent of the commission.

Art.16. The permit for export shall be valid 180 days after the date of issue or for the period of delivery pointed out in the contract which cannot be longer than the term of the issued general license referred to in art.1.

Art.17. The commission shall submit information about the issued permits to the General Customs Directorate and to other departments according their competence.

Art.18. Re-export of arms shall be executed on the basis of a permit for re-export. To acquire a permit for re-export the following documents shall be enclosed:

1. a filled-in sample permit for re-export according to appendix No 6;

2. a certificate for end-user of the arms;

3. a copy of the foreign contract with a clause included about non admitting of re-export without the written consent of the commission;

4. a permit for re-export by the competent bodies of the state of the initial supplier.

Art.19.(1) The permit for export or re-export shall be presented by the exporter at the corresponding customs department together with the customs declaration for export or re-export, filled-in according to the instructions in appendix No 7.

(2) The export or the re-export shall be certified with certified copy of the customs declaration for export, certified by the customs department, filled-in according to the instructions in appendix No 7 and the permit for export (appendix No 4) or for re-export (appendix No 6), where shall be entered under each separate shipment the number and the data of the customs manifest and the number and the data of the bill of export.

C. PERMIT FOR TRANSIT TRANSPORTATION

Art.20.(1) A transit transportation of arms shall be executed on the basis of a permit for transit transportation. For issuing a permit for transit transportation the following documents shall be presented:

1. a filled-in permit for transit transportation according to appendix No 12;

2. a permit for transit transportation through the territory of the state following the Republic of Bulgaria along the route of the transit transportation , issued by the competent bodies.

(2) The documents shall be worked out by the sender of the goods or by an official empowered by him and they shall be presented at the commission not later than 15 days before the entering of the goods on the territory of the Republic of Bulgaria.

(3) The permission or the refusal shall be announced to the applicant in 10 days term after the date of submitting the documents.

(4) The permit shall be valid under the conditions and till the expiry of the term pointed out in it, but not later than 10 days for automobile transport and 15 days for railroad transport.

(5) The outgoing customs department within 10 working days after the certification of the transit transportation shall send one copy of the permit certified by them to the commission and to the General Customs Directorate.

SECTION IV SUBMISSION OF INFORMATION

Art.21. The trade companies of art.1 shall be obliged at request of information by the Interdepartmental council or by the commission to present:

1. data about the employees processing the transactions;

2. a copy of the commercial contract with the foreign partner - middleman, forwarding agent, carrier, end-user or producer;

3. a copy of the concluded commercial contract with the Bulgarian producer or user about the request made for import/export;

4. data (technical characteristics) and description of the technologies and goods - subject to the foreign trade transaction;

5. data about the terms of payment and bank guarantees;

6. information about the foreign trade transaction and their realisation with regard to the permits given;

7. by the decision of the commission it may also require other information which relevant to the foreign trade transaction.

Art.22. At request for permission for import of equipment, materials and parts for introduction of technologies in the Republic of Bulgaria for production of arms, the applicant shall be obliged to present technical specifications and technological documentation, including data referring to the conditions for utilisation of the technology.

Art.23. If the acquired licensed rights or technologies for production of arms are not used or are not used as intended, or if their use is terminated, the end-user in the Republic of Bulgaria shall be obliged to notify the commission about that.

Art.24.(1) The information that has been submitted to the Interdepartmental council and the commission, which is required for issuing the corresponding permits and is not included in the List of facts, data and subjects constituting state secret of the Republic of Bulgaria, shall comprise an official, trade and production secret and shall not be subject to dissemination or submission for use by Bulgarian or foreign individuals or corporate bodies.

(2) The information of para 1 shall be submitted through secret channels.

Art.25. After the customs processing of the last shipment with which the permitted quantity of the permit for export is depleted, import or re-export, the trade company, subject to the foreign trade transaction, shall send in 7 working days term the original of the permit to the commission.

CHAPTER TWO FOREIGN TRADE ACTIVITY IN DUAL-USE GOODS AND TECHNOLOGIES

SECTION I GENERAL PROVISIONS

Art.26.(1) The foreign trade activity in goods and technologies as: nuclear materials, nuclear-connected equipment and technologies with potential application in the field of nuclear arms; initial chemical compounds, equipment and technologies with potential application in the field of chemical weapons; initial elements, equipment and technologies with potential application in the field of biological weapons ad technologies with potential application in the field of rockets - carriers of chemical, biological and nuclear weapons, subject to restrictions referred to in art.4, para 2 of the law, shall be executed on the basis of a license issued by the Interdepartmental council after an assessment that the objectives of art.2 of the law would not be affected. A permit for a transaction with this kind of goods and technologies shall be issued by the commission to an applicant who has an issued license.

(2) The permission or the refusal to be issued a license shall be executed by the Interdepartmental council on the basis of the information submitted and after consultations with other departments according to their competence. The permit or the refusal shall be announced to the applicant in 30 days term after the submission of the application.

Art.27.(1) Foreign trade activity with goods and technologies shall be executed on the basis of a permit for a transaction, issued by the commission.

(2) The permit for import, for re-export and for transit transportation or the refusal a permit to issued shall be announced to the applicant within the following terms:

1. up to 10 days from the date of submitting the documents - in the cases of an issued license as referred to in art.26;

2. up to 30 days from the date of submitting the documents -in the rest of the cases.

(3) The permit for import, export and re-export shall be valid under the conditions and until the expiry of the term of the shipment pointed out it but not more than:

1. 180 days - in the cases and within the terms of validity of an issued license referred to in art.26;

2. 90 days - in the rest of the cases.

(4) The applicant shall in due time inform the commission about all the changes in the terms of the transaction. In case of significant changes the issued permit shall be repealed and a new permit shall be issued according to the general proceedings.

(5) By the decision of the commission it may also require another information related to the foreign trade deal.

SECTION II PROVISIONS AND PROCEEDINGS FOR ISSUING A LICENSE

Art.28.(1) A license for execution of foreign trade activity in goods and technologies shall be issued with a term of validity up to 1 year.

(2) To acquire a license it shall be necessary to submit to the Interdepartmental council the following documents:

1. a court certificate about the circumstances entered in the trade register, containing all the changes following the entry and BULSTAT (as an original or a copy, certified with a fresh stamp of the applicant);

2. information about fulfilled tax duties;

3. a document of the Ministry of Internal Affairs, the Committee for peaceful use of nuclear energy or other competent body pointed out by the commission that the applicant has created conditions and the necessary organisation for work with the specified type of goods and/or technology.

SECTION III PERMIT FOR A PARTICULAR TRANSACTION

A. IMPORT

Art.29.(1) Import of goods and technologies shall be executed on the basis of a permit for import. To acquire a permit for import the following documents shall be presented:

1. a filled-in permit according to appendix No 8 and an application about the end-user according to the sample of appendix No 9;

2. a court certificate about the circumstances entered in the trade register, containing all the changes of these circumstances following the entry, tax registration and BULSTAT (as an original or an official certified copy of the applicant) in the cases when no license is required under art.26.

(2) The commission shall send a copy of the issued permit and application to the end-user, to General Customs Directorate and to the Ministry of Internal Affairs.

(3) The applicant shall be obliged at releasing the shipment to present at the corresponding customs offices a filled-in certificate about the implemented supply according to appendix No 10. The certificate about the delivery carried out shall be issued by the customs office in confirmation of the fact that the goods pointed out in it have been delivered to the Republic of Bulgaria.

(4) Within 10 working days after filing the import General Customs Directorate shall send to the commission one copy of the certificate about delivery carried out together with a copy of the bill of entry.

B. Export

Art.30.(1) Export of goods and technologies shall be executed on the basis of a permit for export. To acquire a permit for export the following documents shall be presented:

1. a filled-in permit for export according to appendix No 11;

2. a certificate for end-user of the goods and/or the technology where the end-user shall point out for what purpose and where the goods and/or the technology would be used;

3. a permit for import by the authorities of the state of the end-user, including non-admittance of re-export without the written consent of the commission;

4. a court certificate about the circumstances entered in the trade register containing all the changes following the entry, a tax registration and BULSTAT (as an original or an official certified copy of the applicant) in the cases when the license of art.26 is not required.

(2) At necessity the permit for export shall e issued after a co-ordination with the Ministry of Internal Affairs and with other departments according to the conceded competence in compliance with art.2 of the law.

(3) The commission shall send a copy of the permit to General Customs Directorate and to the Ministry of Internal Affairs.

(4) Within 10 working days after the date of filing the export General Customs Directorate shall send to the commission a copy of the bill of export.

(5) The applicant shall present to the commission a certificate for delivery carried out or an equivalent document by the end-user, confirming the release of the goods and/or the technology from the customs of the end-user at latest 3 months after the date of entry.

C. Re-export

Art.31.(1) Re-export of goods and technologies shall be executed on the basis of a permit for re-export. To acquire a permit for re-export the following documents shall be presented:

1. filled-in permits for import and export according to appendix No 8 and appendix No 11;

2. a certificate about end-user of the goods and/or technology where the end-user points out for what purpose and where the goods and/or the technology would be used;

3. a permit for import by the competent bodies of the state of the end-user, including non-admittance of re-export without the written consent of the commission;

4. a permit for re-export by the competent bodies of the state initial supplier;

5. a court certificate about the circumstances entered in the trade register, containing all the changes of the circumstances following the entry, tax registration and BULSTAT (as an original or a copy certified with a fresh stamp of the applicant) in the cases when no license of art.26 is required.

(2) The commission shall send a copy of the permit to General Customs Directorate and to the Ministry of Internal Affairs.

(3) Within 10 working days term after the date of filing the re-export General Customs Directorate shall send to the commission a copy of the bill of export.

(4) The applicant shall be obliged to present to the commission a certificate for delivery carried out or an equivalent document by the end-user confirming the release of the goods and/or technology from the customs of the country of the end-user at latest 3 months after the date if its entry.

D. Change of the end-user on the territory of the Republic of Bulgaria

Art.32.(1) The change of the end-user of a goods and/or technology on the territory of the Republic of Bulgaria shall be executed on the basis of a permit for change of the end-user. For issuing a permit for change of the end-user the following documents shall be presented:

1. a filled-in permit by the end-user according to appendix No 9;

2. a court certificate about the circumstances entered in the trade register containing all the changes of the circumstances following the entry, tax registration and BULSTAT (as an original or an official certified copy of the applicant) in the cases when no license of art.26 is required.

(2) The permission or the refusal shall be decided by the commission on the basis of the presented information and the results of the consultations with other departments according to their competence.

(3) The permission or the refusal shall be announced to the applicant within 5 working days from the date of submitting the documents.

(4) The permit shall be valid under the conditions and till the expiry of the term of the supply pointed out in it but not more than 3 months.

(5) The commission shall send through official channels a copy of the issued permit to General Customs Directorate and to the Ministry of Internal Affairs.

SECTION IV PERMIT FOR TRANSIT TRANSPORTATION

Art.33.(1) Transit transportation of goods as: radioactive, explosive, inflammable, oxidising, toxic, infectious and corrosive substances, shall be executed on the basis of a permit for transit transportation. For issuing a permit for transit transportation the following documents shall be presented:

1. a filled-in permit for transit transportation according to appendix No 12;

2. a permit for transit transportation through the territory of the state following the Republic of Bulgaria on the route of the transit transportation, issued by the corresponding competent bodies.

(2) The documents shall be prepared by the sender of the goods or by an official empowered by him and shall be presented to the commission at latest 15 days before the entry of the goods on the territory of the Republic of Bulgaria.

(3) The permit or the refusal shall be announced to the applicant within term up to 10 days after the date of submitting the documents.

(4) The permit shall be valid under the conditions and till the expiry of the term pointed out in it but not more than 10 days for automobile transport and 15 days for railway transport.

(5) Within 10 working days term after the date of certifying the transit transportation the customs department of exit shall send one copy of the permit certified by it to the commission and to General Customs Directorate.

Art.34.(1) At execution of transit transportation of goods apart from the cases of art.33 an application for transit transportation shall be filled-in an according to appendix No 13.

(2) The application of para 1 shall be presented to the customs departments of entry and exit on the territory of the Republic of Bulgaria where its certification shall take place.

(3) Within 10 working days after the date of certifying the transit transportation the customs department of exit shall send one copy of the certified by it permit to the commission and to General Customs Directorate.

CHAPTER THREE PROVISIONS FOR REVOCATION OF ISSUED LICENSES AND PERMITS FOR FOREIGN TRADE TRANSACTIONS

Art.35.(1) An issued license for foreign trade activity in arms and in dual-use goods and technologies and an issued permit for a particular transaction may be revoked respectively by the Interdepartmental council and the commission in case that:

1. the particular requirements or the activity within the framework of the issued license and permits for specific transaction do not comply with the requirements of the legislation of the Republic of Bulgaria and with the obligations taken by it in international agreements or ensuing from its membership in international organisations;

2. the foreign trade transactions with goods and technologies do not ensure protection of the national security and the foreign policy interests of the country and the strengthening of international confidence and stability;

3. the applicant has presented incorrect or incomplete data;

4. the activity does not coincide with the issued permit;

5. the applicant violates the requirements of art.4 of the Law on control of foreign trade activity in arms and in dual-use goods and technologies and of this regulation.

(2) The decision of the Interdepartmental council and of the commission for revocation of the licence and/or the permit shall not be subject to appeal against.

CHAPTER FOUR CHECK OF THE EMPOWERED BODY

Art.36. The Interdepartmental council, the commission and General Customs Directorate shall have the right to check the fulfilment on behalf of the Bulgarian party the obligations in the transaction, ensuing from the regulation and the international agreements concerning the trade with arms and with dual-use goods and technologies.

Art.37. The Interdepartmental council, the commission and General Customs Directorate the shall have the right to attract authorised specialists from other countries for implementing the procedure of control in compliance with obligations assumed by the Republic of Bulgaria in international agreements.

Art.38. The Interdepartmental council and the commission shall have the right to require a confirmation of the receiving of the goods - subject to the export through the official representatives of the Republic of Bulgaria in the country of the end-user.

ADDITIONAL PROVISIONS

§ 1. "Arms" are articles, activities and services, included in the list of art.4, para 2 of the law.

§ 2.(1) The transportation of arms, dual-use goods and technologies to and from the territory of the Republic of Bulgaria respectively to Bulgarian border customs department of exit or entry may be executed by Bulgarian or foreign transport companies.

(2) The Bulgarian carriers shall be able to execute this activity only if they have received license by the Interdepartmental council.

(3) The license for transportation of arms and of dual-use goods and technologies shall be issued for one year.

(4) The foreign carriers or the companies using foreign carriers shall present document for registration and a certificate for suitability of the transport means by which the transportation of arms and dual-use goods and technologies will be carried out.

(5) Bulgarian carriers as referred to in art.2 may execute transportation services in arms, respectively in dual-use goods and technologies to and from the territories of third countries after receiving a permit from the commission for each individual case, in co-ordination with the Ministry of transport. Such permit shall be required regardless of whether a person licensed under the stipulations of this Regulation participates in the foreign trade transaction with arms, respectively with dual-use goods and technologies.

(6) For execution of transportation services on the territory of the country while carrying out foreign trade transactions, permitted by the commission, the bodies of the Ministry of Internal Affairs issue a permit for transportation and perform control according to their competence in compliance with respective legal acts.

§ 3.(1) The Bulgarian transport companies applying to receive a license shall present to the Interdepartmental council the following documents:

1. an application;

2. a court certificate for registration of the company (firm);

3. a permit by the Ministry of Transport for transportation of arms and dual-use goods and technologies;

4. a document by the State inspectorate of shipping, State automobile inspectorate, State railway inspectorate and by the State aviation inspectorate, certifying the suitability of the transport means to carry arms and goods with potential dual use;

5. a document from the Ministry of Internal Affairs that the applicant is able to execute such transport services;

6. a copy of the documents, certifying the tax registration and the registration at the National Statistics Institute;

7. a document for fees paid.

(2) The license issued by the Interdepartmental council or the refusal to be issued a license shall be announced within 30 days after the date of submitting the application.

(3) Within 5 working days term the Interdepartmental council shall notify the commission, the Ministry of Transport, the Ministry of Internal Affairs and General Customs Directorate about the licenses issued or renewed.

§ 4.(1)In the cases as referred to in **§ 2,** art.5 of the Additional Provisions Bulgarian carriers that apply to receive a permit shall present to the commission the following documents:

1. an application;

2. a filled-in permit form according to appendix N 8 and N 11 for transportation of dual-use goods and technologies;

3. a copy of the contract for transportation;

4. a permit for export issued by the competent bodies of the country of the seller;

5.a permit for import issued by the country of the buyer or the end-user;

(2) The permit issued by the commission or the refusal shall be announced within a 15 days term from the date of applying.

(3) Within a 5 working days term the commission shall notify the Ministry of Transport about issued or renewed licenses.

§ 5. The Ministry of Transport shall store information and perform control on Bulgarian carriers that have received a license from the Intradepartmental council and a permit from the commission for transportation in transactions with arms or with dual-use goods and technologies, in accordance with § 2 of the Additional Provisions.

TRANSITIONAL AND FINAL PROVISIONS

§ 6. The effect of the license and the permits issued before the regulation enters into force shall continue till the expiry of their validity and the contracts for transportation, concluded in connection with foreign trade activity in arms and dual-use goods and technologies- till their termination.

§ 7. The regulation shall enter into force on the day of its promulgation in "State Gazette".

NEGOTIATING POSITION

OVERALL POSITION
The Republic of Bulgaria accepts and will implement in full the *acquis* in the field of Industrial Policy.

As a working hypothesis, the Bulgarian Government considers that Bulgaria will become a member of the EU on 01.01.2007.

No derogations or transitional periods in this area will be requested.

ACQUIS ADOPTION AND IMPLEMENTATION
Community Law in the area of "Industrial Policy" sets up the basic principles and guidelines for further development. The Republic of Bulgaria fully accepts the wording and the spirit of Article 130 of the Treaty on European Union, which is further, developed in *Council Decision 96/413/EC,* implying Action Program to Strengthen the Competitiveness of European Industry.

Strategy for Industrial Development, which is a part of the National Plan for Economic Development for the period 2004 - 2006, entirely complies with Article 130 of the Treaty on European Community and *Council Decision 96/413/EC.*

The Industrial policy of Bulgaria will be fully aligned to the acquis in the field of Industrial policy. The Bulgarian side reviews the latest Communications of the European Commission concerning the globalisation of markets and the increasing importance of information technologies.

Bulgaria's Industrial policy is oriented towards improving the competitiveness of the industrial sector, which will be achieved by the following measures:

Restructuring of the enterprises;

Promotion of the industrial co-operation;

Improvement of quality;

Promotion of innovations and technological development;

Creation of favourable investment climate.

The enterprise restructuring implies enhancement of industrial competitiveness through viable enterprises operating in a free market environment, based on the principles of transparency and equality. The measures envisaged to that end are:

Continuation of the privatisation process;

Liquidation and insolvency procedures for enterprises, which are not viable in a competitive environment.

State Aids issues should be addressed to the Chapter 6 Competition policy.

The improvement of the **investment climate** and attracting FDI is also of great importance. The Investment Program 1998 - 2004, adopted by the Government includes investment projects, concerning infrastructure. Their realisation shall facilitate the development and modernisation of the industries. The Commercial Act of the Republic of Bulgaria provides for equal treatment of local and foreign entities regarding their establishment, and the Foreign Investment Act guarantees equal rights and equal treatment of their investment activities.

The administrative capacity for implementation of the 'acquis communautaire' involves:

The Ministry of Economy handles the overall implementation and monitoring of the Industrial policy of the Republic of Bulgaria.

The NGOs - such as branch chambers, unions and associations - take an active part on permanent basis in the formulation of the sector analysis and policies, as well as in the future monitoring of their implementation.

All necessary institutional infrastructures for the implementation of the EU legislation in the area of Industrial policy are or will be in place by the date of accession of Bulgaria to the EU.

* * *

The Bulgarian government proposes the negotiations on this chapter to be provisionally closed on the basis of the existing *acquis*.

Should new elements of the *acquis* make it necessary, Bulgaria recognizes the possibility of opening supplementary negotiations before the end of the Intergovernmental conference.

SCREENING A-LIST

No.	EU Reference
1	384L0450 / OJ L 250 19.09.84 p.17 / 84/450/EEC: Council Directive of 10 September 1984 relating to the approximation of the laws, regulations and administrative provisions of the Member States concerning misleading advertising Incorporated by 294A0103(69) (OJ L 001 03.01.94 p.492)
2	385L0374 / OJ L 210 07.08.85 p.29 / 85/374/EEC: Council Directive of 25 July 1985 on the approximation of the laws, regulations and administrative provisions of the Member States concerning liability for defective products Incorporated by 294A0103(52) (OJ L 001 03.01.94 p.263)

	Incorporated by 294A0103(53) (OJ L 001 03.01.94 p.321) Incorporated by 294A0103(73) (OJ L 001 03.01.94 p.572)
3	385L0577 / OJ L 372 31.12.85 p.31 / 85/577/EEC: Council Directive of 20 December 1985 to protect the consumer in respect of contracts negotiated away from business premises Incorporated by 294A0103(69) (OJ L 001 03.01.94 p.492)
4	387L0102 / OJ L 042 12.02.87 p.48 / 87/102/EEC: Council Directive of 22 December 1986 for the approximation of the laws, regulations and administrative provisions of the Member States concerning consumer credit Amended by 390L0088 (OJ L 061 10.03.90 p.14) Amended by Directive of the European Parliament and of the Council 98/7/EC Incorporated by 294A0103(69) (OJ L 001 03.01.94 p.492)
5	387L0357 / OJ L 192 11.07.87 p.49 / 87/357/EEC: Council Directive of 25 June 1987 on the approximation of the laws of the Member States concerning products which, appearing to be other than they are, endanger the health or safety of consumers Incorporated by 294A0103(69) (OJ L 001 03.01.94 p.492)
6	390L0314 / OJ L 158 23.06.90 p.59 / 90/314/EEC: Council Directive of 13 June 1990 on package travel, package holidays and package tours Incorporated by 294A0103(69) (OJ L 001 03.01.94 p.492)
7	392L0059 / OJ L 228 11.08.92 p.24 / Council Directive 92/59/EEC of 29 June 1992 on general product safety
8	393L0013 / OJ L 095 21.04.93 p.29 / Council Directive 93/13/EEC of 5 April 1993 on unfair terms in consumer contracts
9	394D3092 / OJ L 331 21.12.94 p.1 / Decision No 3092/94/EC of the European Parliament and of the Council of 7 December 1994 introducing a Community system of information on home and leisure accidents Amended by 395D0184 (OJ L 120 31.05.95 p.36)

10	394L0047 / OJ L 280 29.10.94 p.83 / Directive 94/47/EC of the European Parliament and the Council of 26 October 1994 on the protection of purchasers in respect of certain aspects of contracts relating to the purchase of the right to use immovable properties on a timeshare basis

11	395D0260 / OJ L 162 13.07.95 p.37 / 95/260/EC: Commission Decision of 13 June 1995 setting up a Consumer Committee
12	397D0404 / OJ L 169 27.06.97 p.85 / 97/404/EC: Commission Decision of 10 June 1997 setting up a Scientific Steering Committee
13	397D0579 / OJ L 237 28.08.97 p.18 / 97/579/EC: Commission Decision of 23 July 1997 setting up Scientific Committees in the field of consumer health and food safety (Text with EEA relevance)
14	397L0007 / OJ L 144 04.06.97 p.19 / Directive 97/7/EC of the European Parliament and of the Council of 20 May 1997 on the protection of consumers in respect of distance contracts - Statement by the Council and the Parliament re Article 6 (1) - Statement by the Commission re Article 3 (1), first indent
15	397L0055 / OJ L290 23/10/97, P. 18 / Directive 97/55/EC of the European Parliament and of the Council of 6 October 1997 amending Directive 84/450/EEC concerning misleading advertising so as to include comparative advertising
16	398D0139 / OJ L 038 12.02.98 p.10 / 98/139/EC: Commission Decision of 4 February 1998 laying down certain detailed rules concerning on-the-spot checks carried out in the veterinary field by Commission experts in the Member States (Text with EEA relevance)

17	398D0140 / OJ L 038 12.02.98 p.14 / 98/140/EC: Commission Decision of 4 February 1998 laying down certain detailed rules concerning on-the-spot checks carried out in the veterinary field by Commission experts in third countries (Text with EEA relevance)
18	398L0006 / OJ L080 18/3/98, p. 27 / Directive 98/6/EC of the European Parliament and of the Council of 16 February 1998 on consumer protection in the indication of the prices of products offered to consumers (This Directive replaces directive 79/581/EEC on the indication of the prices of foodstuffs amended by directive 88/315/EEC : directive 88/314/EEC on the indication of prices of non-food products and directive 95/58/EC amending directives 79/581/EEC and 88/314/EEC.

TRAVEL TO BULGARIA

There are excellent conditions for tourism in Bulgaria. The Bulgarian Black Sea Coast has become known throughout the world for its wonderful geographical and climatic conditions: a warm sea without sharks, with almost imperceptible tides, well-wooded shores and vast beaches covered with fine golden sand. There are a lot of modern resorts offering excellent conditions for rest and recreations, such as Zlatni Pyassatsi (the Golden Sands), Drouzba, Slunchev Bryag (the Sunny Beach), Rousalka, Albena, Duni, Elenite, St. Constantine and Elena, motels, camping sites and summer camps.

Each of the Bulgarian mountains - Rila, Pirin, the Rhodopes, the Balkan Range, Vitosha, etc., has a charm of its own - their snow-capped peaks sparkling in the sun, covered with thick pine or deciduous forests interspersed with fragrant alpine meadows. There are numerous cosy chalets and pleasant holiday houses, snuggling in the mountains' folds. The mountain resorts of Borovets, Pamporovo, Malyovitsa, Velingrad, Yundola and many others are equally attractive in summer and in winter.

There are more than 500 mineral springs on the territory of Bulgaria and many of them are used for balneotherapy. Health resorts and balneosanatoria were built in Kyustendil, Vurshets, Sandanski, Pavel Banya and in many other places of Bulgaria.

There are 2004 explored and unexplored caves in Bulgaria. In one of them, the Magoura Cave, the unique rock drawings made by people from the pre-historical time can be seen. The Belogradchik rocks, the natural pyramids at Melnik, the Pobiti Kamuni (Stone Forests) near Varna, the Er Kyupria (Devil's Bridges) in the Rhodopes are some of the most curious sights of Bulgaria. Beside the natural beauties of Bulgaria there are countless historical and cultural monuments of Bulgaria's centuries-long history. The Thracian tumulus (burial mound) near Kazanluk and the Proto-Bulgarian Madara Horseman near Shoumen are two of them. Entire towns and villages in Bulgaria are real museums, like Turnovo, Koprivshtitsa, Melnik, Zheravna, Kotel, Tryavna, Nessebur and many other places where memories of the country's past still linger.

MAJOR CITIES

SOFIA

Since 1987 Bulgaria has been divided into eight regions, each named after its administrative capital; with the city of Sofia forming a separate region (called an oblasti with the plural as oblasts) from the province of Sofia, under the name of 'Grad Sofia'.

Location

Situated on the high 'Sofia Plateau' surrounded by imposing mountains such as the 2,000m-high (6,562ft) Mount Vitosha, the city of Sofia cuts an impressive figure in the Bulgarian landscape. Its wide and welcoming yellow boulevards were part of a tasteful refurbishment that the city underwent after the destruction of World War II. Like its other (better known) European counterparts, this capital city has grown up around a cafe culture of sidewalk terraces. The surrounding mountains and forests give Sofia a green and peaceful appearance, but the hustle and bustle of the inner city reveal it to be a thriving metropolis.

Climate

Sofia experiences its highest temperatures and longest hours of sunshine in the summer months of June, July and August. Due to its location in a high-lying and mountainous area, its temperatures stay comfortably below 30°C (86°F). Sofia also, however, experiences its highest rainfall in its summer months, and visitors who intend to set up tents should consider arriving at the end of August.

The city of Sofia harbors ideal conditions for winter sports. Its winters are mild and dry, and snowfalls can virtually be guaranteed from December to April.

Population

With 1.2 million inhabitants, Sofia is the largest city in Bulgaria. The youth, who make up the biggest percentage of this number, enjoy the most visibility and are also the ones who set the busy tempo for which Sofia is known.

Sofia has the highest ratio of Jewish inhabitants within its city walls when compared to any other Bulgarian city. Sofia also sports Bulgaria's only Synagogue, built in the 16th century from the stones of the Jewish cemetery, which had guarded the bones of the deceased members of the Jewish community since their entrance into Bulgaria in the first century AD.

Sports and Activities

The green and mountainous surroundings of Sofia offer ideal hiking opportunities, both for seasoned hikers and beginners who prefer to limit their hikes to short and pleasant walks. In winter this same environment is transformed into a series of busy ski resorts, with Mount Vitosha as the permanent home of Bulgaria's National Ski School.

The artificial Lake Pancharevo near Sofia caters for the swimming desires of both visitors and locals, and is also the scene for various boating activities during the summer months. The popular spa of Bankya, less than 20km (12.4 miles) from Sofia's city center welcomes visitors to its swimming pools, spas and public parks.

The most popular sport in Sofia, and, indeed, in the whole of Bulgaria, is soccer. Avid fans follow every soccer match that features the Bulgarian National team, and nearby Borovets is a World Cup Soccer venue. Sofia's Park Na Svobodata houses a large soccer stadium and holds regular soccer matches organized between local teams.

Attractions

The city of Sofia features a number of excellent Art Galleries and Museums, as well as many historical sites. The Cyril and Methodius Art Gallery houses a fine international collection, while the National Museum of Fine Arts exhibits both ancient and contemporary art. The Sofia Municipal Gallery focuses on local artists, contemporary as well as those from the National Revival period.

The St Alexander Nevski Memorial Church was erected between 1904 and 1912, and commemorates the 200,000 Russians who died in the cause of Bulgaria's liberation. Its architecture is impressive, and its collection of over 170 icons is worth a visit. In summer an arts and craft market gathers in front of the cathedral.

Sites such as the Former George Dimitrov Mausoleum and the former Party House, have also gained popularity with foreign visitors in recent years.

Entertainment

Sofia is a beehive of activity from morning to night, and flaunts an uncountable number of restaurants, cafés and nightclubs. Street cafés are plentiful, and the jazz culture dominates in the night-time cafés and clubs. Most restaurants have not escaped westernization, and pizza in particular is very popular here, although plenty of traditional Bulgarian restaurants remain. Theatre tickets are extremely affordable in Sofia, as they are in most of Bulgaria's major cities, and the theatre and opera season runs from September through to June. Cinemas can be found throughout the city, and mostly play English movies with Bulgarian subtitles. The Vitosha Boulevard is famous for its extensive (and expensive) shopping opportunities.

Parks and Reserves

The whole of Mount Vitosha is a National Park, and chair lifts operate in summer to lift visitors to the top, where a spectacular view can be enjoyed. Foxes, squirrels and elk dwell in its forests.

PLOVDIV

Location

Plovdiv's Rhodope mountains are the highest in Bulgaria, and its entire landscape is categorized by rocky slopes and deep gorges, that offer magnificent views.

Climate

In spite of the notoriously changeable weather patterns of mountainous regions, the region of Plovdiv on the whole enjoys a Mediterranean climate of mild, rainy winters and warm and dry summers. The resorts on top of Rhodope receive substantial and regular snowfalls from December right through to April.

Population

Although Plovdiv is one of Bulgaria's smallest regions, it has the highest population. The Rhodope Mountains that form the lower part of the Plovdiv region are also home to the greatest ethnic diversity among Bulgaria's population. The largest number of Bulgaria's Muslims live in the Rhodope region, as do most of its Slavic inhabitants.

Sports and Activities

The central sport practiced in the mountainous parts of the Plovdiv region is skiing. World-renowned skiing resorts such as Pomporovo, which is the world's southernmost skiing resort, provide the best in skiing facilities, and the varied slopes of the Rhodope Mountains cater for beginners as well as for advanced skiers.

Plovdiv is the second-largest city of Bulgaria, as well as one of its oldest. It was founded in 342BC on top of three hills, and has relics from Roman occupation such as the Roman marble amphitheatre. Its Archaeological Museum houses artefacts dating from the Thracian era, and in Old Plovdiv, 150 of its national revival houses have been declared national monuments. Plovdiv boasts an opera house and national theatre, as well as cinemas and various nightclubs.

Pamporova is not only the world's southernmost ski resort, it is also one of its most popular. It is not difficult to see why. The slopes of the Rhodope mountains as well as the facilities available at the various resorts, make this an ideal winter sport destination, while the various bars and festive restaurants lend Pamporova an atmosphere that is hard to resist.

Economic Activity

The area around the city of Plovdiv is known for its tobacco crops, and its industrious plantations collaborate to make Bulgaria the fourth-largest tobacco exporter in the world.

Tourist Regions

The Bachkovo monastery near Plovdiv is the second-largest monastery in Bulgaria, and draws hundreds of tourists each year. It was built in the 11th century and houses a miracle-working icon of the Virgin Mary and Child inside its church.

The small city of Batak 6km (4 miles) outside of Plovdiv also draws tourists to its church, but for a more macabre reason. During the Turkish oppression of the 19th century hundreds of Batak's citizens hid for days in its small stone church, and dug out a well with their bare hands. They were slaughtered by Turks on the fourth day, and their skulls are still on display in the church.

The most popular tourist region in Plovdiv is Pamporova, which, with its resort hotels and skiing facilities, continues to draw large crowds every winter.

URGAS

LOCATION

Burgas's topography is similar to that of Varna, apart from the fact that its rivers and coastal lakes are, perhaps, even more numerous.

Climate

The region of Burgas enjoys warm and dry summer months and mild winter months, during which the main rainfall descends.

Sports and Activities

Burgas's activities include boating, swimming and fishing, while the Seaside Gardens of the city of Burgas offer pleasant walks.

The city of Burgas is less geared towards tourists than Varna, and is, therefore, a lot more tranquil. The excellent harbor, rail, and air connections to Burgas make this an important port. Burgas sports plenty of art galleries, seafood restaurants, and even a historical Armenian Church. Its Maritime Park is also popular with tourists.

The old town of Nesebur was founded in 600BC by Greek sailors, and has remained a busy coastal port ever since. It houses an 11th Century church of St Stephen, and several Roman, Greek,and even Thracian ruins. It contains
museums and art galleries, and is regarded as a museum town due to the many ruins that extend through its town streets. It has retained the wooden fisherman's cottages that identify Nesebur as the fishing village it was some centuries ago, and on the whole manages to exhibit the many fragments of its past as a happy whole.

Tourist Regions

The colorful history of both Burgas and Nesebur make them oft-visited tourist sites, especially popular with history buffs.

TRANSPORTATION

ROADS

Bulgaria is small enough to travel through by car and main roads are generally in good condition. Traffic drives on the right-hand side of the road, and international traffic signs are used along all roads, although the indicators of cities and towns are worded in the Cyrillic alphabet and may be difficult to understand. To drive in Bulgaria you will need a valid driver's license as well as an international driving permit available at AA (Automobile Association) and other travel branches in your country. Hertz-Rent-a-Car offices are found throughout Bulgaria in the buildings of major hotels. The traffic in Bulgaria is light because petrol is so expensive, and be warned that you are not allowed to drive with any alcohol in your system. Car theft has also recently become a problem in Bulgaria, and valuables should never be left in your car unattended.

BUSES

Buses that run through the whole of Bulgaria are a faster means of travel than trains, but are on the whole also more expensive and irregular. Departure times are not always fixed as sometimes the bus will only leave when full. Private bus companies are now catering for the needs of tourist in supplying a fast and relatively luxurious means of travel, and timetables for these buses can be requested from travel bureaus.

Large cities like Sofia, Plovdiv and Varna have an extensive system of trams and trolley buses that are an ideal and affordable means of public transport within the city. All public transport ceases at midnight.

CABS

Taxis are generally plentiful in major cities like Sofia and Varna, and can be found at predetermined taxi ranks as well as around airports and train stations. The taxi drivers of Sofia are notorious for their unscrupulous dealings, and you will not find a single taxi driver in Bulgaria that runs a meter. Rates per kilometer should always be determined on beforehand to prevent unpleasant surprises, and keep in mind that rates go up by 25% after midnight.

TRAINS

Bulgaria has always had excellent rail connections, right from the construction of the first railway line at Ruse in 1864. Travel by train has also traditionally been the cheapest means of traveling to and through Bulgaria, but since the war in Yugoslavia rail links with the West have been broken. Direct trains still run from Sofia to major cities, while the services to minor towns are cheap and comprehensive, albeit slow. Domestic tickets usually go on sale an hour before the time of departure, but tickets can be bought in advance at travel bureaus. It is recommended that you only travel first class.

AIR TRAVEL

Sofia, Varna and Burgas all have airports, with Sofia functioning as the central airport and Varna and Burgas being serviced mainly from Sofia. Sofia's airport is connected to the airports of all capital cities in Europe, via Balkan Air and the relevant national carrier. The flight time from London to Sofia is around three hours, and from New York closer to six. The flight from Sofia to either Varna or Burgas is under an hour.

PORTS

Varna and Burgas are Bulgaria's main international ports.

HEALTH INSURANCE

The medical policy you have taken out to cover medical costs is not always valid outside of your country. While traveling it is therefore useful to supplement your usual medical insurance with a specific overseas coverage. In Bulgaria, however, emergency aid is provided free of charge in the state-owned hospitals, if a foreign visitor should require it.

IMMUNIZATION

No immunization is needed before you are allowed to enter into Bulgaria, and no immunization is necessary either. If you have a sensitive stomach your General Practitioner at home can prescribe some oral tablets to combat a reaction to the underdone meat and local tap water, although both are safe to consume. If you plan to stay in Bulgaria for longer than a month you will need to undergo an AIDS test.

PHARMACIES

Apteka signs are prominently displayed in towns to indicate the nearest pharmacy. Pharmacies usually close later thhan other stores, and every town has a pharmacy on night-duty, whose address is posted on the doors of the other pharmacists. Although general medicines for headaches, stomachaches and sensitive throats are plentiful, it is advisable for travelers to bring their own supplies of condoms and sanitary towels. Pharmacists are also often able to recommend a reputable local doctor.

DOCTORS AND HOSPITALS

Physicians are highly trained in Bulgaria, and very friendly and capable; but hospitals and clinics do not always have all the facilities that western visitors are accustomed to. If you are in need of a doctor, the reception staff of your hotel can usually recommend one, as can your embassy. Bulgaria has a reciprocal agreement with the United Kingdom which allows British nationals free hospital, medical and dental care. Medicines must be paid for, however.

EMERGENCY TELEPHONE NUMBERS

Police: 166
Ambulance: 150

Fire: 160

SAFETY

The high rise of inflation has resulted in an increase of unemployment and a rise in crime, particularly petty theft as directed against foreigners, who are regarded as possessing stable and valuable currency. Purse snatching and pickpocketing are on the increase in Bulgaria, as are the newly fashionable crimes of car theft and breaking into cars. Police are poorly paid and not always eager to offer assistance to foreigners. It is unwise to walk alone after dark, and one should also be wary of apparently friendly strangers offering tourists lifts at airports.

FOOD AND DRINKS

The Bulgarian meal is based mainly meat dishes, and reveals influences from the various surrounding countries in the spicy preparation of its dishes. A certain similarity to Greek food can also be evinced in the ingredients that are used, such as the use of aubergines and goat's-milk cheese. The most widely eaten of Bulgaria's dishes is the kebapche, which is small, spicy meatballs skewered on a stick. Lamb and pork are the two types of meat most widely used. In the way of vegetables, shopska salat, a salad of tomatoes, cucumber, peppers and feta cheese, often accompanies the main dish of meat. Unusual dishes, such as a soup of cucumber, yoghurt and garlic; or a 'cheese' soup of cheese, potato, cabbage and beans, are acquired tastes.

The most popular drink drunk in Bulgaria is a strong and sweet coffee measured out in small cups, while a glass of yoghurt on ice also seems to provide refreshment. It is interesting to note that lactobacillus Bulgaricus, the bacteria that is responsible for giving Bulgarian yoghurt its unique flavor and consistency, can only be found in Bulgarian air.

Copious amounts of strong spirits such as grape brandy are drunk with the evening meal, and unwary visitors are advised to be aware of its strength. Bulgarian wines are famous in the culinary world, and should be tried when dining out in Bulgaria. Red wine comes from the north of Bulgaria, and white wine from the south.

RESTAURANTS

Restaurants in Bulgaria are mainly geared towards foreign visitors, as Bulgarians eat their main meal during the day and rarely dine out. The westernised fast-food places that have come to proliferate in large cities such as Sofia and Plovdiv, on the other hand, are regularly frequented by the local population, especially the younger generation. Traditional restaurants, however, are still plentiful. Seafood restaurants predictably abound in the Black Sea Coast areas, and Primorsko, near Burgas, specialises in fish soup. Mackerel is a popular fish in coastal areas. Southern kitchens are deft with pork dishes, while offal is a regular feature on northern menus. When a restaurant is very busy, it is customary to share your table with other people.

MONEY

The Bulgarian currency is the Bulgarian lev (BGL) and its plural, leva. Every lev used to consist of 100 stotinki (st), but inflation has led to the elimination of the stotinki. Leva notes are available in denominations of 20, 50, 100, 200, 500, 1000, 5000, and 10000. Leva coins in use are 2, 5, and 10. After the fall of Communism in Bulgaria, new editions of leva notes were printed, and all notes dating prior to 1974 have been declared worthless. To ensure against receiving counterfeit notes, always check for the Bulgarian Lion watermark.

The deregulation of the lev on the exchange market has caused foreign currency, and in particular United States dollars (USD), to become very popular with the Bulgarian population. Black-market currency exchanges and upstart banks vie with airport shop owners and taxi drivers in attempts to separate tourists from their foreign currency.

Local currency may not be taken out of the country.

CREDIT CARDS AND CASH

Bulgaria is still largely a cash economy, and most shops do not have credit card facilities, in spite of displaying Visa and Mastercard posters suggesting the contrary. Very few banks offer cash advances on credit cards, unless they are situated in well known tourist areas, such as Sofia and Varna, and very few offer good rates on such services when they are available. Large international hotels will accept credit cards as payment of hotel bills, and some tourist facilities at Black Sea Coast resorts also recognise credit cards as a form of payment. When accepted, the most welcome credit cards are American Express, Mastercard and Visa. The Mastercard, however, is mostly known as the 'Eurocard', and the Visa as 'Cart Bleue' in Europe. If your card is not recognized it may be necessary to call the bank to confirm their identical identity.

Cash, and in particular foreign cash, is still the most popular form of payment in Bulgaria. It is unwise, however, to publicise the fact that you are in possession of foreign currency, as this will make you a popular target with local criminals. Although taxi drivers and the like might insist on charging in dollars, it is unnecessary and unprofitable to pay in foreign cash. Damaged or broken foreign bills will not be accepted at all.

TRAVELER'S CHECKS

The preferred currencies for exchange in the form of traveller's cheques in Bulgaria are the United States Dollar, Sterling Pound, and, to a lesser extent, French and Swiss Francs. Some banks will even accept Canadian Dollars. Banks such as the Bulgarian Bank of Foreign Trade, the Biochim Commercial Bank, and the Balkanbank, have branches in all major cities and resorts, and change traveller's cheques for a commission that lies between 0.2% and 3%, depending on the region. The Balkanbank, which has 150 branches countrywide, charges USD2.00 per exchange of USD1,000.00 with a minimum charge of USD4.00. First Private Bank also cashes traveler's checks.

Traveler's checks can be cashed at Bulgaria's airports, and at most large hotels, although their service charges will mostly be higher than those of banks. To cash traveler's checks you will need to produce either a valid passport or a sales advice slip from the place where you received your traveler's checks. All international hotels will accept traveler's checks as payment of the bill, although airport shops prefer hard currency. Mastercard, Visa, American Express and Thomas Cook Traveller's Cheques are the most widely recognized.

SERVICE CHARGES

The service charges at banks and exchange bureaus for the exchanging of currency, cashing of traveler's checks and the advancement of cash for credit cards varies tremendously throughout the whole of Bulgaria. This might also have something to do with the fact that the ownership and location of such institutions vary from time to time.

Exchange bureaus are situated in such unlikely places as a movie theatre (the only place for exchange at Karlovo) and a clothing store (in Kazanluk). Small towns such as Melnik and Bansko have no facilities for exchanging currency, leaving the places that do have these facilities free to determine their own service charges. The charges at large bank chains and international hotels, however, are mostly fixed. Most banks in Sofia, such as the Sofia bank, TS Bank and Ekonomi Bank charge 1% commission on exchanging United States Dollars, and 1.5% for other currencies. 'Euro Finance Ltd.' in Sofia will not charge a service charge on cashing American Express, Mastercard, Thomas Cook and Visa Traveller's Cheques. The service charges for cashing traveler's checks are usually lower at Exchange Bureaus than at banks, while the opposite mostly holds true for exchanging currency. Remember to retain the receipt when exchanging foreign currency for lev, so that these can be exchanged for foreign cash again at the border on your return.

VALUE OF MONEY

Although the rate of inflation, with particular regard to consumer goods, has risen sharply in Bulgaria over the past few years, a holiday in Bulgaria need not be expensive for tourists. Prices do rise the nearer you get to busy tourist resorts such as those at the Black Sea Coast, and the closer you take your holiday to the different peak seasons. Prices have been known to rise by 500% in Plovdiv, when its two annual Trade Fairs (in May and September) are in progress.

VISAS AND PASSPORTS

In order to travel to and within Bulgaria the nationals of all countries need a passport valid until at least six months after the date of departure. You do not have to produce a return ticket on arrival. On arrival, however, all visitors have to register at the hotel or guesthouse they are staying at, or, when visiting friends or camping, at the nearest police station. It is also helpful to register with the embassy of your country on arrival, so that they are prepared to assist you in case of medical or legal emergencies. Your embassy can also provide you with a list of addresses of English-speaking facilities, such as doctors and pharmacies. There are also several Bulgarian embassies abroad.

Nationals of the United States of America and members of the European Union can travel in Bulgaria without a visa for up to 30 days, after which they need to have applied for a visa to extend their stay. Nationals of Australia, Bahrain, Hong Kong, Iceland, Israel, Kuwait, Liechtenstein, Norway, New Zealand, Qatar, Saudi Arabia, Singapore, Switzerland, South Africa, Taiwan, UAE, Canada and Japan can visit Bulgaria without a visa if they have pre-arranged a tour of at least three day's duration with Balkantourist or any other authorised agent. Visas are free (but do need to be applied for) to nationals of China, Cyprus, North Korea and Zimbabwe.

There are various types of visas, all varying in price. A Transit Visa, given out if you are only traveling through Bulgaria on your way to another destination, is normally the cheapest, and is available in single and double entry. A Tourist Visa is about the same price and is given out to holiday-makers. A Business Visa also comes in single and double entry, and can be for three or six months The most expensive type of visa is the Express Visa, issued immediately when applied for in person. The most you will ever pay for a visa to Bulgaria is the equivalent of forty pounds. To apply for a visa you will always need to fill out an application form, and give in your passport, a passport photo and the correct amount of money to pay for your visa. For a Business Visa you will also need to fill in an extra form, and be in possession of a legalized invitation from a company in Bulgaria; as well as a letter of confirmation from your own company. If you intend to stay with friends, a legalized invitation from your host in Bulgaria is required. Remember that it can take up to 30 days to process a visa.

SUPPLEMENT

BULGARIA CUSTOMS OFFICES

Burgas
Regional office management (Customs)
Burgas Square Al. Al "№ 1
056 / 876 101
056/843 429
rmd_burgas@d1999.customs.bg
Monday-Friday, 9:00 to 12:30 am / 13:00 to 17:30 pm

Bourgas Airport
Customs post
Burgas, Sarafovo "
056 / 870 330
056/880 263
mp.letishte @ d1999.customs.bg
clock
Served transport: air

Malko Tarnovo
Customs post
Malko Tarnovo municipality. Bourgas Malko Tarnovo MAP
05952 / 3676
05952/2198
mp.malko_tarnovo @ d1999.customs.bg
clock
Served transport: land
Oil
Customs post
Burgas, Oil
056 / 898 847

mp.neftopristanishte @ d1999.customs.bg
clock
Served transport: ship
Port Burgas
Customs post
Burgas Square Al. Al "№ 1
056 / 876 103

mp.pristaniste_center @ d1999.customs.bg
clock
Served transport: ships, railway wagons, trucks, cars

Lesovo
Customs post
Lesovo village municipality. Yambol, MJ Lesovo
0478 / 81 202 81 209
0478 / 81203
mp.lesovo @ d1999.customs.bg
clock

Tsarevo
Customs post
Tsarevo municipality. Burgas
0590/52 458

Petrochemical Plant
Office
Burgas, Petrochemical Plant
056/800 998
056/800 998
mb.nhc @ d1999.customs.bg
Monday-Friday, 9:00 to 12:30 am / 13:00 to 17:30 pm

Bourgas Free Zone
Office
Burgas, Free Zone
056 / 895 178
056/881 051
mb.svobodna_zona @ d1999.customs.bg
Monday-Friday, 9:00 to 12:30 am / 13:00 to 17:30 pm

Sliven
Office
Sliven, Blvd Bansko Shosse 4
044/662 790
044/662 845
mb.sliven @ d1999.customs.bg
Monday-Friday, 9:00 to 12:30 am / 13:00 to 17:30 pm

Yambol
Office
Yambol, Dimitar Blagoev "13, 2nd floor
046/664 241
046/664 241
mb.yambol @ d1999.customs.bg
Monday-Friday, 9:00 to 12:30 am / 13:00 to 17:30 pm

Ruse
Regional office management (Customs)
Ruse, Lipnik "№ 117
082/816 219
082/816 262
Stefan.zlatkov @ d4000.customs.bg
Monday-Friday, 09.00 to 17.30

Razgrad
Office

Razgrad, Beli Lom "№ 40
084/617-015, 617-013
084/617-018
pavel.penchev @ d4000.customs.bg
Monday-Friday, 09.00 to 17.30

Port Rousse
Customs post
Rousse, Rousse Pristanshten Complex - East
082/847-260, 847-255, 827-335 - revisions
082/847-262
nayden.kolchevski @ d4000.customs.bg
Monday-Friday, 09.00 to 17.30 (07.00, revisions to 19.00 hours)

Rousse Free Zone
Customs post
Ruse, "Free Zone" EAD
082/847-286, 847-285
082/847-291
dimitar.hristov @ d4000.customs.bg
Monday-Friday, 07.00 to 19.00

Targovishte
Office
Targovishte Street "Vassil Levski" № 5
0601/69-062, 0601/69-061
0601/65-667
deyan.mavrodiev @ d4000.customs.bg
Monday-Friday, 09:00 to 17:30

Silistra
Office
Silistra, Tsar Shishman "№ 5
086/821-006
086/820-814
georgi.gerov @ d4400.customs.bg
Monday-Friday, 09.00 to 17.30

Port of Silistra
Customs post
Silistra Street, "Port" № 4
086/820-788
086/820-788
gencho.genov @ d4000.customs.bg
Monday-Friday, 09.00 to 17.30

Svilengrad
Regional office management (Customs)
gr.Svilengrad, kv.Petko leader, Iliev ul.Asen № 4
0379/7-30-00
0379/7-32-36
TMU.Svilengrad @ d3100.customs.bg
Monday-Friday, 09.00 to 17.30

Kapitan Andreevo
Customs post
gr.Svilengrad, kv.Petko leader, Iliev ul.Asen № 4
0379/7-12-43
0379/7-15-97
mu3103.delovodstvo @ d3100.customs.bg
clock

"Railway station"
Customs post
gr.Svilengrad, kv.Petko leader, Iliev ul.Asen № 4
0379/7-34-50
0379/7-32-36
mu3102@d3100.customs.bg
clock

Free Zone
Office
gr.Svilengrad, kv.Petko leader, Iliev ul.Asen № 4
0379/7-32-39
0379/7-32-39
mu3106@d3100.customs.bg
Monday-Friday, 09:00 to 17:30

Haskovo
Office
Haskovo, ul.Pravda № 1
038/62-40-19, 038/62-24-49
038/66-27-34
mu3107@d3100.customs.bg
Monday-Friday, 09.00 to 17.30

Kardjali
Office
Kardzhali, ul.Parvi May № 62
0361/6-54-31, 0361/6-54-13
0361/6-54-40
mu3104@d3100.customs.bg
Monday-Friday, 09.00 to 17.30

Svishtov
Regional office management (Customs)
Svishtov, Dunav "10
0631/6-10-40
0631/6-10-50

Monday-Friday, 9:00 to 12:30 am / 13:00 to 17:30 pm

Gabrovo
Office
Gabrovo, str Stancionna "№ 14, PO Box № 6
066/800600
066/800602
Svetozar.Hintolarski @ d4301.customs.bg
Monday-Friday, 9:00 to 12:30 am / 13:00 to 17:30 pm

Gorna Oryahovitsa
Office
Gorna Oryahovitsa 5100, Ivan Momchilov "№ 2A
0618/6-00-55
0618/6-01-43
Dobromir.Popov @ d4302.customs.bg
Monday-Friday, 9:00 to 12:30 am / 13:00 to 17:30 pm

Gorna Oryahovitsa Airport
Customs post
Gorna Oryahovitsa 5100, Ivan Momchilov "№ 2A
0618/6-02-18
0618/6-01-43
Dobromir.Popov @ d4302.customs.bg
Monday-Friday, 9:00 to 12:30 am / 13:00 to 17:30 am

Lovech
Office
Lovech, Street Osamska 235, PO Box 32
068/601356
068/601357
Krasimir.Hadzhiyski @ d4304.customs.bg
Monday-Friday, 9:00 to 12:30 am / 13:00 to 17:30 am

Pleven
Office
Pleven Street Grivishko road "№ 6, floor 2
064/800501
064/801114
Ivaylo.Bankov @ d4306.customs.bg
Monday-Friday, 9:00 to 12:30 am / 13:00 to 17:30 pm

Somovit
Customs post
village Somovit 5959, total. Gulyantsi municipality. Pleven, Ivan Vazov Str № 2
06567/2321
06567/2442
Doychin.Karabulev @ d4307.customs.bg
Monday-Friday, 9:00 to 12:30 am / 13:00 to 17:30 pm

Sevlievo
Office
5400 Sevlievo, Stefan Peshev "№ 161
0675/30643
0675/30643
Jordanka.Kostadinova @ d4309.customs.bg,
Ventsislav.Slavchev @ d4309.customs.bg
Monday-Friday, 9:00 to 12:30 am / 13:00 to 17:30 pm

Fracture
Regional office management (Customs)
Lom 3600, Street Danube "44
0971/66801, 0971/66802
0971/66801
Customs.Lom @ d4200.customs.bg
Monday-Friday, 9:00 to 12:30 am / 13:00 to 17:30 pm

Vratsa
Office
Vratsa 3000, Vasil Kanchov "86
092/660810
092/660810
MB.Vratsa @ d4200.customs.bg
Monday-Friday, 9:00 to 12:30 am / 13:00 to 17:30 pm

Oryahovo
Customs post
gr.Oryahovo 3300, Street Dragoman "1
09171/2173
09171/2173
MP.Oriahovo @ d4200.customs.bg
Monday-Friday, 9:00 to 12:30 am / 13:00 to 17:30 pm

Port of Lom
Customs post
Lom 3600, Street Danube "42
0971/66809
0971/66809
MP.lom @ d4200.customs.bg
clock

Bregovo
Customs post
gr.Bregovo 3790
09312/2274
09312/2274
MP.Bregovo @ d4200.customs.bg
clock

Vidin
Office
Vidin 3700, Street Danube "№ 14
094/600551
094/600551
MB.Vidin @ d4200.customs.bg
Monday-Friday, 9:00 to 12:30 am / pm 13:00 to 17:30

Port - Vidin
Customs post
Vidin 3700, Street Danube "№ 1
094/600548
094/600548
MP.Vidin @ d4200.customs.bg
clock

Vrashka hammer
Customs post
gr.Kula 3800, obsht.Kula, obl.Vidin
0938/2003
0938/2501
MP.Vr_chuka @ d4200.customs.bg
clock

Plovdiv
Regional office management (departure)
Plovdiv, str Kuklensko road "№ 32 pb 4004
032/606 275 606 211
032/606 185
delovodstvo.plovdiv @ d3999.customs.bg
Monday - Friday 9:00 to 18:00

Served transport: road

Kazanlak
Office
Kazanlak Blvd "Rose Valley" № 53 pb 6100
0431/62 049
0431/62 049
MB.Kazanlak @ d3999.customs.bg
Monday - Friday 9:00 to 18:00
Served transport: land
Plovdiv Airport
Customs post
Plovdiv Plovdiv airport
032/601 137
032/628 711
MP.Letishte @ d3999.customs.bg
clock
Served transport: road and air

Pazardjik
Office
Pazardjik, str Plovdiv "p.k 103 4400
034/445 336
034/445 336
MB.Pazardzik @ d3999.customs.bg
Monday - Friday 9:00 to 18:00
Served transport: land

Free Zone Plovdiv
Office
Plovdiv, blvd "Vasil Levski" PO Box 242 A 4,003
032/906 248
032/906 248
mb.szplovdiv @ d3999.customs.bg
Monday - Friday 09:00 to 12:30 13:00 to 17:30
Served transport: land

Smolyan
Office
Smolyan, Hadji Ivan Bechev "№ 1
0301/64 598
0301/64 580
MB.Smolian @ d3999.customs.bg
Monday - Friday 9:00 to 18:00
Served transport: land
Karlovo
Office
Karlovo, Street Gen.Zaimov "28, PO Box 213
4300
0335/96 7369
0335/97 434
mb.karlovo @ d3999.customs.bg
Monday - Friday 9:00 to 18:00
Served transport: land

Stara Zagora
Office
Stara Zagora Quarter Golesh, PO Box 6011
042/613361, 621499, 613331, 613334, 613337
042/621498
mb.starazagora @ d3999. customs.bg
Monday - Friday 9:00 to 18:00
Served transport: land

Radinovo
Office
s.Radinovo 4202, Municipality Maritsa,
manufacturing plant - Agri BULGARIA Ltd.
0318/82 131
0318/82 130
MB.Radinovo @ d3999.customs.bg
Monday-Friday, 9:00 to 12:30 am / 13:00 to 17:30
pm
Served transport: land

Varna
Regional office management (Customs)
Varna Square "Doe" № 2
052 / 689 509, 052 / 689 402
052 / 632 201, 052 / 632 202
yatanasova@customsvarna.com
Monday-Friday, 09.00 to 17.30
Served transport: land

Varna - West
Customs post
Devnya, MJ Varna West
05199 / 7143, 05199/7134, 05199/7135
05199/7144, 05199/7132
prb2002@customsvarna.com
clock
Handling of cargo carried by ships, including
military and special products

Airport - Varna
Customs post
Airport Varna Airport MAP
052 / 511 174
052 / 511 174
prb2003@customsvarna.com
clock
Screening of passengers, accompanied and
unaccompanied baggage, cargo shipments and
processing of military and special products

Port - Varna
Customs post
Varna Square "Doe" № 2
052/689 409
052 / 632 321
prb2005@customsvarna.com
clock
Handling of cargo carried by ships, including
military and special products

Port - Lesport
Customs post
Topoli municipality. Varna - West Industrial Zone
052 / 571 530
052/742 715
prb2006@customsvarna.com
clock

Processing of goods transported by ship

Ferry - Varna
Customs post
Beloslav town - Ferry Complex
05 199 / 34 50
05 199 / 34 50
prb2007@customsvarna.com
Monday-Friday, 08.00 hours - 20.00 hours
Handling of cargo carried by ships and railway wagons, as military and special products
Randy
Office
Shumen Blvd Rishki Pass "№ 54
054 / 830 581
054 / 830 581
mb2008@customsvarna.com
Monday-Friday, 08.00 hours - 20.00 hours
Served transport: land

Dobrich
Office
Dobrich Street Independence "№ 36
058 / 600 504
058/600 504
mb2009@customsvarna.com
Monday-Friday, 09.00 to 17.30
Served transport: land

Balchik
Customs post
Balchik, Primorska "№ 1 p.k.41
0579 / 74043
0579 / 74043
mp2010@customsvarna.com
clock
Processing of goods transported by ship

Sofia office
Regional office management (Customs)
Sofia, PO Box 1202, Street Veslets "№ 84
9859 46 52
02/931 06 97

dvusmenen daily regime - 08.00 - 19.30; Administration - 8-hour day in a five-day working week, 09.00 - 17.30
Goods transported by road and railway transport and excise goods ZADS.

Sofia West
Office
Sofia, PO Box 1271, blvd Rozhen "№ 41
02/938 61 80; 938 71 41
02/38 61 60 141 9387
Valentin.Todorov @ d5999.customs.bg
dvusmenen daily routine: Monday to Friday - 08.00 - 20.00, Saturday - 09.00 - 17.30, Sunday - day off.
Trucks and railway transport
Sofia East
Office
Sofia, PO Box 1870, square in the territory of Botunets METAL SNAB
02/9891903, 02/9895643
02/989 1903

dvusmenen daily routine - 08.00 - 20.00, Sunday - holiday
Goods transported by road and railway transport.
Pirdop
Office
Pirdop, PO Box 2070, Industrial Zone
0728/62 312
0728/62 312

dvusmenen daily operation from 08.00 - 20.00
Imports of copper concentrate from third parties, mining equipment, export of copper cathodes and anodes, sulfuric acid carried by rail and road transport.

Botevgrad
Office
Botevgrad, PO Box 2140, Boulevard March 3 "№ 28
0723/60 087; 66,067
0723/66 576

8-hour mode in five-day work week - 9:00 to 17:30 pm, weekends - Saturday and Sunday.
Processing of import documents, export and transit of goods
Pernik
Office
Pernik, PO Box 2304, Street Vladayska uprising № 1
076/67 0526
076/67 0497
tmupernik@d5999.customs.bg
8-hour mode in five-day work week - 9:00 to 17:30 pm, weekends - Saturday and Sunday.
Processing of trucks and wagons, steel products

Dragoman
Office
Dragoman, PO Box 2210, Street N. Vaptsarov 7
07172/20 42
07172/20 42
dvusmenen mode - from 08.00 am to 20.00 pm
Customs clearance of imported and exported goods by road and railway transport. Dragoman serving free zone.

Dimitrovgrad YU.ZH.
Office
Dragoman, PO Box 2210, Street N. Vaptsarov 7
07 172 / 20 42; 0038110360972
07 172 / 20 42

clock
Customs control of goods imported and exported

by rail transportation and inspection of passengers passing through the state border railway transport.

Kalotina
Customs post
village Kalotina
07 174 / 22 06
07 174 / 22 06
hristo.hristov @ d5999.customs.bg
clock
Customs control of goods, passengers and vehicles crossing the land border with road transport.

Strezimirovtsi
Customs post
Strezimirovtsi village municipality. Pernik Municipality Trun
0773/42 73
0773/42 73
Antoaneta.Rangelova @ d5999.customs.bg
clock
Customs control of goods, passengers and vehicles crossing the land border with road transport.
OPM to BICIS mart Bulgarplod SA Slatina
OPM
Sofia, PO Box 1574, blvd Prof. Tzvetan Lazarov "№ 13
02/979 04 63
02/973 58 84

dvusmenen operation - 7:00 am - 19:00 pm every day
Processing of fresh fruits and vegetables and products processed from those transported by car and train transport.

Southwest office
Regional office management (Customs)
Blagoevgrad, Street Pokrovnishko Shosse
073/8894103, 073/8894112
073/840560, 073/840619
Georgi.Aleksandrov @ d5999.customs.bg
Monday-Friday 9.00 - 12.00 12.30 - 17.30
Served transport: land

Gotse Delchev
Office
Gotze Delchev Street Panairski meadows "№ 18
0751/60411, 0751/60410
0751/60418
Evgeni.Trendafilov @ d5999.customs.bg
Monday-Friday 9.00 - 12.00 12.30 - 17.30
Served transport: land

Tower
Office
Village Tower, 2868 zip code
07425/2171
07425/2413
Vasilka.Tochkova @ d5999.customs.bg
Monday-Friday 9.00 - 12.00 12.30 - 17.30
Served transport: land

Kyustendil
Office
Kyustendil, St. Peter Beron "№ 30
078/551409
078/551409
Vasil.Pechev @ d5999.customs.bg
Monday-Friday 9.00 - 12.00 12.30 - 17.30
Served transport: land
Gueshevo
Customs post

078/551296, 078/551297
078/551298

clock
Served transport: land
Zlatarevo
Customs post

0745/61797, 0745/62097
0745/61797

clock
Served transport: land
Logodaj
Customs post

073/880026, 073/880027
073/880516
clock
Served transport: land

Oltomantsi
Customs post
078/551288, 078/551289
078/551288
Nikolay.Lybikov @ d5999.customs.bg
clock
Served transport: land

Sofia Airport
Regional office management
city of Sofia, Brussels № 1
02/9859 4805, 02/980 4500
02/980 2445
Msa_aerogara@d5999.customs.bg
Monday-Friday, 08.00 hours - 20.00 hours

Sofia airport - passengers
Customs post
city of Sofia, Brussels № 1
02/9859 4880 terminal 2, terminal 4881 02/9859 1

Msa_aerogara@d5999.customs.bg
clock

passengers Sofia Airport - cargo Customs post	city of Sofia, Brussels № 1 02/9859 4821, 02/9859 4823 Msa_aerogara@d5999.customs.bg

USEFUL BULGARIAN ECONOMIC LINKS

Agency for Economic Analysis and Forecasts	www.online.bg/aeaf	The Agency work out macroeconomic forecasts, strategies and national programmes
Privatisation Agency	www.priv.government.bg	Everyhting about the privatisation in Bulgaria- hot projects, list of all companies offered for privatisation etc.
Bulgarian Foreign Investment Agency	www.bfia.org	Investment Statistics, Business Guide, Business Law, Capital Market, Regional Information, Free trade zones, etc.
Bulgarian National Bank	www.bnb.bg	The web site of Bulgarian National Bank
Bulgarian International Business Association /BIBA/	www.biba.mobikom.com	BIBA represents the interests of the international business community vis-a-vis the Bulgarian authorities.
Commodity Exchanges and Wholesale State Commission	www.dksbt.bg	Wholesale markets, Comodity exchanges, Prices, Analyses, Prognoses
Commission for the protection of competition	www.cpc.bg	On this site you can make contact with CPC.
Bulgarian National Securities Commission	www.ssec.bg	All information about bulgarian securities market.
Ministry of Transport and Communications	www.cpt.bg	The site of Ministry of Transport and Communications
Ministry of Agriculture and Forestry	www.mzgar.government.bg	The site of Ministry of Agriculture and Forestry
Ministry of Economy	www.mi.government.bg	The site of Ministry of Economy
Ministry of Finance	www.minfin.government.bg	The site of Ministry of Finance
National Statistical Institute	www.nsi.bg	Bulletins, Time series, Actual Data, Statistical Yearbook
Center for Mass Privatisation	www.bulgarianspace.com	All for the Mass Privatisation in Bulgaria.
Agency for Small and Medium-sized Enterprises	www.asme.bg	Promotion and support of the small and medium enterprises.
Navigation Maritime Bulgaria	www.navbul.com	Transportation of goods between all ports of the world. Established lines for carriage of containers and conventional cargoes to any port and inland destination in Europe, Mediterranean , Black Sea and all over the world.
Bulgarian State Railways	www.bg400.bg/bdz	Services, Projects.
National Information and	www.bulgariatravel.org	All tourist and common information about

Advertising Centre		Bulgaria.
Bulgarian Chamber of Commerce and Industry	www.bcci.bg	Trade Directory, Members of BCCI, Rate of Exchange, Business Opportunities, Web pages of Bulgarian companies, Important Links.
Association of Garments and Textiles Exporters in Bulgaria	www.bgtextiles.org	Your gateway to the Bulgarian producers of apparel, knitwear, textiles, accessories and services
Business Information System "Info Business"	www.info-business.bg	Bulgarian business information.

U.S. AND COUNTRY CONTACTS

U.S. EMBASSY - SOFIA

Ambassador: Ms. Avis T. Bohlen
Deputy Chief of Mission: Mr. Christopher Dell
Political-Economic Counselor: Mr. Steven Blake
Economic Officer: Janet Potash
1, Saborna Street
Sofia, Bulgaria
Tel: (359)(2) 980-5241/8
Fax: (359)(2) 981-8977

Foreign Agricultural Service
Agricultural Attache: Ms. Jamie Rothchild
Agricultural Specialist: Ms. Mila Boshnakova
NDK Administrative Building - 5th Floor
Sofia, Bulgaria
Tel: (359)(2) 951-5561
Fax: (359)(2) 981-6568

U.S. Agency For International Development (USAID)
AID Representative: Mr. John Tennant
Private Enterprise Officer: Mr. Bill Foerderer
Project Development Officer: Mr. Brad Fujimoto
Program Officer: Mr. John Babylon
NDK Administrative Building - 5th Floor
Sofia, Bulgaria
Tel: (359)(2) 951-5670
Fax: (359)(2) 951-5070

U.S. Commercial Service
Commercial Attache: Ms. Susan Weidner
Senior Commercial Specialist: Ms. Uliana Kanelli
Commercial Specialist: Ms. Tsvetanka Kolarova
Commercial Specialist: Mr. Georgi Peev
NDK Administrative Building, 5th Floor
Sofia, Bulgaria
Tel: (359)(2) 963-20-14 , 963-40-62
Fax: (359)(2) 980-68-50

Local Mailing Address:
1, Saborna Street
1000 Sofia, Bulgaria

U.S. Information Service
Public Affairs Officer: Mr. James Hutcheson
18, Vitosha Street
Sofia, Bulgaria
Tel: (359)(2) 980-4838 , 980-3667
Fax: (359)(2) 980-3646

AmCham in Bulgaria
Executive Director: Mr. Philip Philipov
19, Patriarch Evtimii Blvd.,
Sofia, Bulgaria
Tel.: (359) (2) 981-5950, 981-4340
Fax : (359) (2) 980-4206

BULGARIAN TRADE AND INDUSTRY ASSOCIATIONS

Bulgarian Chamber of Commerce and Industry
11-A, Saborna Street
1000 Sofia, Bulgaria
Tel: (359)(2) 87-36-29
Fax: (359)(2) 87-32-09
President: Mr. Bojidar Bojinov
U.S. Desk Officer: Ms. Maria Petrunova

Bulgarian International Business Association
Christos Katzanis
36, Patriarch Evtimii 36 A St.
Sofia 1040, Bulgaria
Tel: (359 2) 981-95-64, 972-21-36, 800-263

Confederation of the Independent Trade Unions in Bulgaria
1, Makedonia Square
1000 Sofia, Bulgaria
Tel: (359)(2) 86-63-92
Fax: (359)(2) 988-5569
Acting Chairman: Mr. Zheliazko Hristov

Bulgarian Industrial Association
16-20, Alabin Street
1000 Sofia, Bulgaria
Tel: (359)(2) 54-50-66

Fax: (359)(2) 87-26-04
Chairman: Mr. Bojidar Danev

Podkrepa Trade Union
2, Angel Kunchev Street
1000 Sofia, Bulgaria
Tel: (359)(2) 85-61
Chairman: Mr. Konstantin Trenchev

Union for Private Economic Enterprise
2a, Suborna Street
1000 Sofia, Bulgaria
Tel: (359)(2) 943-3146
Fax: (359)(2) 943-3156
Secretary General: Mr. Vladimir Pavlov

BULGARIAN GOVERNMENT OFFICES RELATED TO KEY SECTORS

Ministry of Agriculture, Forestry and Agrarian Reform
55, Khristo Botev Boulevard
1000 Sofia, Bulgaria
Tel: (359)(2) 980-7873
Fax: (359)(2) 981-7955
Minister: Mr. Ventsislav Vurbanov

Ministry of Culture
17, Alexander Stamboliiski Street
1000 Sofia, Bulgaria
Tel: (359)(2) 86-111
Fax: (359)(2) 981-8145
Minister: Ms. Emma Moskova

Ministry of Defense
1, Aksakov Street
1000 Sofia, Bulgaria
Tel: (359)(2) 54-60-01
Fax: (359)(2) 987-9693
Minister: Mr. Georgi Ananiev

Ministry of Education and Science
2, Dondukov Boulevard
1000 Sofia, Bulgaria
Tel: (359)(2) 84-41, 87-12-89
Fax: (3590 (2) 87-72-49
Minister: Mr. Vesselin Metodiev

Ministry of Environment and Water
67, William Gladstone Street
1000 Sofia, Bulgaria
Tel: (359)(2) 87-61-51
Fax: (359)(2) 981-1186
Minister: Ms. Evdokia Maneva

Ministry of Finance
102, Rakovsky Street
1000 Sofia, Bulgaria
Tel: (359)(2) 87-06-22
Fax: (359)(2) 980-6863
Minister: Mr. Mouravey Radev

Ministry of Foreign Affairs
2, Al. Zhendov Street
1000 Sofia, Bulgaria
Tel: (359)(2) 71-431
Fax: (359)(2) 971-2413
Minister: Ms. Nadezhda Mihailova

Ministry of Health
2, Sveta Nedelia Square
1000 Sofia, Bulgaria
Tel: (359)(2) 86-31
Fax: (359)(2) 80-00-31
Minister: Mr. Petar Boyadjiev

Ministry of Regional and Urban Development
17, Kiril and Methodius Street
1000 Sofia, Bulgaria
Tel: (359)(2) 83-841
Fax: (359)(2) 87-25-17
Minister: Mr. Evgeny Bakardjiev

Ministry of Industry
8, Slavianska Street
1000 Sofia, Bulgaria
Tel: (359)(2) 87-07-41
Fax: (359)(2) 87-21-90
Minister: Mr. Alexander Bozhkov

Ministry of Interior
29, Shesti Septemvri Street
1000 Sofia, Bulgaria
Tel: (359)(2) 87-75-11
Fax: (359)(2) 87-79-67
Minister: Mr. Bogomil Bonev

Ministry of Justice and European Legal Integration
2, Dondukov Street
1000 Sofia, Bulgaria
Tel: (359)(2) 86-01, 867-32-09
Fax: (359)(2) 67-32-26
Minister: Mr. Vassil Gotsev

Ministry of Labor and Social Policy
2, Triaditsa Street
1000 Sofia, Bulgaria
Tel: (359)(2) 86-01
Fax: (359)(2) 80-06-09
Minister: Mr. Ivan Neikov

Ministry of Trade and Tourism
12, Battenberg Street

1000 Sofia, Bulgaria
Tel: (359)(2) 88-20-11
Fax: (359)(2) 80-39-68
Minister: Mr. Valentin Vassilev

Ministry of Transport
9, Levski Street
1000 Sofia, Bulgaria
Tel: (359)(2) 88-12-30
Fax: (359)(2) 988-50-94
Minister: Mr. Wilhelm Kraus

Bulgarian National Bank
1, Battenberg Sq.
1000 Sofia, Bulgaria
Tel: (359)(2) 85-51
Governor: Mr. Svetoslav Gavriiski

Foreign Investment Agency
3, Sveta Sofia Street
1000 Sofia, Bulgaria
Tel: (359)(2) 980-0518
President: Mr. Iliyan Vassilev

Privatization Agency
29, Aksakov Street
1000 Sofia, Bulgaria
Tel: (359)(2) 987-7579 , 981-1307
Executive Director: Mr. Alexander Sabotinov

Mass Privatization Center
1, Dondoukov Street
1000 Sofia, Bulgaria
Tel: (359)(2) 91-959
Fax: (359)(2) 88-22-67
Executive Director: Mr. Pirin Atanasov

Committee on Energy
8, Triaditza Street
1000 Sofia, Bulgaria
Tel: (359)(2) 988-59-32
Fax: (359)(2) 81-50-29
Acting Chairman: Mr. Ivan Shiliashki

Committee on Posts & Telecommunications
6, Gurko Street
1000 Sofia, Bulgaria
Tel: (359)(2) 949-2322
Fax: (359)(2) 980-3893
Chairman: Mr. Antoni Slavinski

Committee on Standardization and Metrology
21, Shesti Septemvri Street
1000 Sofia, Bulgaria
Tel: (359)(2) 85-91
Fax: (359)(2) 80-14-02
Chairman: Mr. Marius Tsokov

Bulgarian State Railroad
3, Ivan Vazov Street
1000 Sofia, Bulgaria
Tel: (359)(2) 87-30-45, 843-4310
Director: Mr. Jordan Mirchev

Bulgarian Telecommunications Company
8, General Totleben Street
1000 Sofia, Bulgaria
Tel: (359)(2) 94-94-438
Fax: (359)(2) 87-58-85
President: Mr. Marian Dragostinov

General Customs Directorate
1, Aksakov Street
1000 Sofia, Bulgaria
Tel: (359)(2) 80-402
Fax: (359)(2) 79-10-72
Director: Mr. Georgi Kulishev

National Electric Company

5, Veslets Street
1040 Sofia, Bulgaria
Tel: (359)(2) 86-199
Fax: (359)(2) 87-58-26
Chairman: Mr. Konstantin Shushulov

Patent & Trademark Office
52-B G.M. Dimitrov Street
1000 Sofia, Bulgaria
Tel: (359)(2) 71-131
Fax: (359)(2) 70-83-25
Director: Ms. Radoslava Kazandzhieva

COMMERCIAL BANKS

Commercial banks in Bulgaria with a full banking license:

Biochim
6, Vitosha Blvd.
Sofia, Bulgaria
Tel: (359)(2) 86-169
Fax: (359)(2) 981-9151

Bulbank
7, Sveta Nedelia Square
Sofia, Bulgaria
Tel: (359)(2) 84-91, 849-700
Fax: (359)(2) 988-4636

Bulgarian Post Bank
1, Bulgaria Square
Sofia, Bulgaria
Tel: (359)(2) 963-2104
Fax: (359)(2) 963-0482

Corporate Commercial Bank PLC, Sofia
65, Ekzarch Yossif street
Sofia, Bulgaria
Tel: (359)(2) 980-9362
Tlx: (359)(067) 23-593

Express Bank
92, Vladislav Varnenchik Street
Varna, Bulgaria
Tel: (359)(052) 22-30-73
Fax: (359)(052) 23-19-64

First East International Bank
10, Lege Street
Sofia, Bulgaria
Tel: (359)(2) 980-3322
Fax: (359)(2) 80-12-21

Hebros Bank
37, Vazrazdhane
Plovdiv, Bulgaria
Tel: (359)(32) 23-18-76 , 26-42-28
Fax: (359)(32) 56-23-53 , 23-18-76
Sofia Branch (359)(2)988-86-07

International Bank of Trade and Development, Sofia
2, Ivan Vazov street
Sofia, Bulgaria
Tel: (359)(2) 980-60-85, 980-52-49
Fax: (359)(2) 87-30-41

International Orthodox Bank "St. Nikola", Sofia
155, G.S.Rakovski Boulevard
Sofia, Bulgaria
Tel: (359)(2) 980-96-88, 981-65-59
Fax: (359)(2) 980-77-22, 987-65-28

Bulgarian-Russian Investment Bank, Sofia
11A, Suborna Str.
Sofia, Bulgaria
Tel: (359)(2) 860-72-40
Fax: (359)(2) 981-25-26

First Investment Bank, Sofia
10, St. Karadja street
Sofia, Bulgaria
Tel: (359)(2) 910-01
Fax: (359)(2) 980-5033

Creditbank Ltd., Sofia
3, Angel Kunchev street
Sofia, Bulgaria
Tel: (359)(2) 980-00-74
Fax: (359)(2) 981-63-98

Union Bank, Sofia
10-12, Damyan Gruev street
Sofia, Bulgaria
Tel: (359)(2) 987-60-02
Fax: (359)(2) 980-20-04

Teximbank, Sofia
107, Maria Louisa Boulevard
Sofia, Bulgaria
Tel: (359)(2) 33-32-40
Fax: (359)(2) 931-12-07

Capital Municipality Bank, Sofia
6, Vrabtcha street, 2 floor
Sofia, Bulgaria

United Bulgarian Bank
5, Sveta Sofia St.
Sofia, Bulgaria
Tel: (359)(2) 84-70-90
Fax: (359)(2) 988-08-22

FOREIGN BANKS - FULLY LICENSED:

BNP - Dresdner Bank
11, Narodno Sabranie Square
1000 Sofia, Bulgaria
Tel: (359)(2) 980-1237
Fax: (359)(2) 981-6991

Raiffeisen Bank
14, Serdika Street
Sofia, Bulgaria
Tel: (359)(2) 980-8091
Fax: (359)(2) 980-7479

Branches of Foreign Banks:

XiosBank
3, Vitosha Boulevard.
Sofia, Bulgaria
Tel: (359)(2) 980-5654
Fax: (359)(2) 981-8579

ING Bank
World Trade Center - Sofia (Interpred)
7, Levski Str.
Sofia, Bulgaria
Tel: (359)(2) 980-93-03
Fax: (359)(2) 981-53-23

Ionian Bank
20, Alexander Stambouliiski Boulevard
Sofia, Bulgaria
Tel: (359)(2) 86-028, 981-69-59, 981-65-54
Fax: (359)(2) 981-77-79

National Bank of Greece S.A., Sofia
5, Triaditsa Str.
Sofia , Bulgaria
Tel: (359)(2) 981-50-10
Fax: (359)(2) 980-69-56

Bayerisch-Bulgarische Handelsbank, Sofia
36, Alabin street
Sofia, Bulgaria
Tel: (359)(2) 981-05-00, 980-33-03
Fax: (359)(2) 980-5313

Societe Generale, Paris-Sofia
36, Dragan Tsankov street
1040 Sofia, Bulgaria
Tel: (359)(2) 91-941
Fax: (359)(2) 971-29-78

U.S. GOVERNMENT AGENCIES

Trade Promotion Coordinating Council
1-800-USA-TRADE

U.S. Department of State, Office of the Coordinator for Business Affairs
Tel: (202) 746-1625
Fax : (202) 647-3953

U.S. Department of Commerce, Market Access and Compliance
Mr. Paul Marin
Tel: (202) 482-2645
Fax: (202) 501-0787

U.S. Department of Agriculture, Foreign Agricultural Service, Trade and Promotion Office
Tel: (202) 720-7420

U.S. Trade and Development Agency
Mr. Lance Ludman, Project Analyst
Tel: (703) 875-4357
Fax: (703) 875-4009

U.S.-SPONSORED ENTERPRISE FUNDS

ENTERPRISE FUNDS

In November 1989, the Support for East European Democracy (SEED) Act authorized the creation of enterprise funds to help private sector development in the countries of Central & Eastern Europe. They are U.S. Government-financed, non-profit private U.S. corporations modeled after venture capital management companies. The purpose of the funds are to promote the development of the private sector. The enterprise funds primarily make loans to, or investments in small and medium-sized businesses in which other financial institutions are reluctant to invest. The enterprise funds also provide technical assistance for private sector development in the host country.

ALBANIAN-AMERICAN ENTERPRISE FUND

The Albanian-American Enterprise Fund, a 30 million dollar investment fund designed to promote private sector activity in Albania, was established in February 1995. The fund will be capitalized at $30 million in foreign assistance appropriations over a 3-4 year period.

Albanian-American Enterprise Fund
Domenick G. Scaglione, Chairman
14 E. 60th Street, Suite 400
New York, NY 10022
Tel: (212) 702-9102
Fax: (212) 702-0854

BALTIC-AMERICAN ENTERPRISE FUND

The Baltic-American Enterprise Fund was established in January 1995. The Baltic- American Enterprise Fund is capitalized at $50 million and plans to begin funding projects in June of this of 1995. The Fund will establish offices in Tallinn, Riga and Vilnius by the end of 1995 and will provide a variety of financial services to small and medium-sized businesses in the Baltics.

For more information, write or call:

Baltic-American Enterprise Fund
Brewster Campbell Jr., President and Chief Executive Officer
1625 K Street, N.W. Suite 903
Washington, DC 20046
Tel (202) 835-0900
Fax:(202) 835-0955

Office in Estonia:
Parnu mnt. 20a
EE0001 Tallinn, Estonia
Tel: (372) 645-1565
Fax:(372) 645-1556

Office in Latvia:
Brivibas 57-18
Riga LV-1050, Latvia
Tel: (371) 731-0215, 731 -0216
Fax: (371) 731-0217

Office in Lithuania:
Maironio 1, 3rd Floor
2600 Vilnius, Lithuania
Tel: (370) 627-488, 627-471
Fax: (370-2) 614-690

BULGARIAN-AMERICAN ENTERPRISE FUND (BAEF)

The Bulgarian-American Enterprise Fund was established in January of 1992. The Fund was capitalized at $55 million. The BAEF's investment strategies fall into five areas: (1) Micro-Lending: The program is managed by Opportunity International (01) and operates in Sofia, Plovdiv and Velingrad. The enterprises that this program supports are usually small family-operated businesses. Loan size is $1,000-$25,000.

(2) Kompass Program: This program for small and medium-sized business development was organized in cooperation with four Bulgarian banks and is being coordinated by Shorebank in Chicago, which has extensive experience in small business lending. Loan size is $25,000-$250,000.

(3) Small Hotel Program: Historically, tourism has been one of Bulgaria's strongest business sectors. The BAEF uses this program to help private landowners convert their properties into small-business and "bed-and-breakfast style hotels.

(4) The Dairy Program: The Fund is providing a $250,000 line of credit to make loans to dairy farmers. The first six loans, totaling $78,000 were approved by the of 1994.

(5) Venture Capital Investing: In this area, the BAEF is particularly interested in finding joint venture participants and privatization opportunities. Generally investment is limited to established operations, although from time to time the Fund will consider start-up operations. The Fund's staff looks for equity deals in the range of $250,000 to $2,500,000, but will consider deals less than $250,000.

For more information, write or call:

Bulgarian-American Enterprise Fund
Frank Bauer, President and Chief Executive Officer
333 West Wacker Drive, Suite 2080
Chicago, IL 60606
Tel: (312) 629-2500
Fax: (312) 629-2929
Email: baefusa@aol.com

Office in Bulgaria:
Virginia Rollins, Managing Director, Sofia
3 Shipka Street
Sofia 1504, Bulgaria
Tel: (359-2) 44-18-62
Fax:(359-2) 44-30-18
Email: baefsofia@aol.com

Hungarian-American Enterprise Fund (HAEF)

The Hungarian-American Enterprise Fund (HAEF) was created in July 1990. The Fund was originally capitalized at $60 million, but received an additional $10 million in 1991/92 to be used for technical assistance grants. The HAEF has focused its investments in several areas: the consumer goods and services sector, Hungarian businesses that support infrastructure development, facility and equipment upgrades and worker retraining, and small and micro loans. The HAEF has tended to concentrate its financing in equity investments rather than in loans. However, to address the capital needs of smaller enterprises, the HAEF has instituted two small business loan programs. As of June 1994, more than $5 million had been disbursed in 150 commercial loans. Loan amounts range from $10,000 to $100,000. there is also a micro-loan program. Loan amounts in this program range from A$1,000 to $20,0000.

For more information, write or call:

Hungarian-American Enterprise Fund
Eriberto Scocimara, President and Chief Executive Officer
One East Putnam Avenue
Greenwich, Connecticut 06830
Tel: (203) 869-3114
Fax: (203) 869-3556
Email: 102634,3362@COMPUSERVE

Mithra Center
Tartsay Zilmos
Unit 14
Budapest 1126
Tel: (36-1) 214-8160
Fax:(36-1) 214-8159

POLISH-AMERICAN ENTERPRISE FUND (PAEF)

The Polish-American Enterprise Fund began operations in May 1990. The Fund was capitalized originally at $240 million by the U.S. Government with the idea of recovering a large portion of the funds through loan repayment and dividends. Its cumulative investment in Poland now totals more than $346 million in companies which have aggregate sales of over $850 million and net profits in excess of $62 million.

During fiscal year 1996, the fund's small loan and micro lending facilities extended more than 2,400 small business loans, while other initiatives assisted the financing of over 1,100 housing units, and provided equity capital for privatization and buisness expansions.

The Board of Directors of the Polish-American Enterprise Fund has decided to terminate new investment by the fund in established commercial enterprises in order to focus on its core developmental programs including small business loans, micro lending, mortgage lending, and housing development.

The PAEF's program in small business loans was strengthened through the merge of the Enterprise Credit Corporation with the fund's First Polish-American Bank. During fiscal year, the combined activity of the two organizations, now managed by the bank, extended almost 1,000 loans, disbursing a total of $36.8 million. Added to loans made in previous years, the small business loan program has granted loans totaling over $145 million.

The fund's micro lending program is carried out by Fundusz Mikro which attempts to provide loans to the smallest and least-served businesses in Poland. Fundusz Mikro has 30 loan officers operating in 13 outlets located throughout the country who have approved 1,594 loans with an average loan six of 4,800 PLN ($1,800). Thus far, there has been a less than one percent default rate of its loans.

Mortgage lending by the PAEF is accomplished through the Polish-American Mortgage Bank (PAMBank) which in 1996 approved more than 978 loans for over $40 million in support of the housing industry. The total market value of homes financing by PAMBank exceeds $80 million.

In 1994, the PAEF created the Housing Development Corporation (HDC) to finance fledgling real estate developers. The Polish-American Enterprise Fund has been in the forefront of assisting with housing development. Housing development is a key issue for the continuing development of Poland's economy and a risky area for investors. Since 1994, HDC has extended more than $3 million in credit, with almost half of the total disbursement in fiscal year 1996. With the early success of the HDC, it is now cooperating with a Canadian real estate investor to establish the Polish Real Estate Fund with each party contributing $5 million.

For more information, contact:
Ms. Barbara Lundberg, Executive Vice President and General Director
Polsko-Amerykanski Fundusz Przedsiebiorczosci
Al. Jana Pawla II 25
00-854 Warsaw, Poland
Tel: (48-22) 653-4500
Fax: (48-22) 653-4555

ROMANIAN-AMERICAN ENTERPRISE FUND (ROAEF)

The Romanian-American Enterprise Fund was established in July 1994. It was capitalized at $50 million. The Fund's activities include: debt and equity investments in small and medium-sized Romanian private enterprises, a small/micro loan program, technical assistance related to RoAEF investments and programs, promotion of joint ventures with foreign partners (particularly American partners) and policy reform through its loan and inve stment activities.

For more information, write or call:

Romanian-American Enterprise Fund
John Mullen, President and Chief Executive Officer
1800 Diagonal Road
Suite 600
Alexandria, VA 22314
Tel: (703) 684-4435
Fax: (703) 548-9446

Office in Romania:
Fondul Romano-American Pentru Investitii
Obie Moore, Managing Director, Bucharest
4 Vasile Conta Street
Sector 2
Bucharest, Romania
Tel:(40-1) 210-0701, 210-0423
Fax: (40-1) 210-0713
Email: Christina. marine@roaef-dc.roaef.sprint.com

SLOVAK AMERICAN ENTERPRISE FUND

The Slovak American Enterprise Fund was established in 1991 as the Czech and Slovak American Enterprise Fund to assist in the transition of Czechoslovakia to a free-market economy. After 1993, the activities of the Fund were continued to Slovakia by the Slovak American Enterprise Fund. As the first significant foreign investor in Slovakia, the Fund has made more direct investments in Slovakia than any other foreign fund.

To date, the fund has committed approximately $15 million in debt and equity to 30 private Slovak enterprises, and has committed approximately $3 million in loans to 27 private Slovak enterprises through a joint lending program with a private Slovak bank under the American Loan Program. The fund has over $25 million to invest in private Slovak enterprises.

The fund invests capital on a commercial basis in the form of debt or equity with minimum investment of $300,000 and maximum investment of $2.5 million. The fund seeks investment opportunities int he manufacturing and service industry segments, excluding casino, nightclubs, alcohol, tobacco, non-private, start-up or defense-related companies.

Factors that are considered when reviewing financing opportunities include: * Existing enterprises with a sound business plan * Competent and credible management team with a proven track record * Growth potential with continued favorable earnings * Employment growth * Positive environmental impact

The Slovak American Enterprise Fund is actively seeking investment opportunities throughout Slovakia. It intends to focus on target industries which have significant competitive advantages and offer high growth potential. There is a great potential for joint-venture creation as well as expanding existing business relationships.

For more information, contact:
Slovak American Enterprise Fund
Radlinskeho 27
810 05 Bratislava, Slovak Republic
Tel: (421-7) 326-544, 361-580, 362-596
Fax: (421-7) 362-530
Mr. Denis Brown, President
Ing. Iveta Ribanska, Director of Corporate Planning and Marketing

U.S. COMPANIES OPERATING AND INVESTING IN BULGARIA

Abbot Diagnostics
Allen-Bradley
Alta Bulgaria Ltd.
American Continental Cars
Amoco
Amylum Group, Tsaramil Ltd.
Arthur Andersen
AT & T
Boeing
Bulgarian-American Enterprise Fund
Bulgarian Business Systems (Apple Computer IMC)
CB Shipping (Agent of Sea Land)
Citizens Democracy Corps
Coca-Cola, Levents Group
Colgate-Palmolive LTD.
Computerland
Continental Information
Coopers & Lybrand
Curtis Balkan
Cynamid
Dell Computer
DDB Needham Worldwide
Deloitte & Touche
Demax (Rep. of Rockewell International)
DHL
Digital Equipment Corporation
Dow Chemical
Du Pont De Nemours International
Eastern Digital (Rep. of Western Digital)
ECD-Bul (Rep. of Seagate Technology)
EKKO (Rep. of Caterpillar, Bobcat, Ingersoll-Rand)
Eli Lilly & Elanco
Environmental Oil Resources International Ltd.
Ernst & Young
EQE Engineering
Euroenergy Holding (Rep. of McDermott Inc.)
Ford
Freight Solutions International
Genco
Global Communications Group

Great Bear
Good Year
GTS Way (Distributor of Applied Technologies International Corp.)
Honeywell Bulgaria
IBM Bulgaria
IDG Technika Communications Ltd.
Inter Data Systems
International Bank for Investment and Development
In Time Courier Ltd. (Agent of United Parcel Service)
JEF Trading (Nabisco Products)
Johnson & Johnson
antor Management Consultants
Khan Agency (Contractors for Federal Express)
Kodak
KPMG
Kraft Jacobs Suchard
Lanier
Lefkowits & Co.
Link Communication System
Maria Stoeva Ltd.

Margro Services

McDonald's
Merck Sharp & Dohme Idea, Inc.
Microcom International
Mobiltel
Monsanto
Novecon
Oracle
OTIS
Pangaea Ltd.
PBI Advertising
Pepsi Cola
Price Waterhouse
Proctor & Gamble Bulgaria
Rimex (Rep. of J.I. Case)
R.J. Reynolds Tobacco International
Sammex
S & T Bulgaria (Hewlett Packard)
Snelling & Snelling
Sprint-BTC
S.C. Johnson
Sheraton Hotel
Souther Tel Bulgaria
Steelcase Strafor
Texaco
3M
Transimpex (Rep. of Mobil Oil)
Unicorp Systems Ltd.
Unigel Ltd.
Union Food Center International (UFC)
Union Pacific Petroleum Bulgaria Ltd.
Union Television Ltd.
Uniglobe
Unisys
Uni Star (Rep. of Uni Royal)
University of Delaware
Upjohn
Vander Weele Graphics

Westinghouse
Xerox

BASIC TITLES ON BULGARIA

Title	ISBN
Bulgaria A "Spy" Guide - Strategic Information and Developments	1438706448
Bulgaria A "Spy" Guide - Strategic Information and Developments	143300447X
Bulgaria Air Force Handbook	1433004488
Bulgaria Air Force Handbook	1438706456
Bulgaria and NATO Military Cooperation Handbook	1438706464
Bulgaria and NATO Relations Handbook	1433004496
Bulgaria Army Military Strategy Handbook	1433062089
Bulgaria Army Weapon Systems Handbook	1433062089
Bulgaria Army Weapon Systems Handbook	1433062089
Bulgaria Banking & Financial Market Handbook	1438706472
Bulgaria Banking & Financial Market Handbook	143300450X
Bulgaria Business and Investment Opportunities Yearbook	1433004518
Bulgaria Business and Investment Opportunities Yearbook	1438706480
Bulgaria Business and Investment Opportunities Yearbook Volume 1 Strategic Information and Opportunities	1438776357
Bulgaria Business and Investment Opportunities Yearbook Volume 2 Leading Export-Import, Business, Investment Opportunities and Projects	1577519302
Bulgaria Business Intelligence Report - Practical Information, Opportunities, Contacts	1438706499
Bulgaria Business Intelligence Report - Practical Information, Opportunities, Contacts	1433004526
Bulgaria Business Law Handbook - Strategic Information and Basic Laws	1438706502
Bulgaria Business Law Handbook - Strategic Information and Basic Laws	1438769482
Bulgaria Business Law Handbook - Strategic Information and Basic Laws	1433004534
Bulgaria Business Law Handbook - Strategic Information and Basic Laws	1438769482
Bulgaria Business Law Handbook Volume 2 Investment and Trade Laws Volume 2 Investment and Trade Laws	1577518004
Bulgaria Company Laws and Regulations Handbook	1433069563
Bulgaria Constitution and Citizenship Laws Handbook - Strategic Information and Basic Laws	1438778635
Bulgaria Country Study Guide - Strategic Information and Developments	1438706510
Bulgaria Country Study Guide - Strategic Information and Developments	1433004542
Bulgaria Country Study Guide - Strategic Information and Developments Volume 1 Strategic Information and Developments	1438774028
Bulgaria Customs, Trade Regulations and Procedures Handbook	1433004550
Bulgaria Customs, Trade Regulations and Procedures Handbook	1438706529
Bulgaria Department of Defense Handbook	1433004569
Bulgaria Department of Defense Handbook	1438706537
Bulgaria Diplomatic Handbook - Strategic Information and Developments	1433004577
Bulgaria Diplomatic Handbook - Strategic Information and Developments	1438706545
Bulgaria Ecology & Nature Protection Handbook	1433004585
Bulgaria Ecology & Nature Protection Handbook	1438706553

Title	ISBN
Bulgaria Ecology & Nature Protection Laws and Regulation Handbook	1433073404
Bulgaria Energy Policy, Laws and Regulation Handbook	1433071169
Bulgaria Export-Import Trade and Business Directory	1433004593
Bulgaria Export-Import Trade and Business Directory	1438706561
Bulgaria Foreign Policy and Government Guide	143870657X
Bulgaria Foreign Policy and Government Guide	1433004607
Bulgaria Government and Business Contacts Handbook	1438706588
Bulgaria Government and Business Contacts Handbook	1433004615
Bulgaria Healthcare Sector Organization, Management and Payment Systems Handbook - Strategic Information, Programs and Regulations	9781433085819
Bulgaria Immigration Laws and Regulations Handbook - Strategic Information and Basic Laws	143878225X
Bulgaria Industrial and Business Directory	1438706596
Bulgaria Industrial and Business Directory	1433004623
Bulgaria Insolvency (Bankruptcy) Laws and Regulations Handbook - Strategic Information and Basic Laws	9781433085116
Bulgaria Internet and E-Commerce Investment and Business Guide - Strategic and Practical Information: Regulations and Opportunities	1433004631
Bulgaria Internet and E-Commerce Investment and Business Guide - Strategic and Practical Information: Regulations and Opportunities	143870660X
Bulgaria Investment and Business Guide - Strategic and Practical Information	1438706618
Bulgaria Investment and Business Guide - Strategic and Practical Information	143876720X
Bulgaria Investment and Business Guide - Strategic and Practical Information	143300464X
Bulgaria Investment and Business Guide - Strategic and Practical Information	143876720X
Bulgaria Investment and Business Guide Volume 2 Business, Investment Opportunities and Incentives	1577518500
Bulgaria Investment and Trade Laws and Regulations Handbook	1433075571
Bulgaria Labor Laws and Regulations Handbook - Strategic Information and Basic Laws	1438780451
Bulgaria Land Ownership and Agriculture Laws Handbook	1438758723
Bulgaria Mineral & Mining Sector Investment and Business Guide - Strategic and Practical Information	1438706626
Bulgaria Mineral & Mining Sector Investment and Business Guide - Strategic and Practical Information	1433004658
Bulgaria Mining Laws and Regulations Handbook	143307706X
Bulgaria Privatization Programs and Regulations Handbook	1433004666
Bulgaria Privatization Programs and Regulations Handbook	1438706634
Bulgaria Recent Economic and Political Developments Yearbook	1433060361
Bulgaria Recent Economic and Political Developments Yearbook	1433060361
Bulgaria Recent Economic and Political Developments Yearbook	1433060361
Bulgaria Starting Business (Incorporating) in Bulgaria Guide	1433046881
Bulgaria Starting Business (Incorporating) in....Guide	143306491X
Bulgaria Tax Guide	1433004674
Bulgaria Tax Guide	1438706642
Bulgaria Taxation Laws and Regulations Handbook	1433079437
Bulgaria Telecom Laws and Regulations Handbook	1433081563

Title	ISBN
Bulgaria Telecommunication Industry Business Opportunities Handbook	1433004682
Bulgaria Telecommunication Industry Business Opportunities Handbook	1438706650
Bulgaria Transportation Policy and Regulations Handbook	1433064928
Bulgaria: How to Invest, Start and Run Profitable Business in Bulgaria Guide - Practical Information, Opportunities, Contacts	9781433083006

WORLD COMPANY LAWS AND REGULATIONS LIBRARY

Ultimate directories for conducting export-import operations in the country. Largest exporters and importers, strategic government and business contacts, selected export-import regulations and more...

Price: $149 each

TITLE

Afghanistan Company Laws and Regulations Handbook
Albania Company Laws and Regulations Handbook
Algeria Company Laws and Regulations Handbook
Andorra Company Laws and Regulations Handbook
Angola Company Laws and Regulations Handbook
Anguilla Company Laws and Regulations Handbook
Antigua and Barbuda Company Laws and Regulations Handbook
Antilles (Netherlands) Company Laws and Regulations Handbook
Argentina Company Laws and Regulations Handbook
Armenia Company Laws and Regulations Handbook
Aruba Company Laws and Regulations Handbook
Australia Company Laws and Regulations Handbook
Austria Company Laws and Regulations Handbook
Azerbaijan Company Laws and Regulations Handbook
Bahamas Company Laws and Regulations Handbook
Bahrain Company Laws and Regulations Handbook
Bangladesh Company Laws and Regulations Handbook
Barbados Company Laws and Regulations Handbook
Belarus Company Laws and Regulations Handbook
Belgium Company Laws and Regulations Handbook
Belize Company Laws and Regulations Handbook
Benin Company Laws and Regulations Handbook
Bermuda Company Laws and Regulations Handbook
Bhutan Company Laws and Regulations Handbook
Bolivia Company Laws and Regulations Handbook
Bosnia and Herzegovina Company Laws and Regulations Handbook
Botswana Company Laws and Regulations Handbook
Brazil Company Laws and Regulations Handbook
Brunei Company Laws and Regulations Handbook
Bulgaria Company Laws and Regulations Handbook
Burkina Faso Company Laws and Regulations Handbook
Burundi Company Laws and Regulations Handbook
Cambodia Company Laws and Regulations Handbook
Cameroon Company Laws and Regulations Handbook
Canada Company Laws and Regulations Handbook
Cape Verde Company Laws and Regulations Handbook
Cayman Islands Company Laws and Regulations Handbook
Central African Republic Company Laws and Regulations Handbook
Chad Company Laws and Regulations Handbook
Chile Company Laws and Regulations Handbook
China Company Laws and Regulations Handbook
Colombia Company Laws and Regulations Handbook
Comoros Company Laws and Regulations Handbook
Congo Company Laws and Regulations Handbook
Congo, Democratic Republic Company Laws and Regulations Handbook
Cook Islands Company Laws and Regulations Handbook
Costa Rica Company Laws and Regulations Handbook
Cote d'Ivoire Company Laws and Regulations Handbook
Croatia Company Laws and Regulations Handbook
Cuba Company Laws and Regulations Handbook
Cyprus Company Laws and Regulations Handbook
Czech Republic Company Laws and Regulations Handbook
Denmark Company Laws and Regulations Handbook
Djibouti Company Laws and Regulations Handbook
Dominica Company Laws and Regulations Handbook
Dominican Republic Company Laws and Regulations Handbook
Ecuador Company Laws and Regulations Handbook
Egypt Company Laws and Regulations Handbook
El Salvador Company Laws and Regulations Handbook

Equatorial Guinea Company Laws and Regulations Handbook
Eritrea Company Laws and Regulations Handbook
Estonia Company Laws and Regulations Handbook
Ethiopia Company Laws and Regulations Handbook
Falkland Islands Company Laws and Regulations Handbook
Faroes Company Laws and Regulations Handbook
Fiji Company Laws and Regulations Handbook
Finland Company Laws and Regulations Handbook
France Company Laws and Regulations Handbook
Gabon Company Laws and Regulations Handbook
Gambia Company Laws and Regulations Handbook
Georgia Company Laws and Regulations Handbook
Germany Company Laws and Regulations Handbook
Ghana Company Laws and Regulations Handbook
Gibraltar Company Laws and Regulations Handbook
Greece Company Laws and Regulations Handbook
Greenland Company Laws and Regulations Handbook
Grenada Company Laws and Regulations Handbook
Guam Company Laws and Regulations Handbook
Guatemala Company Laws and Regulations Handbook
Guernsey Company Laws and Regulations Handbook
Guinea Company Laws and Regulations Handbook
Guinea-Bissau Company Laws and Regulations Handbook
Guyana Company Laws and Regulations Handbook
Haiti Company Laws and Regulations Handbook
Honduras Company Laws and Regulations Handbook
Hungary Company Laws and Regulations Handbook
Iceland Company Laws and Regulations Handbook
India Company Laws and Regulations Handbook
Indonesia Company Laws and Regulations Handbook
InternationalCompany Laws and Regulations Handbook
Iran Company Laws and Regulations Handbook
Iraq Company Laws and Regulations Handbook
Ireland Company Laws and Regulations Handbook
Israel Company Laws and Regulations Handbook
Italy Company Laws and Regulations Handbook
Jamaica Company Laws and Regulations Handbook
Japan Company Laws and Regulations Handbook
Jersey Company Laws and Regulations Handbook
Jordan Company Laws and Regulations Handbook
Kazakhstan Company Laws and Regulations Handbook
Kenya Company Laws and Regulations Handbook
Kiribati Company Laws and Regulations Handbook
Korea, North Company Laws and Regulations Handbook
Korea, South Company Laws and Regulations Handbook
Kosovo Company Laws and Regulations Handbook
Kuwait Company Laws and Regulations Handbook
Kyrgyzstan Company Laws and Regulations Handbook
Laos Company Laws and Regulations Handbook
Latvia Company Laws and Regulations Handbook
Lebanon Company Laws and Regulations Handbook
Lesotho Company Laws and Regulations Handbook
Liberia Company Laws and Regulations Handbook
Libya Company Laws and Regulations Handbook
Liechtenstein Company Laws and Regulations Handbook
Lithuania Company Laws and Regulations Handbook
Luxembourg Company Laws and Regulations Handbook
Macao Company Laws and Regulations Handbook
Macedonia Company Laws and Regulations Handbook
Madagascar Company Laws and Regulations Handbook
Madeira Company Laws and Regulations Handbook
Malawi Company Laws and Regulations Handbook
Malaysia Company Laws and Regulations Handbook
Maldives Company Laws and Regulations Handbook
Mali Company Laws and Regulations Handbook
Malta Company Laws and Regulations Handbook
Man Company Laws and Regulations Handbook
Marshall Islands Company Laws and Regulations Handbook
Mauritania Company Laws and Regulations Handbook
Mauritius Company Laws and Regulations Handbook
Mayotte Company Laws and Regulations Handbook
Mexico Company Laws and Regulations Handbook
Micronesia Company Laws and Regulations Handbook
Moldova Company Laws and Regulations Handbook
Monaco Company Laws and Regulations Handbook
Mongolia Company Laws and Regulations Handbook
Monserrat Company Laws and Regulations Handbook
Morocco Company Laws and Regulations Handbook
Mozambique Company Laws and Regulations Handbook
Myanmar Company Laws and Regulations Handbook
Namibia Company Laws and Regulations Handbook
Nauru Company Laws and Regulations Handbook
Nepal Company Laws and Regulations Handbook
Netherlands Company Laws and Regulations Handbook
New Caledonia Company Laws and Regulations Handbook
New Zealand Company Laws and Regulations Handbook
Nicaragua Company Laws and Regulations Handbook
Niger Company Laws and Regulations Handbook
Nigeria Company Laws and Regulations Handbook
Niue Company Laws and Regulations Handbook
Northern Mariana Islands Company Laws and Regulations Handbook
Norway Company Laws and Regulations Handbook
Oman Company Laws and Regulations Handbook
Pakistan Company Laws and Regulations Handbook
Palau Company Laws and Regulations Handbook

Palestine Company Laws and Regulations Handbook
Panama Company Laws and Regulations Handbook
Papua New Guinea Company Laws and Regulations Handbook
Paraguay Company Laws and Regulations Handbook
Peru Company Laws and Regulations Handbook
Philippines Company Laws and Regulations Handbook
Pitcairn Islands Company Laws and Regulations Handbook
Poland Company Laws and Regulations Handbook
Polynesia French Company Laws and Regulations Handbook
Portugal Company Laws and Regulations Handbook
Qatar Company Laws and Regulations Handbook
Romania Company Laws and Regulations Handbook
Russia Company Laws and Regulations Handbook
Rwanda Company Laws and Regulations Handbook
Saint Kitts and Nevis Company Laws and Regulations Handbook
Saint Lucia Company Laws and Regulations Handbook
Saint Vincent and The Grenadines Company Laws and Regulations Handbook
Samoa (American) Company Laws and Regulations Handbook
Samoa (Western) Company Laws and Regulations Handbook
San Marino Company Laws and Regulations Handbook
Sao Tome and Principe Company Laws and Regulations Handbook
Saudi Arabia Company Laws and Regulations Handbook
Scotland Company Laws and Regulations Handbook
Senegal Company Laws and Regulations Handbook
Seychelles Company Laws and Regulations Handbook
Sierra Leone Company Laws and Regulations Handbook
Singapore Company Laws and Regulations Handbook
Slovakia Company Laws and Regulations Handbook
Slovenia Company Laws and Regulations Handbook
Solomon Islands Company Laws and Regulations Handbook
Somalia Company Laws and Regulations Handbook
South Africa Company Laws and Regulations Handbook
Spain Company Laws and Regulations Handbook
Sri Lanka Company Laws and Regulations Handbook
St. Helena Company Laws and Regulations Handbook
St. Pierre & Miquelon Company Laws and Regulations Handbook
Sudan Company Laws and Regulations Handbook
Suriname Company Laws and Regulations Handbook
Swaziland Company Laws and Regulations Handbook
Sweden Company Laws and Regulations Handbook
Switzerland Company Laws and Regulations Handbook
Syria Company Laws and Regulations Handbook
Taiwan Company Laws and Regulations Handbook
Tajikistan Company Laws and Regulations Handbook
Tanzania Company Laws and Regulations Handbook
Thailand Company Laws and Regulations Handbook
Togo Company Laws and Regulations Handbook
Tonga Company Laws and Regulations Handbook
Trinidad and Tobago Company Laws and Regulations Handbook
Tunisia Company Laws and Regulations Handbook
Turkey Company Laws and Regulations Handbook
Turkmenistan Company Laws and Regulations Handbook
Turks & Caicos Company Laws and Regulations Handbook
Tuvalu Company Laws and Regulations Handbook
Uganda Company Laws and Regulations Handbook
Ukraine Company Laws and Regulations Handbook
United Arab Emirates Company Laws and Regulations Handbook
United Kingdom Company Laws and Regulations Handbook
United States Company Laws and Regulations Handbook
Uruguay Company Laws and Regulations Handbook
Uzbekistan Company Laws and Regulations Handbook
Vanuatu Company Laws and Regulations Handbook
Vatican City Company Laws and Regulations Handbook
Venezuela Company Laws and Regulations Handbook
Vietnam Company Laws and Regulations Handbook
Virgin Islands, British Company Laws and Regulations Handbook
Wake Atoll Company Laws and Regulations Handbook
Wallis & Futuna Company Laws and Regulations Handbook
Yemen Company Laws and Regulations Handbook
Serbia Company Laws and Regulations Handbook
Zambia Company Laws and Regulations Handbook
Zimbabwe Company Laws and Regulations Handbook

WORLD INSOLVENCY (BANKRUPTCY) LAWS AND REGULATIONS HANDBOOK LIBRARY

STRATEGIC INFORMATION AND BASIC LAWS

UPDATED ANNUALLY: PLEASE CONTACT IBP, INC FOR ISBN NUMBERS

978 ISBN	COMPLETE FULL TITLE
9781433084997	Afghanistan Insolvency (Bankruptcy) Laws and Regulations Handbook - Strategic Information and Basic Laws
9781433085000	Albania Insolvency (Bankruptcy) Laws and Regulations Handbook - Strategic Information and Basic Laws
9781433086793	Algeria Insolvency (Bankruptcy) Laws and Regulations Handbook - Strategic Information and Basic Laws
9781433085017	Angola Insolvency (Bankruptcy) Laws and Regulations Handbook - Strategic Information and Basic Laws
9781433086250	Antigua and Barduba Insolvency (Bankruptcy) Laws and Regulations Handbook - Strategic Information and Basic Laws
9781433085024	Argentina Insolvency (Bankruptcy) Laws and Regulations Handbook - Strategic Information and Basic Laws
9781433086786	Armenia Insolvency (Bankruptcy) Laws and Regulations Handbook - Strategic Information and Basic Laws
9781433085031	Australia Insolvency (Bankruptcy) Laws and Regulations Handbook - Strategic Information and Basic Laws
9781433086779	Austria Insolvency (Bankruptcy) Laws and Regulations Handbook - Strategic Information and Basic Laws
9781433085048	Azerbaijan Insolvency (Bankruptcy) Laws and Regulations Handbook - Strategic Information and Basic Laws
9781433086762	Bahamas Insolvency (Bankruptcy) Laws and Regulations Handbook - Strategic Information and Basic Laws
9781433085055	Bahrain Insolvency (Bankruptcy) Laws and Regulations Handbook - Strategic Information and Basic Laws
9781433086243	Bangladesh Insolvency (Bankruptcy) Laws and Regulations Handbook - Strategic Information and Basic Laws
9781433085062	Barbados Insolvency (Bankruptcy) Laws and Regulations Handbook - Strategic Information and Basic Laws
9781433086755	Belarus Insolvency (Bankruptcy) Laws and Regulations Handbook - Strategic Information and Basic Laws
9781433085079	Belgium Insolvency (Bankruptcy) Laws and Regulations Handbook - Strategic Information and Basic Laws
9781433086748	Belize Insolvency (Bankruptcy) Laws and Regulations Handbook - Strategic Information and Basic Laws
9781433085086	Benin Insolvency (Bankruptcy) Laws and Regulations Handbook - Strategic Information and Basic Laws
9781433086731	Bermuda Insolvency (Bankruptcy) Laws and Regulations Handbook - Strategic

978 ISBN	COMPLETE FULL TITLE
	Information and Basic Laws
9781433085093	Bhutan Insolvency (Bankruptcy) Laws and Regulations Handbook - Strategic Information and Basic Laws
9781433086595	Bolivia Insolvency (Bankruptcy) Laws and Regulations Handbook - Strategic Information and Basic Laws
9781433085109	Bosnia and Herzegovina Insolvency (Bankruptcy) Laws and Regulations Handbook - Strategic Information and Basic Laws
9781433086236	Brazil Insolvency (Bankruptcy) Laws and Regulations Handbook - Strategic Information and Basic Laws
9781433086236	Bulgaria Insolvency (Bankruptcy) Laws and Regulations Handbook - Strategic Information and Basic Laws
9781433085123	Burkina Faso Insolvency (Bankruptcy) Laws and Regulations Handbook - Strategic Information and Basic Laws
9781433086717	Cabo Verde Insolvency (Bankruptcy) Laws and Regulations Handbook - Strategic Information and Basic Laws
9781433085130	Cambodia Insolvency (Bankruptcy) Laws and Regulations Handbook - Strategic Information and Basic Laws
9781433086847	Cameroon Insolvency (Bankruptcy) Laws and Regulations Handbook - Strategic Information and Basic Laws
9781433085147	Canada Insolvency (Bankruptcy) Laws and Regulations Handbook - Strategic Information and Basic Laws
9781433086694	Cayman Insolvency (Bankruptcy) Laws and Regulations Handbook - Strategic Information and Basic Laws
9781433085154	Central African Republic Insolvency (Bankruptcy) Laws and Regulations Handbook - Strategic Information and Basic Laws
9781433086687	Chad Insolvency (Bankruptcy) Laws and Regulations Handbook - Strategic Information and Basic Laws
9781433085161	Chile Insolvency (Bankruptcy) Laws and Regulations Handbook - Strategic Information and Basic Laws
9781433086670	China Insolvency (Bankruptcy) Laws and Regulations Handbook - Strategic Information and Basic Laws
9781433085178	Colombia Insolvency (Bankruptcy) Laws and Regulations Handbook - Strategic Information and Basic Laws
9781433086663	Comoros Insolvency (Bankruptcy) Laws and Regulations Handbook - Strategic Information and Basic Laws
9781433085208	Congo Democratic Republic Insolvency (Bankruptcy) Laws and Regulations Handbook - Strategic Information and Basic Laws
9781433085185	Costa Rica Insolvency (Bankruptcy) Laws and Regulations Handbook - Strategic Information and Basic Laws
9781433086229	Croatia Insolvency (Bankruptcy) Laws and Regulations Handbook - Strategic Information and Basic Laws
9781433085192	Cyprus Insolvency (Bankruptcy) Laws and Regulations Handbook - Strategic Information and Basic Laws
9781433086212	Czech Insolvency (Bankruptcy) Laws and Regulations Handbook - Strategic Information and Basic Laws
9781433086656	Denmark Insolvency (Bankruptcy) Laws and Regulations Handbook - Strategic Information and Basic Laws
9781433085215	Dominican Republic Insolvency (Bankruptcy) Laws and Regulations Handbook - Strategic Information and Basic Laws
9781433086649	Ecuador Insolvency (Bankruptcy) Laws and Regulations Handbook - Strategic Information and Basic Laws
9781433085222	Egypt Insolvency (Bankruptcy) Laws and Regulations Handbook - Strategic Information and Basic Laws

To order and for additional analytical and marketing information, please contacts
International Business Publications, USA at:
P.O. Box 15343, Washington, DC 20003, USA. Phone: (202) 546-210 Fax: (202) 546-32
E-mail: ibpusa@comcast.net

978 ISBN	COMPLETE FULL TITLE
9781433086632	El Salvador Insolvency (Bankruptcy) Laws and Regulations Handbook - Strategic Information and Basic Laws
9781433085239	Estonia Insolvency (Bankruptcy) Laws and Regulations Handbook - Strategic Information and Basic Laws
9781433086625	Ethiopia Insolvency (Bankruptcy) Laws and Regulations Handbook - Strategic Information and Basic Laws
9781433085246	European Union Insolvency (Bankruptcy) Laws and Regulations Handbook - Strategic Information and Basic Laws
9781433086076	Fiji Insolvency (Bankruptcy) Laws and Regulations Handbook - Strategic Information and Basic Laws
9781433085253	Finland Insolvency (Bankruptcy) Laws and Regulations Handbook - Strategic Information and Basic Laws
9781433086199	France Insolvency (Bankruptcy) Laws and Regulations Handbook - Strategic Information and Basic Laws
9781433085260	Gabon Insolvency (Bankruptcy) Laws and Regulations Handbook - Strategic Information and Basic Laws
9781433086311	Gambia Insolvency (Bankruptcy) Laws and Regulations Handbook - Strategic Information and Basic Laws
9781433085277	Georgia Republic Insolvency (Bankruptcy) Laws and Regulations Handbook - Strategic Information and Basic Laws
9781433086175	Germany Insolvency (Bankruptcy) Laws and Regulations Handbook - Strategic Information and Basic Laws
9781433085284	Ghana Insolvency (Bankruptcy) Laws and Regulations Handbook - Strategic Information and Basic Laws
9781433086618	Gibraltar Insolvency (Bankruptcy) Laws and Regulations Handbook - Strategic Information and Basic Laws
9781433085291	Greece Insolvency (Bankruptcy) Laws and Regulations Handbook - Strategic Information and Basic Laws
9781433086168	Grenada Insolvency (Bankruptcy) Laws and Regulations Handbook - Strategic Information and Basic Laws
9781433085307	Guatemala Insolvency (Bankruptcy) Laws and Regulations Handbook - Strategic Information and Basic Laws
9781433086601	Guyana Insolvency (Bankruptcy) Laws and Regulations Handbook - Strategic Information and Basic Laws
9781433085314	Haiti Insolvency (Bankruptcy) Laws and Regulations Handbook - Strategic Information and Basic Laws
9781433086977	Honduras Insolvency (Bankruptcy) Laws and Regulations Handbook - Strategic Information and Basic Laws
9781433085321	Hong Kong Insolvency (Bankruptcy) Laws and Regulations Handbook - Strategic Information and Basic Laws
9781433086151	Hungary Insolvency (Bankruptcy) Laws and Regulations Handbook - Strategic Information and Basic Laws
9781433085338	Iceland Insolvency (Bankruptcy) Laws and Regulations Handbook - Strategic Information and Basic Laws
9781433086144	India Insolvency (Bankruptcy) Laws and Regulations Handbook - Strategic Information and Basic Laws
9781433085345	Indonesia Insolvency (Bankruptcy) Laws and Regulations Handbook - Strategic Information and Basic Laws
9781433086991	Iran Insolvency (Bankruptcy) Laws and Regulations Handbook - Strategic Information and Basic Laws
9781433085352	Iraq Insolvency (Bankruptcy) Laws and Regulations Handbook - Strategic Information and Basic Laws
9781433086137	Ireland Insolvency (Bankruptcy) Laws and Regulations Handbook - Strategic Information

978 ISBN	COMPLETE FULL TITLE
	and Basic Laws
9781433085369	Island of Jersey Insolvency (Bankruptcy) Laws and Regulations Handbook - Strategic Information and Basic Laws
9781433086724	Israel Insolvency (Bankruptcy) Laws and Regulations Handbook - Strategic Information and Basic Laws
9781433085376	Italy Insolvency (Bankruptcy) Laws and Regulations Handbook - Strategic Information and Basic Laws
9781433087080	Ivory Coast Insolvency (Bankruptcy) Laws and Regulations Handbook - Strategic Information and Basic Laws
9781433085383	Jamaica Insolvency (Bankruptcy) Laws and Regulations Handbook - Strategic Information and Basic Laws
9781433087073	Japan Insolvency (Bankruptcy) Laws and Regulations Handbook - Strategic Information and Basic Laws
9781433085390	Jersey Insolvency (Bankruptcy) Laws and Regulations Handbook - Strategic Information and Basic Laws
9781433087066	Jordan Insolvency (Bankruptcy) Laws and Regulations Handbook - Strategic Information and Basic Laws
9781433085406	Kazakhstan Insolvency (Bankruptcy) Laws and Regulations Handbook - Strategic Information and Basic Laws
9781433086120	Kenya Insolvency (Bankruptcy) Laws and Regulations Handbook - Strategic Information and Basic Laws
9781433085413	Kiribati Insolvency (Bankruptcy) Laws and Regulations Handbook - Strategic Information and Basic Laws
9781433086113	Korea Insolvency (Bankruptcy) Laws and Regulations Handbook - Strategic Information and Basic Laws
9781433085420	Kuwait Insolvency (Bankruptcy) Laws and Regulations Handbook - Strategic Information and Basic Laws
9781433086106	Kyrgyz Republic Insolvency (Bankruptcy) Laws and Regulations Handbook - Strategic Information and Basic Laws
9781433085437	Latvia Insolvency (Bankruptcy) Laws and Regulations Handbook - Strategic Information and Basic Laws
9781433087059	Lebanon Insolvency (Bankruptcy) Laws and Regulations Handbook - Strategic Information and Basic Laws
9781433085444	Lesotho Insolvency (Bankruptcy) Laws and Regulations Handbook - Strategic Information and Basic Laws
9781433087042	Liechtenstein Insolvency (Bankruptcy) Laws and Regulations Handbook - Strategic Information and Basic Laws
9781433085451	Lithuania Insolvency (Bankruptcy) Laws and Regulations Handbook - Strategic Information and Basic Laws
9781433086090	Luxembourg Insolvency (Bankruptcy) Laws and Regulations Handbook - Strategic Information and Basic Laws
9781433085468	Macedonia Insolvency (Bankruptcy) Laws and Regulations Handbook - Strategic Information and Basic Laws
9781433086083	Madagascar Insolvency (Bankruptcy) Laws and Regulations Handbook - Strategic Information and Basic Laws
9781433085475	Malaysia Insolvency (Bankruptcy) Laws and Regulations Handbook - Strategic Information and Basic Laws
9781433087110	Malta Insolvency (Bankruptcy) Laws and Regulations Handbook - Strategic Information and Basic Laws
9781433085482	Marshall Islands Insolvency (Bankruptcy) Laws and Regulations Handbook - Strategic Information and Basic Laws
9781433087035	Mexico Insolvency (Bankruptcy) Laws and Regulations Handbook - Strategic Information and Basic Laws

978 ISBN	COMPLETE FULL TITLE
9781433085499	Micronesia Insolvency (Bankruptcy) Laws and Regulations Handbook - Strategic Information and Basic Laws
9781433087097	Moldova Insolvency (Bankruptcy) Laws and Regulations Handbook - Strategic Information and Basic Laws
9781433085505	Monaco Insolvency (Bankruptcy) Laws and Regulations Handbook - Strategic Information and Basic Laws
9781433087028	Mongolia Insolvency (Bankruptcy) Laws and Regulations Handbook - Strategic Information and Basic Laws
9781433085512	Montenegro Insolvency (Bankruptcy) Laws and Regulations Handbook - Strategic Information and Basic Laws
9781433087011	Mozambique Insolvency (Bankruptcy) Laws and Regulations Handbook - Strategic Information and Basic Laws
9781433085529	Nepal Insolvency (Bankruptcy) Laws and Regulations Handbook - Strategic Information and Basic Laws
9781433086441	Netherlands Insolvency (Bankruptcy) Laws and Regulations Handbook - Strategic Information and Basic Laws
9781433085536	New Zealand Insolvency (Bankruptcy) Laws and Regulations Handbook - Strategic Information and Basic Laws
9781433086465	Nicaragua Insolvency (Bankruptcy) Laws and Regulations Handbook - Strategic Information and Basic Laws
9781433085543	Niger Insolvency (Bankruptcy) Laws and Regulations Handbook - Strategic Information and Basic Laws
9781433087004	Nigeria Insolvency (Bankruptcy) Laws and Regulations Handbook - Strategic Information and Basic Laws
9781433085550	Norway Insolvency (Bankruptcy) Laws and Regulations Handbook - Strategic Information and Basic Laws
9781433086205	Pakistan Insolvency (Bankruptcy) Laws and Regulations Handbook - Strategic Information and Basic Laws
9781433085567	Palau Insolvency (Bankruptcy) Laws and Regulations Handbook - Strategic Information and Basic Laws
9781433086564	Panama Insolvency (Bankruptcy) Laws and Regulations Handbook - Strategic Information and Basic Laws
9781433085574	Papau New Guinea Insolvency (Bankruptcy) Laws and Regulations Handbook - Strategic Information and Basic Laws
9781433086557	Paraguay Insolvency (Bankruptcy) Laws and Regulations Handbook - Strategic Information and Basic Laws
9781433085581	Peru Insolvency (Bankruptcy) Laws and Regulations Handbook - Strategic Information and Basic Laws
9781433087127	Philippines Insolvency (Bankruptcy) Laws and Regulations Handbook - Strategic Information and Basic Laws
9781433085598	Poland Insolvency (Bankruptcy) Laws and Regulations Handbook - Strategic Information and Basic Laws
9781433086540	Portugal Insolvency (Bankruptcy) Laws and Regulations Handbook - Strategic Information and Basic Laws
9781433085604	Romania Insolvency (Bankruptcy) Laws and Regulations Handbook - Strategic Information and Basic Laws
9781433086854	Russia Insolvency (Bankruptcy) Laws and Regulations Handbook - Strategic Information and Basic Laws
9781433085611	Saudi Arabia Insolvency (Bankruptcy) Laws and Regulations Handbook - Strategic Information and Basic Laws
9781433086533	Senegal Insolvency (Bankruptcy) Laws and Regulations Handbook - Strategic Information and Basic Laws
9781433085628	Serbia Insolvency (Bankruptcy) Laws and Regulations Handbook - Strategic Information

978 ISBN	COMPLETE FULL TITLE
	and Basic Laws
9781433086526	Sierra Leone Insolvency (Bankruptcy) Laws and Regulations Handbook - Strategic Information and Basic Laws
9781433085635	Singapore Insolvency (Bankruptcy) Laws and Regulations Handbook - Strategic Information and Basic Laws
9781433087103	Slovak Republic Insolvency (Bankruptcy) Laws and Regulations Handbook - Strategic Information and Basic Laws
9781433086519	Slovenia Insolvency (Bankruptcy) Laws and Regulations Handbook - Strategic Information and Basic Laws
9781433085642	Solomon Islands Insolvency (Bankruptcy) Laws and Regulations Handbook - Strategic Information and Basic Laws
9781433086502	South Africa Insolvency (Bankruptcy) Laws and Regulations Handbook - Strategic Information and Basic Laws
9781433085659	Spain Insolvency (Bankruptcy) Laws and Regulations Handbook - Strategic Information and Basic Laws
9781433086984	Sri Lanka Insolvency (Bankruptcy) Laws and Regulations Handbook - Strategic Information and Basic Laws
9781433085666	St. Kitts & Nevis Insolvency (Bankruptcy) Laws and Regulations Handbook - Strategic Information and Basic Laws
9781433086496	Sweden Insolvency (Bankruptcy) Laws and Regulations Handbook - Strategic Information and Basic Laws
9781433085673	Switzerland Insolvency (Bankruptcy) Laws and Regulations Handbook - Strategic Information and Basic Laws
9781433086489	Taiwan Insolvency (Bankruptcy) Laws and Regulations Handbook - Strategic Information and Basic Laws
9781433085680	Tajikistan Insolvency (Bankruptcy) Laws and Regulations Handbook - Strategic Information and Basic Laws
9781433086472	Tanzania Insolvency (Bankruptcy) Laws and Regulations Handbook - Strategic Information and Basic Laws
9781433085697	Thailand Insolvency (Bankruptcy) Laws and Regulations Handbook - Strategic Information and Basic Laws
9781433085703	Togo Insolvency (Bankruptcy) Laws and Regulations Handbook - Strategic Information and Basic Laws
9781433086960	Trinidad and Tobago Insolvency (Bankruptcy) Laws and Regulations Handbook - Strategic Information and Basic Laws
9781433085710	Tunisia Insolvency (Bankruptcy) Laws and Regulations Handbook - Strategic Information and Basic Laws
9781433086953	Turkey Insolvency (Bankruptcy) Laws and Regulations Handbook - Strategic Information and Basic Laws
9781433085727	Tuvalu Insolvency (Bankruptcy) Laws and Regulations Handbook - Strategic Information and Basic Laws
9781433086946	Uganda Insolvency (Bankruptcy) Laws and Regulations Handbook - Strategic Information and Basic Laws
9781433085734	Ukraine Insolvency (Bankruptcy) Laws and Regulations Handbook - Strategic Information and Basic Laws
9781433086939	United Arab Emirates Insolvency (Bankruptcy) Laws and Regulations Handbook - Strategic Information and Basic Laws
9781433085741	United Kingdom Insolvency (Bankruptcy) Laws and Regulations Handbook - Strategic Information and Basic Laws
9781433086328	Uruguay Insolvency (Bankruptcy) Laws and Regulations Handbook - Strategic Information and Basic Laws
9781433085758	USA Insolvency (Bankruptcy) Laws and Regulations Handbook - Strategic Information and Basic Laws

To order and for additional analytical and marketing information, please contacts
International Business Publications, USA at:
P.O. Box 15343, Washington, DC 20003, USA. Phone: (202) 546-210 Fax: (202) 546-32
E-mail: ibpusa@comcast.net

978 ISBN	COMPLETE FULL TITLE
9781433086922	Uzbekistan Insolvency (Bankruptcy) Laws and Regulations Handbook - Strategic Information and Basic Laws
9781433085765	Venezuela Insolvency (Bankruptcy) Laws and Regulations Handbook - Strategic Information and Basic Laws
9781433086915	Vietnam Insolvency (Bankruptcy) Laws and Regulations Handbook - Strategic Information and Basic Laws
9781433085116	Virgin Islands, British Insolvency (Bankruptcy) Laws and Regulations Handbook - Strategic Information and Basic Laws
9781433085772	Zambia Insolvency (Bankruptcy) Laws and Regulations Handbook - Strategic Information and Basic Laws
9781433086458	Zimbabwe Insolvency (Bankruptcy) Laws and Regulations Handbook - Strategic Information and Basic Laws

www.ingramcontent.com/pod-product-compliance
Lightning Source LLC
LaVergne TN
LVHW080034210926
848481LV00011B/3192